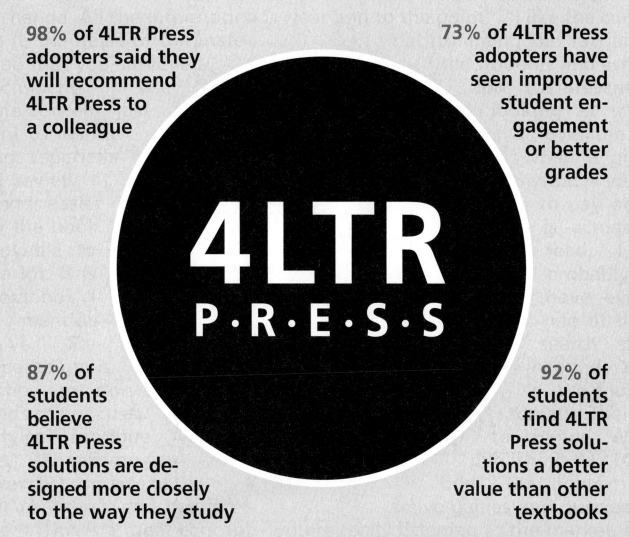
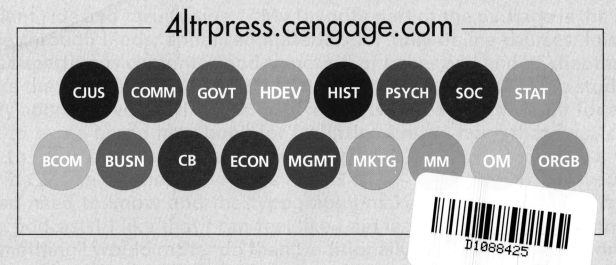
D1088425

WADSWORTH
CENGAGE Learning

CJUS 2009–2010 Edition
Laura B. Myers
Larry J. Myers
Joel Samaha

V.P., Editor-in-Chief: Michelle Julet

Sr. Publisher: Linda Schreiber

Sr. Acquisitions Editor:
    Carolyn Henderson-Meier

Director: Neil Marquardt

Developmental Editors: Colin Grover &
    Jamie Bryant, B-books, Ltd.

Product Development Manager:
    Steven E. Joos

Project Manager: Clara Goosman

Editorial Assistant: John Chell

Brand Executive Marketing Manager:
    Robin Lucas

Sr. Marketing Manager: Michelle Williams

Sr. Marketing Communications Manager:
    Tami Strang

Production Director: Amy McGuire,
    B-books, Ltd.

Content Project Manager: Christy Krueger

Media Editor: Andy Yap

Sr. Print Buyer: Judy Inouye

Production Service: B-books, Ltd.

Sr. Art Director Executive: Maria Epes

Internal Designer: Ke Design

Cover Designer: Yvo Riezebos, Riezebos
    Holzbaur Design Group

Cover Photo: Genevieve Shiffrar

Photography Manager: Deanna Ettinger

Photo Researcher: Charlotte Goldman

For product information and technology assistance, contact us at
Cengage Learning Customer & Sales Support, 1-800-423-0563

For permission to use material from this text or product,
submit all requests online at **www.cengage.com/permissions**
Further permissions questions can be emailed to
permissionrequest@cengage.com

Library of Congress Control Number: 2009928535

SE ISBN-13: 978-1-4390-4393-6
SE ISBN-10: 1-4390-4393-0
IE ISBN-13: 978-0-495-80861-9
IE ISBN-10: 0-495-80861-X

Wadsworth
10 Davis Drive
Belmont, CA 94002-3098
USA

Cengage Learning is a leading provider of customized learning solutions
with office locations around the globe, including Singapore, the United
Kingdom, Australia, Mexico, Brazil, and Japan. Locate your local office at
www.cengage.com/global.

Cengage Learning products are represented in Canada by Nelson Education, Ltd.

To learn more about Wadsworth, visit **www.cengage.com/wadsworth**.
Purchase any of our products at your local college store or at our preferred
online store **www.ichapters.com**.

Printed in the United States of America
1 2 3 4 5 6 7 12 11 10 09

BRIEF CONTENTS

CONTENTS

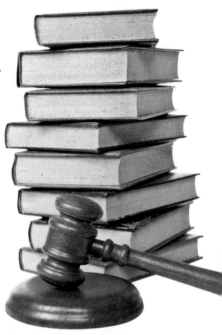

PART TWO PLANNING 58

7 Police and the Law 86

PART THREE THE COURTS 100

8 Courts and Courtroom Work Groups 100

9 Proceedings before Trial 114

10 Conviction by Trial and Guilty Plea   128

11 Sentencing   142

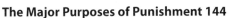

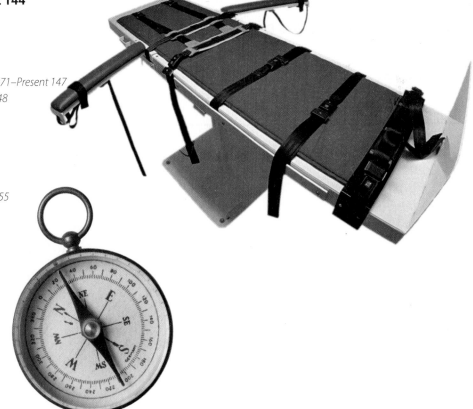

12 Community Corrections 158

13 Prisons, Jails, and Prisoners 174

14 Prison Life 192

PART FIVE   JUVENILE JUSTICE   206

15 Juvenile Justice 206

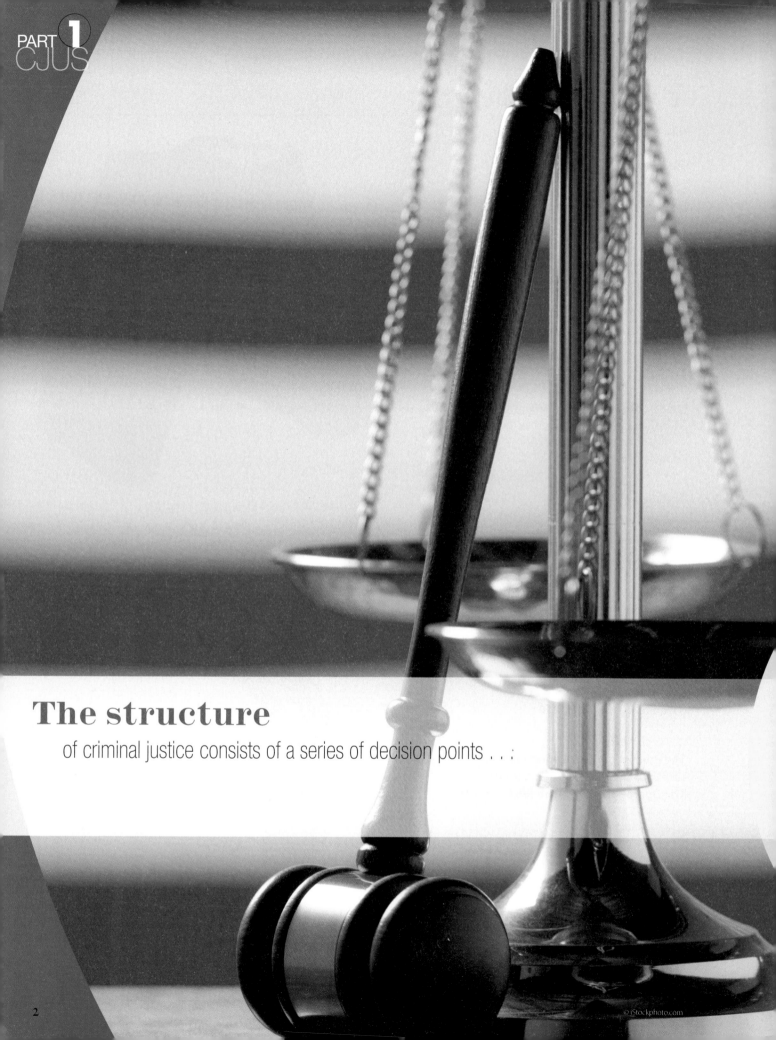

The structure

of criminal justice consists of a series of decision points . . :

I

Criminal Justice in the United States

How complex is criminal justice decision making? What is a proper traffic stop or an arrest? What is a proper charging decision? The following example illustrates the complexity of these decisions. The father of an adult son with mental illness calls the police for assistance with the man because the father cannot control his son's erratic behavior and he is afraid for himself and his son. The father is afraid the son may kill him or kill himself. Two patrol officers respond to the call and have been made aware by the police dispatcher that the person of interest has a mental impairment. The individual is violent and will not respond to the direct commands of the officers. The individual runs toward one of the officers with a large knife. The officer fears for his life. What should the police officer do? Does he know what to do? With the mentally ill, there have to be methods in place for handling actions like this because the individual is not a criminal. In this chapter, complex criminal justice decisions like this one will be discussed.

Learning Outcomes

LO1 Define *criminal justice* and the *criminal justice system*

LO2 Explain the authority and relationships of the major crime control agencies

LO3 Explain the steps in the criminal justice decision-making process

LO4 Discuss the differences in formal and informal decision making used in criminal justice

LO5 Explain the wedding cake model of justice

LO6 Compare the crime control and due process models of criminal justice

LO7 Define and explain the due process and crime control periods from a history of criminal justice perspective

LO1 The Criminal Justice System

Criminal justice is defined as the collectivity of crime control practices, philosophies, and policies used by the police, courts, and corrections to achieve their missions and functions of due process and crime control.[1] The **criminal justice system** is defined as a series of decision points (the criminal justice structure) *and* the decision-making criminal justice process, which takes place in the government crime control agencies.

> **criminal justice** the collectivity of crime control practices, philosophies, and policies used by the police, courts, and corrections to achieve their missions and functions of due process and crime control
>
> **criminal justice system** a series of decision points (the criminal justice structure) *and* the decision-making criminal justice process, which takes place in the government crime control agencies

LO2 Major Crime Control Agencies

the structure of criminal justice consists of a series of decision points in the three major crime control agencies—police, courts, and corrections. Each criminal justice agency is a point where decisions to keep or release individuals from the criminal justice system are made. The dictionary defines a *system* as a "collection of parts that make up a whole." The parts of the criminal justice system consist of the public agencies of crime control (law enforcement, courts, and corrections) at three levels of government (local, state, and federal). Thus, there are local, state, and federal law enforcement agencies; local, state, and federal courts; and local, state, and federal corrections agencies. Table 1.1 provides a general picture of the structure of the U.S. criminal justice system.

LO3 The Decision-Making Process

the crime control agencies make up the structure of the criminal justice system, but there is more to the system than its structure. Criminal justice itself cannot decide anything; rather, it is the framework for decision making. The criminal justice process is all about decision making in the agencies by criminal justice professionals. Like all processes,

criminal justice makes "products." Criminal justice processes people to change their legal status. Both the producers and the products are central to the criminal justice process.

PRODUCERS AND PRODUCTS

Who makes the products? What products do they make? Here are the major producers and products that you will learn about in later chapters:

1. *Law enforcement* officers produce suspects when they arrest (or otherwise focus their investigation on) a person.

Law enforcement ⟩ suspects

Prosecutors ⟩ defendents

Courts ⟩ offenders

Corrections ⟩ ex-offenders

TABLE 1.1 Federal, State, and Local Criminal Justice Agencies			
	LOCAL	**STATE**	**FEDERAL**
Law Enforcement	Municipal police departments County sheriff's offices	Highway patrol	U.S. Marshals Federal Bureau of Investigation (FBI) DEA (Drug Enforcement Administration) ATF (Bureau of Alcohol, Tobacco, Firearms and Explosives) Secret Service
Courts	Municipal courts District trial courts District appellate courts District (county) attorney's office County public defender's office	Supreme court Attorney general's office Public defender's office	U.S. Magistrates Courts U.S. District Courts U.S. Courts of Appeals U.S. Supreme Court U.S. Attorney's offices U.S. Public Defender's office
Corrections	Municipal holding facilities County jails Probation department	State prisons State parole authority	U.S. jails U.S. prisons U.S. probation and parole departments

2. *Prosecutors* produce defendants when they charge suspects with crimes.

3. *Courts* produce offenders when they convict defendants.

4. *Corrections* produce ex-offenders when they release them from custody.[2]

THE FORMAL CRIMINAL JUSTICE PROCESS

Law enforcement starts the formal criminal justice process by deciding whether to investigate a crime and apprehend suspects. The activities of the Las Vegas police in a recent case illustrate the investigative process and the decision to arrest. In September 2007, the police received a tip about a robbery allegedly involving O. J. Simpson, the former NFL football star acquitted in the 1994 slayings of his ex-wife Nicole Simpson and her friend, Ron Goldman. Investigators for the Las Vegas Police Department started an inquiry and met with Walter Alexander who had been named in the tip. He told them about the alleged robbery. He was subsequently arrested, and O. J. Simpson and four other men became the focus of the investigation. Simpson and the other men were arrested for allegedly committing a home invasion and robbery of a sports memorabilia collector who they claimed was in possession of some of Simpson's own personal sports memorabilia.[3] In 2008, Simpson was convicted for his role in the robbery.[4]

Prosecutors continue the process by deciding whether to charge suspects and with what crimes to charge them. Next, prosecutors, defense counsel, and judges all participate in deciding bail, disposition (trial or a plea of guilty), and sentencing of offenders. In the 2008 case of Casey Anthony in Orange County, Florida, investigators and prosecutors worked for several months to determine how to charge Anthony in the disappearance of her three-year-old daughter, Caylee. While the public and Caylee's family clamored for answers, the state attorney's office took the time

(1) Apprehension

(2) Prosecution

(3) Supervision

to build the strongest case possible so that the appropriate charges could be brought against Caylee's mother, Casey. In a homicide case, the prosecutors can take all the time they need. There is no time restraint.[5] In October 2008, an Orange County grand jury indicted Casey on first degree murder and other charges, even though Caylee's body had not yet been located at the time the indictments were handed down.[6]

Corrections professionals decide how to supervise offenders in their custody and participate in deciding if, when, and how prisoners return to society. The process boils down to deciding whether to move people further into the system and when and under what conditions to remove them from it. The treatment of homemaker maven Martha Stewart illustrates the offender reentry process. After completing her prison term for lying about a December 2000 stock sale, Stewart was released from prison in March 2005. After her release, she was confined to her home and had to wear an electronic anklet so that authorities could monitor her location. She remained on home detention at her estate in upstate New York until August 2005. She was permitted to work and entertain under the same conditions as any parolee.[7] Table 1.2 on the next page shows the formal criminal justice process and the progression of decision making by producers.

INTERDEPENDENT DECISION MAKING

Decision making among criminal justice agencies is interdependent. Decisions of one agency affect decisions in other agencies. Take, for example, state laws that restrict police discretion and command police officers to arrest suspects in all alleged cases of domestic assault. Before these mandatory arrest laws, police

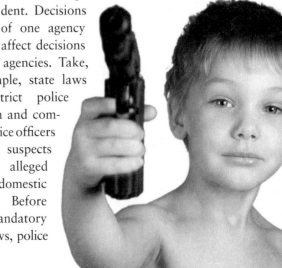

Table 1.2 The Formal Criminal Justice Process and the Progression of Decision Making by Producers

PRODUCER	PROGRESSIVE LEVELS OF DECISION MAKING
Police (Chapters 5–7)	Do nothing Investigate crime Report and record crime Arrest criminal suspect Search criminal suspect Interrogate criminal suspect Release criminal suspect Warn criminal suspect verbally Use force against individuals Intervene to maintain the peace (ordering people to "break it up," "move on," or "keep quiet") Provide service to people (helping lost persons find their way, helping parents find their children, providing an emergency escort)
Prosecutor (Chapters 8–11)	Take no action Divert case or person to another agency Charge person with a criminal offense Recommend bail or detention Negotiate a guilty plea Recommend harsh or lenient sentence
Judge (Chapters 8–11)	Release on bail Detain prior to trial Accept negotiated plea Reject negotiated plea Suspend sentence Sentence to probation Hand down a minimum sentence Hand down a maximum sentence
Probation department (Chapter 12)	Provide little or no supervision Provide minimum supervision Provide medium supervision Provide maximum supervision Report probation violations Do not revoke probation for violations Revoke probation for violations
Prison (Chapters 13–14)	Classify prisoners for type of prison and program Place minimum restrictions on prisoners' liberty and privacy Place medium restrictions on prisoners' liberty and privacy Place maximum restrictions on prisoners' liberty and privacy Issue disciplinary reports Take disciplinary actions Release prisoners Supervise prisoners' reentry into the community

© Nicholas Belton/iStockphoto.com

© Joseph Rafferty/Workbook Stock/Jupiterimages

officers had discretion to take things like age, mental illness, and amount of aggressiveness into account when deciding whether to arrest. Since the laws have been passed, do things like age, mental illness, and amount of aggressiveness matter? Of course they do. But now, prosecutors instead of police officers use their discretionary decision-making power to take them into account when they decide whether to charge arrested men (the assailants are almost always men) with assault. We call the shifting of discretionary decision making from one agency to another the **hydraulic effect**. (When you compress discretion at one decision point in the system, it will pop up at another point.)

Still, decision making is not entirely interdependent. First, criminal justice agencies have a lot of independence. They get their authority and their budgets from different sources. Police departments get their power and money from cities and towns. Sheriff's departments, prosecutors, public defenders, jails, and trial courts get their power and money from counties. Appeals courts and prisons get theirs from states.

Second, agencies set their own policies, rarely if ever coordinating them with other agencies. And most professionals within these agencies do not even think about the effects of their decisions on other agencies. For example, when police officers arrest suspected drunk drivers, child molesters, burglars, and thieves, they are not thinking about how these arrests are going to affect the "system" (giving prosecutors more work, courts heavier caseloads, and prisons more prisoners). Why not? The consequences of their decisions are too far down the line for the officers to worry about them. So, each agency becomes its own little criminal justice subsystem. As criminologist Lloyd E. Ohlin put it:

> *So although full enforcement does exist as a total system, other more abbreviated systems exist within it to respond to the different problems and the infinite variety of persons dealt with by enforcement officials.*[8]

LO4 Formal and Informal Decision Making

hydraulic effect the shifting of discretionary decision making from one agency to another

formal decision making decision making "by the book"

informal decision making decision making "in action"

there are two very different kinds of decision making in criminal justice: decision making "by the book" (**formal decision making**) and decision making "in action" (**informal decision making**) (Table 1.3). Let's look at formal and informal decision making in criminal justice.

FORMAL DECISION MAKING

Formal decision making is decision making according to written rules (decision making "by the book"). Formal decision making is open to public view (arrest, court proceedings), and formal decisions are published, or at least known to the public. The rules come from several sources:

1. U.S. and state constitutions
2. Statutes (written laws) created by the U.S. Congress, state legislatures, and city councils
3. Decisions of state and federal courts
4. Manuals and written policies of courts and crime control agencies (law enforcement, prosecution, and corrections)

TABLE 1.3 Formal versus Informal Decision Making	
FORMAL DECISION MAKING	**INFORMAL DECISION MAKING**
Decisions "by the book" (written rules)	Decisions according to professional judgment (discretionary decision making)
Decisions published or known to the public	Decisions not published and with low visibility
Mission is to provide certainty and predictability in criminal justice	Mission is to provide flexibility to satisfy a need for "play in the joints" of formal criminal justice

Formal decision making consists of applying (and probably often interpreting) these *written* rules of formal criminal justice. Most formal decision making takes place in courts where judges apply laws. But it also takes place in various kinds of departmental and civilian reviews of police misconduct and in disciplinary hearings in prisons.

The most famous example of formal rules is so embedded in our culture that almost everybody can recite it—the *Miranda* warnings—written and published by the U.S. Supreme Court in *Miranda v. Arizona* (1966). If you watch crime news stories or cop stories on TV, you have almost certainly heard the warnings recited. The rules are the way formal criminal justice carries out one of its most important missions—providing certainty and predictability throughout the criminal justice process. We should know what to expect and be able to count on it happening.[9]

INFORMAL (DISCRETIONARY) DECISION MAKING

There is no book of written rules to guide informal decision making, which we call **discretionary decision making**. Discretionary decision making operates according to the judgments of criminal justice professionals guided by their education, training, and experience in the field. Their decision making is low visibility (often completely invisible). Their decisions are not published (and often are not even known to the public).

But do not get the idea that informal criminal justice is not important. It has missions, too, and they are as important as those of formal criminal justice. One of the most important missions is to satisfy the need for flexibility in the vast number of situations that do not fit neatly into the rule book of formal criminal justice. Selective enforcement allows a police officer to take a drunken man passed out in a cold alley to a shelter instead of arresting him. Discretionary decision making lies at the heart of the day-to-day reality of criminal justice. The legal system and society have begun to acknowledge this reality and recognize that not all behavior can be neatly classified into legal or illegal behaviors. At the same time, the system cannot process all criminal activity. Properly utilized discretion allows for individualized justice and permits criminal justice system resources to be used on the most important cases.[10]

Despite the emphasis on discretionary decision making in this book and its importance in day-to-day criminal justice, remember two important points. First, *both* informal and formal decision making are essential. Second, just because the rules are not in writing and decision making according to them is invisible does not mean that discretion is *bad*.

THE COMPLEXITY OF DECISION MAKING

Decision making is a complicated business in the real world of criminal justice. The "book" does not have a list of simple rules telling police officers, prosecutors, defense lawyers, judges, and corrections officers how to solve most of the problems they run into. Only professional judgment, developed through training and experience (with maybe a little luck thrown in), will do.

Also, the goals of criminal justice are multiple, vague, and often in conflict. Police officers are legally commanded to "enforce all the laws." Informally, they cannot (and they *shouldn't*). Prosecutors are told formally to "do justice." Informally, they pursue other goals like winning cases, cracking down on specific crimes, improving efficiency, and saving the people's

FORMAL

1. U.S. and state constitutions
2. Statutes (written laws) created by the U.S. Congress, state legislatures, and city councils
3. Decisions of state and federal courts
4. Manuals and written policies of courts and crime control agencies (law enforcement, prosecution, and corrections)

© Martin L'Allier/iStockphoto.com

© AP Images/Will Hart/NBCU Photo Bank

Andrea Yates was found not guilty by reason of insanity for the drowning deaths of her children. As a result of that verdict, Yates was committed to a state mental hospital, with periodic hearings before a judge to determine whether she should be released. An earlier jury had found her guilty of murder, but the verdict was overturned on appeal.

tax dollars. Judges have to impose sentences that are supposed to punish, incapacitate, and reform individual defendants while protecting the community by sending a message to prevent criminal wannabes from committing crimes. Probation officers are supposed to police and counsel offenders in the community. Corrections officers are supposed to maintain order and prevent escapes from prison, discipline prisoners, and turn them into people who can return to society ready to work and play by the rules.

As if these challenges are not enough, professionals do not have the luxury of time to consider their decisions. They have to decide *right now* how to accomplish their goals. Books do not contain simple solutions that will solve most of the problems criminal justice professionals have to deal with in their daily work.[11] For an illustration of the difficulty of quick decision making, consider the relationship between the police and the mentally ill. Research shows that police officers are more likely to arrest a mentally ill person because the symptoms can be easily criminalized. Bad outcomes with mentally ill individuals, such as jailhouse suicides or street violence resulting in the death or injury of the mentally ill person, have led to policy recommendations and changes in the way police are trained. The goal of these new policies as well as the mental health training for police officers is to help officers recognize the signs of mental illness, respond more appropriately to the mentally ill, and have a wider range of formal and informal options for managing the mentally ill when they are in need.[12] Such policies and knowledge are critical to better informed police decision making in a crisis situation when time is of the essence.

> *Books do not contain simple solutions that will solve most of the problems criminal justice professionals have to deal with in their daily work.*

LEGITIMATE VERSUS DISCRIMINATORY DECISION MAKING

The last dimension to decision making is the criteria. There are two types of criteria. One type, **legitimate decision-making criteria**, consists of criteria that produce legal, fair, and smart decisions. The second type, **discriminatory decision-making criteria**, influences decision making to produce illegal, discriminatory, and harmful decisions.

The legitimate criteria include

- Seriousness of the offense
- Dangerousness of the offender
- Amount and quality of the facts in the case
- Relationship of the offender to the victim

The discriminatory criteria include

- Race
- Gender
- Age
- Class

An enormous amount of research has been conducted on the criteria for decision making. Two points emerge from the "big picture" of all that research:

1. Officials rely on legitimate criteria in *most* cases of *serious* crime at *most* decision points in their decision making.

2. "Racial discrimination emerges *some* of the time at *some* stages of the system in *some* locations, but there is little evidence that racial disparities reflect systemic, overt bias on the part of criminal justice decision makers."[13]

These conclusions leave many gaps in our knowledge, particularly the meaning of the italicized words. The gaps raise a very important question for you to think about when you come to sections focusing on decision-making criteria: "How much discrimination is too much?" Or to put it another way, "How much discrimination is acceptable in a system created and run by *imperfect* people (which of course all of us are)?" Review of police discrimination reveals a form of discrimination that has received significant attention in recent years with the claim that the police racially profile during traffic stops, searches, and arrests. In April 2007, the Bureau of Justice Statistics released a study indicating that while black and Hispanic drivers were just as likely as whites to be stopped by the police, they were significantly more likely to be searched incident to the stop. Beyond the search, black drivers were twice as likely to be arrested as white drivers, and blacks and Hispanics were more likely than whites to experience police use of force. Research on the topic of racial profiling is inconclusive as to whether police are actually discriminating against blacks and Hispanics, but the fact that blacks are more likely to perceive they were mistreated by police is a problem for police community relations.[14]

LO5 The "Wedding Cake" Model of Justice

t he wedding cake model depicts a process in which criminal justice officials decide how to deal with cases according to their informal discretionary definition of "seriousness." Professionals distinguish between "real crime" and "garbage" cases. What determines the difference?

1. Seriousness of the charge (including injury to victims and use of a gun)
2. Past criminal record of the offender
3. Relationship of the victim to the offender
4. Strength of the prosecution's case

Judged by these criteria, it is no surprise that "real crimes" get more attention (as well they should) than "garbage" cases.[15] The tiers of a wedding cake, narrow at the top and increasingly wider toward the bottom (Figure 1.1), represent the decreasing seriousness and increasing numbers of cases.

1. On the small top tier are a tiny number of "celebrated cases."

2. In the second tier are a somewhat larger number of "real crimes."

3. Most "ordinary felonies" are in the third tier.

Racial profiling—regardless of type—is a discriminatory criterion.

FIGURE 1.1
The Criminal Justice Wedding Cake

Tier I:
Celebrated cases

Tier II:
Real crimes

Tier III:
Ordinary felonies

Tier IV:
Misdemeanors

Source: Based on S. Walker, *Sense and Nonsense about Crime and Drugs* (Belmont, CA: Wadsworth, 1994).

© Steven Miric/iStockphoto.com / iStockphoto.com

4. The broad fourth tier represents the vast number of minor crimes.

All three top tiers are **felonies**, crimes that can send convicted offenders to prison for a year or more. First-tier crimes are the "celebrated cases"—the very few felonies that grab public attention because the crime is particularly grisly (Timothy McVeigh who blew up more than a hundred men, women, and children) or because a famous person (Martha Stewart) is charged with committing a crime. In celebrated cases, defendants get all the protections the law allows, including a trial.

Second-tier crimes are "real crimes" (felonies like criminal homicide, rape, aggravated assault, and armed robbery). Of course, some celebrated cases (Timothy McVeigh) are "real crimes," too. But the second tier is reserved for what we will call "pure real crimes" (classified on the seriousness of the offense alone). What makes them serious? They are committed by individuals who have criminal records, are strangers to their victims, use guns, and injure their victims. "Real crimes" are less likely than celebrated cases to go to a full formal trial, but more likely than less serious felony and misdemeanor cases.

Third-tier cases are "ordinary felonies," like burglaries, thefts, and unarmed robberies where no one

got hurt and the victim knew the offender. "Technically," serious felonies in which the event is also a private dispute are classified as "ordinary." Suppose Doug asks his roommate Eli for $25. At the time Eli gives Doug the money, Doug believes the $25 is a gift. A few months later, Eli asks Doug for his $25. When Doug says, "No way, you gave me that $25," Eli grabs Doug's wallet and takes all the money in it, $40. "I'm taking my $25 plus the rest in interest." Police and prosecutors do not call this a "real" robbery, no matter what the law says. So, they either divert it out of the system completely or go for a guilty plea to ordinary theft.

felonies crimes that can send convicted offenders to prison for a year or more

The vast majority of cases are fourth-tier crimes: misdemeanors like simple assault, petty theft, shoplifting, and disorderly conduct. Samuel Walker calls this bottom tier the "lower depths." Practically none of these cases go to trial; they are not worth the cost and effort of formal proceedings. They are disposed of quickly either in preliminary proceedings or by agreements among prosecutors, defendants, and lawyers. In many instances, there are no criminal charges at all; the incidents are considered "problems" the parties should settle between themselves.[16]

LO6 Crime Control and Due Process

two models of criminal justice are commonly used to guide agency missions and professional decisions. These models are built on two missions of our constitutional democracy— crime control and due process.[17] The mission of the crime control model is society's need for enforcement of laws and the maintenance of social order.

© Martin L'Allier/iStockphoto.com

TABLE 1.4 Comparison of the Crime Control and Due Process Models	
CRIME CONTROL	**DUE PROCESS**
Control crime	Fair procedures
Society's needs	Individual's rights
Confidence in police and prosecutor	Distrust of all government power
Negotiation	Adversary court proceedings
Reliability of informal fact-finding	Reliability of formal fact-finding
Discretion by police and prosecutors	Limited discretion by police and prosecutors
Presumption of guilt	Presumption of innocence
Emphasis on early stages of investigation	Emphasis on trial
Conveyer belt	Obstacle course
Fear of criminals	Fear of government

crime control model a model of criminal justice that focuses on the need to protect people and their property

The mission of the due process model is society's need to ensure justice to its citizens or conversely to prevent injustice against its citizens.[18] Table 1.4 shows a comparison of the two models. Most people put crime control high on their list of priorities when it comes to criminal justice. But crime control does not mean controlling crime at any price. We have to respond to crime within the limits placed on government power by the values of our constitutional democracy. Thus, officials fighting crime have to respect the life, liberty, privacy, property, and dignity of all people no matter how much we hate them or what they do.

THE CRIME CONTROL MODEL

The **crime control model** focuses on the need to protect people and their property, partly for the victims' sake, but also for the good of the whole society. If people do not feel safe, they lose their capacity to function and enjoy the rewards that should come from working hard and playing by the rules. At the end of the day, crime control guarantees social freedom by protecting people and their property.

To make good on this guarantee, criminal justice decisions have to sort out the guilty from the innocent, let the innocent go as soon as possible, and convict and punish the guilty (also as soon as possible). Note that *speedy* decisions by themselves are not good enough; they have to be *correct*, too. We do not want to convict innocent people and let guilty ones go free, not just because it is unfair, but because it leads to time-wasting, expensive second-guessing of decisions already made. In other words, we also want decisions to be *right* because we want them to be *final*.[19]

Informal decision making is the best way to ensure speed and accuracy. The crime control model operates like an assembly line-conveyer belt (Figure 1.2) down which moves an endless array of cases, never stopping,

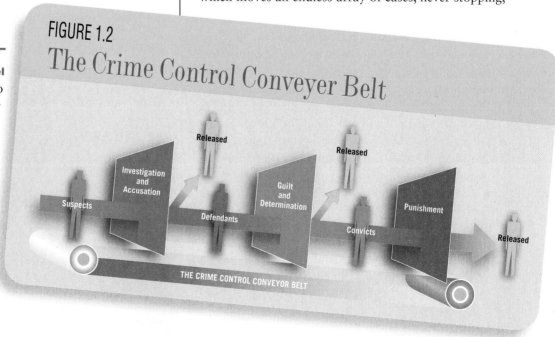

FIGURE 1.2
The Crime Control Conveyer Belt

The crime control model is not too worried about mistakes and unfairness.

carrying the cases to workers who stand at fixed stations and who perform on each case as it comes by the same small but essential operation that brings it one step closer to being a finished product, or, to exchange the metaphor, a closed file.[20]

The **presumption of guilt** (the belief that people caught up in criminal justice are *probably* guilty) fits in with the premium placed on fast and accurate crime control. This is reflected in views such as "the police wouldn't have arrested her and prosecutors wouldn't have charged her unless she'd done something wrong." Therefore, courts shouldn't "handcuff" the police and stymie prosecutors by putting up expensive, time-consuming hurdles to their efforts to find the truth. Give police officers leeway to detain, search, and interrogate suspects so they can sort out the guilty from the innocent. Let prosecutors bargain for guilty pleas to get the guilty to punishment and hopefully redemption as soon as possible. The crime control model emphasizes the early stages in criminal justice—police investigation and guilty pleas.

Finally, the crime control model is not too worried about mistakes and unfairness. Why? First, because it makes three assumptions based on confidence in government power:

1. *Police and prosecutors rarely make mistakes.* They do not base their decisions on personal prejudices even if they are prejudiced. And most suspects are guilty of *something.*

2. *The need for crime control outweighs the suffering of the few innocent people who get caught up in the system.* It is better that a few innocent people get convicted than that guilty people go free.

3. *Sooner or later innocent people are vindicated* (most of the time, sooner). At the end of the day, there is more to fear from criminals going free and innocent people suffering than there is from government power to control crime.

THE DUE PROCESS MODEL

According to the **due process model**, it is more important to guarantee the rights of individuals to fair pro-

cedures than to catch criminals. In fact, the best definition of due process is *fair procedures.* **Fair procedures** mean decision making according to formal rules growing out of the Bill of Rights and the due process clauses of the U.S. Constitution and state constitutions.

The commitment to decision making by formal rules is based on a distrust of government power and the need to control it. Accordingly, we have to throw up barriers to government power at each step in the criminal process to prevent further involvement in this risky business of criminal justice. It should not surprise us that the due process model resembles an obstacle course, not an assembly line.[21]

presumption of guilt the belief that people caught up in criminal justice are *probably* guilty

due process model a criminal justice model founded on the principle that it is more important to guarantee the rights of individuals to fair procedures than to catch criminals

fair procedures decision making according to formal rules growing out of the Bill of Rights and the due process clauses of the U.S. Constitution and state constitutions

adversary process getting the truth by fighting in court according to the formal rules of criminal procedure

presumption of innocence the burden upon government to justify its use of power even against people who turn out to be guilty

Creating due process obstacles (Figure 1.3 on page 14) is based on the idea that you cannot find the truth informally because human failings—like our faulty powers of observation, our self-interest, our emotions, and our prejudices—stand in the way. The model puts great confidence in the **adversary process**—getting the truth by fighting in court according to the formal rules of criminal procedure. So, in the due process model, the trial is the high point of criminal justice. Why? Formal public proceedings reduce the chances that mistakes, emotions, and prejudices will influence decision making because skilled lawyers argue their side of the story in front of neutral judges acting as umpires, and impartial juries decide who is telling the truth.

Distrust of government power and the need to control it also means operating according to the **presumption of innocence**: The government always has the burden to justify its use of power even against people who turn out to be guilty. When all is said and done, the due process model expresses more fear of government than of criminals.

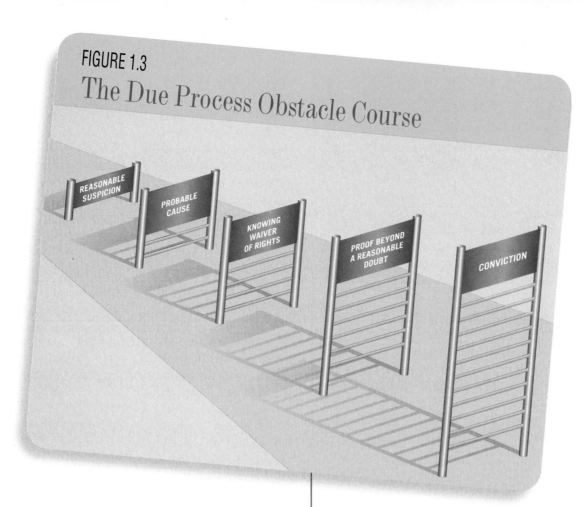

FIGURE 1.3

The Due Process Obstacle Course

REASONABLE SUSPICION

PROBABLE CAUSE

KNOWING WAIVER OF RIGHTS

PROOF BEYOND A REASONABLE DOUBT

CONVICTION

L07 The History of Crime Control and Due Process

t he tension between the values of due process and crime control is as old as criminal justice. One way (there are others) to interpret the history of criminal justice in Western cultures is as a pendulum swinging between a commitment to crime control and a commitment to due process (Figure 1.4).

At one end of the pendulum's swing is the fear of government abuse of power and demands for rules to control it. At the other end is the fear of crime and demands for discretionary power to eliminate it. The fear of government abuse of power has always led to more rules and less discretion. The fear of crime has always produced the opposite—more discretion and fewer rules.

due process revolution

a period in the 1960s during which the U.S. Supreme Court extended the interpretation of the Bill of Rights to apply to state as well as federal criminal proceedings

THE DUE PROCESS REVOLUTION

The **due process revolution** originated in the 1960s. Before this time, the U.S. Supreme Court had interpreted the Bill of Rights to apply only to *federal* criminal proceedings. During the 1960s, the Court adopted an ambitious (some say too ambitious, even unconstitutional) agenda:

1. Expand the rights of criminal defendants.
2. Apply these expanded rights to both federal *and* state criminal proceedings.
3. Include protection for "outsiders"—like poor, minority, and other suspects, defendants, and offenders—within the protection of these expanded rights.

© Bettmann/Corbis

FIGURE 1.4
The Crime Control/Due Process Pendulum

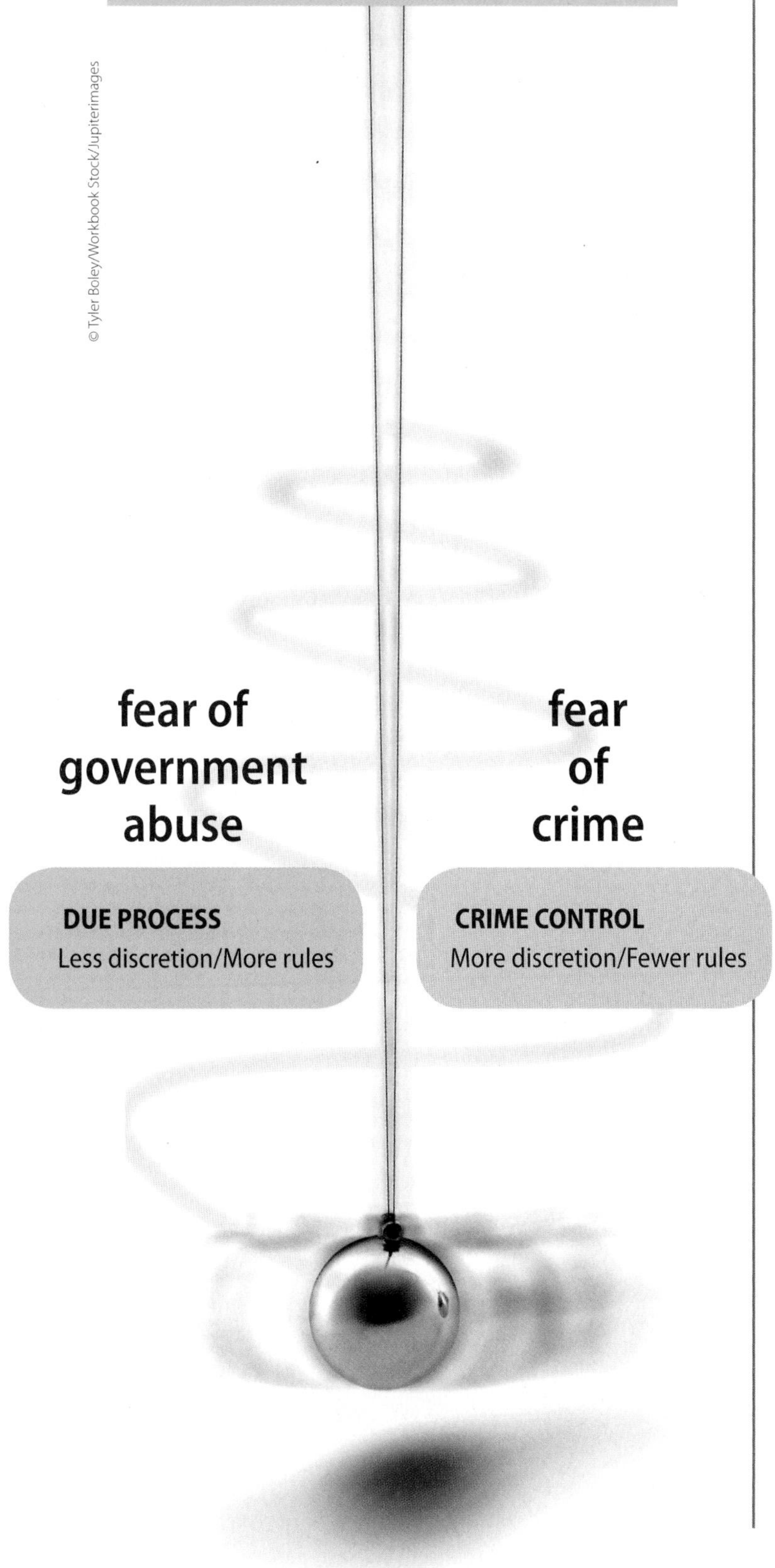

fear of government abuse

DUE PROCESS
Less discretion/More rules

fear of crime

CRIME CONTROL
More discretion/Fewer rules

The 1960s were turbulent times when "the establishment" was under siege. Soaring crime rates, an increasingly militant civil rights movement, growing dissension over an unpopular war in Vietnam, a highly publicized youth counterculture, and rioting in the streets and cities left law-abiding citizens reeling.[22]

THE RETURN TO CRIME CONTROL

One popular interpretation of the problems of the 1960s was that a permissive society with too many safeguards for criminal defendants and not enough punishment for offenders emboldened budding criminals to mock the standards of decency, hard work, and "playing by the rules." These "antisocial renegades" lived for sex, drugs, rock and roll, riots, and, eventually, crime. The popular and political answer was to declare and fight an all-out "war on crime." The elements of this war consisted of more police, more punishment, and fewer rights for criminal defendants.

This resurgence of the value of crime control continued throughout the 1980s and 1990s. And despite reduced crime rates and some public disenchantment with all "domestic wars"—including those on crime and drugs—the belief that law-abiding people are still at war with crime, particularly violent crime and drugs, is very much alive.[23] There is some speculation (but no hard empirical proof) that the September 11 attacks have contributed to a crime control mind-set. But there is also speculation that fighting terrorism has siphoned off energy from crime control to antiterrorism efforts.

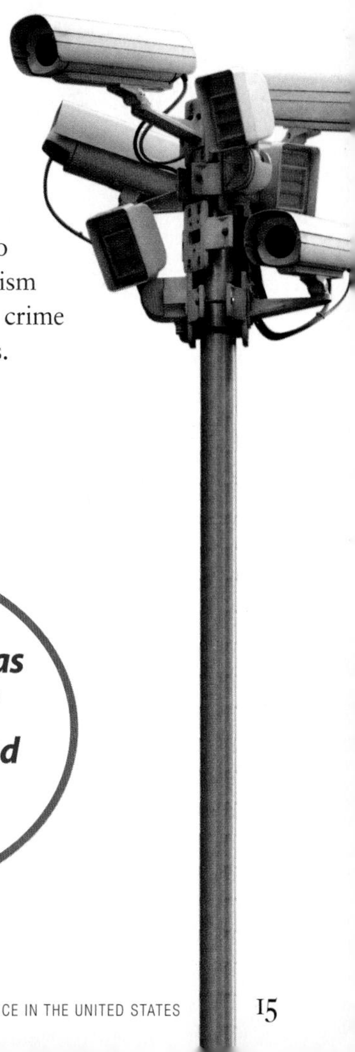

The fear of crime has always produced more discretion and fewer rules.

Crime

is what the courts say crime is when courts make decisions.

2

Crime and Criminals

Is the making of liquor illegal? What is moonshining? Is it still illegal today? Why is it a crime? A man was recently sentenced in the southeast for making and selling moonshine in the 21st century. This hardly seems like a serious crime in modern times. Supporters of this man disagreed with his conviction. They also opposed his sentencing of 18 months to a federal prison. So why did the federal court convict and sentence this man? An understanding of the origins of moonshining laws from the late 1800s reveals some surprising reasons for the laws and why they still stand today. In this chapter, we will explore how crime is defined.

© AP Images/Kevin Goldy

LO1 How Is Crime Defined?

traditionally, crime has been defined as what the criminal law says it is. Criminal law, however, cannot cover all ranges and types of social harms, so defining crime as criminal law is too limited. The criminal law is adapted to the range of social harms through judicial interpretation. The courts determine the social context of the behavior and the situation and how the law might apply in the given situation. Thus, a better definition of crime is what the courts say crime is when courts make decisions.

If we define crime using how courts decide criminal cases, then the meaning of crime is constructed by humans using their own biases and perspectives to define social harm. In January 2009, a federal judge in Tennessee sentenced Marvin "Popcorn" Sutton to 18 months in prison on moonshining and weapons charges. Sutton pled guilty and admitted to selling hundreds of gallons of moonshine to an undercover ABC agent. A barn on his

Learning Outcomes

LO1 Discuss how crime is defined

LO2 Define and explain the major crime types

LO3 Analyze how crime is measured

LO4 Explain the strengths and weaknesses of the measures of crime

property housed three stills, two of which were functional. The federal judge was not swayed by a significant number of supporters who felt that the sentence was too harsh and not justified. Laws prohibiting the production and sale of alcohol by private citizens were created in the late 1800s because the federal government wanted alcohol sales taxed. People who made their own liquor refused to pay the tax and refused to stop making the liquor. They started making their brew at night, becoming known as "moonshiners." Today, the production of home brews has led many to perceive that the production of alcohol is not a crime. The federal judge in Tennessee disagreed with the more than one thousand "Popcorn" supporters who had signed a petition asking the judge for leniency.[1]

There are two competing views on how humans create definitions of crime. The **consensus view** of crime is that people agree on the nature of social harms using social morality to determine rights and wrongs. Not all people agree, however, and not all people use the same values and morals to determine social harm. According to the **conflict view** of crime, different interest groups define social harm according to who has the power to define the laws and social harms at any given point in time.[2] A good illustration of the conflict view is provided by the way the U.S. Supreme Court has defined and redefined criminal law throughout history depending on the views of the majority of the Court and the liberal or conservative backgrounds of the sitting justices. Though the Supreme Court is intended to be unbiased and above influence, the justices are human and use their own backgrounds when they assess the current perspectives of society as they decide cases.

Lanier and Henry point out that although all of these perspectives and definitions are important in defining crime, the definition of crime is even more

complex because all of these issues are part of the definition.[3] Using a prism model, they include consensus and conflict views of social harm, visibility of the social harm, perceptions of the seriousness of the harm, the social response, and individual harm in the determination of what is a crime. When a child is abused, for example, the laws that will be applied to the harm result from both consensus and conflict views because child abuse has been regarded as a serious issue at different times by different groups of people, but it has always been an issue across many different subgroups of society. The hidden aspects of child abuse have traditionally restricted the public's knowledge of the severity and characteristics of the behavior. With increased public attention to child abuse in recent decades, there has been more agreement over the seriousness of child abuse and a greater social response to its signs.

This complex definition of what constitutes crime leads to various uses for crime definitions. Social response agencies focus on different aspects of social harm. The police, for example, focus on behaviors that are known to the police. These behaviors typically involve violent or street crime, committed in poor socioeconomic locations, and they include only those behaviors reported to the police because of their seriousness. Once these behaviors come to the attention of the prosecutor, then seriousness, social values, and consensus and conflict views of crime come into play in determining which cases are charged. Other agencies, such as social services agencies, focus on current behaviors that

CONCENSUS OR CONFLICT

For 24 years, Austrian Josef Fritzl kept his daughter Elizabeth imprisoned in a hidden basement room guarded by eight locked doors. Fritzl assaulted, abused, and raped his daughter, who bore seven children by him. Three of the children were raised by their mother in the makeshift prison, one died shortly after birth and was incinerated by Fritzl, and the remaining three were raised outside of the prison by Fritzl and his wife Rosemarie, who had no knowledge of the underground prison or its inhabitants. When Fritzl allowed one of his secret children to be taken to a hospital, an investigation was initiated and eventually led to Fritzl's arrest and the freeing of his captives. In March of 2009, Josef Fritzl pleaded guilty to six charges including incest, rape, false imprisonment, and murder, and was sentenced to life in prison.

the community regards as serious such as child abuse and domestic violence. So, within any given historical context, there will be certain major types of criminal behavior, and the amount of each of these crimes will be dependent on the mission of the responding agencies as they focus their interventions on these behaviors. As social services agencies began to pay more attention to child abuse, a significant increase in abuse cases became evident. Was more child abuse occurring, or was it just suddenly more visible because the agencies were looking for it? It was suddenly more visible because humans had turned their attention in that direction.

LO2 The Major Types of Crime

Violent crimes are only a tiny slice of the total amount of crime, which generally includes very few murders, a few more rapes, still a few more robberies and burglaries, lots of thefts, and a deluge of drunk and disorderly conduct charges. How can we get a grip on this hodgepodge we call "crime"? One way is to classify crimes into three groups adopted by the official crime statistics you will learn about in this chapter:

Was more child abuse occurring, or was it just suddenly more visible because the agencies were looking for it? It was suddenly more visible because humans had turned their attention in that direction.

VIOLENT

1. *Violent or personal crime* involves actions that can physically hurt or threaten to hurt people. The primary violent crimes in the United States in 2008 included gang-related crimes, drug crimes, and gun crimes.[4] As the 2009 college spring break season commenced, officials in Kansas alerted students to a series of rapes that appeared to coincide with local universities' scheduled vacations. At the time this chapter was written, officials believed that a single perpetrator, Benjamin Appleby, may have been responsible for thirteen rapes documented over an eight-year period. These rapes occurred during school breaks—eight near Kansas State University and five near the University of Kansas. Serial rape is a common form of violent crime, especially in locations with young transient populations such as universities.[5]

Benjamin Appleby, seen here entering a courtroom with lawyer Angela R. Keck, right, and a Johnson County sheriff's deputy, left, was charged with and brought to trial for the murder and attempted rape of Kansas State University student Ali Kemp. Due in part to a videotaped confession made by Appleby two years prior to his 2006 trial, a jury found the defendant guilty on both counts, resulting in a sentence of life in prison. Appleby is still suspected in a number of rapes occurring on or near Kansas university campuses.

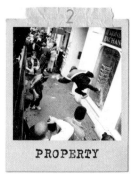

PROPERTY

2. *Property crime* involves actions that take, damage, or destroy or threaten to take, invade, damage, or destroy people's property. Property crimes typically involve some form of theft. In 2007, a new form of property theft emerged with a growing number of copper thefts. As the value of copper increased in recent years, thieves began stripping copper from phone cables and other mechanical devices, which led to phone outages, power outages, and rising construction costs.[6] Numerous youth sports teams were ousted from their playing fields because the copper had been stolen from their field lights.[7]

MORALS

3. *Crimes against public order and morals* include disorderly conduct, public drunkenness, individual drug use, prostitution, and many similar minor offenses (misdemeanors). In early 2008, New York Governor Eliot Spitzer resigned his office when his name surfaced in a federal prostitution case. The prostitutes in the federal case were convicted, but Spitzer was never charged in the case.[8]

Violent crimes and property crimes have two victims—the individual victims of crime and the whole community. How can this be? Think about a few examples. The serial rapist does not just hurt the individuals he attacks. He undermines the whole community's sense of personal safety. The burglar who breaks into your house makes all of us feel unsafe in our homes. The corporation that "cooks" its books and causes you to lose money undermines the public confidence that our market economy depends on.

LO3 and LO4 The Measurement of Crime

today, there are two main sources of crime statistics—police reports and victim surveys—and one much less used and less complete source, offenders' self-reports of crimes they have committed. Each source looks to a different place for the best measure of crime: police, victims, and offenders. Let's look at each of these sources of statistics and then consider their strengths and weaknesses.[9]

OFFICIAL POLICE REPORTS

Basing crime statistics on police reports stems from the belief that the best way to find out about crime is to ask the police. Certainly, this was the belief of the International Association of Chiefs of Police (IACP), a police reform organization that planned the first nationwide collection of crime statistics in the United States. In

In March of 2008, **The New York Times** *broke the story that Eliot Spitzer, governor of New York, had paid $2,000 to meet with Emperors Club VIP escort Ashley Alexandra Dupré for two hours. It was later revealed through further published reports that while in office, Spitzer paid at least $15,000, and up to $80,000, over a period of several years for sexual liaisons with a number of escorts. Two days after* **The New York Times** *story was published, Spitzer resigned as governor amid threats of impeachment, but in November of 2008, prosecutors assigned to the case announced that no criminal charges would be levied.*

1930, the Federal Bureau of Investigation (FBI) collected its first set of data based on official police records, the **Uniform Crime Reports (UCR)**. The FBI depended (and still does) on voluntary cooperation from local police departments to collect and report to the FBI summaries of serious (**Part I offenses**) and minor (**Part II offenses**) offenses. The FBI publishes these statistics every year in *Crime in the United States*. Let's look at the ways Part I and Part II offenses are measured and reported. Then, we will contrast the UCR with a new reporting system, the NIBRS.

Crime Index (Part I) Offenses

The **Crime Index** (Table 2.1) statistic is a summary of raw numbers of crimes and **crime rates** (the number of crimes reported for every 100,000 people). The index consists of eight of the most often reported serious crimes: murder, forcible rape, robbery, aggravated assault, burglary, theft, motor vehicle theft, and arson. In 2007, UCR data revealed that police made 14 million arrests and that violent crime had fallen after rising over the previous two years. An estimated 1,408,337 violent crimes were committed in 2007.[10] There were 10,000 fewer violent crimes in 2007 than in the previous year.[11] Even though overall violent crime rates were down in 2007 and homicide rates were down in major cities, medium-size and small cities saw an increase in homicide rates over the previous year.[12]

According to the UCR, an estimated 9,843,481 property crimes were reported in 2007. Each category of property crime decreased from the 2006 estimates. Losses for property crime victims were estimated to be $17.6 billion.[13]

You should not be surprised to learn that these numbers are not perfect. Why? The reason is that the Crime Index includes only crimes the police know about. So, there are always an unknown number of crimes (the **dark figure of crime**).[14] Also, the UCR overstates serious crime because it counts attempts as if they were completed crimes. In addition, street crime (crimes committed mostly by poor and minority criminals) is overrepresented because white-collar crimes are not included in the index.[15]

Part II Offenses

The less serious offenses in Part II are measured by the raw numbers of arrests for each of the Part II offenses. In Part II, citations and summonses are counted as arrests. Do not view the number of *arrests* as the number of *persons* arrested because the same person might be arrested several times in a year.

National Incident-Based Reporting System (NIBRS)

To improve its statistics, the UCR is shifting from summaries (lump-sum totals of crimes reported to the police and arrests) to incident-based reporting. The new system is called the **National Incident-Based Reporting System (NIBRS)**. (Table 2.2 compares the UCR and the NIBRS.) The NIBRS collects information about two groups of offenses (Table 2.3). Group A includes the 8 UCR index crimes (with some changes in definition) and adds 14 others. Group B includes some specifically named offenses and then a catchall "all other crimes."

The heart of the NIBRS is incident-based

© Diego Cervo/iStockphoto.com

TABLE 2.1 Definitions of Index Crimes

VIOLENT CRIMES

Murder and Nonnegligent Homicide	The willful (nonnegligent) killing of one human being by another. The UCR does not include deaths caused by negligence, suicide, or accident; justifiable homicides; or attempts to murder or assaults to murder, which are classified as aggravated assaults.
Forcible Rape	The carnal knowledge of a female forcibly and against her will. Assaults or attempts to commit rape by force or threat of force are also included; however, statutory rape (without force) and other sex offenses are excluded.
Robbery	Taking or attempting to take anything of value from the care, custody, or control of a person or persons by force or threat of force or violence and/or by putting the victim in fear.
Aggravated Assault	An unlawful attack by one person upon another for the purpose of inflicting severe or aggravated bodily injury. This type of assault is usually accompanied by the use of a weapon or by means likely to produce death or great bodily harm. Attempts involving the display or threat of a gun, knife, or other weapon are included because serious personal injury would likely result if the assault were completed.

PROPERTY CRIMES

Burglary	Unlawful entry of a structure to commit a felony or theft. The use of force to gain entry is not required to classify an offense as a burglary. Burglary is categorized into three subclassifications: forcible entry, unlawful entry where no force is used, and attempted forcible entry.
Larceny/Theft	The unlawful taking, carrying, leading, or riding away of property from the possession or constructive possession of another. It includes crimes such as shoplifting, pocket-picking, purse snatching, thefts from motor vehicles, thefts of motor vehicle parts and accessories, bicycle thefts, etc., in which no use of force, violence, or fraud occurs. In the Uniform Crime Reporting Program, this crime category does not include embezzlement, confidence games, forgery, or worthless checks. Motor vehicle theft is also excluded from this category as it is a separate Crime Index offense.
Motor Vehicle Theft	The theft or attempted theft of a motor vehicle. This offense includes the stealing of automobiles, trucks, buses, motorcycles, motor scooters, snowmobiles, etc. The taking of a motor vehicle for temporary use by persons having lawful access is excluded from this definition.
Arson	Any willful or malicious burning or attempt to burn, with or without intent to defraud, a dwelling house, public building, motor vehicle or aircraft, personal property of another, etc. Only fires determined through investigation to have been willfully or maliciously set are classified as arsons. Fires of suspicious or unknown origins are excluded.

Source: FBI, *Crime in the United States*, 2002 (Washington, DC: FBI, 2003), Appendix II.

© Greg Nicholas/iStockphoto.com

TABLE 2.2 Differences between the UCR and the NIBRS

UNIFORM CRIME REPORT (UCR)	NATIONAL INCIDENT-BASED REPORTING SYSTEM (NIBRS)
Consists of monthly aggregate crime Counts 8 index crimes Records one offense per incident as determined by the hierarchy rule, which suppresses counts of lesser offenses in multiple-offense incident Does not distinguish between attempted and completed crimes Applies the hotel rule to burglary Records rape of females only Collects weapon information for murder, robbery, and aggravated assault Provides counts on arrests for the 8 index crimes and 21 other offenses	Consists of individual incident records for the 8 index crimes and 38 other offenses with details on the • Offense • Offender • Victim • Property Records each offense that occurred in the incident Distinguishes between attempted and completed crimes Expands the burglary hotel rule to include rental storage facilities Records rapes of males and females Restructures the definition of assault Collects weapon information for all violent offenses Provides details on arrests for the 8 index crimes and 49 other offenses

Source: Ramona R. Rantala, *Effects of NIBRS on Crime Statistics* (Washington, DC: Bureau of Justice Statistics, 2000).

reporting. **Incident-based reporting** means that local law enforcement agencies collect detailed information about individual cases for each offense.[16] The details for Group A incidents include the following:

1 *The offense.* Attempts are separated from completed crimes

2 *The victim.* Includes information about age, gender, ethnicity, race, resident or alien status, type of injury, and the relationship of the victim to the offender

3 *The damage to property.* Any property involved

4 *The offender.* Includes details about age, gender, race, and ethnicity

5 *The arrestee.* Includes information about the use of alcohol, narcotics, and other drugs

6 *The witnesses.* Any witnesses

7 *The incident.* A brief narrative describing the incident

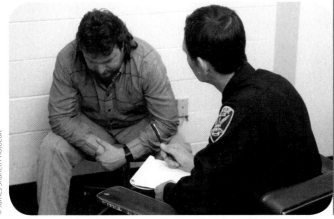

Notice that for Group A incidents, the NIBRS separates attempts from completed crimes (the UCR lumps them together). In addition to the information listed above, it includes details on whether a weapon was used in committing the crime. For Group B incidents, the NIBRS collects only information for arrested persons.

> **incident-based reporting** the collection of detailed information about individual cases by local law enforcement agencies for each offense

States have been slow to adopt the NIBRS. As of September 2007, 31 states were certified to report to the FBI.[17] Nevertheless, that is an improvement over 1997, when the NIBRS covered only 5.7 percent of the population. One reason that the project is taking so long is its size. According to a report of a joint FBI and Bureau of Justice Statistics NIBRS project,

> *Implementation of a project of this scope is an enormous undertaking, particularly so in that it relies so heavily on the internal informational processing and reporting capabilities of local law enforcement agencies.*[18]

VICTIM SURVEYS

Eager to close the gap (which many guessed to be large) between the number of crimes that the police know about and the amount of crime that really exists, criminologists called for a more complete measure of crime. Believing that asking the victims would be the best way to find out how much crime there really is, criminologists developed victim surveys. The most extensive (and most

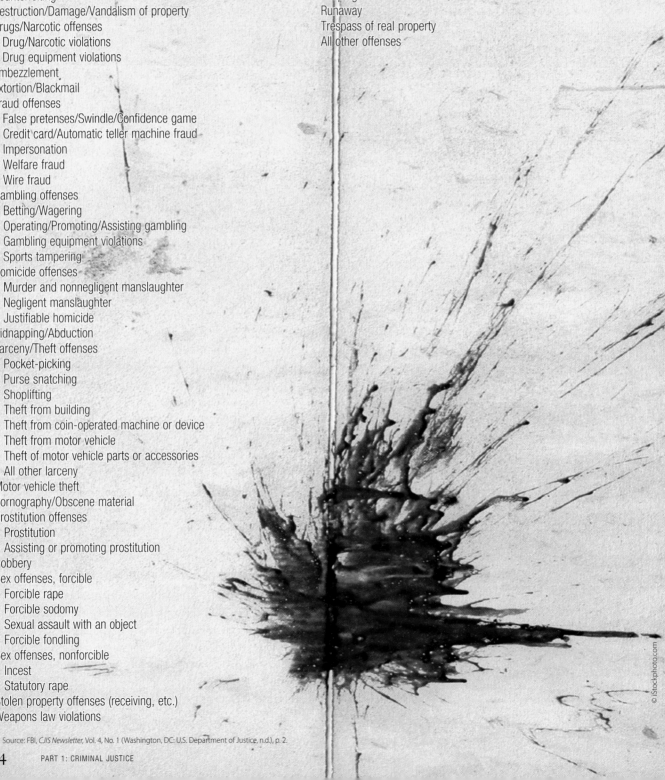

TABLE 2.3 Offenses Covered by the NIBRS

GROUP A (COLLECTS EXTENSIVE DATA ON THE FOLLOWING OFFENSES)

Arson
Assault offenses
- Aggravated assault
- Simple assault
- Intimidation
Bribery
Burglary/Breaking and entering
Counterfeiting
Destruction/Damage/Vandalism of property
Drugs/Narcotic offenses
- Drug/Narcotic violations
- Drug equipment violations
Embezzlement
Extortion/Blackmail
Fraud offenses
- False pretenses/Swindle/Confidence game
- Credit card/Automatic teller machine fraud
- Impersonation
- Welfare fraud
- Wire fraud
Gambling offenses
- Betting/Wagering
- Operating/Promoting/Assisting gambling
- Gambling equipment violations
- Sports tampering
Homicide offenses
- Murder and nonnegligent manslaughter
- Negligent manslaughter
- Justifiable homicide
Kidnapping/Abduction
Larceny/Theft offenses
- Pocket-picking
- Purse snatching
- Shoplifting
- Theft from building
- Theft from coin-operated machine or device
- Theft from motor vehicle
- Theft of motor vehicle parts or accessories
- All other larceny
Motor vehicle theft
Pornography/Obscene material
Prostitution offenses
- Prostitution
- Assisting or promoting prostitution
Robbery
Sex offenses, forcible
- Forcible rape
- Forcible sodomy
- Sexual assault with an object
- Forcible fondling
Sex offenses, nonforcible
- Incest
- Statutory rape
Stolen property offenses (receiving, etc.)
Weapons law violations

GROUP B (COLLECTS DATA ONLY ON PERSONS ARRESTED FOR THESE OFFENSES)

Bad checks
Curfew/Loitering/Vagrancy violations
Disorderly conduct
Driving under the influence
Drunkenness
Family offenses, nonviolent
Liquor law violations
Peeping tom
Runaway
Trespass of real property
All other offenses

Source: FBI, *CJIS Newsletter*, Vol. 4, No. 1 (Washington, DC: U.S. Department of Justice, n.d.), p. 2.

expensive) victim survey in history, the **National Crime Victimization Survey (NCVS)**, was launched in 1972. The NCVS collects detailed information about violent and property crimes and publishes it in an annual report, *Criminal Victimization in the United States.*[19] Obviously, the NCVS does not include homicides because the victims are dead.

How does the NCVS work? Every six months, U.S. Census workers take a telephone poll of a national sample of more than 40,000 households. They ask questions about five topics:

1 *Victimization.* Whether the person was a victim of a crime within the past six months

2 *Victims.* Age, race, gender, educational level, and income of victims

3 *Crime.* Location, amount of personal injury, and economic loss suffered from the crime

4 *Perpetrator.* Gender, age, race, and relationship to the victim

5 *Reporting.* Whether victims reported the crimes to the police and the reasons they did or did not

In its first annual report, *Criminal Victimization in the United States, 1972,* the NCVS proved what researchers and policymakers had always said: A lot more crimes are committed than are reported to the police. Less than half of the victims of violent crimes in 2002 reported them to the police; only 40 percent reported property

3 Types of Reports

✓ Official police reports

✓ Victim surveys

✓ Self-reports

crimes. Why don't victims report crimes? According to criminologist Wesley Skogan:

> *Most victimizations are not notable events. The majority are property crimes in which the perpetrator is never detected. The financial stakes are small, and the costs of calling the police greatly outweigh the benefits.*[20]

This may tell us why victims *don't* report minor offenses. But what about serious crimes? Victims *do* report more violent crimes than property crimes, but still less than half were reported in 2002.

Even though the NCVS uncovers some crimes that were not reported to the police, as with the UCR, there is still a dark figure of crime with the NCVS. Why? For one thing, you *cannot* ask dead victims about homicide, the most violent crime. And interviewers *do not* ask whether you are a victim of other crimes, like commercial burglary, commercial theft, and white-collar crime. Also, victims do not always tell interviewers about the victimizations they are asked about. Why don't victims tell interviewers about their victimizations? Skogan's explanation for why victims do not report crimes to the police may apply here as well. Interviewers have also uncovered other reasons, including embarrassment, apathy, forgetfulness, and knowing the perpetrator.

Sampling problems are another shortcoming in the NCVS. Young black males and illegal immigrants are consistently underrepresented among those interviewed. So are people with certain lifestyles, such as drifters, street

Victims don't report minor offenses.

© Robyn Mackenzie/iStockphoto.com / © Hemera Technologies/PhotoObjects.net/Jupiterimages

know that prisoners have higher victimization rates than the general population.) Wealthy people escape the NCVS by insulating themselves from all kinds of interviews. Another sampling problem is the small number of rapes, robberies, and aggravated assaults reported; for example, the year 2002 sample[21] turned up only 1.1 rapes and 2.2 robberies per 1,000 households. It's hard to make national generalizations based on so few numbers (which is not to say that even one rape or one robbery is not serious). Table 2.4 compares the UCR and the NCVS.

SELF-REPORTS

Self-reports are based on the idea that if you want to know about crimes, ask the people who commit them.

hustlers, and homeless people. And the NCVS does not survey people in prisons, jails, or juvenile corrections facilities. (We

Some prisoners exaggerate their "expertise" and minimize the harm they inflicted on their victims.

Self-reports are surveys of special groups in the general population. Self-reports grew out of a distrust of *all* official statistics.[22] During the 1960s crime boom, some criminologists argued that the steep increase in crime figures was not so much a real increase but a reflection of bias against minorities, poor people, and the youth counterculture that resulted in greater enforcement against them.

In a pioneer self-report survey in the late 1950s, Short and Nye asked nondelinquent schoolchildren and children in juvenile institutions about their delinquent acts. Both groups admitted similar behavior—truancy, stealing less than $2, buying and drinking alcohol, driving without a license, and having sex. After that, self-reports grew rapidly until, by the end of the 1960s, they dominated the study of juvenile delinquency.[23]

Still, finding out about crime by asking prisoners creates problems. First, convicted prisoners do not represent all criminals. Multiple offenders and "unsuccessful" criminals are overrepresented. Second, even a representative sample does not guarantee accuracy.

TABLE 2.4 Comparison of the UCR and the NCVS

	UNIFORM CRIME REPORTS (UCR)	NATIONAL CRIME VICTIM SURVEY (NCVS)
Crimes Included	Index Crimes • Homicide • Rape • Robbery • Burglary • Aggravated assault • Theft • Motor vehicle theft • Arson	Rape Robbery Aggravated assault Simple assault Household burglary Personal theft (purse snatching, pick-pocketing) Motor vehicle theft
Persons Arrested	All offenses	All offenses
Scope	Crimes reported to the police by victims and witnesses Crimes discovered by the police	Nonfatal violent and property crimes against victims 12 years old or older Victims' age, sex, race, ethnicity, marital status, income, and educational level Offenders' sex, race, age, and relationship to victim
Excluded	White-collar crime	Homicide Commercial crimes (nonresidential burglary)
Method	Local law enforcement agencies record crimes reported to or discovered by them and report summary totals to the FBI	U.S. Census Bureau surveys a representative sample of households
Source	Federal Bureau of Investigation (FBI), the law enforcement arm of the Department of Justice	Bureau of Justice Statistics (BJS), the research arm of the Department of Justice

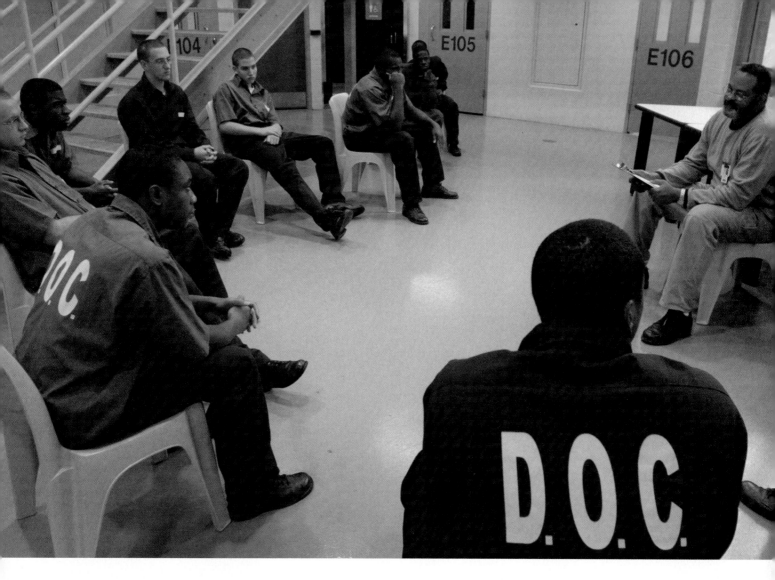
© AP Images/Gary Tramontina

Some prisoners exaggerate their "expertise" and minimize the harm they inflicted on their victims. Many do not trust the researchers or just want to "play games" to relieve the monotony of life in prison. Also, no matter what promises of confidentiality interviewers make, many prisoners still believe what they say will affect their chances for release. So they paint the best possible picture of themselves.[24]

The Canadian criminologist Gwynn Nettler had this to say about self-report surveys after he had reviewed many of them:

> *Asking people questions about their behavior is a poor way of observing it. . . . It is particularly ticklish to ask people to recall their "bad" behavior. Confessional data are at least as weak as the official statistics they were supposed to improve upon.[25]*

An example from Atlanta, Georgia summarizes the problem with the accuracy of crime statistics. In 2004, the Atlanta Police Department obtained an audit of crime data to determine if previous crime rates for the city had been accurate. The agency was concerned that crime had been underreported for some time and that violence in the city was going unheeded because of an inaccurate perception by some that the city was safer than it was. An external auditing company reviewed official crime data, agency data, and the self-reports of police officers and determined that there had been pressure to manipulate official data to make the city seem safer for a series of years, including the time frame leading to the selection of Atlanta for the 1996 Olympics. The agency had underreported crime by discarding incident reports and improperly closing cases. Over half the officers interviewed indicated that crimes had been intentionally downgraded. The goal was to not drive away the tourists. In addition, the city had 15 law enforcement agencies (including university and public transit police) that did not report their crime statistics to the Atlanta Police Department or the FBI. The report indicated that the violent crime rate for Atlanta in 2002 was reported to be almost 7 percent lower than it should have been.[26]

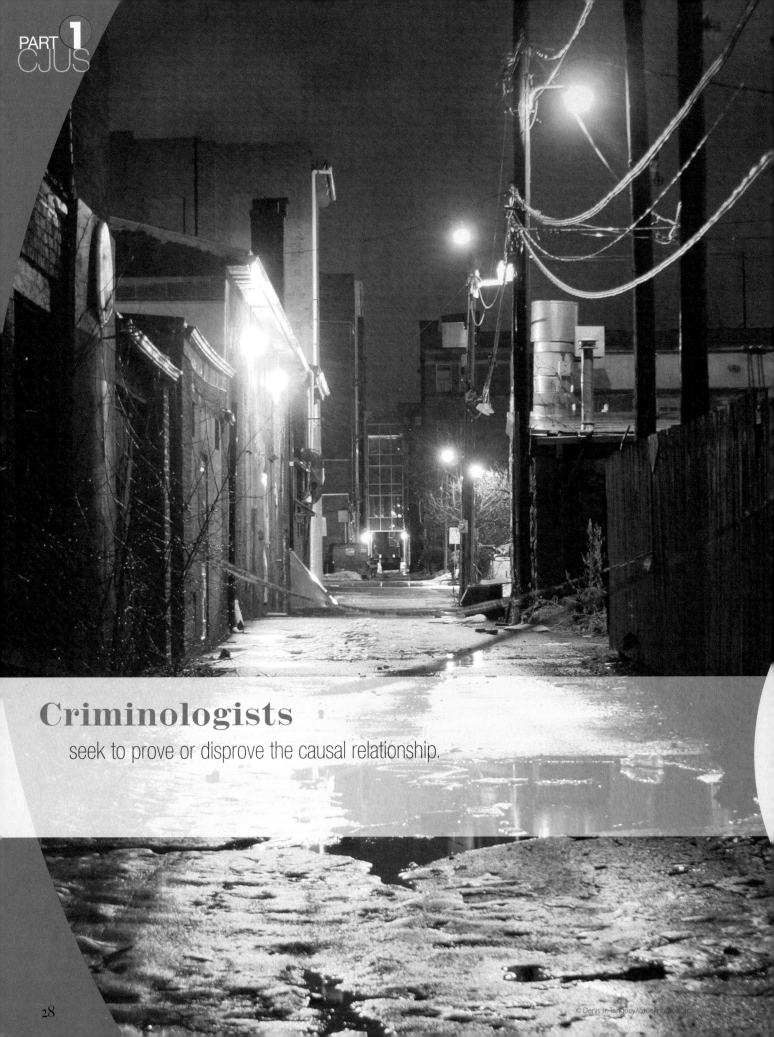

Criminologists

seek to prove or disprove the causal relationship.

3
Explanations of Criminal Behavior

Why a wife kills her abusive husband with a gunshot to the chest is much easier to understand than the killing of nearly 50 female prostitutes by a seemingly normal man. How could a man kill so many women, have sexual intercourse with their dead bodies, and then return home to his loving wife who never suspected what he had been doing over the years. Criminologists, psychologists, sociologists, and legal scholars are just some of the experts who use their knowledge and research to try to understand the criminal mind. In this chapter, we will explore the major theories of crime causation.

LO1 Crime Causation

the modern scientific theories of crime you will read about in this chapter all stem from the natural explanations in the sense that they're based on quantitative, objective observations. The theories focus on relationships between phenomena we can observe.[1] The relationship that criminologists seek to prove (or disprove) is the causal relationship. Causal relationships consist of several elements, two of which we concentrate on here: correlation and theoretical rationale. **Correlation** means that observable phenomena "*tend to vary with each other systematically*," as height and weight do. Positive correlations refer to variations in the same direction (the taller you are, the more you weigh). Negative correlations refer to variations in the opposite direction (the more miles on your car the less money it's worth). Notice that the direction does not have to be true in all cases—it only has to *tend* to be true.[2]

Correlations are necessary to causation because if two phenomena do not vary together, one phenomenon cannot cause the other. But correlation is not enough to prove causation. There has to be a *theoretical rationale*—a sensible explanation for the correlation. Remember this important point: Even if both the elements of correlation and a theoretical rationale are present, cause in theories of crime and criminal behavior is still

> **correlation** observable phenomena that "tend to vary with each other systematically"

Learning Outcomes

LO1 Distinguish among the various views of crime causation

LO2 Explain the classical view of crime causation

LO3 Understand who becomes a victim of crime and the characteristics of crime victims

LO4 Describe the positivist view of crime causation, including social structure and social process theories

LO5 Understand social conflict theories

Correlation

POSITIVE
The more you work, the more money you make.

NEGATIVE
The more you work, the less free time you have.

---

classical (utilitarian) theories theories based on free will and reason

positivist theories theories based on determinism or forces beyond individual control

determinism forces beyond individual control

social conflict theories the idea that crime is whatever the law says it is, and so the focus of criminal theories is on lawmakers and law enforcers instead of lawbreakers

rational choice theory individuals make decisions according to what they believe is in their self-interest

a statement of *probabilities* not *certainties*. But even probabilities are useful. If we identify a rational theory supporting a correlation, we might be able to influence the direction of the relationship between crime and other phenomena. For example, if, as is widely believed, adult criminal behavior is rooted in early childhood, then early childhood intervention can reduce adult crime.

All of the natural scientific theories reflect three very different ways of looking at crime. **Classical theories** (also called **utilitarian theories**) are based on the twin pillars of free will (individuals choose to commit crimes) and reason (they choose to do what benefits them). **Positivist theories** are based on **determinism**—the belief that criminal behavior is controlled by factors beyond the control of individuals. These factors might be within an individual (biologically and/or psychologically) or outside (dependent on social structure and social processes). **Social conflict theories** rest on the idea that crime is whatever the law says it is, and so the focus of these criminal theories is on lawmakers and law enforcers instead of lawbreakers.[3]

LO2 The Classical Theories

during the eighteenth-century Age of Reason (Enlightenment), Jeremy Bentham (influenced by Cesare Beccaria) developed the utilitarian theory of crime causation. This theory was based on two assumptions: First, it is human nature to seek pleasure and avoid pain, a view called *hedonism*. Second, individuals are free to choose to commit (or not commit) crimes (free will). So, for example, if your fear of the pain from getting caught and punished for stealing your friend's MP3 player is greater than the pleasure you anticipate that you will get from stealing it, you will not steal it. In the terminology of classical criminology, your decision not to steal is an example of specific deterrence, and the resulting decisions by other criminal wannabes not to steal are examples of general deterrence.

The whole structure of our criminal law and criminal justice system was built upon these radical assumptions.[4] When crime continued to climb in the 1800s, positivist disillusion with the classical theories produced the positivist theories. And when crime continued its upward climb—and even skyrocketed—policies based on positivist theories were blamed; so, during the 1970s, policies based on the assumptions of classical theory became popular again.

Let's look at two current theories based on classical criminology—rational choice and routine activities theories.

THE RATIONAL CHOICE THEORY

The **rational choice theory** assumes that individuals make decisions according to what

Jeremy Bentham

they *believe* is in their self-interest (even if it's not). The explanation allows for *some* irrational and pathological components in criminal behavior. Rational choice theory consists of three elements:

1. A reasoning criminal
2. A crime-specific focus
3. Separate analyses of criminal involvement and criminal events

The reasoning criminal element assumes offenders commit crimes to benefit themselves. Getting benefits requires rational decision making, even though the decisions are affected by *some* irrationality and pathology. According to the theory, criminals have specific goals, alternative means of obtaining them, and at least some information for choosing the best alternative to achieve their goals.[5]

The crime-specific element assumes decision making is different for each crime. The decision making required for burglary, for example, is different from that needed for robbery, and different kinds of burglaries and robberies require different decision making. So deciding to rob a convenience store or a bank or to mug a person on the street each demands a separate analysis. The decision to commit a commercial burglary is not like the decision to commit a residential burglary. And burglars who target public housing, middle-class neighborhoods, and wealthy enclaves differ as to individual burglars, targets, motivations, and methods. Figure 3.1 shows what motivates armed robbers to commit armed robbery.

The third element divides criminal involvement and criminal

events. Criminal involvement refers to three critical decisions:

1. Deciding generally to get involved in crime
2. Deciding to continue committing crimes
3. Deciding to get out of involvement in crime

The criminal event refers to the decision to commit a specific crime.

An example of rational choice theory is illustrated by the Uncle Hilty case in Conroe, Texas. In 1995, Hilton Crawford set up an elaborate kidnapping plan to abduct the 12-year-old son of a friend. His intent was to hold the child for ransom ($500,000), but he took the child to Louisiana, shot him twice in the head, and buried the body. He chose to commit this crime to help pay off his gambling debts and to live a lavish lifestyle. Crawford was an immediate suspect and blood evidence in the trunk of his car connected him to the crime. He

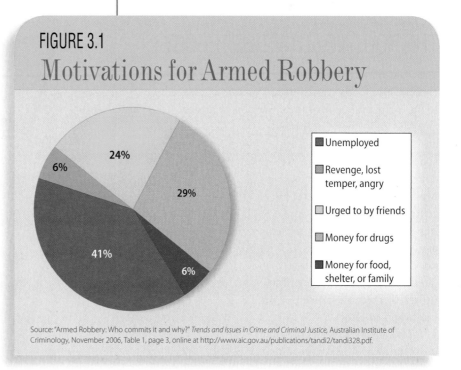

FIGURE 3.1
Motivations for Armed Robbery

- Unemployed
- Revenge, lost temper, angry
- Urged to by friends
- Money for drugs
- Money for food, shelter, or family

24%
6%
29%
41%
6%

Source: "Armed Robbery: Who commits it and why?" *Trends and Issues in Crime and Criminal Justice*, Australian Institute of Criminology, November 2006, Table 1, page 3, online at http://www.aic.gov.au/publications/tandi2/tandi328.pdf.

Hilton Crawford

> **routine activities theory** a focus on the influence of the location of targets and movements of offenders and victims in time and space on decision making by criminals

confessed to the kidnapping and eventually to the murder. Crawford was executed in 2003 by lethal injection.[6]

Policy Implications

Rational choice theory can lead to two contrasting policy approaches to reducing crime. One is to raise the cost of illegal behavior through more arrests, convictions, and stiffer punishments. Raising the price of crime enjoys wide public support and is the current policy of choice. The second approach, increasing the gains from lawful behavior, has not often been tried, and it enjoys little support. Why not? For one thing, we would have to expand the government's activities in a major way, resulting in what some might call unwarranted invasions into areas that are not the government's business. For example, government could set wage controls, guarantee job security, and order more chances for advancement for blue collar employees. That amount of government interference is out of the question in our free market economy, however.

THE ROUTINE ACTIVITIES THEORY

The **routine activities theory,** like classical or rational choice, studies the decision to commit crimes. The focus is the influence of the "location of targets and the movement of offenders and victims in time and space"[7] on the decision to commit a crime. Opportunity and temptation are central to routine activities theory. The theory assumes that offenders' decisions are "not calculated to maximize success, but rather to meet their needs with a minimum of effort."[8]

The theory also assumes that most criminals (like most peo-

ple) are "middling in morality, in self-control, in careful effort, in pursuing advantage."[9] So criminal behavior depends on the situation—specifically, on time, space (perhaps more properly, place), opportunity, and temptation. Situation explanations look at the modus operandi (MO) of offenders.

Let's look at the elements of routine activities theory and its policy implications for fighting crime.

Elements

The theory has three elements, all of which include rational choice:

1. A motivated offender
2. A suitable target
3. The absence of a capable guardian

A motivated offender is "anybody who for any reason might commit a crime." The routine activities theory brings time and space into the foreground and pushes into the background both the individual motivation of criminals and the agencies of criminal justice. Whether money, power, status, sex, or thrills motivate offenders to commit crimes is not the significant inquiry; any motivation will do.

A suitable target is "any person or object likely to be taken or attacked by the offender."[10] This includes anyone or any property in the right place at the right time.

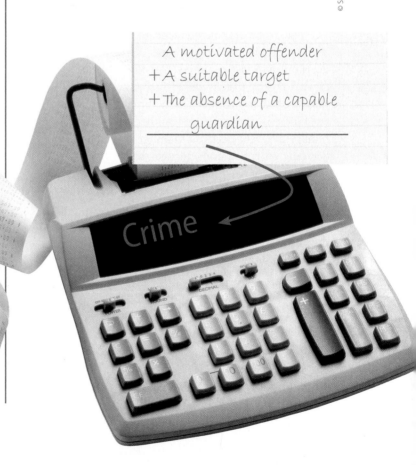

A motivated offender
+ A suitable target
+ The absence of a capable guardian

The capable guardian can be (but usually is not) a police officer or a security guard in a position to protect a target. More likely, because the guardian has to be present at the time, the guardian is someone such as a friend, relative, bystander, or owner of the targeted property. Police typically arrive after the crime is committed.[11]

Angel Maturino Resendiz, the Railroad Killer, is an example of routine activities theory in that he chose to commit crimes as a result of need and opportunity. He is known as the Railroad Killer because he used the railroad to travel across the country. He raped and killed to obtain money for drugs and alcohol. He did not come to the attention of authorities for most of the duration of his crimes because he was an illegal immigrant and moved all over the country. He is believed to have killed up to 15 people using rocks and other basic objects that served his needs at the time. Resendiz was executed in Texas in 2006.[12]

Policy Implications

What have we learned from routine activities theory? Crime is more likely to occur when targets are more "attractive," are not as well guarded, and are more exposed to motivated offenders. For example, since World War II Americans have increasingly spent more time away from home (women working outside the home and single-parent families account for much of this trend). With fewer people at home, homicide, robbery, rape, assault, and burglary rates have climbed. The number of property crimes has also increased as people have acquired more lightweight portable electronic gadgets.[13]

The routine activities theory has stretched criminology beyond motivation and demonstrated the importance of informal social control. But, according to criminologist Gary Lafree, routine activities theory does not

> *offer a ready explanation for the observed timing of observed changes in crime rates. . . . It seems unlikely that the situational variables identified by Clarke and Felson were not also changing when crime rates were . . . high and constant in the 1980s and 1990s. By concentrating on the supply of suitable crime situations, situational theorists end up treating all motivated offenders as equally motivated and all capable guardians as equally capable.[14]*

LO3 Crime Victims and Their Characteristics

routine activities theory includes the role of the victim in crime and is perhaps the dominant theory of victimization. In Chapter 2, we discussed victim statistics derived from the National Crime Victimization Survey (NCVS). When trying to understand the role of the victim in crime, it is important to have knowledge of the typical characteristics of victims and the crimes committed against them. One of the most critical dynamics of victimization is whether the victim knows the offender.

That phrase from the old song "You always hurt the one you love" is more true of criminals and their victims than we like to admit. When it comes to criminals, relationships *do* matter, especially four:

1. *Intimates.* Spouses, ex-spouses, same-sex partners, boyfriends, girlfriends
2. *Relatives.* Parents, children, siblings, grandparents, in-laws, cousins
3. *Acquaintances.* People who know each other, such as friends and people from work, where they shop, where they go for fun
4. *Strangers.* People who do not know each other

Here's some of what we know about crimes involving victims and offenders who have some kind of relationship with each other, from the NCVS in 2006.[15]

- The violent crime rate by victimizations was 11.3 when the crime involved a stranger and 13.0 when the crime involved a nonstranger.

Angel Maturino Resendiz

© Mark Stay/iStockphoto.com

© AP Images/David J. Phillip

- Assault was more likely to be committed by nonstrangers.
- Robbery was more likely to be committed by strangers.
- Rape and sexual assault were more likely to be committed by nonstrangers.
- Nonstranger violent crime is more likely to be committed by a friend or acquaintance than an intimate or relative.

CRIME VICTIMS

Here are the bare facts of criminal victimization for the years 2005–2006:[16]

- There were more than 25 million victimizations.
- Over 6 million were violent crimes and a little more than 18 million were property crimes.
- Young people were violent crime victims at higher rates (47.8 percent for ages 12–15; 52.8 percent for ages 16–19) than any other age group (13.6 percent for ages 50–64).
- There were 27.4 male victims and 23.4 female victims of violent crime for every 1,000 households.
- There were 23.9 white violent crime victims, 32.9 black victims, and 20.4 other victims for every 1,000 households.
- The violent crime rate in households with incomes less than $7,500 was 64.6 for every 1,000 households.
- Crimes of violence were more likely to be committed without a weapon.
- Teens aged 12–19 and young adults aged 20–24 experienced the highest rates of violent crime.
- College and university campuses were the site of 95,270 reported crimes; of these, 97 percent were property crime and 3 percent were violent crime.
- A total of 85,000 persons over the age of 65 were victims of nonfatal violent crime.
- Of all violent crime incidents, 24 percent were committed by an armed offender and 9 percent by an offender with a firearm.

VICTIM PROTECTION AND ASSISTANCE

The U.S. Victims of Crime Act created a $100 million crime victims' fund drawn from criminal fines for federal offenses. The money supports state victim compensation and other programs that assist victims. States have also passed laws to assist crime victims. Most of these statutes provide for violent crime victims who report crimes and cooperate with investigation and prosecution to receive some compensation for medical expenses, funeral expenses, lost wages, and the support of deceased victims' dependents. Unfortunately, the caps on the allowable amounts are so low that the compensation is rarely meaningful.[17]

Some states have established victim-witness assistance programs, usually supervised by prosecutors. These programs provide services like the following:

- *Personal advocacy.* Helping victims receive all the services they are entitled to
- *Referral.* Recommending or obtaining other assistance
- *Restitution assistance.* Urging judges to order, or probation authorities to collect, restitution and helping violent crime victims fill out applications to receive compensation
- *Court orientation.* Explaining the criminal justice system and the role of victims and witnesses in it
- *Transportation.* Taking victims and witnesses to and from court, to social service agencies, and, if necessary, to shelters
- *Escort services.* Escorting witnesses to court and staying with them during proceedings
- *Emotional support.* Giving victims support during their ordeals with crime and with the criminal justice proceedings following it

Thirteen states have even written victims' rights provisions into their constitutions. Typical provisions require the criminal justice system to:

- Treat victims with compassion and respect
- Inform victims of critical stages in the trial process
- Invite victims to attend and comment on trial proceedings

"I feel as if our movement is picking up the steam it needs to carry through all fifty states," said Linda Lowrance, chair of the Victims' Constitutional Amendment Network. But no one has evaluated the *effectiveness* of these provisions, according to John Stein, deputy director of the National Organization for Victim Assistance. Some evidence does show that victim impact statements make people "feel better" about the criminal justice system, even though the statements have little or no effect on the sentencing or punishment of convicted offenders. Roberta Roper, whose daughter was raped and murdered, could not attend the trial of her daughter's murderers because Maryland has no victims' rights law. Forced to watch the trial by pressing her nose against the small pane of glass in a wooden courtroom door, Roper felt she would let her daughter down by not being in court. "By being a presence at the trial, we could as a family, bear witness to the fact that Stephanie lived, and she mattered. We were denied that."[18]

LO4 The Positivist Theories

Positivist theories of crime emerged from the disappointment that arose when tailoring the punishment to fit the crime did not seem to reduce crime. The positivists looked for forces beyond the control of individual choice that caused or determined criminal behavior. Those forces might be within the individual or external. Here we look at three modern descendants of the positivist theories—biological, psychological, and sociological theories.

BIOLOGICAL THEORIES

"Criminals are born not made," concluded the nineteenth-century Italian psychiatrist turned criminologist Cesare Lombroso, launching the first positivist theory of criminal behavior as a biological theory. Lombroso is best known for the atavistic theory that criminals are throwbacks to some primitive age of development. Other early positivists studied faces and body types to find the causes of crime. But Lombroso made a much larger contribution than the atavistic theory suggests; he called for a general theory of crime causation. That general theory became what we know as multiple-factor causation—some factors are determined by biology, others by psychology, and still others by society.[19]

The early positivists gave biological theories a bad name, especially when their focus on external physical traits was dragooned into the service of racists and extreme nationalists to justify genocide and other horrors. But we have come a long way since then. Today, much respectable research on the links between biology and crime exists.[20]

In looking for biological causes of behavior, serial killers provide numerous characteristics to analyze. Dennis Rader, known as the BTK (Bind, Torture, and Kill) killer, was connected to his serial killing through his church work. From 1974 to 1991, the BTK killer would stalk his victims, convince them he was going to only rape them, and then he would strangle them to death. He would strangle them, allow them to regain consciousness, and then strangle them again. He would become more sexually aroused as he progressed through this horrible process. He would then masturbate and ejaculate on the bodies of his victims. Rader also taunted police and the media throughout the many years of his killing spree by sending them the details of his horrific work. In 2005, he sent a floppy disk to a Fox affiliate station in Wichita, Kansas. An analysis of the disk revealed a document from a church. Further investigation led to Dennis Rader who was a member of the church and president of the church council. He was sentenced to ten life terms with no possibility of parole.[21] According to biological theorists, the actions of serial killers such as Rader result not from external forces such as abuse or neglect, but from internal influences such as genetic makeup, hormones, and chemical imbalances within the brain.

© Bettmann/Corbis

Cesare Lombroso

Dennis Rader

© AP Images/Travis Heying/© iStockphoto.com

In February of 1991, while robbing a Domino's Pizza restaurant, Stephen Anthony Mobley shot and killed store manager John Collins. Three weeks later, Mobley was arrested while making his escape from a dry-cleaning store robbery, during which he brandished the same pistol that killed Collins. While being held in jail, Mobley had the word "Domino" tatooed on his back, carried a domino piece in his pocket, and kept a Domino's delivery box in his cell. Mobley was indicted in March of 1991 on malice and felony murder, three counts of aggravated assault, and possession of a firearm in the commission of a crime. After being found guilty on all counts in 1994, Mobley was sentenced to death by lethal injection and was executed on March 1, 2005.

Genetics

"Like father like son" captures the ancient common-sense observation that children resemble their parents. Now, we know empirically that genes *do* affect many behaviors (reasoning, academic achievement, aggression, and hostility). Identical twin studies make it easier to separate the effects of genes and environment, because twins' genes, which are produced by one egg fertilized by one sperm, are identical. Some twin studies have established that genes contribute substantially to criminal behavior.[22] But do not make too much of these results. First, the samples are drawn exclusively from Danish twins, making it difficult to apply the results to other cultures. Second, the evidence for the contribution of genes to *violent* criminal behavior is considerably weaker than it is for less serious offenses.

The execution of Stephen Mobley in 2005 indicates that claims of genetic causes of crime are still met with much skepticism and caution.[23] Mobley's trial for capital murder in 1994 started an international debate when his attorneys attempted to use genetic deficiencies as part of his defense. Nevertheless, he was convicted. The trial and appellate courts rejected the argument that Mobley should not be executed because his crime was due to genetic causes. Subsequently, between 1994 and 2004, attempts to link genetics and crime were made in 27 key cases. Although the Mobley case aroused concerns that irresponsible applications of the genetics and crime link would become rampant, a review of the outcomes of these cases reveals that this has not occurred. Courts still seem to be skeptical of the link, and juries still have political and moral concerns over the genetics and crime relationship.

Biological Markers of Violent Behavior

Criminal behavior, like all behavior, results from complex processes in the brain. Sometimes, permanent conditions (genetics or brain damage) produce the behavior; sometimes temporary conditions (seizures, use of alcohol or other psychoactive substances) produce it. Let's look briefly at the influence of the conditions that have been the focus of most modern research.

Hormones and Male Violence Testosterone, the chief hormone that produces masculine characteristics, has been frequently studied, especially for its role in sexual violence. A wide range of studies, using differing measures of violence, has led to the suggestion of a possible link between testosterone and male aggression.[24] Higher than average amounts of crime committed by athletes have been attributed to the high levels of testosterone in male athletes. This link has also been raised with men and boys who take anabolic steroids to enhance athletic performance. The use of anabolic steroids appears to cause more aggressive and violent behavior.[25] These relationships are correlational and not causative, however. It is just as likely that violent lifestyles lead to high testosterone levels. The conclusion regarding testoster-

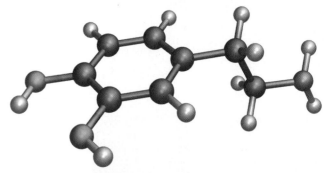

DOPAMINE
activates processes for pleasure and reward

one and aggression is that the hormone is involved in violence but is not the primary factor.[26]

Hormones and Female Violence Although most of the research on hormones and crime is about men, there has also been a long history of interest in female behavior and menstruation. The focus of modern research is on *premenstrual syndrome* (PMS) and whether there is a link between heightened levels of female sex hormones just before the onset of menstruation and violent and aggressive behavior. As with testosterone and aggression, there appears to be a correlation between PMS and aggression, but again PMS does not appear to be the primary factor in aggression by women.[27]

Neurotransmitters There are 50 known *neurotransmitters*, enzymes that translate messages from the brain into action. Researchers have studied a few because they are linked to violent behavior. One of them, dopamine, activates processes for pleasure and reward. Some antipsychotic drugs that affect dopamine levels are used to "quell acute violent outbursts" and as long-term "chemical restraint for violence-prone" inmates of institutions. But these drugs do more than control violence; they also create a number of neurological problems.[28]

The neurotransmitter serotonin has been the most studied in terms of its effect on violent behavior. Since the late 1970s, researchers have reported negative correlations between serotonin concentrations and aggressive, impulsive, sensation-seeking behavior, alcoholism, suicide, and crime. Low levels of serotonin are associated with a lack of control over aggressive impulses.[29]

A lack of control over impulses is illustrated with the case of Jeffrey Dahmer in Milwaukee, Wisconsin. During the 1990s, Dahmer came to the attention of law enforcement on multiple occasions for inappropriate sexual behavior. He was able to convince the courts that he had psychological problems, and he was given probation and allowed to seek treatment. In 1991, one of Dahmer's male victims escaped and went to the police, but Dahmer was able to convince the police that it was just a fight between lovers. The victim was left with Dahmer who killed him later that night and dismembered his body. Dahmer was finally arrested later that year when another of his victims escaped. Police searched his home and found pictures of murdered victims, three severed heads, and body parts. Many of the body parts were found in his refrigerator. In 1992, Dahmer was sentenced to 15 life terms but was killed by another prison inmate in 1994.[30]

Brain Abnormalities and Dysfunctions Recent studies also have shown that abnormal brain development and brain damage are associated with aggressive behavior. Such studies reveal that male offenders with high levels of psychopathic traits such as superficial charm,

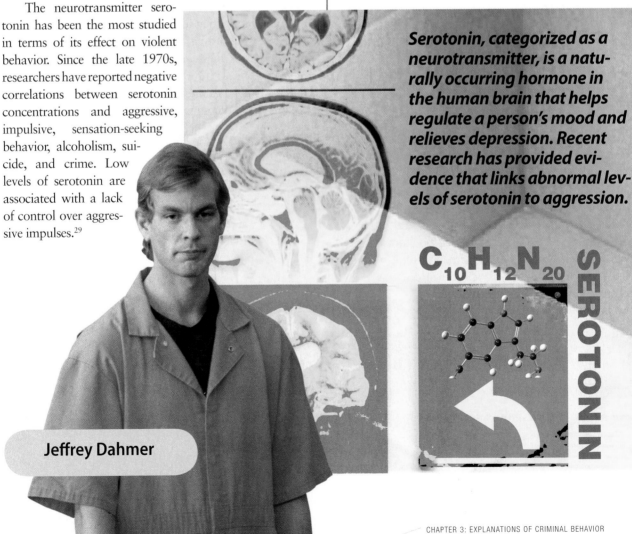

Serotonin, categorized as a neurotransmitter, is a naturally occurring hormone in the human brain that helps regulate a person's mood and relieves depression. Recent research has provided evidence that links abnormal levels of serotonin to aggression.

$C_{10}H_{12}N_{20}$ SEROTONIN

Jeffrey Dahmer

manipulativeness, and absence of remorse or empathy do not differentiate normally between nonemotional and emotional cues. In one study, psychopaths who had been caught and convicted showed abnormal development of the hippocampus compared to successful psychopaths (those not caught) and the normal population. This finding about the hippocampus is important in understanding the regulation of aggression because this part of the brain regulates the fear factor, letting the person know that some things are to be feared and avoided. The result may be "impulsive, disinhibited, unregulated and reward-driven antisocial behavior that is more prone to legal detection."[31]

Diet Recent studies on diet have suggested a link between the modern Western diet and aggression. The modern Western diet has moved from the omega-3 fatty acids essential to brain development and brain health to the less healthy omega-6 fatty acids found in soy, corn, and sunflower oils. Studies on aggressive individuals treated with omega-3 supplements found a significant reduction in violent behavior in comparison with the control group.[32]

Policy Implications

One problem in studying biological markers of violent behavior is that the less intrusive and broadly accepted research methods produce information that is removed from the cause. For example, analyzing urine and hair samples intrude the least on subjects' privacy and dignity, but the results are also the least useful because they blend together relevant neurological processes with unrelated events that happened long before or after a violent event. For another example, painful and risky spinal taps provide a better measure of ongoing brain activity, but they are not related to the start or finish of violent acts.

Conducting this type of research on human subjects also raises ethical concerns. In addition, researchers have to contend with suspicion regarding ethically unacceptable future preventive interventions.[33]

PSYCHOLOGICAL THEORIES

Psychological theories focus on the mental and emotional elements in criminal behavior. There are several kinds of these

INTELLIGENCE

VS.

PERSONALITY

elements, but most theories and research concentrate on two:

1. Intelligence (measured mostly by low IQ)
2. Personality (antisocial and impulsive behavior)

Low Intelligence

The early positivist criminologists believed that low intelligence was one of the causes of crime. In the early 1900s, they used the then new IQ (intelligence quotient, which was obtained by dividing mental age by chronological age) to identify feebleminded inmates—those with IQs below the mental age of 12. The wave of IQ testing that swept through U.S. prisons seemed to back up their belief.

After these studies, low intelligence disappeared as an explanation for criminal behavior—until 1977 when Hirschi and Hindelang reported that their review of research showed that the link between IQ and delinquency was at least as strong as between race or social class and delinquency.[34] They conceded, however, that the link was *indirect*. Kids with low IQs fail in school, and academic failure is linked to future delinquency and adult criminality. But that did not make the link any less real.

Before dying in prison in 1996, Ottis Elwood Toole lived as a notorious murderer, arsonist, rapist and cannibal. Toole is believed to have murdered at least seven people, and in December of 2008, he was identified as the likely killer of Adam Walsh, son of America's Most Wanted host John Walsh. Despite years of criminal success and police evasion. Toole's IQ was estimated at just 75, well below the average offender IQ of 92. The IQ of Toole's frequent partner in crime Henry Lee Lucas was also lower than average, estimated at 84.

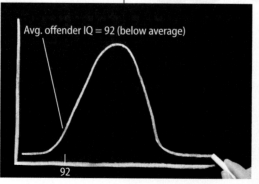

Avg. offender IQ = 92 (below average)

92

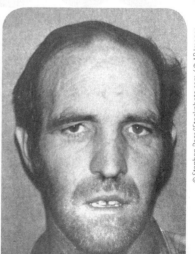

A number of subsequent studies in the United States and other countries found similar results. But none was more strong, confident, or controversial than Richard Herrnstein and Charles Murray's *The Bell Curve*.[35] Herrnstein and Murray, after extensively reviewing the IQ-crime research, found that offenders have an average IQ of 92 (8 points below average). Other studies showed that serious offenders' scores are lower than those of minor offenders, and that low IQ scores in small children are linked to later delinquency and adult offending.[36]

Personality

When you think of personality you probably think of words like *aggressive, argumentative, timid, withdrawn, friendly, likable,* and others that describe behavioral and emotional traits that hold true most of the time. Sheldon and Eleanor Glueck compared 500 delinquent and nondelinquent Boston boys during the 1940s and 1950s.[37] They concluded that the "delinquent personality" does not depend so much on a list of characteristics as it does on the *relationship* among characteristics. These characteristics include being more extroverted, vivacious, and impulsive and less self-controlled than nondelinquents. Delinquents also tend to be more hostile, resentful, defiant, suspicious, and destructive. Delinquent youths are less likely to fear failure and are less concerned about meeting conventional expectations. They do not respond to authority and are more socially assertive. Delinquents often say that they are not recognized or appreciated.

Researchers have built and administered elaborate tools aimed at sorting out how delinquent and criminal personalities differ from nondelinquent and noncriminal personalities. Despite many claims that they do a good sorting job, these tools suffer from many methodological problems that raise questions about their accuracy. Too often, it is not possible to determine whether the differences are because of environment or personality. Consequently, these tools are not very useful in proving (or disproving) a link between personality and crime.

In 2003, Gary Ridgway was sentenced to 48 life sentences with no possibility for parole for the homicides of 48 female prostitutes or teen-aged runaways in the Seattle, Washington area. Ridgway, known as the Green River Killer,

dumped the bodies in and around the Green River in Washington during the 1980s. DNA evidence eventually linked him to the crimes. Ridgway claimed he had an addiction to prostitutes. After burying some of his victims, he would return later and have sexual intercourse with the dead bodies, a practice known as necrophilia. In total, he confessed to 49 killings, but investigators and the families of victims believe he killed many more. Ridgway's criminal actions could be the result of personality disorders, biological abnormalities, or even brain abnormalities that might account for his sexual dysfunction.[38]

SOCIOLOGICAL THEORIES

Criminologists are wary of explanations of criminal behavior based on the individual's biology, psychology, and free will. They look instead for links between criminal behavior and the structure and processes of society; in social institutions like neighborhoods, family, churches, and schools; in demographics like social status, race, gender, age, and education; and in community values.

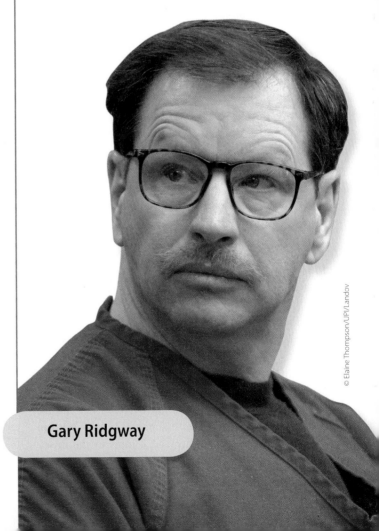

Gary Ridgway

Social Structure Theories

Social structure theories link individual criminal behavior to social class and structural conditions like poverty, unemployment, and poor education. According to social structure theorists, crime is located mainly in lower-income classes because flaws in the social structure increase the odds that individuals in that part of society will commit crimes. Emile Durkheim explained crime as the result of the breakdown of social norms—the **anomie theory**.[39] A society in transition, Durkheim said, weakens the bonds that ordinarily control our natural (but not always desirable) urges; crime follows that weakening. Two forms of the theory—strain and opportunity theories—were developed to describe conditions specific to the United States.

The Strain Theory

According to Merton's **strain theory**, society establishes goals that we all try to achieve—the goals "worth striving for."[40] In U.S. culture, the most important goal is getting rich. Indeed, it's not enough just to get rich—the goal is to get as rich as possible. Although society establishes the goals, the social structure blocks some people from achieving them. This blockage creates a strain that leads more people in the lower classes than in the upper classes to commit crimes.

Strain falls especially hard on the lower classes. For them, the social structure itself stands in the way of success. In contrast, in the upper classes, it takes only moderate talent and effort to achieve success through the work ethic. The contradiction between the culture and the social structure is the essence of Merton's strain theory. The reason for higher crime rates in the lower classes is not cultural (everyone wants to get rich and everyone has a similar work ethic), but rather lies in the social structure: the lower classes do not have their fair share of opportunities to get rich by hard work.

Social Process Theories

Social structure theory does not pretend to explain all criminal behavior. After all, crime occurs in all social classes, and most people in the lower classes do not commit crimes. **Social process theories** look for explanations of crime in social processes (interactions among members) of families, peer groups, schools, churches, neighborhoods, and other social institutions. There is a great deal of empirical research linking experiences with these institutions to criminal behavior. For example, most prison inmates come from single-parent homes, have relatives and friends who have served time in prison, are school dropouts or underachievers, and have poor work skills and employment records.

Social process theorists agree that criminogenic forces in society affect behavior, but they disagree over *how*. **Social learning theories** assume individuals are born as blank slates and can learn any values and behavior. **Social control theory** assumes everybody is born with the desire to break the rules. **Labeling theory** assumes the criminal justice system creates criminals. Whether individuals have actually broken the law does not matter. Society's actions shape the self-image and behavior of people who have been labeled criminals.

Social Learning Theories Sutherland formulated the most prominent social learning theory: differential associ-

Emile Durkheim

ation theory. According to Sutherland, criminal behavior, just like any other behavior, depends on our associations with other people. If we associate more with lawbreakers than with law-abiders, chances are we will commit crimes. Some associations are stronger than others. The more intense the relationships, the more we learn from them and the longer we retain what we have learned. Our families and our friendships teach us the most enduring lessons about how to behave. People in low-income neighborhoods who associate with "street criminals" learn to act like street criminals, not because people who live in poor neighborhoods are "bad" but because that is the way social beings behave. By the same reasoning, corporate criminals learn criminal behavior, too.[41]

The Social Control Theory Social control theory assumes that people are rule breakers by nature. As Hirschi put it, "The question 'Why did they do it?' is simply not the question the theory is designed to answer. The question is, 'Why don't we do it?' There is much evidence that we would, if we dared."[42] Why do we obey rules when we are rule breakers by nature? We obey because our ties to established institutions of social control (families, peer groups, churches, and schools) check our natural desire to break rules and satisfy our selfish interests. When ties to these institutions weaken, criminal behavior is likely to follow. Social bonds do not reduce our desire to get what we want; they reduce the chance we will give in to our desire.[43]

Hirschi identified four elements in the social bond that curb the natural desire to break rules. First, attachment to others makes us sensitive to their opinions. Attachment to those whose opinions we care about (parents, teachers, coaches, neighbors, and friends) predicts best whether we will follow rules. Second, commitment to the conventional order keeps us in line. The stronger our desire to get a job, get an education, and protect our reputation, the greater the chances we will follow the rules. Third, involvement in legal activities leaves us less time to get into trouble. Fourth, the stronger we believe in the conventional order, the less likely we are to break its rules.

Control theory is an appealing explanation for crime trends since 1950, a period that has seen ties to traditional institutions weakened. Empirical evidence strongly supports the argument that juveniles and young adults with strong ties to their families and schools are less likely to commit crimes. Of course, this does not explain what caused the weakening of ties in the first place and why ties were stronger in the 1950s than in the 1990s.[44]

The Labeling Theory According to Becker, individuals do not commit crimes because they cannot manage the stresses in society, because they associate with other criminals and learn crime from them, or because they break the social bonds that would keep in line their urges to break rules.[45] Instead, outsiders—"moral entrepreneurs" like police, courts, and corrections officers trying to control crime—turn deviant episodes by individuals into criminal careers. In other words, the criminal justice system creates criminals. Whether "criminals" have actually broken the law does not matter. What does matter is that once the "system" says they are criminals, they act like criminals. Society's actions shape their self-image.

Labeling theory shifts the emphasis from lawbreakers to lawmakers and law enforcers. This shift draws attention to the possible harmful effects of contacts with criminal justice agencies. The theory had a direct influence on public policy during the 1960s and 1970s with the creation of programs that diverted people out of the criminal justice system into alternative social programs.[46]

If our close friends show disdain for the legal system, we too are less likely to play by the rules. Because of strong attachment amongst members, street gangs reinforce unlawful attitudes.

© A. Ramey/PhotoEdit / © Wendy Idele/Nonstock/Jupiterimages

© Mark Evans/iStockphoto.com

© Inmagine/Inspirestock/Jupiterimages

emotional debate) and nonviolent pressure are the means most often used. The group(s) with the most power and resources win(s) the battles. Rather than being an honest broker in the conflict over interests, government represents the interests of the most powerful group(s).[47] Examining the opposite perspective can aid in understanding conflict theory, so we present consensus theory first.

THE CONSENSUS THEORY

Durkheim stated two propositions relevant to understanding the sociology of criminal law:

1. Crime is conduct "universally disapproved of by members of each society. Crimes shock sentiments which, for a given social system, are found in all healthy consciences."

2. "An act is criminal when it offends strong and defined states of the collective conscience."[48]

Empirical evidence from modern times supports Durkheim's consensus hypothesis. Blacks and whites, ethnic groups, men and women, rich and poor, young and old, and well-educated and poorly educated people agree on what conduct amounts to serious crime. In 1983, researchers asked a selected sample to rank the seriousness of various crimes. The answers displayed a broad consensus that violent crimes are considered most serious, property crimes are less serious, and public-order crimes are the least serious.[49] This is similar to the rankings in most criminal codes (see Figure 3.2).

THE CONFLICT THEORY

Consensus theory dominated mainstream criminology until the 1950s, when conflict theories reemerged. The conflict theorists challenged the notion that consensus is the "normal" state of society. Instead, **conflict theory** assumes that conflict is the normal state of society. It assumes further that social control requires active constraint, sometimes in the form of coercion. Common values and interests cannot maintain social control because they do not exist. Society is divided into competing classes and interest groups; the most powerful ones dominate legislatures and criminal justice agencies. They write criminal laws that further their interests and impose their values on the whole society. They use these laws to maintain their dominance and control conflict.[50]

Conflict theory maintains that criminal law does not reflect absolute, agreed-on principles or universal moral values. Instead, criminal law defines, and criminal justice agencies preserve and protect, the interests and values of the dominant social groups. Criminal law

conflict theory conflict is the normal state of society and social control requires active constraint, sometimes in the form of coercion

LO5 Social Conflict Theories

throughout history, two contrasting views of the nature of society have prevailed in social theory. According to the consensus perspective, consensus is the normal state of society. The consensus of values and the need to uphold them are the glues that hold society together. That does not mean there is total agreement. One reason we have government is to mediate among groups with competing values. In the mediation, the state is the honest broker representing the values of the whole society, not those of any particular group(s).

According to the conflict perspective, conflict is the normal state of society. Conflict over interests (groups' wants and needs) and the efforts to satisfy them is how society operates. Conflict is rarely violent; revolution and civil war are hardly ever the means of choice to resolve conflict. Instead, debate (sometimes very heated and

and procedure are means of preserving the dominant group(s)' definition of social order.[51]

THE RADICAL THEORY

Dissatisfaction with consensus and conflict theory, and with mainstream criminology and criminal justice, contributed to the creation of a "new," or radical, criminology in the 1960s. Radical criminology maintains that mainstream criminologists and criminal justice professionals are apologists, if not lackeys, for a capitalist ruling class that dominates the state. Radicals disagree over whether the dominant class consciously exploits the working class or whether the structure of capitalist society inevitably determines their exploitative actions. Instrumentalists contend that the ruling class consciously decides to exploit. According to structuralist radical theory, capitalists do not *know* they are exploiters. In the 1960s and 1970s, radical criminologists developed a coherent radical criminal justice theory based on the following propositions:

1. The state's primary purpose is to protect the dominant class in society.

2. This purpose requires controlling the lower classes.

3. The ruling class exploits the working class by wringing profit from overworked laborers.

4. Criminal law controls workers so that capitalists can get richer and secure protection for their accumulated riches.

5. Brute force is not always necessary to protect these interests and control the workers.

6. Capitalists sometimes have to commit crimes to maintain the existing power arrangements. So police officers violate individuals' rights, government abuses its power, corporations fix prices, and so on. They try not to do this too often because it threatens the myth that law is neutral, evenhanded, and fair.

7. Workers commit crimes mainly out of necessity. They prey on other workers, and sometimes capitalists, to survive: They steal what they cannot earn. Or, out of frustration with existing unjust arrangements, they erupt in violence against others. Occasionally, they commit "heroic crimes," like attacking the power structure. Their crimes are not bad or evil; they are utilitarian actions necessary to survive in a capitalist society.[52]

> According to structuralist radical theory, capitalists do not *know* they are exploiters.

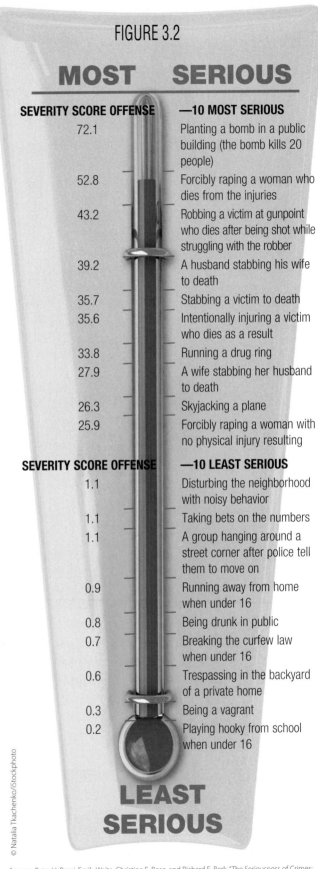

FIGURE 3.2

MOST SERIOUS

SEVERITY SCORE OFFENSE	—10 MOST SERIOUS
72.1	Planting a bomb in a public building (the bomb kills 20 people)
52.8	Forcibly raping a woman who dies from the injuries
43.2	Robbing a victim at gunpoint who dies after being shot while struggling with the robber
39.2	A husband stabbing his wife to death
35.7	Stabbing a victim to death
35.6	Intentionally injuring a victim who dies as a result
33.8	Running a drug ring
27.9	A wife stabbing her husband to death
26.3	Skyjacking a plane
25.9	Forcibly raping a woman with no physical injury resulting

SEVERITY SCORE OFFENSE	—10 LEAST SERIOUS
1.1	Disturbing the neighborhood with noisy behavior
1.1	Taking bets on the numbers
1.1	A group hanging around a street corner after police tell them to move on
0.9	Running away from home when under 16
0.8	Being drunk in public
0.7	Breaking the curfew law when under 16
0.6	Trespassing in the backyard of a private home
0.3	Being a vagrant
0.2	Playing hooky from school when under 16

LEAST SERIOUS

© Natalia Tkachenko/iStockphoto

Source: Peter H. Rossi, Emily Waite, Christine E. Bose, and Richard E. Berk, "The Seriousness of Crimes: Normative Structure and Individual Differences," *American Sociological Review* 39(1974).

No behavior can be criminal
without a specific law defining it as a crime.

4

Criminal Justice and the Law

In 2001, Andrea Yates, the mother of five children ages 6 months to 7 years, called 911 to report that she had drowned all of her children in the bathtub. When police arrived, she calmly and unemotionally told police what she had done and showed the bodies of her children to the responding police officers. Andrea told the police, "I killed my children." Andrea's calm reaction to what she had done and the capacity to kill not one but five of her children led many to believe that she intended to kill her children and that she should be punished severely for her crimes. Yet, there was evidence of mental illness and a history of long-term mental problems that might have been the underlying reason for the deaths of these children. Should Andrea Yates have been sentenced to death for her crimes or should she have been found guilty but insane by the courts? This is not an easy determination by the courts or by a jury that hears such a case. In this chapter, you will learn about the legal issues surrounding the insanity defense.[1]

LO1 The Sources of Criminal Law

"**n**o crime without law" and "No punishment without law" are two of the most ancient principles of our criminal law. Crime control in a constitutional democracy depends on these principles. If we lived in a pure democracy, the majority could do whatever it pleased, but we live in a *constitutional* democracy, which limits what the majority can do. The U.S. Constitution sets those limits. Thus, no behavior can be criminal without a specific law defining it as a crime, and the criminal justice system can take no actions except by the authority of law. The sources of this authority are the national and state constitutions, federal and state statutes, and court decisions interpreting these constitutions and statutes.[2]

Informally, the constitutional and legal framework and authority are broad and flexible enough to allow plenty of "play in the joints" of discretionary decision making. Legal terms, like all other words, are at best imperfect symbols of what they represent. No written rule defining criminal behavior can precisely

Learning Outcomes

LO1 Discuss the sources of criminal law

LO2 Understand how substantive criminal law defines a crime and the legal responsibility of the accused

LO3 Differentiate between excuses and justification defenses for crime

LO4 Explain the classifications and grading of crime

LO5 List the similarities and differences between criminal law and civil law

LO6 Explain the importance of due process in the criminal justice system and understand how criminal procedure protects the rights of the accused

criminal law tells private individuals what behavior is a crime and lays down the punishment for it

criminal procedure tells government officials the extent and limits of their power to enforce the criminal law, and it sets out the consequences for illegal official actions

principle of economy applying criminal law by relying on the least expensive or invasive response to misbehavior

describe all the behavior it's intended to prohibit. No provision defining the power of criminal justice agencies can fully account for all the actions that power allows. No rule can cover all contingencies that may arise after it's written. Finally, no rule, however clear and predictive, can—or should—eliminate the influences of ideology, economics, social structure and processes, and individual personality. In short, the tension between formal rules and informal, discretionary decision making—between formal and informal criminal justice—also applies to criminal law and criminal procedure.

This chapter examines the constitutional and legal framework in day-to-day criminal justice operations. Both criminal law and the law of criminal procedure affect these operations. **Criminal law** tells private individuals what behavior is a crime and lays down the punishment for it. **Criminal procedure** tells government officials the extent and limits of their power to enforce the criminal law, and it sets out the consequences for illegal official actions.

LO2 Defining Crime and Legal Responsibility

Criminal law defines what behavior is criminal and spells out the punishment for committing crimes. In every society, there are people whose behavior we should condemn, but to condemn is not necessarily to criminalize. To be blunt, we distinguish (and we *should*) between "creeps" and criminals. Everybody agrees that murder, rape, robbery, burglary, and theft should be crimes. But we also agree that creeps who cheat on their girlfriends or boyfriends and lie to their friends should not go to jail. Why?

Criminal law has very high costs. It costs a lot of money, takes a lot of time, intrudes deeply into privacy and liberty, and more often than not fails to produce the result we want. Or if it does yield the desired result, we often can achieve that result at a lower cost with less expensive, less restrictive social control mechanisms like the disapproval of family, friends, and others we love and respect; informal discipline within social institutions like schools and workplaces; and private lawsuits. Hence, we generally rely on the least expensive or invasive response to misbehavior. We call this limit on the use of criminal law the **principle of economy**.

The principle of economy is not the only way we limit the power of government to define crime. Let's look at two others:

1. The elements of crime
2. The defenses to crime

We will also look at how we establish legal responsibility and then at the means for making sense of criminal law—classifying and grading crimes. Later in the chapter, we will look at constitutional limits on government power when we analyze criminal procedure and the rights of the accused.

THE ELEMENTS OF CRIME AND LEGAL RESPONSIBILITY

All serious crimes (criminal homicide, rape, robbery, burglary, theft, and the like) consist of three elements, which establish legal responsibility for legal behavior:[3]

1. The criminal act (the physical element—*actus reus*)
2. The criminal intent (the mental element—*mens rea*)
3. The concurrence of the criminal act and the criminal intent (the relationship element)

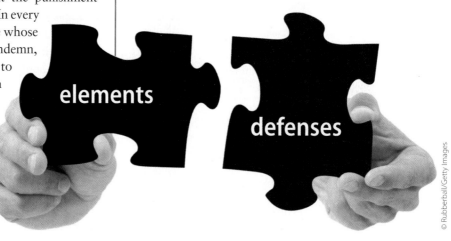

© Rubberball/Getty Images

A few crimes, such as criminal homicide, require a fourth element:

4. Causing a particular result (for example, causing death in homicide)

The Constitution also commands that all crimes have to contain one of these elements—a criminal act—*and* that to convict defendants, the prosecution has to prove all the elements in the crime beyond a reasonable doubt. A legislature does not have to include a criminal intent when it enacts a statute defining a crime, but if it does, then the prosecution has to prove intent beyond a reasonable doubt.

Beyond the Constitution, the criminal law has established limits of its own through long tradition (about 800 years). These limits take the form of the elements in the preceding list, and you probably know by watching or reading crime dramas how very much alive these elements of crime still are. Because they are so entrenched, the principles are a form of command themselves. *Serious* crimes always contain at least the first three elements, and sometimes the fourth. Let's look at these elements of crime that are so old and still so much alive in our criminal justice system.

The Criminal Act

The first element is the criminal act. Our criminal law cannot punish people for what they *wish*, or *hope*, or *intend*, or for who they are (their inherited condition); it can only punish them for what they *do*. But this does not mean you have to complete a crime to satisfy the act requirement. Ralph Damms committed attempted murder when he chased his wife Marjorie with a gun he forgot to load, caught up with her, pointed the gun at her head, and pulled the trigger several times. "It won't shoot! It won't shoot!" he shouted.[4] It's also a crime (conspiracy) to agree to commit a crime even if you never start to commit it. So a woman who agreed to buy "X" (the

When white separatist Matthew Hale attempted to change the name of his Illinois-based extremist organization to World Church of the Creator in 1996, he was successfully sued by an Oregon-based religious group for trademark infringement. Hale openly denounced and in 2002 filed a class action lawsuit against the trial's presiding judge, Joan Lefkow, claiming that she was personally biased against him. In January of 2003, Hale was arrested for soliciting an undercover FBI informant acting as his bodyguard to kill Judge Lefkow. Upon his conviction in April of 2005, Hale was sentenced to 40 years in prison.

drug Ecstasy) was guilty of conspiracy even though the deal fell through. It's also a crime to encourage someone else to commit a crime (solicitation), even if that person turns you down cold. So when Harold Furr offered Donald Owens $3,000 to kill his wife Earlene, he was found guilty of solicitation even though Owens flatly refused the offer.[5] It's also a crime merely to have in your possession a long list of items, including certain types of weapons, drugs, and pornography, even if you do not use, sell, or for that matter do anything with them. Notice what all these crimes have in common—they all include some action: pulling the trigger, agreeing to buy Ecstasy, asking a friend to kill, and taking possession of, say, a gun.

Making crimes out of attempt, conspiracy, solicitation, and possession is justified as a way to prevent *future* harm. In other words, we are punishing someone for what he *might* do, not for what he has done. There used to be strong objections to punishing someone to prevent future harm, but we are living in an age of prevention, as the "war on terror" after 9/11 and the "war on drugs" since the 1980s remind us.

purposeful intent (sometimes called specific intent) you did it and/or caused a criminal result on purpose

knowing intent you know you're committing an act or causing a harm, but you're not acting for that purpose

reckless intent consciously creating a risk of causing a criminal harm

negligent intent unconsciously creating an unreasonable risk of harm

"Criminal act," as defined by the law, also includes the failure to act—but only if there is a legal duty to act. This is called a *criminal omission*. There are two kinds. Most common is the failure to report when the law requires you to (not filing your income tax return or reporting an accident). Less common is the failure to intervene to help someone in danger—for example, a father who stands by while the mother abuses their baby. Legal duties can arise out of specific statutes (like income tax laws), contracts (such as an agreement to take care of a sick person), and special relationships (parents and minor children, doctors and patients).

One critical limit to the criminal law's generous definition of act is that the act has to be voluntary. So holding a loaded gun on Doug to force him to take Michelle's Ecstasy was not stealing. Nor, a court decided, was it murder in a bizarre case in which a sleepwalking mother killed her daughter Pat with an axe. (The mother was dreaming she was killing a man who was attacking Pat.)

The Criminal Intent

In all serious crimes, like murder, rape, robbery, burglary, and theft, a criminal intent has to trigger the criminal act. The mental element is complicated because there are four levels of criminal intent (see Table 4.1):[6]

1. Purposeful
2. Knowing
3. Reckless
4. Negligent

Purposeful intent (sometimes called specific intent) means just what it sounds like—you did it on purpose and/or caused the result in crimes like murder that include the element of cause. **Knowing intent** means you know you are committing an act or causing a harm, but you are not acting for that purpose. For example, a doctor who performed a hysterectomy on a pregnant woman to save her life knew he would kill the fetus, but he did not remove the uterus for the very purpose of killing the fetus.

Reckless intent means consciously creating a risk of causing a criminal harm. Consider Bill who knew from a mechanic that his motorcycle brakes were bad and that his bike could only manage his weight and not the additional weight of another person. He took his girlfriend Taylor for a ride on the bike without informing her of the risk. So Bill created the risk of harming or killing Taylor every time they rode the bike together, and he did it even though he was aware of the danger.

Negligent intent is like reckless intent in that it means taking actions that create a risk of causing harm. But *negligent* is unconsciously creating a risk, meaning that you *should* know (or as it's often phrased, "a reasonable person *would* know") you are creating a risk, but, in fact you do not know. For example, Tara bought a car she found through a Minneapolis newspaper ad. She drove off in the

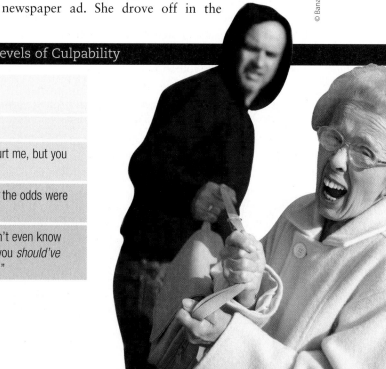

LEVEL OF CULPABILITY	DEFINITION
Purposeful	"You did (or caused) it on purpose."
Knowing	"OK, so you didn't do it because you *wanted* to hurt me, but you *knew* you *were* hurting me."
Reckless	"OK, so you didn't *want* to hurt her, but you *knew* the odds were very high you *could* hurt her—and you did."
Negligent	"OK, so you didn't *mean* to hurt him, and you didn't even know how high the odds were you *would* hurt him, but you *should've* known the odds were very high—and he got hurt."

TABLE 4.1 Everyday Definitions of Model Code Levels of Culpability

Selling alcohol to customers under 21 years of age is an example of a strict liability offense.

**LEGAL RESPONSIBILITY =
ACT
INTENT
RELATIONSHIP**

car without having a safety check, which would have revealed that the brakes were shot. On the way home, she hit and killed a pedestrian when the brakes failed. Tara was negligent: she did not know about the brakes, but she should have known not to drive a car she knew nothing about.

Strict Liability Offenses

Most minor crimes do not require intent; the act is enough. We call these crimes without intent **strict liability offenses**. Our criminal law did not recognize strict liability until the Industrial Revolution when public transportation, factories, and large-scale consumer purchasing created high risks to health and safety. Shared managerial responsibility characterized these new enterprises and made the requirement of personal and individual culpability meaningless. The requirement of criminal intent prevented the punishment of those responsible for these serious injuries, incurable diseases, and deaths. Legislatures responded by adopting strict liability offenses, which incur liability without mental fault. Some examples of strict liability offenses are serving alcohol to underage drinkers, causing drug-related deaths, having sexual intercourse with underaged people, and violating motor vehicle safety regulations.

The Concurrence of Act and Intent

The element of concurrence means criminal intent has to trigger the criminal act.[7] For example, Ronald hates Keith. He plans to kill Keith but changes his mind because he does not want to go to prison. As luck would have it, two months after Ronald abandons his plan to kill Keith, Lisa accidentally hits Keith with her new SUV and kills him. Ronald is delighted when he hears that Keith is dead, but he is not guilty of murder. Why not? Ronald's intent to kill Keith did not trigger Lisa's act of running over him.

Causing a Criminal Harm

In crimes that include an element of cause, the prosecution has to prove two kinds of cause: factual cause and legal cause. **Factual cause** means that the result would not have happened if it were not for (but for) the defendant's actions. More technically, the defendant's actions triggered a chain of events that eventually led to a criminal result. For example, Kirby and his companion robbed Ben and left him on a country road late at night. Cody, a college student driving back to school, accidentally hit and killed Ben. If Kirby and his companion had not left Ben on the road, Cody would not have hit and killed him. So they are the factual cause of Ben's death.

But factual cause is not enough to prove causation; there has to be legal cause, too. **Legal cause** asks whether it's fair to blame defendants for the consequences of the chain of events their actions triggered. It's up to the jury to decide the "fair to blame" question. The jury (and probably you, too) decided it *was* fair to blame Kirby and his companion for Ben's death. But what about this example? In a jealous rage, Cameron shoves Rob who loses his balance and falls against the sharp edge of a glass table, suffering a nasty gash in his leg. Rob refuses to go to the doctor because he does not want to spend the money. Finally, after nearly a day, he is so weak from losing blood that he goes to a hospital emergency room where he receives a transfusion. He develops an infection from a dirty needle used in the transfusion and dies three weeks later. Is Cameron guilty of criminal homicide? Probably not, because it's not fair to blame him for Rob's negligent (possibly reckless) failure to get help *and* the

strict liability offenses crimes without criminal intent

factual cause the result wouldn't have happened if it weren't for the defendant's actions

legal cause asks whether it's fair to blame defendants for the consequences of the chain of events their actions triggered

they committed the crimes, but argue that they should be acquitted anyway. In **defenses of justification**, defendants admit they are responsible for their actions but argue that, under the circumstances, their actions were justified. In other words, the *rightness* of their actions justifies what they did. The classic justification defense is self-defense: "I killed Ronald because he was about to kill me." In **defenses of excuse**, defendants admit what they did was wrong but argue that, under the circumstances, they were not *responsible* for their actions. In other words, the wrongfulness of their actions is *excused*. The classic excuse is insanity: "Killing Steve was wrong, but I was insane when I killed him." Let's take a closer look at the defenses of justification and excuse.

THE DEFENSES OF JUSTIFICATION

The defenses of justification include self-defense, the defense of home and property, and consent. They are all *grudging* exceptions to the government's jealous monopoly on the use of force—that is, to the idea that you cannot take the law into your own hands.

"Kill or be killed" is the idea behind the self-defense exception to the ban on taking the law into your own

In June of 2006, Susan Polk was convicted by jury on a second degree murder charge in connection with the death of her husband, Frank Polk, four years prior. After 30 years of marriage, Susan filed for divorce in 2001, a proceeding which devolved into deep resentment and mutual allegations of domestic violence. In October of 2002, Frank Polk was found stabbed and beaten to death, and after first denying involvement, Susan admitted that she killed him, claiming self-defense. At her trial, two of Polk's three sons testified against their mother, asserting that the murder was premeditated. After the guilty verdict was revealed, Susan was sentenced to a prison term of 16 years to life.

---

defense of alibi
defendants have to prove they couldn't have committed the crime because they were somewhere else when the crime was committed

defenses of justification defendants admit they're responsible for their actions, but argue that, under the circumstances, their actions were justified

defenses of excuse
defendants admit what they did was wrong but argue that, under the circumstances, they weren't responsible for their actions

hospital's negligent use of a dirty needle.

LO3 The Defenses of Crime

even if the prosecution proves all the elements of a crime beyond a reasonable doubt, defendants can avoid conviction if they can prove one of three kinds of defenses:[8] alibi, justification, or excuse.

In the **defense of alibi**, defendants have to prove they could not have committed the crime because they were somewhere else when the crime was committed. In the defenses of justification and excuse, defendants admit that

hands. But defendants can avoid conviction only if they can prove three conditions existed at the time they fought back.

1. They did not provoke the attack.

2. They reasonably believed the attack was going to happen right then (it was imminent).

3. They used only enough force necessary to repel the attack.

The third condition points to two unacceptable reasons for taking the law into your own hands:

1. *Preemptive strikes*. To prevent future attacks, such as killing someone who is going to kill you next week

2. *Retaliation*. To pay back someone who tried to kill you last week

Preemptive strikes and retaliation are always the government's business, never that of private individuals.

Now that you have learned some of the basics of some of the justifications, let's look at the excuses (the act was wrong, but the defendant was not responsible).

THE DEFENSES OF EXCUSE

The defenses of excuse are based on the idea that the law should make allowances for the imperfections and frailties of human nature. The criminal law does not like these defenses very well, although it allows a long list of them, including age; duress; entrapment; insanity

Newspaper heiress Patty Hearst was kidnapped in 1974 by a left-wing urban militia. After ransom attempts failed, Hearst was coerced into joining the group and was later arrested for participating in armed robbery. She was sentenced to 35 years in prison but was later granted clemency by President Jimmy Carter. Could her lawyers have used the excuse of duress to win the case?

or diminished capacity, the best-known excuse; and a number of so-called syndromes, such as PMS (premenstrual syndrome). The law's hostility to excuse defenses is formally hidden, but you can detect it in the failure of almost every defendant who pleads them in an attempt to escape conviction.

> **entrapment** efforts by law enforcement officers to get people to commit crimes

Age

The excuse of age (immaturity) reaches far back into the English common law brought by the colonists to America. The common law recognized three categories of maturity:

1. Individuals too young under all circumstances to be criminally responsible

2. Individuals mature to the extent that they might or might not be criminally responsible

3. Individuals mature enough to be criminally responsible in nearly all circumstances

The law still recognizes these categories. In most states, the categories are synchronized with the jurisdiction (authority) of juvenile courts. So juvenile courts have exclusive jurisdiction up to age 15 or 16. Between 16 and 18, juveniles can either be tried as juveniles or be certified (transferred) to the regular criminal courts for trial as adults. Certification is most common when juveniles are accused of murder, rape, aggravated assault, robbery, and drug-related offenses.

Duress

If someone forces you to commit a crime, you might have the excuse of duress. In some states, duress is a defense to all crimes except murder; in others, it excuses only minor crimes. States also differ as to the definition of duress. Some say only threats to kill the defendant will excuse the crime; others say threats to seriously injure will do. Threats to damage reputation or to destroy property are not enough in any state. Most states say defendants must show that they faced immediate harm if they refused to commit the crime.

Entrapment

Defendants who use **entrapment** as an excuse claim that they were encouraged by police officers to commit the

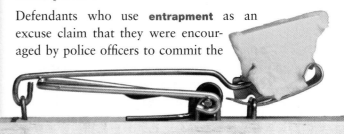

In 2007, former Idaho Senator Larry Craig was arrested at the Minneapolis-St. Paul International Airport on suspicion of lewd conduct. According to the police report, Craig entered a men's bathroom stall and signaled to an undercover agent in an adjacent stall in an attempt to instigate sexual activity.

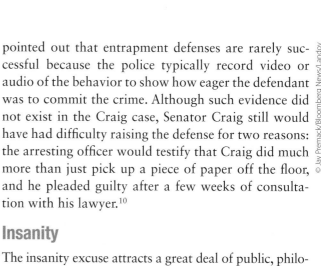

crime and that they would not otherwise have done so. Law enforcement encouragement occurs most often in crimes where there are no *complaining* witnesses (prostitution, gambling, pornography, official wrongdoing, and drug crimes) because officers have to use deception to detect these crimes. Allowing the excuse of entrapment reflects an intolerance of government pressures on law-abiding people to commit crimes they would not have committed without the pressure. Notice that *encouragement* is not entrapment. So for the purpose of getting people to commit crimes, officers can ask people to commit crimes, form personal relationships with them, promise them benefits, and supply or help them get contraband. How do we separate encouragement from entrapment?

Most courts use the predisposition test to decide when officials have crossed the line between encouragement and entrapment. According to the test, if the defendant was ready and willing to commit the crime (predisposed) and the officer only provided her with the opportunity to commit it, that is encouragement, not entrapment. The crucial question is where the criminal intent originated. If it originated with the defendant, then the government did not entrap but only encouraged the defendant.[9] A potential entrapment case involved Senator Larry Craig who accused his arresting officer of entrapment when he was arrested for trying to engage in lewd behavior in a Minnesota airport restroom. CNN's legal analyst Jeffrey Toobin was dubious that Craig would have been successful had he chosen to pursue an entrapment defense. Toobin pointed out that entrapment defenses are rarely successful because the police typically record video or audio of the behavior to show how eager the defendant was to commit the crime. Although such evidence did not exist in the Craig case, Senator Craig still would have had difficulty raising the defense for two reasons: the arresting officer would testify that Craig did much more than just pick up a piece of paper off the floor, and he pleaded guilty after a few weeks of consultation with his lawyer.[10]

Insanity

The insanity excuse attracts a great deal of public, philosophical, religious, and scholarly attention, but it plays only a tiny part in the day-to-day operations of criminal justice. Defendants rarely plead insanity and rarely succeed if they do. Even if they do succeed, they do not automatically "walk." In some jurisdictions, the verdict is "not guilty by reason of insanity"; in others, it's "guilty but insane." Guilty but insane means that the defendants will go to prison but with the chance for treatment while incarcerated. Not guilty by reason of insanity means they are not guilty, but they still are not free to go. After a verdict of not guilty by reason of insanity, special proceedings are held to decide whether the defendants are mentally ill and dangerous. If they are (and it's a rare court that finds they are not), they are confined to maximum security hospitals (really just prisons) until they are no longer dangerous, which usually means a long time and often for life. John Hinckley Jr., who attempted to assassinate President Reagan in the early 1980s, is typical. He is still detained in a maximum security hospital (although he is allowed occasional weekend furloughs).

In a crime similar to that of Andrea Yates, Lashuan Harris was seen dropping her three young sons into the San Francisco Bay. Harris pleaded innocent to three counts of murder and was found not guilty by reason of insanity. Here, DaMarcus Harris, cousin of Lashuan Harris, holds flowers in front of a makeshift memorial at Pier 7 in San Francisco on October 21, 2005.

Insanity is a legal, *not* a medical, term; it means a mental disease (for example, paranoia) or defect (retardation) that impairs reason and/or will. There are three main tests of insanity:

1. The right-wrong test
2. The right-wrong test supplemented by the irresistible impulse test
3. The substantial capacity or American Law Institute (ALI) test

The **right-wrong test** focuses on reason. The test, sometimes called the *M'Naughten rule*, comes from a famous English case. In 1843, Daniel M'Naughten had the paranoid delusion that the prime minister, Sir Robert Peel, had masterminded a conspiracy to kill him. M'Naughten shot at Peel in delusional self-defense but mistakenly killed Peel's personal secretary. The jury acquitted M'Naughten. On appeal, the House of Lords—England's highest court of appeal—formulated the right-wrong test. The test evaluates whether two necessary elements were present at the time the crime was committed:

1. A mental disease or defect caused such damage to the defendants' capacity to reason.
2. Either they did not know what they were doing, or if they knew what they were doing, they did not know it was wrong.[11]

Several jurisdictions have supplemented the right-wrong test with the **irresistible impulse test**. The irresistible impulse test focuses on defendants' willpower, or their capacity to control their actions at the time of the crime. The test evaluates whether two necessary elements existed:

1. The defendants suffered from a mental disease or defect.
2. It caused them to lose the power to choose between right and wrong.

In other words, the defendants know what they are doing, they know it's wrong, but they cannot stop themselves from doing it.

The **substantial capacity test** focuses on both reason and will. Formulated by the American Law Institute, it evaluates whether two necessary elements existed at the time of the crime:

1. The defendants had a mental disease or defect.
2. It caused them to lack substantial capacity to either appreciate the wrongfulness (criminality) of their conduct or to conform their conduct to the requirements of the law.

Notice that the test focuses on substantial capacity; in other words, the mental disease or defect does not have to totally destroy the defendants' reason or will.

The case of Andrea Yates referred to at the beginning of this chapter is an interesting example of the application of the insanity defense. Recall that Yates called the Houston (Texas) police and admitted that she drowned all five of her children in the bathtub. There was evidence of intent, mental illness, rationality, reason, and irrationality. Was Andrea Yates sentenced to prison or death for this crime, or did her attorneys prove she was insane? Actually, both outcomes occurred. In Texas, to use the insanity defense, the defense must prove that the defendant was not only mentally ill but also at the time of the crime the defendant did not know the actions were wrong.

In 2002, in her first trial, Yates was found guilty of capital murder and sentenced to life in prison. The jury believed she intended to kill her children. On appeal, Yates was granted a new trial because an expert witness had testified that Yates knew what she was doing because *Law & Order* had recently aired an episode in which a mother killed her children and was exonerated using the insanity defense. After the first trial, it was discovered that the *Law & Order* episode had never aired and Yates could not have seen it. In the second trial in 2006, the jury accepted the mental illness evidence and determined that Yates did not know what she was doing at the time of the event. Yates was acquitted of the capital murder charges and was immediately committed to a state mental hospital.[12]

right-wrong test an insanity defense focused on whether a mental disease or defect impaired the defendants' reason so that they couldn't tell the difference between right and wrong

irresistible impulse test a test of insanity that focuses on whether mental disease affected the defendants' willpower (their capacity to control their actions at the time of the crime)

substantial capacity test a test of insanity that focuses on whether a mental disease substantially impaired the reason and/or will of the defendants

Harvey Milk

Syndromes Affecting Mental Capacity

Excuse defenses based on syndromes that supposedly affect mental capacity began to appear in the 1970s. One famous syndrome excuse case took place in the late 1970s when Dan White, a San Francisco police officer and member of the city council, shot and killed gay activist and city council member Harvey Milk and Mayor George Moscone. White's lawyer introduced the junk food syndrome, popularly called the "Twinkie defense." He argued that junk food had affected White's mental faculties because eating junk food aggravated White's depression, thereby diminishing his capacity enough to reduce his responsibility. The jury returned a verdict of manslaughter, and White was sentenced to a relatively short prison term. After his release from prison, he committed suicide.

Women occasionally have claimed premenstrual syndrome (PMS) as a defense to excuse their crimes. There are three legal obstacles to pleading the PMS defense:

1. Defendants have to prove that PMS is a disease; little medical research shows it is.

2. The defendant has to actually suffer from PMS; there are hardly ever any medical records to document it.

3. PMS has to cause the mental impairment; there is still too much skepticism about PMS to accept that it excuses criminal conduct.

LO4 The Classification of Crimes

he urge to make sense of criminal law is ancient. That urge has produced many schemes of classifying and grading the content of criminal law. Here we will look at two classification schemes; a third scheme—crimes and torts—will be discussed in the next section.[13]

In March of 2009, entertainer Chris Brown was charged with felonious assault and making criminal threats following an altercation with girlfriend and fellow entertainer Rihanna. According to the office of the Los Angeles District Attorney, these charges carry a maximum sentence of four years and eight months in prison. After pictures of Rihanna's injuries were released, public opinion swayed in her favor, causing many to prematurely presume Brown's guilt.[14]

FELONY, MISDEMEANOR, AND VIOLATION

Crimes classified according to the type and duration of punishment are called felonies, misdemeanors, or violations. These are ancient classifications, demonstrating that the past still influences today's criminal law. The great legal historian Frederic William Maitland maintained that the reasons for old classifications may have died a long time ago, but their ghosts rule us from the grave. He meant that even when classifications have outlived their usefulness, they still shape how we think and what we do. Dividing crimes into felonies and misdemeanors is one example. Until 1600, felonies were all punishable by death. Today, we divide **felonies** into capital felonies, punishable by death or life imprisonment, and ordinary felonies, punishable by one year or more in prison. So felonies include serial killers at one extreme and individuals who steal $500 at the other. The breadth of its scope makes the classification largely meaningless in any sociological sense. It serves mainly as an administrative device to determine who gets the death penalty, life imprisonment, or incarceration in a state prison.

Misdemeanors are minor offenses punishable either by fines or by up to one year in jail. Common misdemeanors include simple assaults and battery, prostitution, and disorderly conduct. Most jurisdictions divide misdemeanors into gross misdemeanors (30 days to one year in jail) and petty misdemeanors (a fine and/or up to 30 days in jail). **Violations** are punishable by a small fine, and they do not become part of your criminal history. (Remember that criminal history is one of the major legitimate criteria for decision making in criminal justice.) The most common violations are traffic offenses.

MALA IN SE AND MALA PROHIBITA

This classification sorts crimes according to whether they are perceived as "evil." This old arrangement overlaps the felony, misdemeanor, and violation categories and defines some crimes as inherently bad (the Latin *mala in se*). Crimes such as murder and rape fall into this category. Other behavior is a crime only because the law says so (the Latin *mala prohibita*). Parking in a no parking zone is *malum prohibitum*.

LO5 Criminal versus Civil Law

Some harms are the basis for lawsuits even though they are not crimes. These private or civil lawsuits differ from criminal actions in several respects. In criminal cases, the government and the defendant are the parties to the case. So the title of the criminal case is *State* (or *U.S., Commonwealth,* or *People*) *v. Munckton* (defendant). In private personal injury actions (called **torts** or **civil cases**), plaintiffs sue wrongdoers (defendants) to get money (called **damages**) as compensation for their injuries. Torts or civil cases carry the names of the parties to the lawsuit; the plaintiff's name is first, as in *Chan* (plaintiff) *v. Gonzalez* (defendant).

Criminal cases rest on the notion that crime harms society generally, leaving individual injuries to tort or civil actions, but almost all crimes against persons and property are also torts. A burglary, for instance, consists of the tort of trespass; a criminal assault consists of the tort of criminal assault. For litigants to bring a civil case, they must have standing. Standing means that the litigant must have a personal stake in the outcome. Civil cases differ from criminal cases in the standard of proof. Civil cases require only a preponderance of the evidence instead of the criminal case's more stringent standard of proof, beyond a reasonable doubt. Also, in criminal cases

there are extensive due process guarantees for the defendant. Most of these guarantees do not apply in a civil case. Litigants and defendants, for example, are not entitled to counsel.[15]

Criminal prosecutions and civil actions may arise out of the same event, but criminal and civil proceedings are not mutually exclusive. Victims can sue for, and the government can prosecute, injuries arising out of the same conduct. For example, in 1995, O.J. Simpson was acquitted of criminal charges in the deaths of his ex-wife, Nicole Brown Simpson, and her friend Ronald Goldman. In 1997, the victims' families brought a civil suit against Simpson, and he was found liable for the wrongful deaths of the victims. Simpson was ordered to pay more than $33 million in restitution to the families.[16]

LO6 Due Process

Criminal law tells private individuals what they cannot do and lets them know the punishments for committing crimes. The law and rules of criminal procedure tell public officials what powers they have to enforce the criminal law, the limits of their powers, and the consequences for abusing them. The law of criminal procedure is the formal side of decision making in criminal justice agencies. It lays down rules for decisions made by officials at each step in the criminal process. The bedrock of the criminal process is the principle of due process of law. **Due process** means the right to fair procedures. Four provisions in the U.S. Constitution limit the power of government to create criminal laws and set punishments; notice that two of them guarantee due process.

The **ex post facto clause** bans retroactive criminal laws. Retroactive criminal laws make a crime out of

misdemeanors minor offenses (simple assaults and battery, prostitution, and disorderly conduct) punishable either by fines or up to one year in jail

violations crimes punishable by a small fine; they don't become part of your criminal history

mala in se inherently evil behavior

mala prohibita behavior that is criminal only because the law defines it as a crime

torts (civil cases) private personal injury actions

damages money for personal injuries awarded by courts

due process the right to fair procedures

ex post facto clause clause in the U.S. Constitution that bans retroactive criminal laws behavior that was not criminal before the law was passed. For example, if a state passes a statute on January 2, 2009, raising the drinking age from 18 to 21, the state cannot prosecute a 19-year-old who bought a beer on New Year's Eve in 2008. Why not? People have to have fair warning their behavior is a crime; ex post facto laws obviously do not do that.

An example of due process is the **void-for-vagueness doctrine**. According to this doctrine, vague laws deny individuals life, liberty, and property without due process of law because the laws do not give individuals fair warning. In *Lanzetta v. New Jersey*, the U.S. Supreme Court explained that a law so vague that individuals "of common intelligence" have to "guess" what it means "violates the first essential of due process of law."[17]

In addition to guaranteeing due process, the Fourteenth Amendment also bars states from denying individuals **equal protection of the laws**. Equal protection means that criminal laws can treat groups of people differently only if the different treatment is *reasonable*. Distinctions based on race, ethnicity, religion, and national origin are *never* reasonable. Distinctions based on gender can be reasonable if there is a really good reason for the distinction; in other words, distinctions are *sometimes* reasonable. For example, a statute making it a crime for women (but not men) to smoke in public violated the equal protection clause. On the other hand, the U.S. Supreme Court ruled that California's statutory rape law, which applied only to men, did not violate the equal protection clause. Why not? California has a "compelling interest" in reducing "the tragic human costs of illegitimate teenage pregnancies."[18]

RIGHTS OF THE ACCUSED

Constitutional limits on criminal law are commands; criminal justice officials have no choice but to obey them. However, as you will learn, constitutional commands leave plenty of room for discretionary decision making when it comes to applying the commands to particular cases. The basic rights guaranteed during the trial process begin with the Sixth Amendment's protection of a speedy and public trial.[19] The Sixth Amendment also guarantees the right to an impartial jury. The accused also has the right to be tried in the jurisdiction where the crime was committed. The accused must also be informed of the charges against her. In addition, the accused has the right to be confronted with the witnesses against her so that she can prepare a proper defense.

One of the best-known rights of the accused is the right to counsel. For those who cannot afford an attorney, the state must provide one to them. The problem for indigent defendants is that you get what you pay for, and state-provided legal defense does not compare in quality or outcome to personal legal counsel.

Other rights of the accused include the Fifth Amendment's protection against double jeopardy, meaning that the defendant cannot be tried twice for the same crime if acquitted in the first trial. The defendant also cannot be compelled to testify against himself. Finally, the Supreme Court has determined that due process guarantees that evidence obtained in an illegal search and seizure cannot be used at trial.

CRIMINAL TRIAL PROCEDURE

With all of these due process protections (guarantees) in place, the general procedure for a criminal trial begins with the selection of the jury.[20] The jury is chosen through a process known as *voir dire*, which is intended to ensure that the defendant's right to an impartial jury is protected. Once a jury has been selected, opening statements begin. In their opening statements, the prosecution and defense provide an outline of what they will present during the trial. After opening statements are completed, the prosecution presents the case against the accused. After each witness testifies, the defense has the right to cross-examine the witness. After cross-examination, the prosecution can conduct a redirect examination of the witness to clarify or correct a point made during the cross-examination.

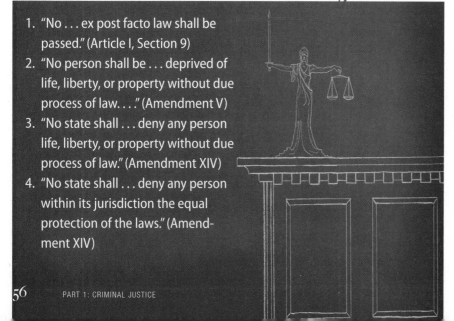

1. "No . . . ex post facto law shall be passed." (Article I, Section 9)
2. "No person shall be . . . deprived of life, liberty, or property without due process of law. . . ." (Amendment V)
3. "No state shall . . . deny any person life, liberty, or property without due process of law." (Amendment XIV)
4. "No state shall . . . deny any person within its jurisdiction the equal protection of the laws." (Amendment XIV)

© Comstock Images/Jupiterimages

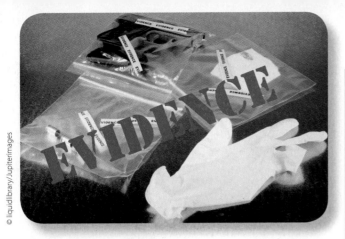

The defense then presents its case. It does not have to prove the innocence of the accused. Due process protections place the burden on the state (government) to prove guilt. The prosecution has the burden to establish proof of legal responsibility beyond a reasonable doubt. The defense only has to show that the prosecution has not done so. The defense does this by challenging either the truth of the prosecution's evidence or the legality of that evidence. After the defense has presented its case, the prosecution can present rebuttal evidence.

The role of the judge during the trial is to rule on motions by the prosecution and defense regarding evidence to be presented and questions to be asked of the witnesses. The judge rules on these motions and questions using due process rules to protect the accused from the power of the state. Commonly, in criminal cases judges must rule on defense motions that claim evidence was obtained illegally and therefore should be excluded from the trial.

The role of the jury is to listen to the cases presented by the prosecution and the defense and then make a decision. Once the cases have been presented, the judge will charge the jury and instruct the jurors about how they are to make their decision. The jury must be told what the law means and how it is to be applied. The jury will then be allowed to deliberate and return a verdict. If the jury deliberates for more than a day, the judge may decide to sequester the jurors until they reach a decision.

The sequestering of a jury is rarely used but will be used in high profile cases with much sensitivity. The second trial of Andrea Yates, referred to earlier in this chapter, went to the jury in the late afternoon. There was significant national and international media attention for this trial given the circumstances of the case, the drowning of five young children and the issue of the insanity defense being a primary factor in the retrial. After three hours of deliberation on the first day, the jury indicated that they needed more time to reach a verdict in the case. The judge decided to sequester the jury for the night to protect them from the influence of the media.[21] Sequestering means the jury will stay in hotels overnight, away from public and media influence. If the jurors cannot reach a decision, the judge may ask them to reconvene and try again. Once the judge decides that reconvening will not produce a verdict, the judge can dismiss the jury and call for another trial. If the jury does reach a decision, the verdict will be announced in open court. Once the verdict is returned, the jury will be polled to determine whether each juror individually agrees with the verdict. Sentencing usually occurs at a later time to allow for post-trial motions and hearings.

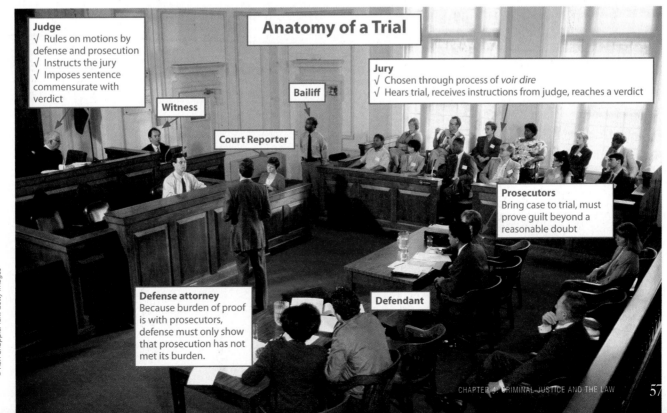

Anatomy of a Trial

Judge
√ Rules on motions by defense and prosecution
√ Instructs the jury
√ Imposes sentence commensurate with verdict

Witness

Court Reporter

Bailiff

Jury
√ Chosen through process of *voir dire*
√ Hears trial, receives instructions from judge, reaches a verdict

Prosecutors
Bring case to trial, must prove guilt beyond a reasonable doubt

Defense attorney
Because burden of proof is with prosecutors, defense must only show that prosecution has not met its burden.

Defendant

Policing in the United States

has gone through several eras.

5

Missions and Roles of the Police

The Department of Homeland Security (DHS) was added to the federal law enforcement structure after the events of 9/11 to aid in the fight against threats to the United States. One of the goals of DHS is to enhance information sharing with partners. Modern law enforcement stresses the need for agencies and organizations to partner with each other to accomplish their missions. An example of information sharing with partners is illustrated by a DHS research project on regional planning efforts for disaster threats that integrates information sharing and planning efforts among law enforcement, emergency management, fire and rescue, federal, state and local governments, business, faith-based organizations, educational institutions, nongovernmental organizations, the financial industry, utilities, and other relevant groups.[1] The lack of information sharing has been documented as a major problem in previous large-scale disasters such as 9/11 and the Hurricane Katrina response. In this chapter, we will explore the history of law enforcement and the transition to a more modern and comprehensive function that integrates various types of law enforcement, levels of government, and other response agencies.

Learning Outcomes

LO1 Recount the early development of policing and how policing evolved in the United States

LO2 Identify the various levels of law enforcement and the main types of law enforcement agencies

LO3 Understand the police organizational structure

LO4 List the missions and basic responsibilities of the police

LO1 Evolution of Policing in the United States

Since municipal police departments were first established in the nineteenth century, policing in the United States has gone through several eras. Here, we look at the origins of policing and its evolution through the twentieth century.

constable/night watch system a police system consisting of two elements—constables and night watch—in every local community

municipal police department system a formalized police force responsible to a central office and on duty "24/7"

THE CONSTABLE/ NIGHT WATCH SYSTEM, 1066–1850

Policing in the United States traces its roots to medieval England. After the Norman Conquest in 1066, King William created the **constable/night watch system**, a police system based in the local community. It consisted of two elements—constables and night watch—in every local community. That system, which lasted until 1829 in England, came to the American colonies and then endured in the United States until the 1850s.[2]

Constables worked for the courts. They were paid fees for serving warrants and summonses and arresting suspects. They also made money by helping to prosecute criminals. Night watchmen (they were all men) were supposed to patrol the neighborhood from dusk to dawn, calling out the hours ("8 o'clock and all is well!"), making sure the street lamps were lit, watching for fires, breaking up fights, and arresting "suspicious persons." Night watch was a public duty, but you could hire substitutes to do it for you. The constable/night watch system had two things going for it: it was cheap and it was weak. In the mid 1800s, these were seen as advantages by Americans who hated government taxes and government power as much as they feared crime. But, as mobs of urban rioters increased in number and intensity between 1830 and 1860, Americans' dislike of government began to lessen, and their fear of disorder grew.

THE MUNICIPAL POLICE DEPARTMENT ERA, 1851–1920

After three major riots in four years, Boston had had enough. In 1838, the city established a **municipal police department system**, a formalized police force responsible to a central office and on duty "24/7." Most cities rapidly followed Boston's example. Although riots triggered the creation of police departments, city residents and city government quickly came to view them as a convenient tool for missions such as controlling traffic, finding lost children, managing drunks, and dealing with the homeless and hungry.[3]

The New Police Departments Introduced Four New Features

First, they were formally organized with a military-like hierarchy; orders were issued from the chief at the top and carried out by officers on the beats below. Informally, though, except for riot control, patrol officers spent most of their time alone walking beats and acting on their own initiative with no orders; in this way, they differed from soldiers who acted in groups under specific orders.

Second, the new departments were part of the executive branch of city government, not the courts as the constable/night watch system had been. This meant the end of fees collected for serving court documents. Instead, police officers were paid salaries (and the salaries were high enough to lure many skilled laborers onto the force). But, as part of the executive branch, police were now divorced from preparing and prosecuting cases, which isolated them from the courts and prosecutors and generated antagonism among the three major criminal justice agencies.[4]

In 1066 the constable/night watch system is initiated.

1066

1308

Dante Alighieri's epic poem *The Divine Comedy*, written circa 1308, is an allegoric saga depicting the Christian afterlife. Criminals' hellish fates are decided according to the types of crimes they committed in life—a mythological precursor to the criminal justice system.

1448

Vlad III, Prince of Wallachia, known commonly as Vlad the Impaler, came to rule Wallachia (southern Romania) in 1448. He is best known for unrelenting brutality toward and torture and execution of his political opposition.

Third, officers wore uniforms. This made them the first (and for a long time the only) public officials everybody could identify as public officials. Officers hated and bitterly fought wearing uniforms, which they considered un-American. Uniforms were for lackeys of kings and queens, not for Americans who believed part of being an American was being able to dress as you pleased. Besides, uniforms made them readily identifiable not just by residents who needed them but by "street toughs looking for trouble" and probably, more important, by superior officers making sure officers were walking their beats and not hanging out in saloons and billiard rooms.[5]

Fourth, police practiced **proactive policing**, meaning they were supposed to prevent crime before it happened by going out looking for suspicious people and behavior. This was the opposite of the **reactive policing** used in the constable/night watch system, where constables and watchmen acted only after they were asked and paid to do it. Walking the beat (patrol) was supposed to scare off criminal wannabes and make victims more likely to report crimes since they had closer contact with the police. In addition, good salaries were supposed to help motivate officers to investigate crimes.[6]

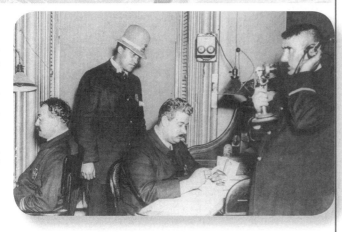

The major downside of municipal control was that police departments became the arms of the dominant political machines. So they participated in partisan politics, and that participation was often corrupt—like manipulating ballot boxes. Partisan politics was not the only corrupting influence. Money, too, often lured departments as well as individual officers into making deals with houses of prostitution, saloons, gambling establishments, and other vice operations.

Nevertheless, on balance, police departments had several strengths. Communities supported them because officers policed the neighborhoods where they lived. They took charge of "whatever emergencies and crises crossed their paths." They provided needed services, such as ambulances, soup kitchens, garbage collection, and homeless shelters.

Early in the twentieth century, however, public attention began to focus on the problems of policing as a new wave of reform, called the Progressive Era, swept across the country. A rash of investigations in cities throughout the United States from about 1895 to 1920 uncovered widespread incompetence and corruption in most city police departments.[7]

At the same time, policing was changing from an all-purpose public service to the narrow mission of criminal law enforcement. This shift reflected a change in thinking by social welfare reformers and some police chiefs who no longer viewed unemployed people as members of the "dangerous classes," saving that description for criminals only. Police missions may have changed, but police officers stayed the same. As the twentieth century opened, the typical urban police officer in the United States was a recent immigrant with little or no education, who had been appointed by a local politician and was expected to enforce the law according to the politician's wishes.

THE REFORM MODEL ERA, 1921–1960

Recognizing this political domination, corruption, and lack of training, three California police chiefs

In 1605, Guy Fawkes and a host of co-conspirators attempted to blow up England's House of Parliament, killing King James I and the Protestant aristocracy. The attack, known as the Gunpowder Plot, was unsuccessful.

1605

1610

Elizabeth Báthory was a Hungarian countess who abducted, tortured, and killed at least 80 women and girls before her imprisonment in 1610. She was never tried in court.

in the 1920s, August Vollmer, O. W. Wilson, and William Parker, encouraged what they called the **reform model of policing**. According to this model, the police are the "gatekeepers" to the criminal justice system; they decide who enters the system and who does not. So the police mission is clear and narrow: arrest people for committing the FBI's Index Crimes.[8]

By the 1950s, all of the following elements in the reform agenda were accepted and in place, at least in the larger departments:

1. *Centralization of police authority.* Police chiefs began to really run their departments.
2. *Shift from foot to motorized patrols.* Officers moved into squad cars.
3. *Technological advances.* Fewer officers could cover more territory because of squad cars, two-way radios, and telephone call boxes.
4. *Paramilitary organization.* Chiefs were in charge of a strictly disciplined hierarchy with formal authority descending from the top through the ranks to patrol officers.
5. *Specialized units.* These were mainly vice squads with the power to control police corruption throughout the department.
6. *UCR data.* FBI Uniform Crime Reports data became the measure of police performance.
7. *Reactive, incident-driven policing.* Responding to calls became the distinctive method of policing.
8. *Restrictions on police discretion.* Department rules, such as those regarding use of force and high-speed chases, lessened police discretion.
9. *Focus on criminal law enforcement.* The focus shifted from maintaining order and providing service to enforcing criminal law.[9]

Public confidence in the reform model remained high, and support from police professionals and politicians remained strong—but not without challenge. A small band of police chiefs around the country and their supporters in academic circles criticized the reform model, both during the reform era and later, for the following reasons:

1. Despite some reduction in the mid to late 1990s, crime rates taken in the long run have remained at historic highs.
2. Criminal justice is ineffective because even if the police arrest suspects, the likelihood is small that they will serve time in prison.
3. Police tactics such as patrol, rapid response, follow-up investigation, and arrest do not work well either to control crime or to reduce fear of crime.
4. Private security is outpacing public police as a means of controlling crime, fear, and disorder.[10]

THE TURBULENT 1960s

During the 1960s, the police became easy scapegoats caught in the middle of disorder, riots, and crime-plagued cities. Of course, police could not remove or even significantly reduce deep racial, ethnic, class, and gender inequalities. Nor could they realistically be expected to calm the culture wars between social conservatives and social liberals that had ebbed and flowed long before the 1960s and are still very much alive today. Police actions did not create these divisions even if they sometimes helped to bring them into sharp and painful focus.

Not surprisingly, "law and order" was a major theme of the 1964 presidential election campaign. President Johnson created the President's Commission on Law Enforcement and the Administration of Justice. The Crime Commission gave serious attention to six police problems:

1. The multiple and conflicting missions of policing
2. The fragmented nature of law enforcement
3. The poor training and minimal education of police officers
4. Police corruption, brutality, and prejudice
5. The separation of the police from the communities they serve

In May of 1718, dreaded pirate Blackbeard (Edward Teach) took control of the Charleston, South Carolina port, demanding medicine in exchange for the release of hostages.

© Doris Kindersley/Doris Kindersley RF/Getty Images

1718

In 1838, French thinker Auguste Comte created the study of sociology as a remedy for contemporary social ills. Because of this inception, the development of advanced sociological theories and paradigms, such as those found in criminal justice, became possible.

1838

© Mary Evans Picture Library/Alamy

1851–1920

In 1851, the municipal police department era begins.

1851

© Karen Mower/iStockphoto.com

6. The lessening of the public support that effective policing depends on[11]

By the late 1960s, police officers were frustrated, angry, and fed up with highly publicized and unrelenting criticism by the "reformers." But they had other complaints, too: poor pay, dictatorial chiefs, urban riots, unrealistic demands to solve the nation's social problems, and U.S. Supreme Court opinions that "handcuffed the police instead of the criminal." These complaints had one lasting effect—urban police unionization. Regardless of whether their complaints were justified and whether unions were the answer to their complaints, departments in almost all large cities, with the big exception of those in the South, became unionized. According to Walker, the union movement "won dramatic improvement in salaries and benefits for officers along with grievance procedures that protected the rights of officers in disciplinary hearings." Not everyone favored unionization—and it still has its share of critics. Some reformers believed that unions "resisted innovation and were particularly hostile to attempts to improve police community relations."[12] Nevertheless, the union movement represents a major concrete result of the troubled 1960s.

That is not all the 1960s left us. President Johnson's Crime Commission sparked great research activity. Thanks to evaluation research and police department cooperation with researchers, our knowledge of policing has advanced enormously. More than courts and corrections, police departments have allowed and participated in evaluations of their work, even when research has criticized their practices. They have also worked with researchers to set up and conduct experiments that have led not just to better understanding but to improvements in policies and practices. So, clearly, the legacy of the 1960s includes more than riots, crime, and disorder.

THE COMMUNITY POLICING ERA, 1970 TO THE PRESENT

The social unrest of the late 1960s, coupled with the crime boom, shook the confidence of practitioners, leading them to wonder if crime and disorder were beyond the control of law enforcement as it operated under the reform model. Scholars highlighted the failings of the most widely used reform model strategies, further shaking the confidence of police professionals and prompting them to reassess their strategies.[13]

In this time of professional reassessment and scholarship evaluating the effectiveness of reform model policing, the community policing era was born. Several successful community policing experiments; strong support from President Clinton, who signed bills creating the federal programs into law; and billions of federal dollars approved by both major political parties have made community policing the *talk*, if not the *walk*, of policing in 2009.

Community-oriented policing (COP) boils down to three elements:

1. The community and the police working together to accomplish the

1875

In April of 1875, Henry McCarty was arrested in Silver City, New Mexico, for stealing some cheese. This was to be the first of many encounters with the law for outlaw gunslinger Billy the Kid.

In the fall of 1888, notorious serial killer Jack the Ripper murdered five prostitutes in and around London, England. Never apprehended, the true identity of the Ripper remains unknown.

1888

1893

In 1893, Émile Durkheim developed the concept of anomie to explain the cultural consequence of mass-specialization within a complex society. The concept was later interpreted in criminology as a social disorder resulting in deviance.

missions of crime control, order maintenance, and other social services to the public

2. Identifying, analyzing, responding to, and evaluating community problems (including not just crime but disorder) by focusing on causes, not just specific incidents of crime and disorder

3. Bringing in other government agencies and private community resources from business and community service organizations to participate in working on problems

LO2 The Main Types of Law Enforcement Agencies

Public police agencies in the United States are organized along the lines of our federalist system of government with crime control divided (not always harmoniously) among national, state, county, and municipal agencies. The enormous numbers of for-profit private law enforcement agencies further complicate this structure. Let's look at the broad outlines of the organizational levels of federal, state, county, and municipal law enforcement agencies in the United States.

FEDERAL LAW ENFORCEMENT AGENCIES

In 2004, there were nearly 105,000 federal officers authorized to make arrests and carry firearms (see Table 5.1). (For security reasons, the total does not include Federal Air Marshals and CIA Security Protective officers; it also excludes officers assigned outside the 50 states).[14] Let's look at a few of the largest agencies, including:

- the Federal Bureau of Investigation (FBI)
- the Drug Enforcement Administration (DEA)
- the Department of Homeland Security (DHS)

TABLE 5.1 Number of Federal Law Enforcement Officers, 2004	
FEDERAL AGENCY	**NUMBER OF OFFICERS**
U.S. Customs and Border Protection	27,705
Federal Bureau of Prisons	15,214
Federal Bureau of Investigation	12,242
U.S. Immigration and Customs Enforcement	10,399
U.S. Secret Service	4,769
Drug Enforcement Administration	4,400
Administrative Office of the U.S. Courts	4,126
U.S. Marshals Service	3,233
U.S. Postal Inspection Service	2,976
Internal Revenue Service, Criminal Investigation	2,777
Veterans Health Administration	2,423
Bureau of Alcohol, Tobacco, Firearms and Explosives	2,373
National Park Service	2,147
U.S. Capitol Police	1,535

Source: Bureau of Justice Statistics, *Federal Law Enforcement Officers*, 2004 (Washington, DC: Bureau of Justice Statistics, July 2006), Highlights, Table 1.

On June 2, 1899, Butch Cassidy (Robert Parker), The Sundance Kid (Harry Longabaugh), and their Wild Bunch gang robbed a Union Pacific train in Wyoming, resulting in a massive, though unsuccessful, man hunt.

1899

In 1902, Sir Arthur Conan Doyle's *The Hound of the Baskervilles* was published. Featuring iconic detective and deductive thinker Sherlock Holmes, this novel epitomizes keen policing and investigation.

1902

1921–1960

In 1921, the reform model era begins.

1921

Federal Bureau of Investigation (FBI)

The FBI's mission statement reads:

> *The mission of the FBI is to protect and defend the United States against terrorist and foreign intelligence threats, to uphold and enforce the criminal laws of the United States, and to provide leadership and criminal justice services to federal, state, municipal, and international agencies and partners.*[15]

Its top 10 priorities are as follows:

1. Protect the United States from terrorist attack
2. Protect the United States against foreign intelligence operations and espionage
3. Protect the United States against cyber-based attacks and high-technology crimes
4. Combat public corruption at all levels
5. Protect civil rights
6. Combat transnational and national criminal organizations and enterprises
7. Combat major white-collar crime
8. Combat significant violent crime
9. Support federal, state, county, municipal, and international partners
10. Upgrade technology to successfully perform the FBI's mission[16]

The FBI has 56 field offices in major metropolitan areas throughout the United States and Puerto Rico, and each of these offices is responsible for federal law enforcement within its region. Some examples of the FBI's field office work during the week ending February 27, 2009, (see "Sample . . .") illustrate the diverse nature and scope of the work performed by the FBI.

© AP Images/Stephen J. Boitano

Top 10 FBI Priorities

© Popperfoto/Getty Images

1929

In 1929, Italian-American Mafioso Al Capone orchestrated the Saint Valentine's Day Massacre in an attempt to eliminate the gang of "Bugs" Moran, Capone's rival in bootlegging and smuggling. While several mobsters were killed, Bugs escaped.

© Hulton Archive/Getty Images

Bonnie Parker and Clyde Barrow were infamous for interweaving a torrid love affair and a triumphant stint in bank robbery. After living lives of burglary, murder, and jailbreak, Bonnie and Clyde were shot to death by a posse of Texas and Louisiana officers on May 23, 1934.

1934

On June 30 of 1934, John Herbert Dillinger successfully robbed the Merchants National Bank in South Bend, Indiana, of $29,890—one of many such heists. Less than a month later, Dillinger was shot dead outside the Biograph Theater in Chicago, Illinois.

© AP images/Dayton Daily News

1934

In February 2009 in his first federal budget, President Obama proposed increased funds for the Department of Justice, which funds the FBI, for the fight against terrorism. His budget provided $8 billion for the FBI, including $425 million in enhancements and $88 million for the National Security Division to address the President's highest priority: protecting the American people from terrorist acts. Funding supports the detection and disruption of terrorists, counterintelligence, cyber security, and other threats against our national security.[17]

Drug Enforcement Administration (DEA)

The DEA's mission is:

"*to enforce the controlled substances laws and regulations of the United States and bring to the criminal and civil justice system of the United States, or any other competent jurisdiction, those organizations and principal members of organizations involved in the growing, manufacture, or distribution of controlled substances appearing in or destined for illicit traffic in the United States; and to recommend and support non-enforcement programs aimed at reducing the availability of illicit controlled substances on the domestic and international markets.*[18]"

To carry out its mission, the DEA has the following responsibilities:

- "Investigation and preparation for prosecution of major interstate and international controlled substance violators

- Investigation and preparation for prosecution of criminals and drug gangs who perpetrate violence in our communities and terrorize citizens through fear and intimidation

- Management of a national drug intelligence program in cooperation with federal, state, local, and foreign officials to collect, analyze, and disseminate strategic and operational drug intelligence information

- Seizure and forfeiture of assets derived from, traceable to, or intended to be used for illicit drug trafficking

- Coordination and cooperation with federal, state, and local law enforcement officials on mutual drug enforcement efforts and enhancement of such efforts through exploitation of potential interstate and international investigations beyond local or limited federal jurisdictions and resources

- Coordination and cooperation with federal, state, and local agencies, and with foreign governments, in programs designed to reduce the availability of illicit abuse-type drugs on the U.S. market through crop eradication, crop substitution, and training of foreign officials

- Responsibility, under the policy guidance of the secretary of state and U.S. ambassadors, for all programs associated with drug law enforcement counterparts in foreign countries

- Liaison with the United Nations, Interpol, and other organizations on matters relating to international drug control programs"[19]

The DEA is part of the war on drugs effort in the United States. Several high-profile cases in 2009 illustrate the nature and scope of the work performed by the DEA (see "Sample . . .").

In 1938, Robert Merton co-opted the sociological theories of Durkheim in development of the Strain Theory of deviant motivation. Merton's theory was later elaborated upon by notable thinkers Albert Cohen, Robert Agnew, Steven F. Messner, and Richard Rosenfeld.

Throughout the Great Depression, hardboiled crime fiction delighted readers with atmospheric suspense, snappy dialogue, and explosive plots. Raymond Chandler's 1939 novel *The Big Sleep* epitomizes the hardboiled genre.

1938

1939

1960–Present

Throughout the 1960s, urban crime rates soared.

1960s

Sample of DEA's High-Profile Cases in 2009

- **New York: Podiatrist Charged with Selling Pills Obtained by Writing and Filling Phony Prescriptions**. Levine faces up to 25 years in prison for drug, weapons charges.
- **New York: Sing Sing Correction Officer Indicted on Top Narcotics Charges**
- **California: Operation Rock Solid Culminates in the Arrest of 31 Individuals**. Drug dealers and members of the Crips Street Gang arrested in a joint operation between DEA's MET and Oceanside Police Department.
- **Michigan: Two Michigan Men Arrested in Large Marijuana Conspiracy**. 1,400 pounds of marijuana seized in joint investigation by DEA and Flint Area Narcotics Group (FANG).
- **Michigan: Michigan Doctor and Pharmacist among Men Indicted in Huge Prescription Drug Scheme**. Physician alleged to have illegally distributed more than 1 million dosage units.

Source: U.S. Drug Enforcement Administration, http://www.usdoj.gov/dea/pubs/news_releases.htm.

Other Federal Law Enforcement Agencies

Some of the other federal law enforcement agencies include the following:

- *U.S. Marshals Service.* The Marshals Service is a separate agency within the Department of Justice. The marshals protect the federal courts, judges, and jurors; guard federal prisoners from arrest to conviction; investigate violations of federal fugitive laws; serve summonses; and control custody of money and property seized under federal law.[20]

- *U.S. Customs and Border Protection.* Customs inspectors examine all cargo and baggage entering the country. Special agents investigate smuggling, currency violations, criminal fraud, and major cargo frauds. Special customs patrol officers concentrate on contraband, such as drugs and weapons, at official border crossings, seaports, and airports.[21] The work of the U.S. Customs and Border Protection agency is illustrated in their work at airports throughout the United States.[22] In just one week in early 2009, officers of the U.S. Customs and Border Protection agency encountered numerous incidents at Dulles International Airport near Washington, DC (see "Examples. . .").

- *Bureau of Alcohol, Tobacco, Firearms and Explosives (ATF).* According to the ATF's mission statement, this agency is:

> *a principal law enforcement agency within the United States Department of Justice dedicated to preventing terrorism, reducing violent crime, and protecting our Nation. The*

On November 22, 1963, Lee Harvey Oswald assassinated President John F. Kennedy during a motorcade in Dallas, Texas. Harvey fled to a nearby movie theater, but he was apprehended by police and shot to death by vigilante Jack Ruby before he could be tried.

In 1966, Ronald Akers and Robert Burgess synthesized the work of Gabriel Tarde and Edwin Sutherland into a complete social learning theory. In their work, Akers and Burgess outlined a variety of deviant behaviors and analyzed their development.

On the night of August 8, 1969, four disciples of Charles Manson infiltrated the house of director Roman Polanski and brutally murdered his eight-month pregnant wife, Sharon Tate—one of many such murders by Manson's Family. Manson himself was convicted of murder and conspiracy.

In 1970, the community policing era began.

1970

1963

1966

1969

men and women of ATF perform the dual responsibilities of enforcing Federal criminal laws and regulating the firearms and explosives industries. We are committed to working directly, and through partnerships, to investigate and reduce crime involving firearms and explosives, acts of arson, and illegal trafficking of alcohol and tobacco products.[23] "

In 2008 and 2009, a series of 70 arson fires in Pennsylvania led to the development of a task force including the ATF to help investigate the arsons and bring an end to the serial fires. Arson investigators with the ATF worked with the Coatesville Police Department, Chester County (Pennsylvania) District Attorney's Office, Pennsylvania State Police, and the FBI to arrest those responsible for setting close to 70 fires in and around the Coatesville community. Although two arrests had been made as of March 2009, the fires continued. The integration of the federal ATF with other local, state, and federal agencies shows how the resources of multiple agencies can be used to manage a significant crime such as this series of arsons.[24]

Examples of Incidents Handled by U.S. Customs and Border Protection Officers at Dulles International Airport

- Officers found two sausages in a shrink-wrapped puzzle box that a woman from Amsterdam had declared as a child's gift. The woman was fined $500.
- A traveler from Ethiopia was fined $300 for attempting to smuggle five pounds of dried beef hidden inside a dry bread package.
- A woman carrying four pounds of pork sausage from the Netherlands was fined $300 for repeatedly failing to report the meat.
- A man from Vietnam was fined $175 for failing to declare six packages of pork sausage—even after CBP officials offered him several opportunities to change his declaration.
- A traveler arriving from Paris had 34 Cuban cigars—including 25 Petit Cazzadores—taken away by officers.
- Two people—including a minor—were busted for bringing bottles of absinthe

Throughout the 1990s and into the 2000s, former criminal lawyer and Mississippi House Representative John Grisham's suspenseful courtroom-based novels, such as 1993's *The Client*, met sweeping popular and critical acclaim.

Former NFL running back O.J. Simpson's criminal trial for the 1994 murders of Nicole Brown Simpson and Ronald Goldman has been described as the trial of the century—one of the most publicized criminal cases in history. Simpson was acquitted of all charges.

Simpson's 1994 acquittal didn't put an end to his legal troubles, however. In 2008 he was sentenced to a total of 33 year in prison for the armed robbery of sports memorabilia. See Chapter 1 for more information.

1990s-2000s

1994

without an Alcohol and Tobacco Tax and Trade Bureau-approved label in from Europe. Another minor was caught trying to bring in two bottles of vodka from Germany.

- A woman who arrived from London had $34,700 seized after repeatedly refusing to declare $35,000 in U.S. currency she was hiding in her bag. Officers gave her a $300 humanitarian release, and she will have to file a petition to get the rest of her money. Travelers carrying more than $10,000 in U.S. currency equivalence must declare the amount.

- The most serious offense was the arrest of a 40-year-old Colombian man traveling from Panama who was charged with importing five kilograms or more of cocaine into the country.

- Officers arrested four people with outstanding warrants from Montgomery, Fairfax, Arlington, and Loudoun counties.

- During the 2008 fiscal year, CBP officers arrested 111 passengers on arrest warrants from local, state, and federal jurisdictions and issued 172 civil penalties for failure to declare prohibited agriculture products.

Source: WTOP. 2009, February 26. Sausages, Cigars and Porn - A Wacky Week at Dulles. Retrieved March 9, 2009, from WTOP.com: http://www.wtop.com/?nid=25&sid=1611830.

Department of Homeland Security (DHS)

The events of 9/11 resulted in a huge new addition to the structure of federal law enforcement—the Department of Homeland Security (DHS)—in 2002. In 2005, the DHS announced a six-point agenda to ensure that its policies, operations, and structures would be able to address the potential threats—both present and future—that face our nation. The agenda was intended to result in changes that would:

1. Increase overall preparedness, particularly for catastrophic events

2. Create better transportation security systems to move people and cargo more securely and efficiently

3. Strengthen border security and interior enforcement and reform immigration processes

4. Enhance information sharing with our partners

5. Improve DHS financial management, human resource development, procurement, and information technology

6. Realign the DHS organization to maximize mission performance[25]

To achieve its mission and support the agenda, the department realigned to focus on the following goals:

- Centralize and improve policy development and coordination

- Strengthen intelligence functions and information sharing

- Improve coordination and efficiency of operations

- Enhance coordination and deployment of preparedness assets[26]

The highlights for the DHS under the new presidential administration in 2009 revealed that Obama's priorities for DHS would be:

- Safeguard the nation's transportation system

- Enhance cyber security and technology research and development through partnerships with government, industry, and academia

- Strengthen border security and immigration services

- Support state homeland security activities[27]

STATE LAW ENFORCEMENT AGENCIES

All states have law enforcement agencies with statewide authority. They go by various names, but common ones are the State Police, State Highway Patrol, and State Bureau of Investigation. As the number of motor vehicles proliferated after 1910, the need for highway traffic control generated new calls for state police. Some states, including Texas, Pennsylvania, Connecticut, and Massachusetts, added a state trooper division to their existing organization. Most states, however, never overcame opposition to a centralized state police agency with comprehensive powers, but they did adopt special state highway patrol agencies with authority limited to traffic law enforcement. State highway patrol officers have only limited authority to perform general law enforcement duties, such as investigating crimes occurring in a state trooper's presence or crimes taking place on or near state highways.

Technological advances in traffic devices, alcohol testing, and communications systems all require officers to have greater ability and more training than their predecessors. Increasing numbers of states are setting

statewide entry requirements and training standards for police officers, either through agency-established academies or in conjunction with institutions of higher learning. Following training, line officers advance in rank through either civil service or merit plans. In addition to enforcement agencies and training institutions, most states maintain "crime lab" or "criminalistics" services; some support investigative units.

COUNTY LAW ENFORCEMENT AGENCIES

Sheriffs' departments enforce the criminal law in most rural and unincorporated portions of the more than 3,000 counties in the United States. In most instances, sheriffs do not interfere in municipal law enforcement because most incorporated towns and cities have their own police forces. Sheriffs' departments have two other duties. They maintain the county jails, which hold pretrial detainees and most people sentenced for misdemeanors. They are also officers of the county court. In that capacity, the sheriff's office supplies bailiffs to provide security and management of detainees on trial, transports prisoners to and from court, and serves court papers (summonses, forfeiture and eviction notices, and court judgments).

MUNICIPAL POLICE DEPARTMENTS

Municipal police departments do the lion's share of policing and consume most of the law enforcement budget in the United States, and they are the subject of most of what you will learn about police and policing in this book (see Table 5.2). A majority of local officers perform the patrol function while the remaining

officers engage in criminal investigation. Municipal or metropolitan agencies can be quite large (New York City, for example), and their main duties and services include arrest, routine patrol, criminal investigation, traffic law enforcement, crowd and traffic control, and issuance of special licenses and permits.[28]

LO3 The Organizational Structure of Policing

Police departments have a formal structure but use an informal decision-making style; we will examine these seemingly inconsistent characteristics.

FORMAL POLICE STRUCTURE

Formally, law enforcement agencies resemble military organizations; we call this the **military model of policing**. Police departments use a hierarchical command structure, meaning that authority flows from the chief at the top who gives orders to officers on the beat who carry out the orders. Officers wear uniforms, and they are divided into ranks with military-sounding names like commander, captain, lieutenant, and sergeant. Also, disobeying orders is called insubordination, and it leads to punishment just as it does in the military. The police mission is described as fighting "wars" against

TABLE 5.2 Expenditures on Federal, State, and Local Law Enforcement Agencies, 2003	
State	$66.1 billion
Municipal	$93.9 billion
Federal	$35.3 billion

Source: Bureau of Justice Statistics, *Justice Expenditure and Employment in the U.S. 2003* (Washington, DC: Bureau of Justice Statistics, April 2006), Table 1.

"enemies" who commit crimes, use drugs, and otherwise cause trouble.

THE INFORMAL POLICE DECISION-MAKING PROCESS

The military model describes the formal, outward structure of police organization, but the informal reality of its decision-making process in its day-to-day operations is very different. Whereas soldiers wait for specific orders from officers before they act and most orders are highly specific ("Go over that hill and attack that bunker"), police officers are left on their own to carry out vague commands like "keep the peace" or "settle problems." Soldiers work together. They cannot, do not, and should not decide whether to move into an area, shoot at the enemy, or carry out other operations. In contrast, except for large public gatherings, demonstrations, disturbances, and riots, police officers work alone or with a single partner.[29]

In day-to-day operations, police departments resemble hospitals, universities, and law firms more than military organizations. Police chiefs make sure that they have enough personnel, money, and support so that the officers can do their jobs. But the "big" decisions (arrest or let go) are left to the officers.[30]

The military model does describe our image of the police as well as their image of themselves. But that image causes problems. The military image and the belief that "all's fair in war" leads some police officers to use excessive force or illegally invade the privacy and liberty of anyone they consider the "enemy." The enemy—people in the community in this case—may adopt the same maxim, putting the police in danger.

LO4 Responsibilities of the Police

the police have three missions that define their basic responsibilities: criminal law enforcement, order maintenance, and public service not related to either criminal law enforcement or maintaining order.

Criminal law enforcement may be the most publicized mission, but it is in the other two—maintaining order and providing services not related to crime or disorder—that discretionary decision making looms largest. Officers also spend most of their time on those two missions, and most taxpayers' dollars go to them. Let's look more closely at each of the three police missions.[31]

CRIMINAL LAW ENFORCEMENT

Criminal law enforcement is a "rare" police mission, but that does not mean it is unimportant. Guarding the gates of the criminal justice system and starting the criminal justice process in motion by deciding who will and who will not pass through those gates is by any measure very important.[32] The police produce the first product of criminal justice decision making—the criminal suspect. Without that product, the criminal process

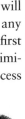

MISSION

1. Criminal law enforcement

2. Order maintenance

3. Public service not related to either criminal law enforcement or maintaining order

maintaining order a police mission in which police are supposed to "do something right now to settle problems"

1. Preventing crime from happening in the first place
2. Investigating crimes and identifying suspects after crimes have been committed
3. Finding and catching suspects after they are identified
4. Helping prosecutors build a case against defendants

ORDER MAINTENANCE

Maintaining order means police are supposed to "do something right now to settle problems."[33] Notice three major differences between maintaining order and criminal law enforcement:

1. "Do something" calls for discretionary decision making that includes a lot more choices than just arresting someone.

would never start. The criminal law enforcement mission boils down to four duties or responsibilities:

2. "Settle problems" also allows a wide range of discretionary decision making. Problems include more than crimes, and "settle" means more than putting the criminal justice process in motion.
3. "Right now" means to settle the problem in minutes. Criminal law enforcement takes days—sometimes weeks or even months—stretching from investigation before an arrest and the arrest itself by patrol officers to follow-up investigation by detectives.

PUBLIC SERVICE

A police department is the only government agency on call every day, all day, all year. So it makes sense for people to call the police to solve all kinds of problems: to report fights, drunkenness, rowdy kids, prostitution, and panhandling on the streets; to stop a feud between neighbors outside; to settle a domestic disturbance and a noisy party inside; to find lost children and rescue animals in distress anywhere; or to find the nearest hospital.[34]

Test coming up? Now what?

With CJUS you have a multitude of study aids at your fingertips. After reading the chapters, check out these ideas for further help.

Review cards include all learning outcomes, definitions, and summaries for each chapter.

Printable Flash Cards give you three additional ways to check your comprehension of key criminal justice concepts.

Other great ways to help you study include **Interactive Quizzing, Downloads, Games,** and **Video Activities.**

You can find it all at **4ltrpress.cengage.com/cjus.**

Police use an array

of tactics to control crime.

6

Policing Strategies

Policing strategies have evolved in modern times to include technology enhancements, specialized task forces, policy development based on crime statistics, research-based crime initiatives, and more comprehensive strategies that integrate resources, the community, and other agencies. Community policing strategies have incorporated the community in crime prevention and crime response. New advances in DNA technology have been used to investigate and convict criminals, as well as to exonerate innocent people who were convicted of crimes they had not committed. In this chapter, we will explore the major forms of policing strategies used in modern policing.

LO1 Strategies of Crime Control

now that you have learned about police missions, we will take the next logical step and examine police strategies for carrying out their missions. Two reactive strategies—preventive patrol and criminal investigation—have dominated U.S. policing since the 1800s. Uniformed police officers patrol the streets to prevent crimes. Detectives investigate crimes to catch suspects for prosecution, conviction, and punishment. For most of their history, both strategies have followed a **one-size-fits-all approach to crime control**—react the same way to all crimes in all places at all times. Since the 1970s, however, a convincing body of research has clearly shown the limits of the one-size-fits-all approach.

Those research findings began to appear as the crime and social disorder boom combined with citizens' fear of violence, guns, and illegal drugs to create a public mood of "enough is enough." Frustrated and angry, the public sent a strong message to politicians and cops: "Do something *now*!" Police leaders got the message, and they responded. One response was to refine patrol and investigation. Another was to supplement preventive patrol and criminal investigation with proactive policing strategies—a bolder, more provocative, and more

> **one-size-fits-all approach to crime control** law enforcement reacts the same way to all crimes in all places at all times

Learning Outcomes

LO1 Understand the main functions of police patrol, investigation, and special operations units

LO2 Discuss the concept of patrol and its effectiveness

LO3 Discuss key issues associated with the criminal investigative function

LO4 Explain the various police support functions

LO5 Understand the concept of community policing

LO6 Describe various community policing strategies

crime-attack strategies police focus on specific types of suspicious people in specific places at specific times to prevent or interrupt crimes and arrest suspects for committing specific crimes

community policing strategy a strategy based on the idea that the police can best carry out their missions by helping communities help themselves by getting at the causes of and finding solutions to community problems

preventive patrol officers move through their beats on foot or in vehicles, making themselves visible to control crime and reassure law-abiding people that they're safe

controversial response. **Crime-attack strategies** (the narrowest) focus on specific types of suspicious people in specific places at specific times to prevent or interrupt crimes and arrest suspects for committing specific crimes. Some call these narrowly tailored crime-attack strategies "smarter law enforcement." But how "smart" crime-attack strategies really are depends on the answers to empirical questions about their effectiveness, constitutional questions about whether they violate rights of privacy and liberty, and ethical questions about whether they intrude upon dignity and autonomy in a free society.

There is also a far more ambitious and sweeping proactive strategy afoot. The **community policing strategy** is based on the idea that the police can best carry out their missions by helping communities help themselves, not (or at least not *just*) by enforcing the criminal law but by preventing crime, reducing the fear of crime, maintaining order, *and* improving the quality of community life by getting at the causes of and finding solutions to community problems.[1] In this chapter, we will look at each of these strategies and at how technology is changing law enforcement.

LO2 Patrol

Patrol is at the heart of what police do, so let's take a closer look at what patrol involves and the various types of patrol.

PATROL: THE "BACKBONE" OF POLICING

Preventive patrol consists of officers moving through their beats mak-

In April of 2009, Jiverly Wong entered the American Civic Association immigration center in Binghamton, New York and opened fire on its occupants. After wounding four and killing 13 with his two pistols, Wong turned one of the weapons on himself. In the days that followed, Binghamton police were criticized for an allegedly sluggish response to the incident: though they arrived on the scene three minutes after the first emergency calls were made, they did not enter the immigration center for nearly 40 minutes. Broome County District Attorney Jerry Mollen defended the police, stating that there was nothing the police could have done to save those who died.

ing themselves visible.[2] It has two objectives: controlling crime and reassuring law-abiding people that they are safe. Patrol cars either move slowly (prowling) to prevent crime or speed through the streets, with sirens screaming and red lights flashing, to pursue suspects. Crime control assumes that just seeing uniformed officers and knowing they might appear anytime will prevent criminal wannabes from committing crimes. Having officers on the beat also improves the chance that they might see and catch criminals in the act. The second objective, reassuring law-abiding citizens that they are safe, also assumes the effectiveness of the visible presence of uniformed officers.

Traditionally, faster patrol was assumed to be better. At least, that is what police used to think about their response to calls. They assumed that the faster they got to crime scenes, the more criminals they could catch, the more injuries they could prevent, and the more satisfied the public would be. Departments relied on two tactics to speed up response time: (1) the emergency 911 telephone number and (2) a computer-assisted automobile vehicle monitoring (AVM) system.[3]

Then several empirical studies shattered the belief that faster is better. Researchers discovered that police response time has no effect on apprehension, charge, and conviction rates. They also found that people's satisfaction does not depend on how fast police answer calls.[4]

Police departments dropped the one-size-fits-all approach to calls, adopting instead a **differential response approach**. With this approach, their response varied according to the type of crime. They used rapid response for serious crimes like rape and robbery and other responses, like 30-minute delays, telephone reporting, walk-in reporting, and scheduled appointments, for less serious offenses.[5]

Types of Preventive Patrol

There are two main types of patrol: vehicle patrol and foot patrol. Foot patrol dominated the first century of public policing. Then came the car, which by the 1940s had replaced foot patrol. Vehicle patrol was the dominant form until the 1970s when foot patrol and the hybrid bicycle came back into use. (The hybrid bicycle has a few of the advantages of vehicles and practically all the benefits of foot patrol.) Let's look at vehicle patrol, foot patrol and single-officer patrol.[6]

Vehicle Patrol How does vehicle patrol work in practice? It depends on the city or town, the beat, the time of day, and the individual officer. Vehicle patrol has serious drawbacks. It contributes to poor police-community relations, especially in poor neighborhoods, where many residents regard the police as a hostile occupational force. Isolated in their cars, with windows rolled up to protect them from the smells, the dangers, and even the temperatures, the police seem out of touch and definitely not able to communicate effectively with the people they serve.[7]

Beginning in the 1970s, a series of empirical evaluations uncovered several deficiencies in preventive patrol besides isolation and poor community relations. Prisoners told interviewers that the presence of police did not frighten them; obviously, it did not deter them from committing crimes.[8] Attempts to increase perceived police presence by letting officers use squad cars for their personal use had little, if any, deterrent effect. Patrol cannot stop crimes committed inside buildings. Even when preventive patrol deters, its effect is limited to main streets and buildings, leaving side and back streets, alleys, and even the backs of buildings on main streets unaffected.

These evaluations also found that crimes of passion are largely beyond the reach of preventive patrol.

Enraged or demented individuals do not take patrol officers into account when their impulses explode into violence. Also, skilled criminals quickly discover where the police concentrate their efforts and avoid those places or at least wait until a squad car drives by before they make their moves.

The most famous (and probably the most influential) study of preventive patrol, the Kansas City Preventive Patrol Experiment, tested the effectiveness of this dominant police strategy. Researchers divided 15 beats into three groups matched for similar crime rates and demographic characteristics. For one year, the police applied three patrol strategies to each group. In the control group, they applied traditional preventive patrol; one car drove through the streets whenever it was not answering calls. In group 2, proactive patrol, they greatly increased patrol activity; cars drove through the beats two to three times more often than in the control group. In group 3, reactive patrol, they eliminated preventive patrol entirely; a patrol car stayed at the station until someone called for assistance.

Before and after the experiment, interviewers asked businesspeople and neighborhood residents about whether they had been crime victims, their opinion of the quality of law enforcement, and their fear of crime. To the surprise of many, no matter what the strategy:

- Crime rates stayed the same.
- Rates of reporting crime to the police remained constant.
- People's fear of crime stayed the same.
- Opinions about the effectiveness of police services did not change.
- Respect for the police increased in the control beats (traditional preventive patrol!).[9]

Foot Patrol Police returned to the old practice of patrolling on foot in the 1970s and 1980s because it brought them closer to the community. Why does getting closer to the community matter? Does foot patrol make police more "street smart," reduce crime and disorder, and reduce the fear of crime, too? Two major evaluations tried to answer these questions. In Flint, Michigan, foot patrol reduced the fear of crime and actual crime rates. It was

> Crimes of passion are largely beyond the reach of preventive patrol.

differential response approach an approach that varies police mobilization according to the type of crime

When it comes to officers on patrol, 1 is greater than 2.

- Saved money
- Resulted in fewer resisting-arrest situations
- Resulted in fewer assaults against officers
- Resulted in fewer injuries to officers
- Generated fewer citizen complaints
- Completed about the same number of traffic warnings, field interrogations, business checks, arrests, and crime report filings[11]

preliminary investigation patrol officers collect information at crime scenes and write incident reports describing what they learned

incident reports written reports describing what patrol officers found during preliminary investigations

so popular that in spite of Flint's severe financial problems, the city voted three times for special tax increases to expand the program. On the other hand, the Newark Foot Patrol Experiment produced mixed results. Fear of crime went down and public satisfaction with police went up, but crime rates stayed the same.[10]

Single-Officer Patrol Patrol is labor-intensive: it relies heavily on people, not labor- and cost-saving equipment. Salaries make up 80 percent of police budgets, making patrol the most expensive police operation. This is particularly true of two-officer patrols, which prevailed in American policing until the 1980s. Faced with declining budgets, the cost-effectiveness of one-officer patrols appealed to budget-conscious administrators, who saw the chance to cut the cost of patrol in half. But officers vigorously opposed the idea because they strongly believed that they were safer with partners backing each other up. When the Police Executive Research Foundation evaluated one-officer patrols in San Diego, however, it found this was not true. The study reported that compared to two-officer units, one-officer units:

LO3 Criminal Investigation

Let's look more closely at what happens during preliminary and follow-up criminal investigations and the roles of patrol officers and detectives in each.

PRELIMINARY INVESTIGATION

Most departments divide a criminal investigation into a preliminary investigation by patrol officers and a follow-up investigation by detectives. In **preliminary investigations**, patrol officers collect information at crime scenes and write **incident reports** describing what they learned. Police departments and prosecutors rely heavily on incident reports in deciding whether to continue the criminal process. Incident reports that contain "good" information, such as (1) the names and addresses of several witnesses, (2) the names and addresses of suspects (or at least good descriptions of them), and (3) detailed descriptions of stolen property, raise the chances of successful prosecution and conviction.

Detective investigations almost never lead to the identification of unknown criminals.

Patrol officers make most arrests. They arrest suspects either at the scene of the crime or later based on identifications from victims or witnesses. Detectives, on the other hand, make only a small number of arrests, and detective investigations almost never lead to the identification of unknown criminals. As a result of these findings, many police departments now train patrol officers to conduct more extensive investigations. Some departments even provide patrol officers with feedback from prosecutors' offices regarding the final outcome of cases the officers investigated.

In a **follow-up investigation**, detectives conduct an investigation after the preliminary investigation by patrol officers. In TV shows and movies, the detectives always solve the crime and catch the bad guys, but researchers who have studied detectives in real life tell a more complicated story. First, most cases are not solved by detective work. Then, how are they solved?

1. Patrol officers have already arrested the suspect.
2. Detectives have identified suspects before they get the case.
3. Arrested suspects confess to other crimes they have committed.[12]

A new tool in criminal investigation is the use of DNA technology. **DNA** is the building block for your entire genetic makeup, which is unique. Every cell in your body has the same DNA. DNA is a highly effective law enforcement identification tool because every person's DNA is unique (except for identical twins). So, just like fingerprints, DNA evidence collected at crime scenes can point the finger at or eliminate a suspect.

When labs link DNA from one crime scene with evidence at another crime scene using CODIS (Combined DNA Index System), they can link these crimes to a single suspect anywhere in the country. **CODIS** is a software program that operates databases of DNA profiles from convicted offenders, crime scene evidence from unsolved crimes, and missing persons. It can electronically link crime scenes.[13]

Keep in mind that before evidence containing DNA can solve crimes, three conditions have to be met:

1. Criminals have to leave evidence containing DNA behind, either at the crime scene or on the victim or the victim's clothes.
2. A trained technician has to search for the evidence.
3. Investigators have to find evidence containing DNA.[14]

Just a tiny amount of DNA can help to solve a crime. For example, a car thief in Finland was caught by analyzing a DNA sample of his blood found inside a mosquito. When criminal investigators searched a stolen car that police had recovered, they found a mosquito that had sucked blood. After testing the blood, investigators were

follow-up investigation detectives conduct an investigation after the preliminary investigation by patrol officers

DNA the building block for each individual's unique genetic makeup

CODIS (Combined DNA Index System) a software program that operates databases of DNA profiles from convicted offenders, crime scene evidence from unsolved crimes, and missing persons

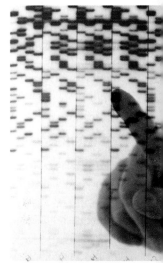

Crime is not distributed evenly in place and time.

© Jeff Greenberg/Alamy

"hot spots" patrol patrol that gives some locations, like intersections and buildings, special attention at certain times because these areas generate a substantial portion of calls for law enforcement services

police crackdowns sudden increases in police activity at particular places during "hot" days and times

displacement effect crime moves to another location during crackdowns and comes back after the crackdown

able to link the sample to a man who was registered in their police database.[15]

PROACTIVE POLICING AND SPECIAL OPERATIONS UNITS

Preventive patrol and criminal investigation have their limits, but those limits are mainly due to strategies based on a one-size-fits-all approach to crime control—respond to all crimes in all places at all times in the same way. We have already seen how research led to refinements in patrol and investigation. The same research also led to the adoption of proactive crime-attack strategies (officers initiate actions to prevent crime and catch criminals) tailored to specific crimes and types of criminals, in particular places, at certain times. Let's look at some of these strategies, including "hot spots" patrol and police crackdowns.

"Hot Spots" Patrol

"Hot spots" patrol is based on a simple idea: Because crime is not distributed evenly in place and time, some addresses at certain times need special attention. For example, the city of Minneapolis found that more than half of the 911 calls reporting serious crimes came from only 3 percent of its 115,000 addresses (hot spots). All rapes came from 1.2 percent of the addresses, all robberies from 2.2 percent, all car thefts from 2.7 percent, and all domestic disturbances from 9 percent. So trying to give every resident an equal share of patrol was not smart. Lawrence Sherman assisted the Minneapolis Police Department in designing the Minneapolis Hot Spots Patrol Experiment to test how "smart" hot spots patrol is.[16]

To evaluate hot spots patrol, Sherman and his colleagues at the Crime Control Institute collected addresses based on calls for assistance and crimes reported to the police during one year.[17] Then, the police applied "three hours a day of intermittent, unpredictable police presence" to a random selection of the "worst" hot spot intersections in the city. Robbery fell 20 percent, and crimes overall fell 13 percent at these intersections. The number of fights and disturbances was cut in half in the experimental areas. The Minneapolis police officers on hot spots patrol just drove around; they did not get out of their cars to talk to people or to interrogate suspects. According to Sherman, "more aggressive efforts may have reduced crime even further—or made it worse."[18]

Crackdowns

Lawrence Sherman and Dennis Rogan also found that calls to the police came on "hot" days of the week at "hot" times of the day.[19] **Police crackdowns** consist of sudden increases in police activity at places during these "hot" days and times.

How effective are crackdowns? The evidence is mixed. According to Sherman, "most addresses, and even most blocks, in any city go for years without any crime—even in high-crime neighborhoods."[20] Some research shows crackdowns on drunk driving, robbery, drug dealing, and prostitution reduce crime—but (and it is a big but) only at the crackdown location and only for a short time. The problem is that crime moves to another location (a result called the **displacement effect**) and then comes back to its old location after the crackdown. However, Sherman's review of evaluations of crackdowns in 18 U.S. locations and five other countries showed that 15 worked with little evidence of displacement. For example, in London, England, there was no evidence that a crackdown on prostitution pushed prostitutes to other areas of the city.[21]

The Pasadena (Texas) Police Department, just outside Houston, provides an example of a special unit designed to crack down on specific crime issues in a community. The Pasadena Police Department has a special unit or task force, as some agencies call these units, to deal with gangs and street crime. According to the department's website:

> *The Gang Task Force and Street Crimes Unit continues to serve as a model for law enforce-*

ment agencies across the State of Texas. The unit was formed in 1993 to investigate gang-related activity and develop an aggressive program combining suppression and intervention tactics. In 2004, the Street Crimes Unit was formed and combined with the Gang Task Force to serve as a proactive crime fighting and investigations unit on the street level. This unit serves as a supplement to the Detective Division, often solving crimes before a report can be made and forwarded to a Detective for investigation.

GTF Officers receive extensive training in this specialized area and work closely with area agencies at all levels. The Gang Task Force also works with the Texas Gang Investigators Association, an organization that has helped produce legislation aimed at providing better tools to fight gang crime.

In cooperation with the Police Administration, GTF has developed new programs that integrate education and intervention with proven investigative procedures and aggressive enforcement tactics.[22]

In March of 2009, NFL running back Ryan Moats was stopped by a Dallas Police Department officer after he ran a red light en route to Baylor Regional Medical Center in Plano, Texas. Though Moats explained to the officer that he was rushing to see his mother-in-law who was dying from breast cancer, the officer held him for 13 minutes, and even drew his weapon. Moats was released after a nurse at the medical center confirmed the urgency of the situation, but by the time he reached Baylor, his mother-in-law had died. The detaining officer was placed on administrative leave for the incident, and later resigned from the department.

AP Images/David J. Phillip

Crackdowns raise questions about the right balance between crime control and individual liberty and privacy in a constitutional democracy. Crackdowns intrude deeply into people's daily lives, interfering with their right to come and go as they please and to be let alone by government. Some residents complain that crackdowns turn their neighborhoods into "police states." Young black men complain that officers "hassle" them simply because they are young, black, and in the neighborhood. Inevitably, crackdowns affect innocent people who have no intention of committing crimes or causing trouble.[23]

LO4 Support Functions

Patrol and criminal investigation are assisted by numerous administrative support functions that allow the police function to operate. Police officers are sworn personnel, and support function personnel are typically nonsworn. Administrative support functions include communications/dispatch, personnel, records, training, research and planning, public information, and property.[24]

Communications/dispatch involves the 911 response by trained dispatchers who direct police response according to incoming emergency calls. The dispatcher plays a key role by conveying critical information to the patrol officer responding to the call. A primary responsibility of the dispatcher is to screen calls to distinguish between calls that actually involve crimes and need a police response and calls that require some other type of response.

The personnel department recruits, hires, retains, and terminates police personnel. This department maintains personnel records, evaluates personnel performance, and administers health, safety, and benefit programs for personnel.

The records division collects and maintains paper and computerized records of police activity. This function is essential for the successful prosecutions of cases because the entire criminal justice process relies on these records. A police department maintains a host of records including arrest reports, incident reports, accident reports, juvenile reports, field interrogations, witness statements, suspect interviews, and other critical pieces of information that help reconstruct a case or other police activity.

The training division is responsible for the pre-service and in-service training of personnel. Pre-service training is recruit training that takes place in the police

police support functions

communications/dispatch
personnel
records
training
research & planning
public information
property

academy. Typically, larger agencies have their own police academies, and smaller agencies send their new personnel to state-run academies or regional training centers. In-service training may be done in house or at state or regional locations and includes education on new techniques (use of Tasers) or specialized topics (domestic violence or the mentally ill offender). The amount of yearly in-service training and/or the topics covered may be mandated (required) by state law. In Texas, for example,

> *Section 1701.351(a) of the Texas Occupations Code requires that each peace officer shall complete at least 40 hours of continuing education programs once every 24 months. The commission may suspend the license of a peace officer who fails to comply with this requirement.*[25]

These 40 hours must include training in cultural diversity, special investigative topics, and crisis intervention. Cultural diversity and crisis intervention have been key topics for police personnel in the last decade, as police have had to deal with more conflicts sparked by cultural differences and with various crisis situations.

The research and planning division of a police department is responsible for short-term and long-term strategic planning and staying current with new laws, practices, and standards. This division may also do crime analysis, write grant proposals, and administer grants. Writing grant proposals has become increasingly important as law enforcement agencies look to federal and state grants to obtain funding for implementing new strategies, hiring and/or educating personnel, and securing new state-of-the-art technologies and resources. One federal government program, for example, Public Safety Partnership and Community Policing Grants, funds projects under the following guidelines:

> *As originally authorized, the grantor agency may use at least 85 percent of program funds to hire or rehire career law enforcement officers and procure equipment and/or technology (if such expenditures can be shown to result in an increase of officers deployed in community-oriented policing because of time savings achieved from the equipment or technology); up to 15 percent of program funds may be used for grants that support programs or projects to (a) increase the number of officers involved in activities focused on interaction with members of the community on proactive crime control and prevention, (b) provide specialized training to officers to enhance conflict resolution, mediation, problem solving, service and other skills needed to work in partnership with members of the community, (c) increase police participation in multidisciplinary early intervention teams, (d) develop new technologies to assist State and local law enforcement agencies in reorienting the emphasis of their activities from reacting to crime to preventing crime, (e) develop and implement innovative programs to permit members of the community to assist law enforcement agencies in the prevention of crime, including programs to increase the level of access to the criminal justice system utilized by victims, witnesses and ordinary citizens, (f) establish innovative programs to minimize the time that officers must be away from the community while awaiting court appearances, (g) establish innovative programs to increase proactive crime control and prevention programs involving officers and young persons, (h) establish new administrative and managerial systems to facilitate the adoption of community-oriented policing as an organization-wide philosophy, (i) establish and coordinate crime pre-*

vention and control programs (involving law enforcement officers working with community members) with other Federal programs that serve the community and its members to better address their comprehensive needs, and (j) support the purchase by a law enforcement agency of no more than one service weapon per officer newly deployed in community-oriented policing. Three percent of program funds may be used to provide technical assistance, training, research or other studies in support of program objectives.[26] **"**

The Guardian Angels is an international volunteer organization dedicated to community-oriented crime prevention and patrol. Founded February 1979 in New York City, Guardian Angels trains unarmed citizens to intercept violent crime and make citizen's arrests, and to lead educational workshops for school and businesses. While new Guardian Angels chapters often meet resistance from city government officials, the group has generally been accepted as a positive aid to community-oriented policing.

The public information unit is responsible for communicating with the public and the media. Many police agencies have a designated public information officer who conducts this function. The dissemination of information about crimes to the media is an important function that must be maintained by qualified personnel who know how to transmit information needed by the public without hindering criminal investigation processes. This division also holds press conferences, maintains the department website, and releases crime-related data. The Houston (Texas) Police Department website, for example, at http://www.houstontx.gov/police/ provides information needed by the public as well as prospective job seekers. The information includes accident report forms, crime prevention information, crime statistics, the agency mission statement, and news releases. The crime statistics section of the Houston Police Department website includes data spreadsheets of crime numbers for each month.[27]

The property division is responsible for maintaining the evidence and property from each case. Evidence must be kept in a secure location until the case comes to trial or is otherwise terminated. This function is critical because the chain of custody must be maintained between the investigator who obtains the evidence and the use of the evidence at trial.

LO5 Community-Oriented Policing

touted by police management, criminal justice academics, and politicians, **community-oriented policing (COP)** is first and foremost concerned with establishing a working relationship with the community. It reflects a partnership between police and the communities they serve to identify and solve community problems. The idea is that partnerships between police and the community can reduce crime and increase security. COP emphasizes shifting decision-making power from top executives at headquarters down to local precincts. Residents are viewed as the main line of defense against crime, disorder, fear, and the deterioration of the quality of life in their neighborhoods. So, in community-oriented policing, residents identify and participate in the solutions to the problems in their neighborhood. When police talk to residents, they find residents do not always put serious crime at the top of their list of concerns; instead, they often say that fear is as important as victimization, and what to police seem like minor problems (kids hanging out on corners, drunks in the street, and graffiti) may trigger as much fear as serious crime does.[28]

> **community-oriented policing (COP)** a police strategy primarily concerned with establishing a working relationship with the community

LO6 Community Policing Strategies

a key to community policing is that police cannot do it alone, but they can help communities help themselves. Many programs or strategies qualify as part of community policing and involve contributions from the public or education of the public

TABLE 6.1 Externally Focused COP Programs

EXTERNALLY FOCUSED CHANGE—REORIENTATION OF POLICE OPERATIONS AND CRIME PREVENTION

1. Department sponsorship of community newsletter
2. Additional officers on foot, bicycle, or horse patrol
3. Use of storefronts for crime prevention
4. Use of a task unit for solving special problems in a targeted area
5. Victim contact program
6. Crime prevention education of the general public
7. Fixed assignment of officers to neighborhoods or schools for extended periods
8. Permanent reassignment of some sworn personnel from traditional patrol to crime prevention
9. Use of citizen survey to keep informed about local problems
10. Neighborhood watch
11. Business watch
12. Increased hiring of civilians for non–law enforcement tasks
13. Community service officers (uniformed civilians who perform support and community liaisons)
14. Unpaid civilian volunteers who perform support and community liaison activities

Source: Jihong Zhao, Nicholas P. Lovrich, and T. H. Robinson, "Community Policing: Is It Changing the Basic Functions of Policing? Findings from a Longitudinal Study of 200+ Municipal Police Agencies," *Journal of Criminal Justice*, 29(5)(2001):365–377.

TABLE 6.2 Internally Focused COP Programs

INTERNALLY OR MANAGERIALLY FOCUSED CHANGE

1. Reassessment of rank and assignments
2. Reassignment of some management positions from sworn to civilian personnel
3. Addition of the position "Master Police Officer" to increase rewards for line officers
4. Formation of quality circles (problem-solving among small groups of line personnel)

Source: Jihong Zhao, Nicholas P. Lovrich, and T. H. Robinson, "Community Policing: Is It Changing the Basic Functions of Policing? Findings from a Longitudinal Study of 200+ Municipal Police Agencies," *Journal of Criminal Justice*, 29(5)(2001):365–377.

regarding crime and crime prevention. Tables 6.1 and 6.2, taken from a survey of more than 200 police departments in cities with populations over 25,000, give you some idea of how broad (and flexible) community policing is.[29]

For example, a community newsletter sponsored by a police department shows the commitment of the police department to the community. Several examples of a community policing newsletter can be viewed on the website of the Oak Park (Illinois) Police Department (http://www.oak-park.us/Police_Department/Resident_Beat_Officer.html). These newsletters contain news about recent meetings and activities in the community in regard to safety and security issues. They include requests for block captains from the community and announcements of block parties. A Crime Watch section indicates the nature of recent crime activity in the area, what the residents should be looking for, and how to deal with such activity.

Many police agencies using community policing strategies have added officers to foot, bicycle, or horse patrol. In the summer of 2008, the Columbus (Ohio) Police Department added more officers to its mounted unit that was nearly disbanded a few years earlier due to budget cuts. The unit was expanded in the belief that mounted patrols would reduce crime in heavy crime areas of the city. The officers and their horses enhance police-community relations by making connections with children and adults. The mounted police are also able to make typical arrests that a vehicle patrol unit makes on city streets. The officers and their horses are trained to deal with aspects of their work that might scare a horse such as the noise of fireworks or smoke from a bomb.[30]

A very common community policing strategy for a neighborhood or community is a neighborhood watch program. Police departments like the San Diego (California) Police Department provide community relations officers and police service officers to any neighborhood interested in starting a neighborhood watch program. These officers will help neighborhood residents create the program. The San Diego Police Department gives residents the following description of a neighborhood watch program and what it will do for them:

Neighborhood Watch is a crime prevention program that enlists the active participation of residents in cooperation with law enforcement to reduce crime, solve problems, and improve the quality of life in your area. In it you will get to know and work with your neighbors, and learn how to:

- *Recognize and report crimes and suspicious activities,*
- *Protect yourself, your family, and your property,*

- *Protect your neighbor's family and property, and*
- *Identify crime and disorder problems in your area, and work with SDPD personnel to solve them.*[31] **"**

TRADITIONAL PATROL		COMMUNITY-ORIENTED PATROL
police ←	decision making →	police and the community
centralized ←	organization →	local
from the chief down to the officers ←	authority →	officers at the beat level
crime control ←	mission →	crime control, fear reduction, order maintenance, and improved neighborhood living conditions
respond to specific incidents ←	strategy →	respond to underlying causes of community problems

NEIGHBORHOOD CRIME WATCH

WE IMMEDIATELY REPORT ALL SUSPICIOUS ACTIVITIES TO OUR POLICE DEPARTMENT

There is a fine line
between appropriate and excessive use of force.

7

Police and the Law

The use of force by police officers is one area of liability pertaining to the legalities of policing. How much force is excessive? In an effort to develop strategies to control individuals without use of lethal force, the Taser, an instrument that delivers an electrical shock to individuals in the effort to subdue, has been criticized as causing more harm that it should. In fact, some claim that Tasers can lead to death in some cases. In this chapter, we will explore how law is used to manage the actions of police officers in every aspect of their jobs.

LO1 Arrests

many police actions call for balancing government power to control crime and individuals' right to be left alone by the government. These actions include making arrests and other seizures of individuals; conducting searches of persons, houses, and people's belongings; and interrogating suspects. Let's begin by examining the police authority to arrest. Later we will discuss searches and interrogations and the circumstances under which police may use force.

REASONABLE ARREST

Not all police actions that affect our right to come and go as we please amount to an arrest. An **arrest** occurs when the police take someone into custody without that person's consent. So, if an officer comes up to you and asks, "Who are you and what are you doing here?" you have not been arrested. But if the officer comes up to you and says, "You're under arrest," takes you to the station, books you, takes your "mug shot," and locks you up overnight, you *have* been arrested. In the first example, you are free to decline to answer—and even to walk away. (You may feel the pressure of a moral and civic duty to stay and answer, but you are not *legally* bound to do so.) In the second example, by arresting you, the police officer has made a seizure, so under the Fourth Amendment to the U.S. Constitution it has to be reasonable (see Table 7.1). What is a reasonable arrest? The answer boils down to three elements:

arrest taking an individual into custody without his or her consent

Learning Outcomes

LO1 Understand what an arrest is and when an arrest is reasonable

LO2 Explain when searches can be made without a warrant

LO3 Understand the exclusionary rule and the situations in which it applies

LO4 Explain the *Miranda v. Arizona* decision and how the *Miranda* warnings are used

LO5 Describe how the USA Patriot Act of 2001 changed the guidelines for electronic surveillance of suspected terrorists

LO6 Understand the objective standard of reasonable force

LO7 Explain what constitutes excessive force and describe deadly and nondeadly force

LO8 Explain police corruption

1. *Probable cause.* Officers must have an objective basis for an arrest.

2. *Reasonable force.* Officers cannot use excessive force to make an arrest.

3. *Warrant.* Officers have to get a warrant before they enter a house to arrest someone.

Thus, the Fourth Amendment ban on unreasonable seizures protects you, meaning the officer has to back up her actions with probable cause *and* use only reasonable force in taking you into custody.[1]

Whether an arrest is reasonable comes down to the objective basis for the arrest (probable cause) and the manner of the arrest (the use of an arrest warrant and/or reasonable force). Let's look at the elements of probable cause and the warrant requirement (we will discuss the use of force later in the chapter).

TABLE 7.1 The Bill of Rights and Police Powers

AMENDMENT	RIGHTS PROTECTED
Fourth Amendment	The right of the people to be secure in their persons, houses, papers, and effects against unreasonable searches and seizures shall not be violated, and no warrants shall issue but upon probable cause, supported by oath or affirmation, and particularly describing the place to be searched and the persons or things to be seized.
Fifth Amendment	No person . . . shall be compelled in any criminal case to be a witness against himself, nor be deprived of life, liberty, or property, without due process of law. . . .
Sixth Amendment	In all criminal prosecutions, the accused shall enjoy the right . . .to be confronted with the witnesses against him . . . and to have the assistance of counsel for his defense.
Fourteenth Amendment	No state shall make or enforce any law which shall abridge the privileges or immunities of citizens of the United States; nor shall any state deprive any person of life, liberty, or property, without due process of law; nor deny to any person within its jurisdiction the equal protection of the laws.

Probable Cause

The Fourth Amendment says that arrests are unreasonable unless officers back them up with probable cause. **Probable cause to arrest** means there are enough facts for a reasonable officer in light of her expertise to believe the person she is arresting has committed, is committing, or is about to commit a crime.[2] What kinds of facts are needed to make the cause for the arrest "probable"? Officers definitely must have more than a hunch, but they do not have to have proof beyond a reasonable doubt. Practically speaking, officers have to have enough facts to justify detaining a suspect long enough to give prosecutors time to decide if there is enough evidence to charge the person with a crime.

Notorious for his struggles with substance abuse and resulting legal troubles, Robert Downey Jr. was last arrested in April of 2001 on suspicion of being under the influence of drugs. Downey was sent into drug rehabilitation and served three years of probation. Using this time to overcome his addiction, Downey has since reclaimed his status as one of Hollywood's leading actors.

© AP Images/Nick Ut

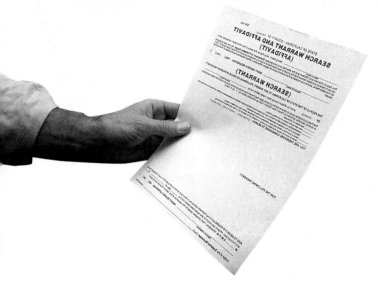

© Tony Freeman/PhotoEdit

Arrest Warrants

The vast majority of arrests are reasonable without warrants.[3] There is one big exception, however: police cannot enter a home to arrest a suspect without a warrant. According to the U.S. Supreme Court, entering homes is the "chief evil" the Fourth Amendment protects against, and "a principal protection against unnecessary intrusions into private dwellings is the warrant requirement imposed by the Fourth Amendment on agents of the government who seek to enter the home for purposes of search or arrest."[4]

LO2 Searches without Warrants

Wherever people have a reasonable expectation of privacy, government intrusions are searches and thus are restricted by the Fourth Amendment. Remember, though, that the Fourth Amendment bans only *unreasonable* searches. What constitutes a reasonable expectation of privacy is left to the courts to decide on a case-by-case basis. In *Katz v. U.S.*, FBI agents bugged a public telephone booth to listen to bookie Charles Katz giving odds on college football games in his gambling operation.[5] According to the U.S. Supreme Court, "One who occupies a public telephone booth, shuts the door, and pays the toll that permits him to place a call is entitled to assume that his conversation is not being intercepted."

Although this may sound to you like strong support for privacy rights, the U.S. Supreme Court quickly indicated in a series of cases that the reasonable expectation of privacy is very narrow. According to the Court, none of the following actions is a search, so the decision to undertake them is left to the discretion of individual law enforcement officers:

- Looking for evidence in plain view
- Obtaining bank records, including savings and checking accounts and loans[6]
- Getting a list of all numbers dialed from or to a specific telephone[7]
- Looking through trash for criminal evidence[8]
- Wiring a paid informant for sound so that law enforcement officers can listen to conversations[9]

According to the plain-view doctrine, it is not a search if officers' discovery of evidence meets three conditions:

1. Officers discover the evidence by means of their ordinary senses—sight, smell, hearing, and touch.
2. Officers have a right to be where they are and are doing what they have a right to do.
3. Officers discover the evidence inadvertently.

Applying these conditions, the U.S. Supreme Court decided that a plain-view discovery had occurred when officers stopped a car for running a red light and saw a plastic bag of marijuana on the front seat.[10] But it was not a plain-view discovery when officers used a

In April of 2008, a swarm of Texas police officers and SWAT teams infiltrated the Yearning for Zion Ranch, a secluded compound owned and operated by the Fundamentalist Church of Jesus Christ of Latter Day Saints. After they received several hoax phone calls alleging child abuse at the ranch located on the outskirts of Eldorado, Texas, law enforcement professionals moved swiftly to organize the raid, which resulted in the removal of many women and nearly every child from the ranch into state custody. In May of 2008, the Third Court of Appeals in Austin, Texas ruled that the state had knowingly obtained search warrants on the basis of false information, and in June, the dislodged women and children were allowed to return to the compound.

© AP Images/Tony Gutierrez

high-powered telescope to see into the apartment of a suspect hundreds of feet away or when they turned a TV set upside down to get its serial number so that they could check to see if the TV was stolen. According to the Court, the first case involved a plain-view discovery because the officers discovered the marijuana by their ordinary sense of sight while they were doing what they had a right to do in a place they had a right to be. In the second case, officers relied on a technological enhancement of their sense of sight to look into the apartment; therefore, their action was not a plain-view discovery. In the third case, the discovery was not accidental: the officers had to upend the TV to get the serial number.

REASONABLE SEARCHES

As with reasonable arrests, the U.S. Supreme Court has filled many pages with decisions explaining what is a *reasonable* search. But for us, the answer boils down to this. In the everyday work of police officers, a search is reasonable if the officers:

1. Have probable cause
2. Get a warrant backed up with probable cause before they search a house
3. Conduct the search at the time they arrest a suspect
4. Get consent to search if they do not have probable cause

The vast majority of searches are conducted at the time of arrest or with consent, meaning that most searches are made without warrants.

Probable cause to search is similar to probable cause to arrest, except that the facts and circumstances have to support a reasonable belief that the officers will find evidence of crime, weapons, or contraband on the person or places they search. Of course, a reasonable belief does not mean that the officers will find any of

> The Constitution does not require that officers' beliefs turn out to be *right*; it only requires that their beliefs be *reasonable*.

these items. The Constitution does not require that officers' beliefs turn out to be *right*; it only requires that their beliefs be *reasonable*.[11]

LO3 The Exclusionary Rule

the exclusionary rule throws out "good" evidence because of "bad" police behavior. It prevents the government from using confessions obtained in violation of the right against self-incrimination, evidence gathered by unreasonable searches and seizures, evidence obtained in violation of the right to counsel, and eyewitness identifications acquired by unreliable procedures.[12]

The justification for the exclusionary rule is to deter unconstitutional police behavior. Before *Mapp v. Ohio* (1961), which applied the exclusionary rule to state and local law enforcement, police officers rarely obtained warrants.[13] By 1987, the narcotics division of the Chicago Police Department ordered that "virtually all preplanned searches that are not 'buy busts' or airport-related searches occur with warrants." The exclusionary rule also "punishes" officers. Getting evidence thrown out can negatively affect both assignments and promotions. Some officers lie in court so that their illegally seized evidence will not be thrown out. Admittedly, this limits the effectiveness of the exclusionary rule, but strong responses by both the police department and the courts have reduced the instances of police perjury.

The U.S. Supreme Court has established several exceptions to the exclusionary rule.[14] Under the good faith exception, evidence can be used when it was obtained under what appeared to be an acceptable warrant, but the warrant is later found to be invalid for reasons that the police could not have determined at the time. The inevitability of discovery exception arises when evidence is obtained illegally, but a legal search was already under way that would inevitably have found the evidence anyway. The public safety exception permits the police to seize evidence illegally during a threat to public safety because the threat outweighs the need to maintain constitutional safeguards. The last exception, the independent source exception, allows evidence seized illegally to be used if it is seized a second time with a proper warrant.

LO4 The *Miranda* Warnings

in addition to arrests and searches, another police action that raises constitutional questions is the interrogation of suspects. According to the Fifth Amendment, "No person shall be compelled in any criminal case to be a witness against himself." Police interrogation has long been controversial. Supporters believe that a safe society depends on questioning suspects. Critics argue that a free society does not convict people with evidence out of their own mouths. Supporters of interrogation reply that it does not just convict the guilty, it frees the innocent, too. Critics argue that police use unethical tactics like lying, deceit, and tricks to get confessions; officers reply that interrogating criminal suspects is not (and should not be treated like) a conversation between friends and that pressure is not the same as force.

In one of its most famous cases, *Miranda v. Arizona*, the U.S. Supreme Court held that the Fifth Amendment requires police to give suspects in custody four warnings before interrogating them:

1 You have a right to remain silent.

2 Anything you say will be used against you.

3 You have a right to a lawyer.

4 If you cannot afford a lawyer, one will be provided for you.[15]

Many people do not understand what the *Miranda* decision means to them during a police contact. In pre-arrest questioning, the police do not have to give the *Miranda* warnings because the person has not been arrested.[16] The warnings typically will not be given until the person starts to incriminate himself. The officer will give the warnings at that point so that the incriminating statements can be used later at trial. In post-arrest questioning, the person must receive the *Miranda* warnings. Once the person has been Mirandized and waives the right, the person may choose to re-invoke the right at any point and stop the questioning.[17]

Even when suspects have been taken into custody, the **public safety exception** allows officers to interrogate them without giving the *Miranda* warnings if giving the warning would endanger the officers or other people nearby. Note, too, that even coerced confessions are admissible unless police coercion caused the suspects to incriminate themselves. Most suspects waive their right to remain silent and agree to be interrogated.

Ernesto Miranda

public safety exception
Miranda warnings are not required if giving them could endanger officers or others nearby; also an exception to the exclusionary rule that allows police to seize evidence illegally if it poses a threat to public safety

LO5 The USA Patriot Act of 2001

the restrictions on arrest and search and seizure were lessened substantially with the USA Patriot Act of 2001. The Act was a result of the September 11, 2001 terrorist attacks on the United States. It expanded the powers of law enforcement by allowing less restrictive use of wiretaps and search warrants to help combat terrorism and cybercrime. Though criticized heavily by civil libertarians, the Act allows nationwide roving wiretaps. No longer are law enforcement officers limited to specific phones or computers. One wiretap order covers any phone or computer without the officers having to prove in court that access has direct relevance to the investigation.

The Act also applies to Internet use. Just by telling a single judge that the information might be relevant to an ongoing investigation, the government can have access to an individual's use of the Internet, whether or not the person is an investigation target. The Act also permits the expanded use of the Foreign Intelligence Surveillance Act (FISA) for domestic surveillance when the probable cause standard cannot be met. Information obtained through the surveillance can then be shared with the FBI.[18]

Many critics argue that the Patriot Act violates constitutional rights. The American Civil Liberties Union (ACLU), for example, contends that it violates the right to confidentiality in inmate-attorney communications because the government now is permitted to monitor these communications if there is reasonable suspicion that the communications involve terrorism.[19] (**Reasonable suspicion** means that the facts and circumstances are such that law enforcement officers, in light of their training and experience, would suspect that a crime might be afoot.) According to the Electronic Privacy Information Center (EPIC):

> *The USA PATRIOT Act, or USAPA introduced a plethora of legislative changes which significantly increased the surveillance and investigative powers of law enforcement agencies in the United States. The Act did not, however, provide for the system of checks and balances that traditionally safeguards civil liberties in the face of such legislation.*
>
> *Legislative proposals in response to the terrorist attacks of September 11, 2001 were introduced less than a week after the attacks. President Bush signed the final bill, the USA PATRIOT Act, into law on October 26, 2001. Though the Act made significant amendments to over 15 important statutes, it was introduced with great haste and passed with little debate, and without a House, Senate, or conference report. As a result, it lacks background legislative history that often retrospectively provides necessary statutory interpretation.*
>
> *However, the USA PATRIOT Act retains provisions appreciably expanding government investigative authority, especially with respect to the Internet. Those provisions address issues that are complex and implicate fundamental constitutional protections of individual liberty, including the appropriate procedures for interception of information transmitted over the Internet and other rapidly evolving technologies.[20]*

In order to quell charges that it infringed too heavily on the privacy of law-abiding citizens, many of the Patriot Act's provisions were written with sunset clauses, which established dates by which the provisions had to be renewed. If they were not renewed, they would be expunged from the Act. In March of 2006 however, President George W. Bush signed into law a bill that made many of these sunsetting provisions permanent. In late 2007, federal judges in New York and Oregon attempted to counter these measures, voiding certain provisions of the Patriot Act that they ruled to be unconstitutional.

LO6 Police Use of Reasonable Force

the defining characteristic of police is the legitimate use of force. Police use legitimate force to gain control of resisting or fleeing suspects and to protect themselves or others from injury and death. Clearly, force is required for police work to bring people under con-

THE USA PATRIOT ACT . . .

- Resulted from the terrorist attacks of September 11, 2001.
- Expanded the powers of law enforcement.
- Allowed more leniency in wiretapping and search warrants.
- Made the tracking of Internet use easier.
- Permitted surveillance without probable cause.
- May violate constitutional rights.

© Bulent İnce/iStockphoto.com / © iStockphoto.com

trol when necessary, but how much force is too much? Throughout most of U.S. history, states followed the ancient common-law rule that allowed officers to use deadly force when it was necessary to apprehend fleeing felons. By the 1960s, many police departments had adopted rules that restricted the common-law rule. The gist of these rules is that officers can use deadly force only when (1) it is necessary to apprehend "dangerous" suspects and (2) it does not put innocent people in danger. In *Tennessee v. Garner,* the U.S. Supreme Court "constitutionalized" these rules into an **objective standard of reasonable force.**[21] According to this standard, the Fourth Amendment permits officers to use the amount of force necessary to apprehend suspects and bring them under control. The standard is objective because it does not depend on an officer's intent or motives. So, if an officer uses a reasonable amount of force, the fact that he used that force out of malice or prejudice does not make it unreasonable. By the same token, no amount of good intentions and noble motives will make the use of excessive force reasonable. In the next section, we will look more closely at excessive force—a measure of police violence and brutality.

LO7 Excessive, Deadly, and Nondeadly Force

xcessive force means that officers use more than the amount of force necessary to get control of suspects and protect themselves and others.[22] Before we examine excessive force in more detail, you need some facts to help you keep the discussion in balance. First, police rarely use any force at all in making Fourth Amendment seizures. Why not? They do not have to because suspects usually submit to police authority without resistance (see Figure 7.1). And when police do use force, they do not often cause serious injury. According to a national sample of individuals aged 16 and over who were subjected to police use of force, 12 percent said they suffered broken bones or had teeth knocked out; 13 percent said they received cuts and bruises; and over 63 percent said they either received no medical care or treated themselves.[23]

Police use of excessive force (or the perception of excessive force) has sparked some of the worst riots in American history—Harlem in 1935, Watts in 1965, Miami in 1980, and Los Angeles in 1992. The police use of force against motorist Rodney King in 1991 and the riots following the acquittal in 1992 of the officers who used that force set off a huge public debate about police use of force (legitimate or not). For once, Americans actually saw the police use force instead of just hearing descriptions of it (by chance, a young guy trying out his new camcorder recorded a group of LAPD officers using clubs, boots, and other means to keep King down). Seeing the tape night after night on TV etched the picture in viewers' minds.

The beating of King, the acquittal of the officers, and the death and destruction caused during the riots highlighted three points about police use of force:

1. The legitimate use of coercive force—the defining characteristic of police work—is critical to effective police work.

2. The need for *legitimate* force is also the source of the *excessive* use of force.

3. The *perception* that police use excessive force routinely is held by many members of racial minority groups.[24]

Since the Rodney King incident, police have been accused of excessive use of force against racial minorities on numerous occasions. In 2006, for example, UCLA students marched in protest against university police. The students insisted that the police were guilty of excessive force because they had used a Taser five times against Mostafa Tabatabainejad, a fourth-year Middle Eastern and North African studies and philosophy student. Police claimed the student would not leave a building in a timely manner. The incident and the resulting protest brought significant international attention to the issue and the institution.[25]

> **objective standard of reasonable force** Fourth Amendment permits officers to use the amount of force necessary to apprehend suspects and bring them under control

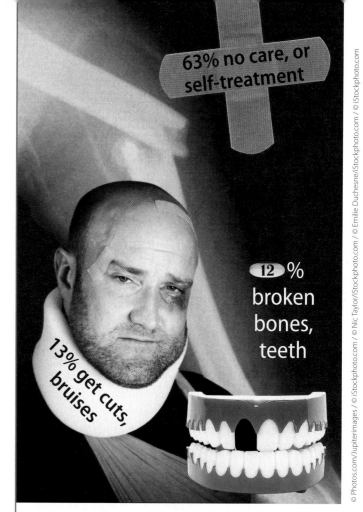

63% no care, or self-treatment

12% broken bones, teeth

13% get cuts, bruises

less-than-lethal force
force that is enough to "cause the suspect to fall to the ground" but is not deadly

Such examples of excessive force have shown us what we *know* (and *do not* know) about the kinds and amounts of force police use in their day-to-day operations, about department use-of-force policies, and about the effectiveness of these policies and practices. In this section, we will look at the types of force police use and will consider when that force may become excessive.

THE TYPES OF FORCE

Let's look at three kinds of force that police use: less-than lethal force, hot pursuits, and deadly force.

Less-than-Lethal Force

Less-than-lethal force is enough force to "cause the suspect to fall to the ground." This type of force can be accomplished with physical force, the traditional nightstick and gun threat, tear gas, mace, pepper spray, Tasers, and other new technologies such as nets and foam. Many of these less-than-lethal modalities have been adopted to some degree by most law enforcement agencies, but not without problems. Many of these modalities, including the Taser, have been used without proper testing of their safety, efficiency, and effectiveness.[26]

The use of the Taser by law enforcement continues to receive harsh criticism as being excessive, especially when it causes harm to the victim. Law enforcement contends that the Taser brings people under control without a physical confrontation that potentially might cause harm to both the civilian and the officer, but victims and victim advocates claim that the electric charge is extremely painful, if not deadly. As an example of the benefits claimed for the Taser, the Burlington (Vermont) Police Department says the Taser has resulted in less lost time due to officers harmed from physical confron-

tations. The year before the Taser was adopted, the agency spent $150,000 in lost time for officers hurt while subduing suspects. The year following the adoption of the Taser, no hours were lost due to officer injuries related to subduing suspects. On the other side of

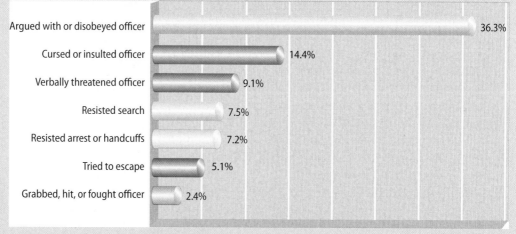

FIGURE 7.1

Actions Taken by Individuals 16 and Over during Officers' Use of Force

Action	Percent
Argued with or disobeyed officer	36.3%
Cursed or insulted officer	14.4%
Verbally threatened officer	9.1%
Resisted search	7.5%
Resisted arrest or handcuffs	7.2%
Tried to escape	5.1%
Grabbed, hit, or fought officer	2.4%

Source: Bureau of Justice Statistics, *Contacts between Police and the Public* (Washington, DC: Bureau of Justice Statistics, February 2001), p. 28, Table 28.

In September of 2008, New York City Police Lieutenant and 21-year veteran of the force Michael Pigott responded to an emergency call about a naked man behaving erratically in his apartment. Officers chased the man, Iman Morales, through his apartment building and out onto a ledge. After a short standoff, Pigott ordered a police sergeant to Taser Morales, despite that doing so violated department protocol. When he was Tasered, Morales fell 10 feet to the sidewalk below the ledge and died instantly from severe head trauma. Eight days after the incident, Pigott was discovered dead with a self-inflicted bullet wound to the head.

the debate, Amnesty International USA points to 250 deaths associated with the use of the Taser from 2001 to 2006. Victim advocates, such as those who work with the mentally ill, claim that the Taser is not a proper tool to use with mentally ill offenders or with those with physical conditions that can be aggravated by the use of the Taser, resulting in significant injury or death.[27]

Hot Pursuits

A police pursuit with a vehicle occurs when a police officer initiates a traffic stop or house check and the target of the stop or check flees in a vehicle and the police give chase. This is a controversial use of force because innocent bystanders can be hurt or killed in the pursuit and also because evidence indicates that excessive force may

be more likely to occur at the end of a chase. In an attempt to reduce chase problems, police agencies have responded with hot pursuit policies that establish a continuum that indicates when a pursuit is appropriate.[28]

Under state law in Pennsylvania, for example, every police agency must now "have a written emergency vehicle-response policy governing procedures under which an officer should initiate, continue or terminate a pursuit." The 2007 Pennsylvania Police Pursuit Report documented a 9 percent decrease in police pursuits as a result of the law and the resulting pursuit policies. The Report contained the following data:

> • *No police or uninvolved persons were killed as the result of pursuits in 2007 or 2006.*
>
> • *652 of the pursuits resulted in crashes, with 218 of those crashes resulting in injuries.*
>
> • *Nearly half of all the pursuits (943) were initiated because of traffic violations, including speeding. The other most common reasons for police to initiate pursuits were stolen or suspected stolen vehicles (296); felony criminal offenses (289), and driving under the influence or suspected DUI (234).*
>
> • *1,387 pursuits resulted in the apprehension of the fleeing motorist.*[29]

Deadly Force

The most extreme use of police authority is deadly force. Police officers are trained in shooting for just this type of

In July of 2008, former Ultimate Fighting Championship light heavyweight champion Quinton "Rampage" Jackson was arrested for reckless driving after he led pursuing officers on a high-speed chase. Driving a Ford F-350 with his picture on the side, Jackson drove on the wrong side of the street and on sidewalks, nearly hitting several pedestrians, striking several vehicles, and causing other property damage. After he was arrested, Jackson announced that he had become severely depressed after losing a title fight to fellow light heavyweight Forrest Griffin, and he was escorted to a mental health institution. Jackson was ordered to perform community service and attend therapy until his sentencing in January of 2010.

© PA Photos/Landov

© Jon Kopaloff/Getty Images

© Stock Connection Distribution/Alamy

force, but statistically, the use of deadly force is a rare occurrence. The debate about the use of firearms by law enforcement tends to focus on when and when not to use this level of extreme force. When the decision to discharge a weapon is made, there are more consequences than just the physical harm to the suspect. Not only is there potential for collateral damage to bystanders and other officers, but there is also potential for political harm to police-community relations if the use of deadly force is questioned.

The legal governing force for use of deadly force is the landmark case of *Tennessee v. Garner*, which allows the use of deadly force only when there is an imminent threat to life.[30] Law enforcement agencies now have strict policies for use of force that comply with the *Garner* requirements, and all incidents of deadly force are evaluated against the standard.[31]

A 2004 review of deadly force by law enforcement, including county, city, and constables, in Houston, Texas, revealed that one in three shootings from 1999 to 2003 involved an unarmed person. Although all of these shooting were ruled justified, the review indicated the potential reasons for these unarmed shootings and how such shootings could be prevented.[32] The report concluded:

Several patterns emerged among the 65 shootings of unarmed people that experts said could be addressed with updated policies, alternative weapons and training:

MOONLIGHTING: *Twelve people, including teenagers cruising a parking lot and a man pilfering shingles from a construction site, were shot by off-duty officers working security jobs for extra pay. Some of these officers had been assigned to desk duty for years.*

BUY BUSTS: *At least eight people were shot by narcotics officers. Raids or other planned operations led to the wounding of three bystanders and the death of another. Two people were shot in the back. In some cases, citizens claimed*

that undercover officers did not adequately identify themselves before firing.

MENTALLY ILL: *At least 10 mentally ill people shot were unarmed or carrying objects such as screwdrivers and pieces of wood. In all cases, responding officers either lacked stun guns or did not try to use them.*

INSIDE VEHICLES: *At least 36 were shot while in cars or trucks. Most were shot by sheriff's deputies, some of whom put themselves in harm's way and then fired in self-defense.*

LO8 Police Corruption

olice corruption is a form of occupational crime: it involves misusing police authority for private gain. Corruption can be limited to one or two officers or be spread throughout a whole department. And it can range from something as minor as a patrol officer accepting a free cup of coffee from a neighborhood restaurant to things as serious as a top official extorting thousands of dollars a month from vice operations or an officer targeting only Hispanics for arrest.[33] There are several explanations as to why police corruption occurs. One is the rotten apple theory, which says that there are a few bad officers that recruitment and training cannot identify. Another is that some officers start out as idealists but become "bad" because of the socialization processes of training and field experiences.

Whatever the causes, the misuse of police authority is the key to understanding police corruption and unethical actions by law enforcement officers. The defining characteristic of the policing profession is the potential use of coercion. Police officers can misuse their authority coercively to accomplish their own personal goals.[34] Let's look first at how officers may come to misuse their authority and then at the types of police corruption. We will conclude by discussing some possible remedies for police corruption.

HOW POLICE CORRUPTION CAN OCCUR

The effort to control the misuse of authority begins with the hiring of police officers. The goal of hiring is to find personnel who can manage authority in a professional manner, according to law. How does the hiring process determine these qualities? While perfect accuracy is not possible and some wrong hires will be made, the process should produce recruits with strong value systems. Those who choose to become police officers choose to do so for multiple reasons. Some recruits want the power and authority of the job and can potentially misuse this authority. Other recruits choose policing for the social service aspect of the job and are more likely to manage the authority appropriately. Written testing, oral interviews, and scenario responses can all help in selecting the right recruits. But hiring is only the first step. Even when the best personnel are hired, some good officers may become unethical in their actions after they are hired. How does that happen?

The demands of police work and the culture of law enforcement can be shocking to some police rookies. Their perception of police work may be far from the reality, and as they learn the true nature of the job, rookies may undergo a variety of psychological transformations. Formally, police agencies value hierarchy, procedure, and cohesion. New recruits quickly learn however that the informal realities of the job are quite different from the formal instruction they received in the police academy. Rookies are often guided into the informal police culture by experienced officers who are willing to share real-life stories and useful tips. Though they are usually granted some time to observe and adjust, recruits eventually enter a phase called the Encounter, in which they must respond appropriately to the expectations of colleagues and citizens. It is in this phase that recruits truly begin to realize the nature of policing. The gun and the badge, thought by new recruits to be symbols of authority and respect, will mean something very different to civilians and criminals, who may challenge the recruits' authority and show little respect for law enforcement. The recruits' colleagues may expect them to adopt certain informal practices that may challenge their value systems, from accepting free food to more serious offenses, such as overlooking the corrupt behavior of fellow police officers.

After going through this period and coming to terms with the realities of the job, the recruits will enter a new phase, the Metamorphosis, in which they will have to choose whether to compromise their beliefs to conform to the realities or to maintain their value systems in the face of a complex profession. The options in the Metamorphosis include "going with the flow" and transforming psychologically and socially to the norms

of the agency. Another option is to maintain a strong value system and to either ignore the norms or try to change the system. Trying to change an informal system in a police agency can be difficult. A whistleblower in a police agency will likely encounter significant resistance. Connecticut state troopers, for example, testified to their state legislature in early 2008 regarding the culture of their organization in response to whistleblowing:

> . . . there is a discouraging culture of reprisal and intimidation threatening the morale and integrity of the 1,200-member Division of State Police. Legislators, including Rep. Christopher L. Caruso, D-Bridgeport, co-chairman of the legislative Government Administration & Elections Committee, said they were shocked by revelations of retribution from command staff inflicted on troopers who had pending complaints requiring whistleblower protections. . . . Trooper Steven Rief, president of the State Police Union and Sgt. Andrew Matthews joined other troopers, past and present, complaining to the committee that whistleblowers are routinely transferred and intimidated. . . . the climate is self-perpetuating because the management hierarchy is made up of veterans "with old ways of thinking" who don't change. . . . "If we're willing to die for perfect strangers, who's protecting our rights?" Matthews said. "If I have to lay my life on the line, I'll do that. Our badge was tarnished already, but I'm trying to bring a shine to it. . . . I have been isolated in my cruiser for the last year," Matthews said, adding that relying on the state Attorney General's office for protection hasn't helped. . . . "It seems that our whole system to protect the integrity of the State Police has failed," said Rep. James A. O'Rourke III, D-Cromwell. . . . "There definitely needs to be stronger safeguards for these courageous men and women who stepped forward and exposed wrongdoing or incompetence," [Attorney General Richard] Blumenthal said in an interview.[35]

As a last resort, officers may decide to look for a job in another police agency with fewer internal problems or to get out of the profession altogether, which unfortunately

results in fewer honest police officers patrolling our communities.[36]

Understanding the contingencies of a law enforcement agency also help us understand how a good officer can become corrupt or unethical. Contingencies are the balance of good and bad norms in an agency. If there is a high degree of rule violations, unethical behavior, poor leadership, bad morale, and other issues, then personnel are more likely to change over time. Not all agencies have an imbalance of contingencies, and all personnel in an agency do not face the same pressures. Those officers who do face negative contingencies will face moral experiences where they will be confronted with the options of doing the job right or making unethical choices. Their colleagues may expect the officers to make the unethical choices because they do it as well. Some officers will offer justifications, saying that it is all right to do these things because pay is bad or because people do not understand. Under such pressure, the officer will begin to justify his own behavior. He will not see it as wrong; he will see it as justified behavior under the circumstances. Finally, the officer will start down a slippery slope, beginning with minor actions that would probably merit only a reprimand, then sliding further into more unethical behavior over time. Some officers' consciences will not allow them to live with themselves if they commit even minor infractions, so they stop, but others do not listen to that "inner voice" and proceed onward until they get caught, often causing severe legal and reputation problems for themselves, their agency and their community.[37]

TYPES OF POLICE CORRUPTION

From a legal perspective, police corruption definitely involves the violation of law by police officers. In the worst case, a police officer willfully deprives a person of her legal rights. Examples of such actions include the excessive use of force; unlawful stops, arrests, or searches; sexual assault; deliberate fabrication of evidence; and any other act that results in the loss of liberty or rights to another.[38]

Discrimination by a police officer against a person based on sex, gender, race, color, national origin, religion, sexual orientation or disability is also considered a form of corruption. **Racial profiling**, in which law enforcement decisions are made on the basis of race or ethnicity, is an example of discriminatory law enforcement behavior.[39] Less than half of the states now have laws prohibiting police officers from engaging in racial

profiling. Racial profiling leads to disproportionate rates of stopping, detaining, and/or searching minority drivers. Minority drivers in several communities have charged that they were the victims of racial profiling, leading to legislative action requiring agencies to report and explain disproportionate numbers in their data.[40]

Corruption also includes actions that enhance the personal gain of the individual officer:

- Accepting bribes from citizens who habitually violate noncriminal statutes or ordinances (e.g., traffic laws)
- Accepting bribes from those who violate the law in order to make money (i.e., prostitutes, drug dealers)
- Accepting money in exchange for police services or protection
- Fraud
- Embezzlement
- Nepotism
- Extortion
- The actual commission of felony crimes[41]

REMEDIES FOR POLICE CORRUPTION

Possible remedies for police corruption include incarceration, heavy fines, restitution, revocation of the badge, and even civil remedies such as public apology. But these are punitive measures. One positive approach to dealing with police corruption and misconduct relies on training and other socialization measures to prevent and to change police behavior. For example, advocates for the positive approach argue that training officers to be unflappable in the face of unpleasant behavior can be very effective. Taking an insult without reacting wins more respect and obedience than responding emotionally.

Listen Up!

CJUS was designed for students just like you—busy people who want choices, flexibility, and multiple learning options.

CJUS delivers concise, focused information in a fresh and contemporary format. And . . . CJUS gives you a variety of online learning materials designed with you in mind.

At **4ltrpress.cengage.com/cjus**, you'll find electronic resources such as **Printable Flash Cards, Interactive Quizzing, Downloads, Games,** and **Video Activities** for each chapter. These resources will help supplement your understanding of core criminal justice concepts in a format that fits your busy lifestyle.

Visit **4ltrpress.cengage.com/cjus** to learn more about the multiple CJUS resources available to help you succeed!

The American court system

strives to be as efficient and effective as possible.

8

Courts and Courtroom Work Groups

The 1962 film adaptation of To Kill a Mockingbird stars Gregory Peck as Atticus Finch (left) and Brock Peters as defendant Tom Robinson.

In the classic book, *To Kill a Mockingbird*, the story of Southern justice in the early part of the twentieth century is portrayed in a fictional account of defending the accused during a period of racial tensions and the culture of the south. In this story, racial prejudice outweighs the truth. Atticus Finch, the defense attorney, proves that the black defendant did not commit the crime of rape. Regardless, the defendant is convicted, revealing that justice is not a simple process. Thus, if finding the truth is not simple, how is it accomplished? Understanding the court system and the organizational behavior of the courtroom work group will help us understand how the fictional court in *To Kill a Mockingbird* functioned, as well as how real courts function today.[1]

After arrests, decision making moves from police departments to courts. The formal and informal stories of courts and how they operate are very different. In the *formal* story, aggressive prosecutors fight for the "people," vigorous defense lawyers fight for their clients, and neutral judges act as umpires to make sure their work group accomplishes its mission to find the truth by due process of law. Judges let both sides fight *hard* but make sure they fight *fair*. Juries convict the guilty and free the innocent. In the *informal* version of the story, the courtrooms are almost always dark and empty; they are lit up and occupied only for the rare trial and to ratify decisions already made in judges' chambers, in halls, and even in closets and restrooms.[2]

In this chapter, we will look at the criminal court structure, criminal court missions, and courtroom work group roles.

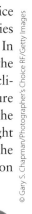

Learning Outcomes

LO1 Describe the structure of the various U.S. court systems

LO2 Explain the difference between trial courts and appellate courts

LO3 Describe how a case gets to the U.S. Supreme Court

LO4 Understand the courtroom work group and its organizational mission

LO5 Discuss the selection and qualifications of judges

LO6 Identify the role played by prosecutors in the courtroom work group and understand how prosecution offices are organized and managed

LO7 Identify the role played by defense counsel in the courtroom work group

LO1 The Structure of the Court System

i n our federal system, there are national and state courts separated into three tiers (see Figure 8.1 on the facing page):

1 *Lower courts (trial courts of limited jurisdiction).* They have the power to decide the facts and apply the law in misdemeanor cases and conduct pretrial proceedings in felony cases.

2 *Felony courts (trial courts of general jurisdiction).* They have the power to decide the facts and apply the law in felony cases.

3 *Appellate courts (appeals courts).* They have the power to review trial courts' application of the law to the facts.

LOWER COURTS

Lower courts (called by many different names, such as misdemeanor, superior, municipal, county, justice of the peace, and magistrate's courts) only have the power (jurisdiction) to decide misdemeanors and conduct preliminary proceedings in felony cases. That is why they are called courts of **limited jurisdiction**. Jurisdiction is defined as the types of cases, the court procedures, and the geographic region the court has authority over. Formally, defendants in lower criminal courts have the same rights as defendants in felony courts. In practice, most cases are tried less formally than in felony courts, and they are tried without juries. Lower criminal courts are not courts of record—they do not keep written records of proceedings.[3]

Lower courts decide minor (but in numbers by far the most) cases, like traffic offenses, drunk and disorderly conduct, shoplifting, and prostitution. This makes them the first and only contact most people ever have with criminal courts.

Besides deciding minor criminal cases (as fast or as slow as due process requires),

limited jurisdiction
when courts only have the power to decide misdemeanors and conduct preliminary proceedings in felony cases

general jurisdiction
courts that can decide all felony cases from capital murder to theft and also review the decisions of lower courts

lower criminal courts conduct four important pretrial proceedings in both misdemeanor and felony cases:

1. They decide whether to release defendants on bail.
2. They assign lawyers to indigent (poor) defendants.
3. They preside over preliminary hearings to test the government's case against defendants.
4. They decide whether confessions, searches, and seizures can be admitted as evidence.

FELONY COURTS

Felony courts (usually called district or circuit courts) are where felony cases are tried. They are courts of **general jurisdiction**, meaning they can decide all felony cases from capital murder to theft and also review the decisions of lower courts. Felony courts are courts of record, and they follow the rules of the adversary process more than proceedings in lower courts do.[4]

GEOGRAPHIC AND HIERARCHICAL JURISDICTION

Geographic jurisdiction is the political boundary of a court's authority. The court's jurisdiction may cover a city, a county, or even a region. When a defendant goes to trial, the trial will be held in a court in the political bounded area in which the crime occurred. If the crime occurred on federal land, such as a federal park or an Indian reservation, then the federal court will have jurisdiction over the crime. If the crime was committed on a military base, the case will be tried by the federal military court with jurisdiction.

Hierarchical jurisdiction centers on the role of the court. Hierarchy refers to the difference between appellate and trial courts. Trial courts are triers of fact. The judge or jury in a trial court listens to facts and determines the guilt or innocence of the defendant. Appellate

FIGURE 8.1

The Structure of the U.S. Judicial System

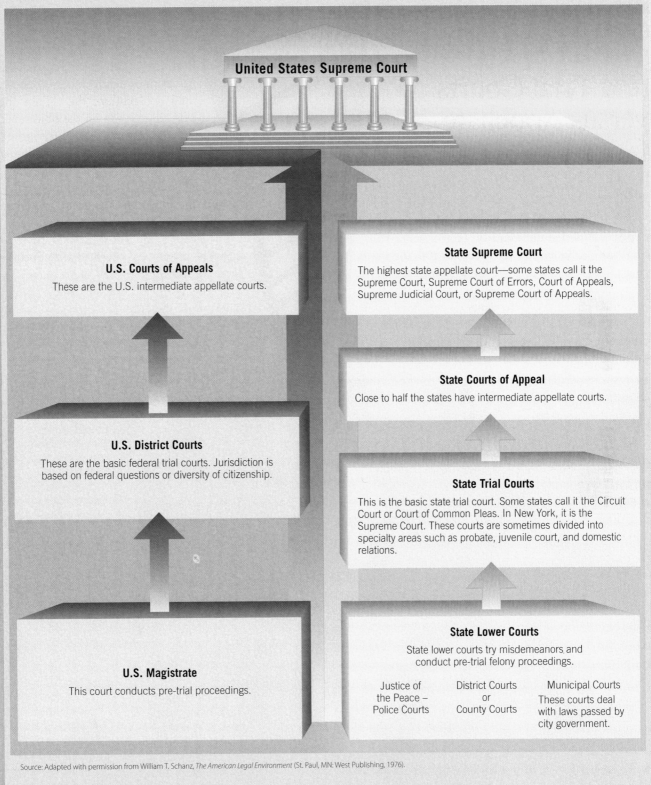

United States Supreme Court

U.S. Courts of Appeals
These are the U.S. intermediate appellate courts.

State Supreme Court
The highest state appellate court—some states call it the Supreme Court, Supreme Court of Errors, Court of Appeals, Supreme Judicial Court, or Supreme Court of Appeals.

U.S. District Courts
These are the basic federal trial courts. Jurisdiction is based on federal questions or diversity of citizenship.

State Courts of Appeal
Close to half the states have intermediate appellate courts.

State Trial Courts
This is the basic state trial court. Some states call it the Circuit Court or Court of Common Pleas. In New York, it is the Supreme Court. These courts are sometimes divided into specialty areas such as probate, juvenile court, and domestic relations.

U.S. Magistrate
This court conducts pre-trial proceedings.

State Lower Courts
State lower courts try misdemeanors and conduct pre-trial felony proceedings.

Justice of the Peace – Police Courts

District Courts or County Courts

Municipal Courts
These courts deal with laws passed by city government.

Source: Adapted with permission from William T. Schanz, *The American Legal Environment* (St. Paul, MN: West Publishing, 1976).

courts listen to matters of law and not facts. Appellate courts determine if the law was applied correctly.[5]

LO2 Trial Courts versus Appellate Courts

t he main distinction between trial (lower criminal and felony) courts and appeals courts is that **appellate courts** do not decide questions of guilt or innocence. They review the proceedings of the trial court to make sure the trial court followed the rules of procedure and did not violate the defendant's constitutional rights. Defendants do not have to (and most do not) appear when appellate courts hear their cases. Proceedings in the appellate court are the most formal of all three levels of courts.[6]

Most states and the federal judiciary have two levels of appellate court—intermediate (usually called *courts of appeals*) and last resort (usually called *supreme courts*). When a case is appealed, the intermediate appellate court reviews the objections made by the defense and prosecution, the rulings the trial court made on the objections, and whether the government proved its case beyond a reasonable doubt. Supreme courts review the most serious cases, such as death penalty cases, the most complicated legal questions, and all constitutional questions.

There is no constitutional right to appeal a trial or intermediate appellate court's decisions, but all states have created a statutory right to review. Many states allow the automatic appeal of death sentences. Overturning the decisions of the lower courts does not automatically close a case. The government can retry defendants.[7]

Oyez! Oyez! Oyez!

FAST FACTS ON THE U.S. SUPREME COURT

- The Supreme Court first assembled on February 1, 1790, in New York City.
- The Supreme Court Bench consists of one Chief Justice and eight Associate Justices, all of whom are nominated by the President of the United States.
- Once confirmed by the Senate, Justices serve for life.
- The Supreme Court building is open to the public from 9:00 a.m. to 4:30 p.m. Monday through Friday.
- In 1960, the Court heard only 2,313 cases. Today its yearly caseload sits at over 10,000.
- Justice William O. Douglas holds the record for longest tenure: he served from 1939 until 1975, a total of 36 years and six months.
- The nine Justices are seated on the Bench by seniority: the Chief Justice sits in the center chair while the least senior Justices sit at the extremities.
- White quill pens are placed on counsel tables each day that the Court sits, as has been done since the earliest sessions of the court.
- In 1967, Thurgood Marshall became the first African-American appointed to the Supreme Court, and in 1981, Sandra Day O'Connor became the first woman appointed.

When the Court is in session, the 10 a.m. entrance of the Justices into the Courtroom is announced by the Marshal. Those present, at the sound of the gavel, arise and remain standing until the robed Justices are seated following the traditional chant:

"The Honorable, the Chief Justice and the Associate Justices of the Supreme Court of the United States. Oyez! Oyez! Oyez!

All persons having business before the Honorable, the

Supreme Court of the United States, are admonished to draw near and give their attention, for the Court is now sitting. God save the United States and this Honorable Court!"

LO3 The U.S. Supreme Court

according to the U.S. Constitution, Article III, Section 1:

> *The judicial Power of the United States, shall be vested in one supreme Court, and in such inferior Courts as the Congress may from time to time ordain and establish. The Judges, both of the supreme and inferior Courts, shall hold their Offices during good Behavior, and shall, at stated Times, receive for their Services a Compensation which shall not be diminished during their Continuance in Office.*

This is all the Constitution has to say about the federal courts, except for a few words guaranteeing a jury in all criminal trials (Article III, Section 2) and defining treason (Article III, Section 3). The Judiciary Act of 1789 created the U.S. Supreme Court, but the Court assumed to itself the source of its greatest power—the power of judicial review (the Court's power to decide whether federal and state laws and court decisions violate the U.S. Constitution).

The U.S. Constitution is the "supreme law of the land;" unfortunately, it does not come with an instruction manual telling us what its provisions mean. Many provisions do not need an instruction manual because they are perfectly clear—for example, the minimum age requirement for the president (35), members of the Senate (30), and members of the House of Representatives (25). But some are not so clear—for example, due process of law, equal protection of the laws, unreasonable searches and seizures, and others you will learn about in the remaining chapters.

LO4 The Courtroom Work Group

We all know courts are supposed to administer justice according to the rule of law. That is their formal mission or their due process mission, but courts also have informal missions. One is crime control—the public expects courts to make sure guilty people are

Instruction Manual

The U.S. Supreme Court's decisions are our instruction manual. But most cases never reach the Supreme Court. You need to be clear about several points regarding cases that reach the Court for decision:

1. There is no constitutional right to have the Court review a case.

2. The Court does not decide whether a person is guilty or not.

3. Almost everything the Court does is secret, except for the lawyers' arguments before the Court, the briefs they file, and the Court's published opinions.

4. Criminal cases come to the Court by way of two petitions. (They are called petitions because there is no right to the Court's review.) The **petition for a writ of habeas corpus** asks the Court to order some official (usually a prison warden or jail supervisor) to come to a trial court and justify a prisoner's imprisonment. The **petition for a writ of certiorari** asks the Court to order a lower court to send up the record of its proceedings for the Supreme Court to review. The Court issues the writ if four justices vote to issue it.[8]

The Court usually agrees to review cases for two reasons:

1. A conflict exists among the U.S. circuit courts (the intermediate federal appellate courts) on the law's position on the issues.

2. An important constitutional question has not been resolved.

The U.S. Supreme Court denies the vast majority of petitions it receives. See the official website of the U.S. Supreme Court for information on rules and cases.[9]

convicted and punished. Another is social justice—the public expects courts to do what is "best" for victims and offenders. A third informal mission stems from the reality that courts are not just legal institutions, they are

petition for a writ of habeas corpus a request of the Court to order some official (usually a prison warden or jail supervisor) to come to a trial court and justify a prisoner's imprisonment

petition for a writ of certiorari a request of the Court to order a lower court to send up the record of its proceedings for the Supreme Court to review

> *The courtroom work group's mission is to keep the organization running smoothly, efficiently, and, above all, harmoniously.*

courtroom work group

the professional group of prosecutors, judges, and defense lawyers

social organizations made up of a professional **courtroom work group**—prosecutors, judges, and defense lawyers.[10] The courtroom work group's mission is to keep the organization running smoothly, efficiently, and, above all, harmoniously. This informal mission, called the court's organizational mission, dominates the everyday operations of our criminal courts. Let's look more closely at the organizational mission.

THE ORGANIZATIONAL MISSION

Courts are not just legal organizations following the rules; they are complex social organizations that place a high premium on accomplishing their mission of smooth, efficient, and harmonious decision making. This mission is difficult to accomplish in adversary proceedings, especially when courts face heavy criminal caseloads, which most of them do. So discretion and negotiation, not adversary proceedings and written rules, are the means to accomplish the organizational mission. But it is not just necessity and convenience that encourage the use of discretion and negotiation; they are more pleasant, too, as you are about to find out as we examine the operations of the courtroom work group.

The general public is largely unaware of the importance of the negotiation process in courts and how often plea bargaining is used. Part of the courtroom work group process involves educating clients about their role in the negotiation process and what it means to them. For example, an educational website for people seeking legal assistance provides the following information to users:

> *A plea bargain is an agreement in which the prosecutor and defendant arrange to settle the criminal case against the defendant. The defendant pleads guilty or no contest to the charges in exchange for some agreement from the prosecutor as to the sentencing. In some cases the prosecutor will agree to charge a lesser crime or dismiss some of the charges against the defendant in exchange for a guilty plea. The vast majority of criminal cases are resolved by plea bargains.[11]*

The courtroom work group—judges, prosecutors, and defense attorneys—carries out the organizational mission of deciding (disposing of) cases, most often through negotiation. The members of the courtroom work group have a lot more in common than the due process mission suggests. Decision making takes place within a close working and personal environment. Judges, prosecutors, and defense attorneys see one another regularly and have similar backgrounds and career ambitions.[12]

To the courtroom work group, defendants are outsiders (even to their own lawyers). Once defendants are charged, judges, prosecutors, and defense lawyers usually agree that defendants are guilty of *something*. So, all that is left for the group to do is agree on a punishment. This is usually not hard to do because:

- There is a large volume of cases, and they all have deadlines.
- Most cases are routine.
- The group definitely prefers friendly negotiation to disputation.
- The pull of other business makes negotiation attractive.

Against the strong pull of these realities, due process and crime control definitely have to compete with the time and effort the group commits to informal decision making. The mission to dispose of cases and the desire to maintain good work group relationships soften formal role conflicts among prosecutors, defense counsel, and judges.[13]

The "justice" negotiated behind the scenes in the courthouse corridors, judges' chambers, or even the restroom is far more typical than the criminal trial that looms so large on TV and movie screens. "Justice by consent" dominates the reality of criminal courts, not the criminal trial. This reality that due process and crime control, as well as social justice, have to fit in with the work group's organizational and personal agenda confuses those who are not part of it, often to the point of exasperation. The deals that prosecutors and defense attorneys make and judges approve are inconsistent (or appear to be) with both due process and crime control.[14]

As parts of an organization, judges, prosecutors, and defense attorneys do not oppose one another in competing for the truth. They are a team, negotiating the best settlement possible with minimal dispute and maximum harmony within the courtroom work group. They have the thankless job of doing what they can to

.5

balance an array of competing, often irreconcilable, demands and values. Such balancing rarely satisfies anyone, because no one gets everything he or she wants—that is what settlement (as opposed to victory) means. In the adversary system, the goal is victory, and there is always a winner—or at least it seems that way from the outside. In negotiation, the goal is settlement, and the result is always at best "only half a loaf." Do not think that negotiation and settlement have to mean injustice. They usually represent the best outcome possible in the real world.[15]

LO5 The Selection of Judges

ven though we pride ourselves on being a "government of laws" and not of individuals, judges play a major policy-making role in American criminal justice. How judges are selected and the qualifications for judicial selection are important to the court process.

States select judges by four methods: popular election, appointment, the merit (Missouri Bar) plan, and a mixture of methods. Missouri created the merit plan idea in 1940 to overcome the widespread use of political patronage in judicial selection. Under the **merit system** (see Figure 8.2), a commission made up of lawyers, citizens, and an incumbent judge draws up a list of nominees. From this list, the governor appoints judges to fill a short initial term. After their term expires, the judges have to be elected. The merit system does not *eliminate* political influence, but it does *minimize* it by eliminating the need for fund-raising, advertising, and making campaign promises.[16]

Supporters of the merit system argue that impartial decision making depends on knowing the law and the ability to judge according to the law. Elections and their dependence on party loyalty stand in the way of impartial decision making. Supporters of the elective

FIGURE 8.2
Model Merit System Plan for Selecting State Judges

PHASE ONE	PHASE TWO	PHASE THREE	PHASE FOUR	PHASE FIVE

Option 1

Judicial appointment system established by statute or by state constitutional amendment

A constitutional amendment or state statute utilizes the force of law to underscore and codify a particular aspect of the process, e.g., removing political parties from all nomination processes

Executive order systems permit successive administrations to design the process or alter levels of influence over the commission without formal approval from the legislature

Option 2

State governor establishes a judicial appointment system by executive order

Nominating Commission

- Comprised of both lawyers and lay persons
- AJS recommends 5 members; in practice, state commissions vary from 5 to 24 members
- Responsible for recruiting, investigating, interviewing, and evaluating candidates for judgeships
- Commission carries out screening duties independent of formal control by governor or legislators
- Commission is subject to anti-discrimination rules
- Commissioners appointed by governor, bar associations, judges, legislators, or existing members. Appointments made on a nonpartisan or bipartisan basis
- Staggering terms of service
- Term limits of service
- Commissioners prohibited from applying for judgeships for specified number of years after leaving commission
- In most states, commissioners prohibited from holding paid public office or any official political party position
- Commission should encompass the diversity of the jurisdiction and the bar

Commission submits a list of nominees to appointing authority

- Appointing authority typically vested in state governor
- Commission produces a list of best-qualified nominees only
- Final list of nominees made public, and public comment invited
- Appointing authority constrained to appoint only from list of nominees recommended by commission
- AJS recommends commissions submit no more than 5 and no less than 2 nominees per vacancy, though in practice maximum and minimum number varies by state law or executive orders
- Deadlines established for appointing authority to act on submitted nominees. Typically, appointing authority must act within 30 days or responsibility passes to Chief Justice or the presiding judge

Candidate appointed to bench by governor

Nominee may be subject to confirmation by state senate, entire state legislature, or an executive council

Retention Mechanism

- Judges retained through an uncontested retention election OR
- Judges reappointed through nominating commission and appointing authority

On retention election ballots, the sole question presented to voters is whether or not Judge X shall be retained in office ("Vote Yes or No")

Reappointment systems may consider other nominees in addition to the sitting judge in order to form a recommendation

Establishing a formal state-sponsored and funded judicial performance review and evaluation provides information to voters in public comments sessions and retention elections

Source: American Judicature Society, *Model Merit Selection Plan in Theory and Practice* (Des Moines, IA: American Judicature Society, 2003). Reprinted with permission.

system promote its democracy, arguing that elected judges are responsive and responsible to the community they serve. Voters will (and should) throw out judges who do not respond to community values.[17]

The characteristics of the judges who are selected depend in part on which judicial selection process is used. Elected judgeships generally go to judicial candidates who emphasize public image, loyalty to a political party, and other characteristics more often associated with politics than with the judiciary. Selection procedures based on appointment allow for careful examination of qualifications but do not exclude political considerations. Although all judicial selection processes are susceptible to some type of human bias, the attempt to select the "best" judge, while taking human bias into account, can focus on the following qualifications:

- ☑ Neutrality
- ☑ Fair-mindedness
- ☑ Above-average knowledge of the law
- ☑ Strong analytical and logic skills and the ability to be lucid
- ☑ Personal integrity
- ☑ Good physical and mental health
- ☑ Judicial temperament
- ☑ Sensible handling of judicial power

Each of these characteristics permits a wide range of interpretation for decision makers selecting judges. Judicial temperament, for example, means different things to different people. Does judicial temperament mean an aggressive and assertive authoritarian judge with strict control over court proceedings or a quiet judge who remains neutral with courtroom actors, listens carefully to all perspectives, and makes decisions through thoughtful interactions with everyone in the court? Both types of judges may be considered "good" judges by different people.[18]

But what makes a "bad" judge? Bad actions and behavior can be classified into three categories:

- ⊗ *Bias*. A judge does not seek the right answer but makes decisions to reward friends or punish enemies.
- ⊗ *Laziness*. A judge who avoids trials and/or does not stay current on the law.
- ⊗ *Incompetence*. A judge who avoids reasoned decisions to avoid exposing judicial incompetence.[19]

In July 2008, former Alaskan Senator Ted Stevens was indicted by a federal grand jury on seven counts of failing to properly disclose the receipt of gifts with an estimated value of $250,000. Though Stevens was convicted on all counts in April 2009, Judge Emmet Sullivan overturned the indictment completely, citing grave misconduct on the part of the prosecution. Further, because they withheld exculpatory evidence, Judge Sullivan initiated a criminal contempt investigation into the six-member prosecutorial team.

Ethics is also a primary area of concern, and a failure in this area can lead to the removal of a judge from office. In 2008, a California judge was removed from the bench for claiming—and then lying about—reimbursements for judicial education courses that she did not take and was not authorized to take. Citing the judge's lack of integrity, a judicial commission found that she was guilty of willful misconduct and removed her from the bench.[20]

LO6 The Role of Prosecutors

prosecutors are a vital link between police and courts and between courts and corrections. Police bring arrests to prosecutors, not to judges. Prosecutors, not judges, decide whether these cases ever get to court. As a result, prosecutors have enormous power. By deciding not to charge, prosecutors can stop a police investigation in its tracks, rendering courts and corrections powerless. Even when they charge, prosecutors direct the course of events inside the work group by the crimes they decide to charge defendants with, the plea arrangements they make with defense attorneys, and the sentences they recommend to judges.[21]

Prosecution in the state system in the United States is local; generally, counties elect prosecutors. The federal system is different. The president appoints federal prosecutors (U.S. attorneys) for all 94 federal districts. Let's look next at the formal and informal missions of prosecutors, and the structure and management of prosecutors' offices.

FORMAL AND INFORMAL MISSIONS

Prosecutors pursue multiple and conflicting missions. Formally, they are the chief law enforcement officers in the criminal courts. Along with administering justice, prosecutors are also office administrators, formulating policy and managing cases and their office staff. They are also careerists. They have their eye on gaining higher public office, entering high-paying prestigious private practice, or maybe just keeping their comfortable work group relations until they retire.

Most of us think of prosecutors as law enforcers. This is not surprising because that is how they are most often portrayed in the news and TV dramas. In the real world, prosecutors' power to choose what crimes and

suspects to prosecute is an essential part of law enforcement. Prosecutors use various standards to measure how successfully they are accomplishing their law enforcement mission. Using their powerful discretion, for example, they may decide that welfare and corporate fraud deserve high priority and measure their success by the number of convictions they win, the ratio of convictions to acquittals, or the types and lengths of sentences offenders get.

In Harrisonburg, Virginia, for example, District Attorney Marsha Garst was elected to a third four-year term in 2008. When taking her oath of office, she promised that her priorities would be unsolved murders, drugs, gangs, and domestic violence. According to a media report:

> *Cracking down on methamphetamine dealers also remains high on Garst's list of goals. Drug addiction, Garst said, also leads to property crimes and domestic violence.*
>
> *"We want to drive dealers out of this county," she said. "It devastates families."*
>
> *On combating domestic violence and gangs, Garst pointed to members on her staff dedicated to those issues.*
>
> *The office has a domestic violence prosecutor and a Project Safe Neighborhoods prosecutor to focus on gangs.*
>
> *Her office, she said, also strives to improve how it deals with the public it serves.*
>
> *"I want to make sure we are still responsive, and we couple very aggressive prosecution with fairness."[22]*

Prosecution offices are organizations, which means that high on their list of priorities are efficiency, economy, and smooth-working relations among staff members and between the staff and other public agencies and the community. As heads of these organizations, prosecutors put a premium on cases and crimes that

Marsha Garst

In January 2009, Donna Hockman stood trial for murder in the shooting death of her boyfriend, Dustin Stanley. During closing arguments, Virginia prosecutor Marsha Garst (left) showed the jury a photo of Stanley and one of his children. The Rockingham County Circuit Court jurors returned a first-degree murder verdict against Hockman and recommended she serve a life sentence.

© AP Images/Pete Marovich

produce the greatest impact for the quickest and most economical processing. Prosecutors as administrators also favor rules that foster routine, regular, and predictable results. So they emphasize the uniformity of cases, rather than the uniqueness of individuals.[23]

STRUCTURE AND MANAGEMENT

The management and structure of a prosecution office vary according to the size of the jurisdiction, geography, resources, and technology. Every jurisdiction has a chief prosecutor, usually elected to a four-year term. In small jurisdictions, prosecutors work alone or with a few assistants who know one another personally and work together closely. These prosecutors usually have their own private practices, too. In large jurisdictions, prosecutors' offices are large agencies with lots of assistant district attorneys (ADAs) whom chief prosecutors rarely see and probably do not even know. Chief prosecutors (DAs or county attorneys) in states, and U.S. attorneys in federal jurisdictions, hardly ever appear in court. They set general office policy, deal with the public, and manage relations with other criminal justice agencies.

The Los Angeles District Attorney's Office is the largest in the United States. The Office maintains a tremendous number of personnel to serve Los Angeles County. According to its website:

> The District Attorney of Los Angeles County is the lawyer for the people, a non-partisan official who is elected every four years. The District Attorney's Office prosecutes felony crimes throughout Los Angeles County. Deputy district attorneys also prosecute misdemeanor crimes in unincorporated areas and in 78 of the 88 County cities. The staff of approximately 2,105 includes 1,017 deputy district attorneys, 277 investigators, and 811 support personnel, comprising the largest local prosecutorial agency in the nation.[24]

Most assistant prosecutors are fresh out of law school. They are usually appointed because of the law school they graduated from, where they ranked in their class, and their political connections. Democrats usually appoint Democratic assistant prosecutors; Republicans appoint Republicans.

Most assistant prosecutors do not make prosecution a life career. They stay fewer than five years and then go into private practice. When they leave, most do not go to prestigious corporate law firms; rather they usually stay in criminal law practice, often becoming defense attorneys. A few become judges, but they hardly ever run for political office.

Prosecution offices assign assistant prosecutors according to two operating systems. In **prosecutor horizontal case assignment** offices, assistants are assigned to manage one stage of the prosecution—drafting criminal charges, working on pretrial motions, negotiating pleas, trying cases, or handling appeals. Under **prosecutor vertical case assignment**, assistant prosecutors are assigned to manage all stages of specific defendants' cases from charge at least through trial and often through appeal. Horizontal system assistants get to be experts in criminal procedure (arraignment, preliminary hearing, pretrial motions, and trial); vertical system assistants become experts in criminal law (homicide, rape, burglary).[25]

prosecutor horizontal case assignment a system in which assistant prosecutors are assigned to manage one stage of the prosecution—drafting criminal charges, working on pretrial motions, negotiating pleas, trying cases, or handling appeals

prosecutor vertical case assignment a system in which assistant prosecutors are assigned to manage all stages of specific defendants' cases from charge at least through trial and often through appeal

LO7 The Role of the Defense Counsel

defense lawyers, like the other members of the courtroom work group (and all other criminal justice professionals for that matter), pursue formal and informal missions. We are familiar with their formal mission to defend their clients. Their informal mission is to bargain with prosecutors to get the best deal for their clients. Another important informal organizational mission is to get along with the courtroom work group.

"In all criminal prosecutions, the accused shall enjoy the right to . . . have the Assistance of Counsel for his defense," so the Bill of Rights to the U.S. Constitution commands. To this, the U.S. Supreme Court has added: Defendants have the right to *effective* counsel. And the lawyers' code of ethics says that defense lawyers have to "zealously" defend their clients. So formally, defense lawyers have the constitutional duty and professional responsibility to make sure the government plays by the rules. Specifically, that means seeing to it that the government proves every element of its case beyond a reasonable doubt based on evidence that was legally obtained.

An effective and zealous defense can go so far as to impede the search for the truth. Indeed, defense counsel are ethically required to do so. The Constitution makes it mandatory for the prosecution to prove guilt. Accordingly, defense attorneys may not reveal that a client is guilty even if the attorney knows that the client committed the crime. [26]

In the 1960s, Abraham Blumberg called the practice of criminal defense law "a confidence game."[27] According to Blumberg, organizational pressures generated by the courtroom work group lead criminal defense lawyers to abandon their role of zealous advocate for the accused. Relationships with judges and prosecutors, he believed, outweigh the needs of clients. To maintain good relations, judges, prosecutors, and defense lawyers join together in an "organized system of complicity."[28]

It is true that defense lawyers, especially public defenders, are not just lawyers; they are members of the courtroom work group. The government pays public defenders, so it is no surprise that some people view them as agents of the government—a suspicion shared by indigent defendants. The "friendly adversary" relationship between defense counsel and their supposed opponents—prosecutors—feeds this suspicion. Opponents, after all, are not supposed to be friends.[29]

Can lawyers vigorously defend clients they have never seen before and probably will never see again, especially when a vigorous defense might antagonize professional peers with whom they have ongoing relationships? Some empirical evidence suggests that defense lawyers can wage a hard fight in the adversary system, drive a hard bargain in plea-negotiating sessions, and still maintain close professional, peer, and personal relationships with prosecutors and judges. Defense lawyers should not (and most do not) take personally either the fights over defending clients in court or the arguments for clients out of court. After all, as defense attorneys—and prosecutors—understand, the adversary system is based on the idea that the truth will emerge if both sides present their most vigorous arguments.[30]

Even after his 2005 death, defense attorney Johnnie Cochran remains one of the most recognizable lawyers in America. Most known for his defense of O. J. Simpson, Cochran also represented musicians Michael Jackson, Sean "Diddy" Combs, and Snoop Dogg; athletes Jim Brown and Marion Jones; and actor Todd Bridges. Cochran was often lauded for his charismatic wordplay and his advocacy for victims of alleged police abuse.

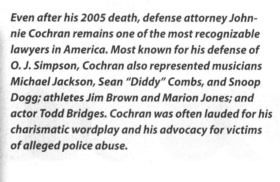

Can lawyers vigorously defend clients they have never seen before and probably will never see again?

THE CJUS SCRAPBOOK

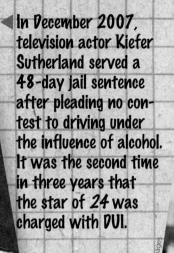

In December 2007, television actor Kiefer Sutherland served a 48-day jail sentence after pleading no contest to driving under the influence of alcohol. It was the second time in three years that the star of *24* was charged with DUI.

With 18 seasons, *Law and Order* is the longest running crime series in television history. The "justice" negotiated behind the scenes in the courthouse corridors, judges' chambers, or even the restroom, is far more typical than the criminal trial that looms so large in each episode.

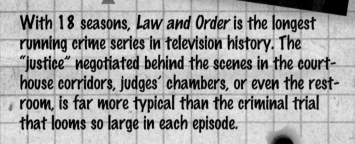

In March 2005, Brian Nichols was on trial for rape in an Atlanta, Georgia, courthouse. Midway through the trial, Nichols overpowered and took the gun of a female deputy, then shot the judge and a court reporter, wounding them both. During his subsequent escape, Nichols wounded a federal agent and killed a sheriff's deputy. Nichols was captured after taking a woman hostage and was found guilty on 54 charges, including murder, in November 2008. The next month, Nichols was sentenced to multiple life sentences after a jury split 9–3 in favor of giving him the death penalty.

© AP Images/Glendale Police Department

© Jessica Burstein/NBCU Photo Bank via AP Images

© iStockphoto.com / ©Radius Images/Jupiterimages

© John Spink

The pretrial process

can be complex but is necessary to ensure a fair trial.

9

Proceedings before Trial

Learning Outcomes

LO1 Understand the pretrial process in criminal cases, including the role of prosecutorial discretion

LO2 Recognize when the right to counsel applies and in what types of cases

LO3 Understand the bail process and the legal right to bail

LO4 Understand the context of pretrial detention

LO5 Explain how the government's case against a defendant is tested

LO6 Understand the authority to try a defendant

Bernard Madoff, the New York financier who organized the biggest Ponzi scheme in modern history, bilked a long list of investors out of an estimated $65 billion. Madoff was arrested in late 2008 and was ordered to home confinement, instead of jail, to await the series of hearings that would ultimately end in a plea of guilty to all charges. In January 2009, after he allegedly mailed a million dollars worth of jewelry to family and friends, federal prosecutors filed a motion to revoke Madoff's $10 million bail and send him to jail. The motion was unsuccessful however, leaving Madoff on house arrest. This second failure to jail Madoff infuriated victims and individuals around the world who believed that he should have been detained. They were concerned that under house arrest, Madoff was still able, and was actively working, to hide his abundant assets from the court. While the public's demand for jail was extremely loud and clear, the federal courts were bound by the **Bail Reform Act**, a federal law that governs pretrial detention. Only two factors can be used to make a pretrial detention decision:

1. Is the accused a danger to the community?
2. Does he or she pose a flight risk?

The federal judge in Madoff's case did not believe he met both of these criteria. The most severe outcome of the pretrial detention decision is detention by jailing.

> **Bail Reform Act** a federal law governing pretrial detention

In this courtroom sketch, Bernie Madoff delivers an address to the judge.

© AP Images/courtroom art, Elizabeth Williams

Once release is granted, the most severe outcome is house arrest. Even though the public believed house arrest was too lenient, it was in fact more severe than other outcomes in similar cases. According to the most recent Bureau of Justice statistics, 70 percent of defendants in federal fraud cases were released after their initial court hearing. Of those, less than 2 percent were ordered to the most severe conditional term of house arrest. Thus, under federal law, Madoff's house arrest was not typical. When Madoff pled guilty in March 2009, his bail was revoked and he was detained in a federal correctional facility to await his sentencing later in the year.[1]

LO1 The Pretrial Process

TABLE 9.1 Decisions and Decision Makers from Arrest to Sentencing

DECISION MAKERS	DECISIONS
Prosecutor	Charge with a crime Divert to social services agency Dismiss case Test case by grand jury or judge Plea-bargain Try case Recommend sentence
Judge	Set bail Assign counsel Bind over for trial Rule on motions and objections before, during, and after trial Sentence defendants
Bail bondsman	Put up money bail Pursue defendants who fail to appear
Grand jury	Indict "No bill" (decline to indict)
Defense counsel	Advise defendant on how to plead Plea-bargain with prosecutor Develop strategy to defend client's interest
Defendant	Plead guilty or not guilty Accept plea bargain
Court personnel	Conduct bail investigation Conduct presentence investigation and report
Trial jury	Convict Acquit

Only one out of ten people arrested for committing a felony goes to prison. Table 9.1 shows the decisions and decision makers who determine whether arrested suspects go free or become defendants and possibly convicted offenders. Figure 9.1 shows the funnel effect of decision making after arrest. In this chapter, you will learn about the decision making behind this funnel effect, including the decision to charge, the appointment of defense counsel, the decision to detain or release defendants before trial, testing the government's case against defendants, and arraignment and pretrial motions.

THE DECISION TO CHARGE

Prosecutors have *nearly* total discretion to make three decisions:

1. To charge or—just as important—not to charge suspects with crimes

2. The specific crime to charge suspects with, such as first- or second-degree murder

3. Whether to transfer the case from the criminal justice system to a social services program, such as drug treatment—a process known as diversion

The decision to charge starts formal court proceedings (adjudication). Once adjudication starts, prosecutors represent the government in all the following proceedings:

1. Deciding whether to bail or detain defendants

2. Presiding over grand jury reviews and presenting the government's case in preliminary hearings

3. Presenting the government's case in trials

4. Negotiating guilty pleas with defense lawyers

FIGURE 9.1
The Funnel Effect after Arrest

100 Violent crimes	**100** Property crimes	**100** Drug offenses	**100** Public order offenses
79 Prosecuted	82 Prosecuted	80 Prosecuted	84 Prosecuted
50 Convicted	62 Convicted	58 Convicted	66 Convicted
12 Imprisoned	9 Imprisoned	12 Imprisoned	5 Imprisoned

Source: Bureau of Justice Statistics, *Sourcebook of Criminal Justice Statistics, 1991* (Washington, DC: Bureau of Justice Statistics, 1992), Table 5.53.

© Don Nichols/iStockphoto.com

5. Negotiating sentences with judges and defense lawyers

Prosecutors' discretion to charge is wide but not total.[2] One reason it is not total is that prosecutors share the decision to charge (or just as important, the decision *not* to charge) with other decision makers, including:

- Members of the public who complain to the police
- Patrol officers who respond to the complaints
- Detectives who investigate complaints to gather evidence and witnesses
- Victims and other witnesses who provide testimony and other information
- Judges who conduct the first appearance and other preliminary proceedings
- Grand jurors who hand up indictments
- Defendants who agree to plead guilty, or refuse to plead guilty, to a specific crime

The 2008 homicide of Eve Carson, president of the University of North Carolina student body, illustrates how complex a charging decision can be. In this case, both federal and state law had been violated. In January 2009, federal prosecutors decided to seek the death penalty in the case. A grand jury indicted Demario James Atwater on federal charges of carjacking resulting in death, carrying and using firearms in relation to carjacking, being a felon in possession of a firearm, and possessing a short-barreled shotgun not properly registered to him. In addition, at the state level, Atwater was charged with first-degree murder in Orange County,

North Carolina, as was 18-year-old Lawrence Alvin Lovette Jr. Atwater will face the death penalty at both the state and federal levels, but Lovette will not face the death penalty because he was 17 at the time of the crime.[3]

In Chapter 2, the case of Marvin "Popcorn" Sutton, the mountaineer sentenced in 2009 for violating federal liquor and firearms laws, was introduced as an example of how criminal laws are created to stem certain behaviors, and how unusual some of these laws appear in modern times. In this chapter, Popcorn Sutton's case also illustrates how public demand and prosecutorial discretion do not always match. There was significant support for Sutton and a noticeable lack of support for the laws used to prosecute the "moonshiner." Prior to sentencing, the public and Sutton's defense attempted to sway the court from sentencing the man in accordance with the prosecutor's charges. Sutton was old and ill, and supporters suggested that even a short prison sentence would do more harm

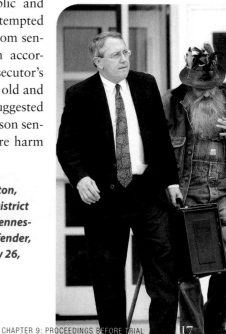

Marvin "Popcorn" Sutton, right, leaves the U.S. District Court in Greeneville, Tennessee, with his public defender, Tim Moore, on January 26, 2009.

© AP Images/Greeneville Sun, Phil Gentry

than good. During his sentencing, Sutton told the judge that he would rather die at home than go to prison.[4] When he was sentenced to 18 months in federal prison, Sutton's supporters reacted strongly, asserting that the court's decision served no legitimate purpose. In March 2009, Popcorn Sutton committed suicide just days before he was to report to federal prison.

Let's look further into what influences the decision to charge.

The Influences on the Decision to Charge

The decision to charge is the most discretionary decision (meaning the least subject to review) in all of criminal justice.[5] Most experts believe prosecutors need this broad discretion because not all arrests should result in criminal charges. Some victims do not want prosecution. In other cases, there may not be enough evidence to prove the defendants are guilty beyond a reasonable doubt. Sometimes counseling or other noncriminal responses may be more appropriate. Maybe resources can be spent better on prosecuting other cases.[6]

What criteria do prosecutors use in deciding whether to charge and what to charge suspects with? One is formal—the strength of the case against the suspect. Three are informal—the seriousness of the offense, the criminal history (dangerousness) of the suspect, and the organizational pressure to win cases.

The Strength of the Case

The "**strength of the case**" refers to the amount of evidence against the suspect. All the research puts this criterion at the top of the list of influences on prosecutors' decision to charge. So answers to these questions are important: Are there witnesses? Are they believable? Will they show up in court? Is there physical evidence? If there is, is it admissible? If the evidence adds up to what prosecutors believe is proof beyond a reasonable doubt, they will charge the suspects; if it does not, they will not. Of course, the evidence has to be obtained legally, or it will be thrown out.

Prosecutors *are* concerned about evidence, but about the amount of evidence, not its admissibility. Their concern boils down to whether the police obtained enough physical evidence (like stolen property) or witnesses to prove guilt beyond a reasonable doubt. For every case that prosecutors drop because police violated suspects' constitutional rights, they drop 20 because the police did not get enough evidence to prove the suspects are guilty.[7]

Let's now turn to the informal (extralegal) influences on the prosecutor's discretionary decision to charge.

Informal Influences

There are three extralegal influences on the prosecutor's decision to charge:

1. Seriousness of the offense
2. Dangerousness of the defendant
3. Organizational pressure to "win" cases

The real world of criminal justice justifies the wide discretion of prosecutors to charge. Most statutes cannot account for variations in individual cases. Legislatures pass many criminal laws, making crimes out of virtually everything that "bothers" particular groups without regard to whether the laws can be enforced. Some prosecutors believe that criminal codes are "society's trash bin." The charging process gives prosecutors a way to scour it. Also, prosecutors have to "individualize justice." Possessing an ounce of marijuana for personal use is not the same as possessing 150 ounces for sale. Prosecutors do, and probably should, respect the wishes of victims who want to forgive those who have harmed their persons and property. Burglars who break into stores to steal compact disc players have not caused the same harm as those who break into homes in the dead of night, terrorizing occupants in their beds.

 ≠

The importance of individualizing justice can be illustrated by a case involving crimes committed by the mentally ill. There has long been considerable debate over whether mentally impaired offenders should be eligible for the death penalty, because their impaired mental judgment may make it impossible for them to meet the legal requirement of intent. In 2005, a Virginia jury sentenced Daryl Atkins to the death penalty even though his case had been reviewed by the U.S. Supreme Court, which had determined that the mentally ill as a class should be excluded from death penalty consideration. The jury's decision that Atkins possessed intent despite his mental impairment lends credence to the argument that justice must be individualized and that categories of people cannot be treated differently by the law. Each case must be decided on a case-by-case basis.[8]

As for the second informal influence—the suspect's dangerousness—sometimes not prosecuting suspects can serve justice better than prosecuting them. A minor property offender who is willing to return a stolen television set and pay for the inconvenience to the victim probably fares better if not prosecuted. Scarce resources demand that prosecutors set priorities because they cannot prosecute all cases. Accordingly, they prosecute the most serious crimes and, among the most serious crimes, pick the most "dangerous" offenders.

Organizational pressure to win cases also influences the screening process. The promotion policy in the prosecutor's office encourages prosecutors to accept only "strong" or "winnable" cases. Promotions are based on conviction rates, and the policy gives more credit to convictions than to guilty pleas. The stronger the case, the better the chance for a guilty verdict, and the better the "stats" for promotion. The policy discourages prosecutors from taking risks on weaker cases. It treats high ratios of not guilty verdicts as an indicator of incompetence. At the

Daryl Atkins

same time, it gives credit to prosecutors for rejecting cases, because the rejections reduce the caseload of an overworked court.

THE FIRST APPEARANCE

After prosecutors file charges, defendants make their first appearance in court. (Do not confuse the first appearance with the arraignment discussed later; the first appearance comes *before* arraignment.) Misdemeanor defendants frequently enter pleas at the first appearance; felony defendants hardly ever do. The first-appearance judge does three things:

1 Reads the charges against defendants and informs them of their rights

2 Appoints lawyers for indigent (poor) defendants

3 Decides whether to bail or detain defendants prior to trial and sets the initial terms for bail or detention

LO2 The Right to Counsel

Until the 1960s due process revolution, a lawyer's job was to represent people once they got to court, not before they were charged or after they were convicted. Since the due process revolution, which extended constitutional protections, even police departments and corrections agencies have to hire lawyers, because the Constitution protects people on the street, in police stations, and when they are locked up before trial. The right to a lawyer reaches even into prison cells—and to the death penalty.

Here, we will concentrate on counsel for suspects and defendants. The Sixth Amendment to the U.S.

retained counsel a lawyer paid for by the client

appointed counsel lawyers assigned to people who can't afford to hire their own

Constitution provides: "In all criminal prosecutions, the accused shall enjoy the right . . . to have the assistance of counsel for his defense." U.S. courts have always recognized criminal defendants' Sixth Amendment right to **retained counsel** (a lawyer paid for by the client), but they did not recognize the right to **appointed counsel** (lawyers assigned to people who cannot afford to hire their own) until well into the 1930s. At that time, the U.S. Supreme Court held that the Sixth Amendment guarantees poor defendants a right to a lawyer at their *trial* in *federal* courts. The Court said nothing about a right to counsel either *before* trial in federal courts or to any proceedings at all in *state* courts.[9]

The U.S. Supreme Court confronted the right to counsel in *state* courts in *Betts v. Brady* (1942).[10] Betts was convicted of robbery and sentenced to prison. At his trial, he had asked for a lawyer, claiming that he was too poor to afford one. The judge denied his request because Carroll County, Maryland, the site of the trial, provided counsel only in murder and rape cases. Hearings on Betts's petition for habeas corpus eventually reached the Supreme Court. The Court decided that the denial of counsel deprives a defendant of a fair trial only in "special circumstances."

So, after the *Betts* decision, most indigent defendants (defendants too poor to hire their own lawyers) had to rely on counsel *pro bono* (lawyers willing to represent clients at no charge). That was supposed to

change when the U.S. Supreme Court overruled *Betts v. Brady* in *Gideon v. Wainwright* (1963),[11] after accepting the handwritten petition for certiorari submitted by Clarence Gideon (a Florida drifter).

Let's look more closely at when the right to counsel applies, the meaning of the Sixth Amendment's words "all criminal prosecutions," the right to "effective" counsel, the standard of indigence for obtaining counsel, and how the defense of the poor works in practice.

WHEN THE RIGHT TO COUNSEL APPLIES

The Sixth Amendment guarantees the right to counsel in all criminal "prosecutions." What proceedings are prosecutions? Certainly, trials and appeals, when defendants most need special legal expertise, would be considered "prosecutions," and we will discuss them in the next section. But what about before trial? According to the Supreme Court, the right attaches to all "critical stages" of criminal proceedings. Table 9.2 shows the stages in the criminal process and indicates the ones the U.S. Supreme Court has declared critical stages. It is clear from the table that defendants have the right to counsel to represent them at all procedures after the first appearance.

But a great deal happens in the police station *before* the first appearance. Does a defendant have a right to a lawyer during police interrogation and identification procedures (lineups, show-ups, and photo identification)? The U.S. Supreme Court first applied the right to a lawyer in police stations in *Escobedo v. Illinois* (1964).[12] The Court held that the right to counsel attached at the accusatory stage of a criminal case—namely, when the general investigation focused on a specific suspect. According to the Court, that point was reached in *Escobedo* when the police made up their minds that Danny Escobedo had committed the murder they were investigating. After they made up their minds

Clarence Earl Gideon

TABLE 9.2 "Critical Stages" and the Right to Counsel

STAGE OF PROCESS	RIGHT TO COUNSEL?
Investigative stop	No
Frisk for weapons	No
Arrest	No
Search	No
Custodial interrogation	Yes
Lineups before charge	No
First appearance	No
Lineup after charge	Yes
Grand jury review	No
Preliminary hearing	Yes
Arraignment	Yes
Pretrial hearings	Yes
Trial	Yes
Appeals	Yes

he was the murderer, Chicago police officers tried to get him to confess by interrogating him. During the interrogation, Escobedo asked to see his lawyer, who was in the police station. The officers refused. Eventually, he confessed and was tried and convicted with the help of the confession. The Supreme Court said the confession was not admissible because it was obtained during the accusatory stage when Escobedo was without the help of his lawyer.[13] Just two years later, in *Miranda v. Arizona* (1966),[14] the Court decided that police officers have to tell suspects that they have a right to a lawyer during custodial interrogation.

THE MEANING OF "ALL CRIMINAL PROSECUTIONS"

Having considered what kinds of proceedings are prosecutions, let's now look at what kinds of cases are included (see Table 9.3 on the next page). In *Powell v. Ala-*

bama, the U.S. Supreme Court held that due process commands that appointed counsel represent poor defendants in capital cases.[15] In *Gideon v. Wainwright* (1963), the Court extended the right to counsel to poor defendants prosecuted for felonies against property.[16] In 1972, the Court went further, ruling that all poor defendants prosecuted for misdemeanors punishable by jail terms have a right to an appointed lawyer. In *Argersinger v. Hamlin* (1972), Jon Richard Argersinger, a Florida indigent, was convicted of carrying a concealed weapon, a misdemeanor punishable by up to six months' imprisonment, a $1,000 fine, or both.[17] A Florida rule limited assigned counsel to "non-petty offenses punishable by more than six months imprisonment." The Court struck down the rule, holding that states have to provide a lawyer for defendants charged with any offense punishable by incarceration no matter what the state's criminal code calls it (misdemeanor, petty misdemeanor, or felony).

Notice that the Court in *Argersinger* did not say that poor people have a right to a lawyer paid for by the government in *all* criminal cases. Why not? The Court was well aware of a practical problem: there is not enough money to pay for everyone to have a lawyer. Of course, strictly speaking, constitutional rights cannot depend on money, but, as a practical matter, money definitely affects how many people get their rights in real life. We know that many poor people who have a right to a lawyer do not get one because counties and other local governments simply do not have the money to pay for them. After all, many taxpayers do not want their tax dollars spent on lawyers for "criminals." This mix of practical reality and constitutional rights surfaced in *Scott v. Illinois* (1979).[18] The Court specifically addressed the question, "Does the right to assigned counsel extend to offenses that do not actually result in prison sentences?" The Court answered no.

THE RIGHT TO "EFFECTIVE" COUNSEL

In 1932, the U.S. Supreme Court said that due process requires not just counsel but effective counsel. But the Court did not tell us

TABLE 9.3 The Leading Right to Counsel Cases

CASE	YEAR	DEFINITION
Powell v. Alabama	1932	Appointed counsel for poor, illiterate, "ignorant," isolated defendants in state capital cases
Johnson v. Zerbst	1938	Appointed counsel in *federal* cases at trial (not before or after)
Betts v. Brady	1942	Appointed counsel in state cases under "special circumstances"
Chandler v. Fretag	1954	*Retained* (paid for) counsel in all criminal cases
Gideon v. Wainwright	1963	Appointed counsel in state felony cases (overruled *Betts v. Brady*)
Argersinger v. Hamlin	1972	Appointed counsel in misdemeanors punishable by over six months' incarceration
Scott v. Illinois	1979	No right to counsel for sentences that don't result in actual jail time

what "effective" means, so lower federal courts and state courts stepped in and adopted what has been called the "mockery of justice standard." Under this standard, only lawyers whose behavior is so "shocking" that it turns the trial into a "joke" are constitutionally ineffective.

In actual cases, appellate courts have ruled that lawyers were not constitutionally ineffective even when the lawyers slept through trials, came to court drunk, could not name a single precedent related to the case they were arguing, or were released from jail to represent their clients. The courts held that the lawyers had not turned the proceedings into a joke and, thus, had not met the mockery of justice standard. When one defendant claimed he got ineffective representation because his lawyer slept through the trial, the judge said, "You have a right to a lawyer; that doesn't mean you have a right to one who's awake." That decision was affirmed by the reviewing court.

Courts and commentators have criticized the mockery of justice standard for being too subjective, vague, and narrow. The standard's focus on the trial excludes many serious errors lawyers make preparing for trial. Besides, in the overwhelming majority of cases disposed of by guilty pleas, the standard is totally irrelevant.

Most jurisdictions have abandoned the mockery of justice standard, replacing it with the "reasonably competent attorney standard." According to this standard, judges measure lawyers' performance against the "customary skills and diligence that a reasonably competent attorney would perform under similar circumstances." Attorneys have to be more diligent under the reasonably competent attorney standard than under the mockery of justice standard. Nevertheless, both the mockery of justice and the reasonably competent attorney standards are "vague to some appreciable degree and . . . susceptible to greatly varying subjective impressions."

In *Strickland v. Washington* (1984), the U.S. Supreme Court tried to clarify the reasonably competent attorney test by creating a two-pronged (reasonableness and prejudice) test to evaluate the effectiveness of counsel.[19] Under the first prong (reasonableness), defendants have to prove that their lawyer's performance was not reasonably competent, meaning that the lawyer was so deficient she "was not functioning as the 'counsel' guaranteed the defendant by the Sixth Amendment." Under the reasonableness prong, reviewing courts have to look at the totality of the facts and circumstances to decide whether the defense lawyer's performance was reasonably competent. Reviewing courts have to start with a presumption in favor of the defense lawyer's competence, meaning they have lots of leeway to make tactical and strategic decisions that fall within the wide range of available professional judgment. As long as defense counsel's

didn't meet with a lawyer

choices fall within that wide range, representation is presumed to be reasonable.

Even if the defendant proves his lawyer's performance was unreasonable, he still has to prove the second prong of the test (prejudice). This prong requires defendants to prove that their lawyer's incompetence was *probably* responsible for their conviction.

In general, courts are reluctant to get involved in the touchy question of judging the performance of defense attorneys. Why? For one thing, judges fear that too much interference can damage not only professional relationships but also the professional independence of defense lawyers and even the adversary system itself. Furthermore, judges who criticize defense lawyers are criticizing fellow professionals, lawyers who appear in their courts regularly.

THE STANDARD OF INDIGENCE

The U.S. Supreme Court has never defined "indigence" or explained how poor a defendant has to be to qualify for appointed counsel. However, U.S. courts of appeals have established some general guidelines on how to determine whether defendants are poor enough to qualify for a lawyer paid for by the government:

1. Poor defendants do not have to be completely destitute.
2. Earnings and assets count; help from friends and relatives does not.
3. Actual, not potential, earnings are the measure.
4. The state can tap defendants' future earnings to get reimbursement for the costs of counsel, transcripts, and fees for expert witnesses and investigators.

Indigent defense is provided by three types of attorneys:

1. **Public defenders.** Full-time defense lawyers paid for by local taxpayers
2. **Assigned counsel.** Lawyers in private practice selected from a list on a rotating basis either for a fee or *pro bono* (donated time)
3. **Contract attorneys.** Private attorneys under contracts with local jurisdictions to represent indigent defendants for an agreed-upon fee[20]

THE REALITY OF THE CRIMINAL DEFENSE OF THE POOR

How does the defense of the poor work in practice? Only 5 percent of all indigent defendants see a lawyer before their first appearance. This means that poor defendants usually do not get any legal advice before they are interrogated, have to stand in lineups, or are charged with crimes. Furthermore, the most inexperienced and least-trained lawyers usually defend the poorest defendants.

LO3 The Legal Right to Bail

almost all misdemeanor defendants and nearly two-thirds of all felony defendants remain free after they are charged, largely through the system of bail. **Bail** is the release of defendants until their cases are decided. In 1682, the Pennsylvania Constitution included a provision copied by the rest of the states. It commanded that all prisoners are "bailable" except in capital cases "where proof is evident."[21] Originally, a defendant had to produce one or more individuals who would guarantee that the defendant would show up in court. By 1900, money had replaced individuals as a guarantee. At first, defendants had to put up the full amount of bail. If defendants showed up for their court date, they got their money back. Soon, the money bail system replaced the demand for the full amount or direct financial surety. The Eighth Amendment to the U.S. Constitution bans "excessive bail," but the U.S. Supreme Court has not done much in the way of telling us what "excessive" means. So the kinds and amounts of bail are left mainly up to the states.

Let's look further at the money bail system.

THE MONEY BAIL SYSTEM

Under the money bail system, defendants pay bondsmen 10 percent of the total amount of bail; the bondsmen are legally liable for the full amount if defendants do not appear. Even if defendants show up, they do not get their 10 percent back—it is the bondsmen's fee. Technically, when defendants fail to appear on private bail bonds, courts can collect the full amount from the bondsmen, who then can recoup the amount paid from defaulting defendants. In practice, this rarely happens. Intricate and entrenched informal rules ensure that bondsmen will not forfeit the amount of bail bonds.[22]

Formally, the amount of bail money is supposed to be just enough to make sure defendants show up in court. Extensive empirical research during the 1960s challenged the fairness of the money bail system in practice.[23] First, affluent defendants were freed on bail; poor defendants were kept in jail.[24] Some spent more time in jail waiting for trial than the length of the sentence for the crimes they were charged with.[25] Second, it is expensive to run jails, and local communities had to pay for feeding, housing, and supervising detained defendants and caring for them if they became sick. Third, detention affected the outcome of poor defendants' cases because they could not help their lawyers as well as defendants out on bail. Many were sentenced to jail and prison instead of probation. Fourth, they tended to be sentenced to longer terms than bailed defendants because they could not show that they were working, maintaining community ties, and obeying the law while they waited for trial.[26]

This research and the political temper of the 1960s led to a powerful bail reform movement. The heart of the movement was to shift bail decision making away from money and toward the characteristics of individual defendants. In 1961, the Manhattan Bail Project set off a wave of changes throughout the country. The Project staff personally interviewed arrested defendants

Former Illinois governor Rod Blagojevich points emphatically as he is escorted from a press conference.

© Frank Polich/Reuters/Landov

preventive detention
detaining defendants to protect public safety

test the government's case an independent review of the prosecutor's decision to charge to make sure there's enough evidence to put the community and the defendant to the time and expense (and for defendants, the additional burden of stigma and stress) of criminal prosecution

to find out if they had ties to the community that would ensure they would show up in court. If they did, they were released solely on their promise to appear in court. Release in exchange for a promise to appear is called "release on recognizance" (ROR). Many states and the federal government passed laws shifting decision making away from money to ROR and other nonmoney conditions of release on bail.

An interesting example of the release of a charged individual on recognizance is the 2008 case of Illinois governor Rod Blagojevich. Governor Blagojevich was charged with federal corruption for allegedly conspiring to sell or trade President-elect Barack Obama's vacant senate seat. He was released on a signature bond, which means he will forfeit a $4,500 bond if he fails to appear in court. The court also ordered Blagojevich to relinquish his passport and his identification card as a firearm owner.[27]

LO4 Pretrial Detention

Whether getting individuals to vouch for defendants, demanding money from the defendants, or getting promises from them, the purpose of bail was clear—making sure the defendants came to court. Beginning in the 1980s, there was a growing demand to add a second purpose to bail—protecting public safety by preventing defendants on bail from committing crimes. In line with public safety, the federal government and many states amended their bail laws to provide for **preventive detention** (detaining defendants to protect public safety).

Setting conditions to ensure public safety may include banning defendants from certain neighborhoods or places, prohibiting them from carrying weap-

ons, and requiring them to report to court periodically. But if judges decide these conditions (or others) are not sufficient to protect the community, they can lock up defendants before and during trial. For example, the U.S. Bail Reform Act of 1984 directs judges to order defendants jailed if after a hearing they decide "no conditions or combination of conditions will reasonably assure . . . the safety of any other person and the community."[28] In fact, most bailed defendants show up (eventually) in court, and few commit new crimes while on bail.

LO5 Testing the Government's Case

after the first appearance, the assignment of counsel, and the decision on bail, the prosecutor has to test the government's case before it can go to trial. **Test the government's case** means that an independent review of the prosecutor's decision to charge is conducted to make sure there is enough evidence to put the community and the defendant to the time and expense (and for defendants, the additional burden of stigma and stress) of criminal prosecution. The two testing devices are the preliminary hearing and the grand jury review (see Table 9.4 on the next page).[29]

THE PRELIMINARY HEARING

Preliminary hearings follow the initial appearance. The length of time between the first appearance and the preliminary hearing ranges from a few days in

preliminary hearings judges review prosecutors' charging decisions to determine whether there's probable cause to continue the case against the defendant

indictment a formal written accusation by the grand jury

grand jury a jury that determines whether there is enough evidence to indict

some jurisdictions to a few weeks in others. The formal function of the preliminary hearing is to test the government's case against defendants. It offers the first opportunity for judicial screening of cases—cases that up to this point only police and prosecutors have reviewed.

At **preliminary hearings**, judges review prosecutors' charging decisions to determine whether there is probable cause to continue the case against the defendant. If judges decide that cases deserve further action, they *bind over* defendants (order them to answer the charges against them). If they determine that the prosecution's case lacks probable cause, they dismiss the charges. Although prosecutors can recharge in the future, as a practical matter, they rarely reopen cases dismissed at preliminary hearings.

THE INDICTMENT BY A GRAND JURY

The government can also initiate criminal proceedings and test probable cause by **indictment**, a formal written accusation by a grand jury; this is an ancient practice originating in medieval England. **Grand jury** proceedings can be held in place of preliminary hearings, or they can follow preliminary hearings as a second screening device.

Dismissals at preliminary hearings do not prevent grand juries from reconsidering probable cause to send a case to trial. In other words, if a magistrate dismisses a case, prosecutors can bring the case to a grand jury for

Renowned American aviator Charles Lindbergh leaves court after testifying to a grand jury about the payment of a $50,000 ransom for his son, who was kidnapped on March 1, 1932.

another try, in the hope that they will win a more favorable outcome. On the other hand, if a judge binds over a case, a grand jury can decide not to indict. Grand juries are composed of private citizens chosen to serve from one to several months. Traditionally, 23 sat on a grand jury; 12 to 16 most commonly sit today. Compared to the unanimous verdict usually required to convict, it takes a simple majority of grand jurors to indict.

Indicting by grand jury screening and binding over in preliminary hearings rest on the same objective basis: probable cause. Nevertheless, preliminary hearings and grand jury proceedings differ in several important ways (see Table 9.4). Grand jury hearings are not adversarial proceedings: only the government presents evidence. Defendants cannot offer evidence or appear before grand juries. Furthermore, preliminary hearings are open and public; grand jury proceedings are secret and closed. There are severe penalties for grand jurors or others who "leak" information presented to a grand jury. Finally, magistrates preside over preliminary hearings; prosecutors oversee grand jury proceedings.

Bernard Madoff, the financier charged with defrauding investors of billions of dollars, waived his right to a grand jury review so he could plead guilty to all charges. The defendant is required to waive the right to a grand jury indictment if the defendant chooses to plead.[30]

TABLE 9.4 Contrasts between Preliminary Hearing and Grand Jury Review

PRELIMINARY HEARING	GRAND JURY REVIEW
Public	Secret
Adversarial	Presents only the government's case
Judge presides	Prosecutor presides
Judge decides facts	Grand jurors decide facts

INDICTMENT (FORMAL WRITTEN ACCUSATION)

© Hulton Archive/Getty Images

grand jury indictments. Despite its tenacious and occasionally truculent critics, the grand jury remains an alternative to an information and a preliminary hearing in serious and sensitive cases. In these cases, prosecutors can receive support and share the responsibility with the grand jury, a body that represents the community.

THE INFORMATION

Prosecutors can bypass the grand jury and initiate proceedings following their own review of probable cause in an instrument called a **bill of information**.[31] Most states using the information procedure require that a preliminary hearing follow the filing of an information. The preliminary hearing prevents a criminal prosecution from proceeding solely on the prosecutor's probable cause determination. In other words, the preliminary hearing in information jurisdictions screens what a grand jury review screens in indictment jurisdictions.

A SUMMARY OF THE TESTS

The preliminary hearing, the indictment, and the information represent different ways to test the government's case against defendants before trial. The preliminary hearing places the decision in the magistrate's or judge's hands; the information, in the prosecutor's hands; and the indictment, in the hands of the community's representatives, the grand jurors. Each has a check on its authority to initiate the criminal process. A grand jury can review and reverse a preliminary hearing's decision to bind over or a prosecutor's information, and magistrates can review

LO6 The Authority to Arraign

if the government passes the tests posed by preliminary hearing bind overs, grand jury indictments, or prosecutorial informations, the criminal court has the authority to try the defendants. It exercises that authority by arraigning the defendants. **Arraignment** consists of bringing the defendants to open court, reading the charges against them, and demanding that they plead not guilty, guilty, or *nolo contendere* (no contest) to the charges.[32] The arraignment and plea to the charges formally set the stage for the criminal trial. Informally, they provide the opportunity either to start, continue, or ratify a plea agreement already reached.

During the period between arraignment and the trial, the prosecution and the defense can file pretrial motions that lead to pretrial hearings. Most states require that the defense make objections to the indictment or information, request the prosecution's evidence (known as *discovery*), and object to the government's evidence (*fruits* of illegal searches and seizures) before trial. The government can also request discovery in the form of a pretrial motion.

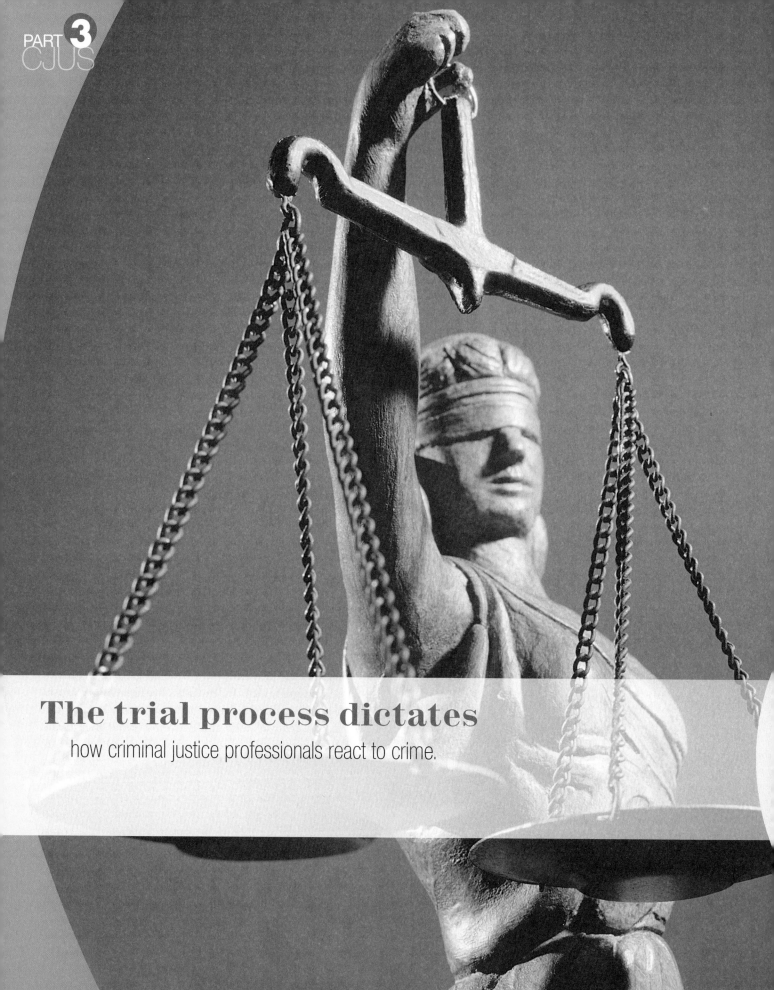

The trial process dictates
how criminal justice professionals react to crime.

10
Conviction by Trial and Guilty Plea

© Gene Blevins/Reuters/Landov

Learning Outcomes

LO1 Explain the use of juries in the trial process

LO2 Summarize the trial process

LO3 Define the concept of a speedy trial

LO4 Explain what is meant by the term *plea bargain* and identify the types of guilty pleas

LO5 Recognize how and why plea bargaining occurs

LO6 Explain the roles of the prosecutor, defense attorney, judge, and defendant in plea negotiations

California wildfires destroy a tremendous amount of property and take numerous human lives every year. When those wildfires are intentionally set, the crime of arson has been committed. What would a trial jury do in the case of a California wildfire arsonist on trial for setting these horrific fires? The March 2008 trial of the arsonist responsible for the deaths of five firefighters resulted in a homicide conviction, and the jury recommended the death penalty for the crime. Even though he did not knowingly murder the firefighters, the defendant was eligible for the death penalty because the deaths resulted from his arson, and multiple deaths were involved.[1] In this chapter, we will review the trial process and the special role of juries in that process.

Criminal trials are the high point of formal criminal justice. They are public morality plays pitting good against evil, containing moments of high drama, and displaying the gory details of the horrors people are capable of inflicting on each other. Yet trials are actually rather rare. All estimates indicate that more than 90 percent of criminal cases are completed with a plea bargain.[2] According to the Bureau of Justice Statistics, 95 percent of felony convictions were obtained through a guilty plea. The remaining 5 percent of cases were decided by a jury or judge.[3] With a guilty plea, *punishment* is the issue, not *guilt* (the courtroom work group already knows the defendant is guilty). In informal, low-visibility, private negotiations, the members of the work group work out what the punishment will be. In these cases, court proceedings just ratify formally and publicly what the courtroom work group has already decided informally in private. Table 10.1 depicts the number of persons convicted of a felony in state courts during 2004.

TABLE 10.1 Number of Persons Convicted of a Felony in State Courts in 2004

MOST SERIOUS CONVICTION OFFENSE	NUMBER	PERCENT
All offenses	1,078,920	100%
Drug offenses	362,850	34%
Possession	161,090	15
Trafficking	201,760	19
Property offenses	310,680	29%
Burglary	93,870	9
Larceny	119,340	11
Fraud/forgery	97,470	9
Violent offenses	194,570	18%
Murder/nonnegligent manslaughter	8,400	1
Rape/sexual assault	33,190	3
Robbery	38,850	4
Aggravated assault	94,380	9
Other violent	19,750	2
Other offenses	177,810	17%
Weapon offenses	33,010	3%

Source: Durose, M. R., & P. A. Langan, *Felony Sentences in State Courts, 2004* (Washington, DC: Bureau of Justice Statistics, 2007), p. 2 (http://www.ojp.usdoj.gov/bjs/pub/pdf/fssc04.pdf).

In this chapter, we will look first at conviction (disposition) by formal trial, where juries are used to determine the outcome, and then at disposition by informal negotiation, where punishment is the issue.

Trials send messages to officials throughout the criminal justice system about the vast majority of cases that never get to trial. Expectations about what happens in trials shape police decisions to arrest, prosecutors' decisions to charge, defense lawyers' willingness to negotiate, and defendants' decisions to plead guilty. Juries are the people's representatives in the "halls of justice," guarding against undue, improper, and vindictive government action. Leading jury experts have called this the "halo effect."

The Sixth Amendment to the U.S. Constitution guarantees the right to a trial "in all criminal prosecutions by an impartial jury of the State and district" where the crime was committed. In a jury trial, the jury decides the facts—whether the government's evidence proves the defendant is guilty beyond a reasonable doubt. The verdict (from the Latin "to tell the truth") is the jury's decision on that important question. Judges decide the law, meaning they apply the rules of the adversary system. A defendant who does not want a jury to decide the facts can have a bench trial, in which the judge decides both the facts and the law. Let's look more closely at trial by jury and the makings of a fair trial.

LO1 The Role of the Jury

Criminal trials are powerful symbols. For good or ill, the trial teaches a public, visible, and potent lesson about the integrity, fairness, and effectiveness of the criminal justice process. A criminal trial is also a search for the truth. According to the adversary process, the government has to prove the defendant is guilty beyond a reasonable doubt.

The Halo Effect

THE JURY AS A POLITICAL INSTITUTION

Juries are the democratic element of the court system; they represent the community and its values. In clear-cut cases, formal law, not informal politics, governs. But in cases that can go either way, extralegal influences enter the jury room and affect jurors' deliberations and decisions.[4]

"I just stuck to the facts," most jurors say about their vote. And empirical studies show they are not lying. But *unconsciously* their value judgments affect their interpretation of the facts—but only in close cases. We call this unconscious influence of value judgment the **liberation hypothesis**. According to Harry Kalven and Hans Zeisel in their classic study of the jury, determining the truth and making value judgments are intertwined.[5] In close cases, the facts are not clear-cut. The possibility that the facts may be read in two sharply contrasting ways is heightened by the adversary process—the prosecution spins the facts only toward "guilty," and the defense spins them only toward "not guilty."

JURY NULLIFICATION

Sometimes a jury returns a "not guilty" verdict even though the jurors believe the defendant is guilty of the crime. In effect, the jurors choose to nullify a law that they believe is either immoral or wrongly applied. This action is called **jury nullification**.

Jury nullification has occurred throughout history when juries have perceived the government to be enforcing morally wrong or unpopular laws. In the mid-1800s, for example, northern juries refused to prosecute defendants who had harbored slaves in violation of the Fugitive Slave Laws, and in the Prohibition era (1920–1933), defendants accused of violating laws against alcohol were found not guilty. Current examples include the acquittals of mercy killers and defendants tried for minor drug offenses.

Courts do not like jury nullification and try to prevent jurors from knowing that they can nullify. Jurors typically learn about nullification from legal dramas on television, novels, or news stories about juries that have nullified. Judges worry that if jurors are aware of their right to nullify, juries will have too much power and many cases may result in hung juries. On the other hand, juries that use this power can actually balance the power of the prosecutor and provide feedback on prosecutor priorities that might not be aligned with community sentiment.[6]

© Jose Manuel Gelpi Diaz/iStockphoto.com

JURY SELECTION

The Sixth Amendment guarantees the right to an impartial jury. According to the U.S. Supreme Court, this means that jurors have to be selected at random, from a "fair cross section of the community." To satisfy the random selection requirement, jurisdictions establish a jury list using names taken from one of several sources—voter registration lists, actual voter lists, tax rolls, telephone directories, or even lists of driver's license registrations. The jury list excludes minors, people who cannot speak or write English, convicted felons, and persons who have recently moved to the community. According to the Supreme Court, a fair cross section does not require that jurors "mirror the community and reflect the various distinct groups in the population."[7] For example, a jury does not have to include 8 percent Hispanic jurors just because the population of the community is 8 percent Hispanic. Furthermore, a fair cross section means only that recognized races, ethnic groups, and genders may not be excluded from the chance to participate; it does not mean that they actually have to sit on juries.

Many states "excuse" some potential jurors from jury *duty*—and jury service is a duty, not a choice. Excuses include poor health, old age, being a student, being a caregiver, knowing the defendant, economic hardship, and transportation problems. Members of some occupations, like attorneys, doctors, dentists, government workers, emergency workers, and members of the military, are also excused in many states.[8]

From the jury list, the jury panel (people from the jury list actually called for jury duty) is selected. The next step is the voir dire, the

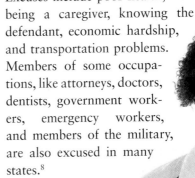

process of questioning the prospective jurors to pare the panel to an actual jury. The voir dire gives prosecutors and defense counsel the chance to get the jurors they want and to exclude the ones they do not want. They can remove jurors either through challenges for cause or through peremptory challenges. Both the prosecution and the defense can use challenges for cause to exclude as many prospective jurors as they like, as long as they can show prejudice to the judge's satisfaction. Examples of prospective jurors who might be successfully challenged for cause include impoverished retirees in an investment fraud case, bar owners in a drunk-driving case, and victims of previous burglaries in a burglary case. The prosecution and the defense also have a specific number of peremptory challenges that they can use to remove prospective jurors without having to give a reason why.[9]

TWELVE-MEMBER JURIES AND UNANIMOUS VERDICTS

Most of us think of juries as having 12 members and their verdicts as being unanimous. That was true for centuries but not anymore. In *Williams v. Florida* (1970), the Supreme Court held that six-member juries did not violate the Sixth Amendment.[10] According to the Court, the Sixth Amendment aims to ensure accurate, independent fact-finding by preventing government oppression. Having only six members, the Court concluded, does not affect a jury's effectiveness. Not everyone agrees. Empirical research shows that six-member juries are less reliable, do not save time, and are a lot less likely to represent a cross section of the community.[11]

Juries with fewer than 12 members are most common in misdemeanor cases, but seven states also allow them in noncapital felonies. What about five-member juries? The Court drew the line at six in a unanimous decision in *Ballew v. Georgia* (1978).[12] Justice Blackman concluded that statistical data demonstrated:

1. Progressively smaller juries are less likely to foster group deliberation.
2. Smaller and smaller panels raise doubts about the accuracy of jury verdicts.
3. Verdicts will vary as juries become smaller.
4. The variance will hurt the defense.
5. The opportunity for minority representation decreases with the size of juries.

The Supreme Court has also decided that the right to a jury trial does not include the right to a unanimous verdict. According to the Court in *Apodaca v. Oregon* (1972), neither an 11-to-1 nor a 10-to-2 vote to convict in a felony case violates the Sixth Amendment.[13] Why not? The commonsense judgment of peers does not depend on whether all jurors agree to convict. In a companion case, *Johnson v. Louisiana* (1972), the Court rejected the argument that proof beyond a reasonable doubt requires a unanimous verdict; instead, the Court held that a 9-to-3 guilty verdict in a robbery case complied with the right to an impartial jury.[14]

Critics of the *Apodaca* and *Johnson* decisions argue that unanimity instills confidence in the system, ensures participants' careful deliberation, and guarantees the hearing of minority viewpoints. Furthermore, unanimity prevents government oppression and supports the established legal preference for freeing 100 guilty persons rather than convicting one innocent individual. Finally, unanimity comports better with the requirement that criminal convictions rest on proof beyond a reasonable doubt. Most states seem to agree. Despite the Court's green light on the constitutionality of less than unanimous verdicts, only two states also allow less than unanimous verdicts (11–1 and 10–2) in noncapital felony cases.[15]

Though 12-member juries are still common, they are not legally necessary. This image depicts the jurors serving on musician Michael Jackson's 2005 child molestation trial. Seven felony counts of child sexual abuse and two counts of administering an intoxicating agent to a minor were levied against Jackson by Gavin Arvizo, who spent time at the pop star's home when he was 13 years old. Jackson vehemently denied the charges, and in June 2005, was acquitted on all counts.

© AP Images/Aaron Lambert

LO2 The Criminal Trial Process

f air trials require an atmosphere that does not prejudice the jury against defendants. To guar-

132   PART 3: THE COURTS

them to be gagged and bound to maintain "order in the court."[17]

PROVING GUILT "BEYOND A REASONABLE DOUBT"

Although it is probably not obvious to most outsiders, the elaborate rules for every procedure in the criminal trial are all aimed at deciding whether defendants are guilty. Whether they are guilty depends on proving guilt beyond a reasonable doubt.

Proof beyond a reasonable doubt is the burden that prosecutors have to carry to turn defendants into offenders. Defendants do not have to prove their innocence, and they do not have to help the state prove its case. They can even throw roadblocks in the way of the government's efforts to prove its case. In other words, defendants are innocent until proven guilty; they enjoy a presumption of innocence. To win acquittal, all that defendants have to do—and only if they choose to—is cast a reasonable doubt on the government's case.[18]

THE TRIAL

We have already discussed the first step in a trial—choosing a jury. Now let's look at the remaining steps: the lawyer's opening statements, the examination and cross-examination of witnesses, the introduction and presentation of evidence, the lawyers' closing arguments, the jury charge, and jury deliberations.

Opening Statements

In their opening statements, prosecutors and defense lawyers give an overview of their side of the case.[19] The goal is to begin the persuasion process to sway the jury in the direction desired by the prosecution or the defense. Prosecutors use the opening statements to give the jury a road map of what they are going to prove. This helps juries follow the case because prosecutors cannot always present their evidence in a logical order. If they can follow the case, jurors are less likely to get confused, bored, and irritated by evidence that does not make sense without the opening statement. Defense lawyers can use their opening statement to take advantage of weaknesses in the prosecution's view of the case.

According to the Center for Criminal Justice Advocacy, which provides free training information to new lawyers, the opening statement must contain a hook to sway the jury in the direction the attorney

antee an atmosphere that minimizes prejudice, trial judges can transfer the trial to a calmer location (change of venue). They can also sequester the jury (put the jurors in hotel rooms under guard where they cannot read newspapers, watch TV, talk on the telephone, or have access to computers). Trial judges can also put gag orders on the press and lawyers and even keep reporters out of the courtroom.

In 2008 in Florida, for example, the prosecution requested a gag order in the highly publicized case of Casey Anthony, who was accused of murdering her three-year-old daughter Caylee. Although motions for gag orders are usually brought by the defense to protect the rights of the defendant, in this instance the prosecution asked for the gag order claiming that Anthony and her family were using the media to prejudice the case in their favor. The court denied the motion, saying that although the prosecution's claim had merit, it did not rise to a level of "being a serious and imminent threat to the administration of justice." Attorneys in the case, however, were admonished to not make extra-judicial comments that might prejudice the case.[16]

In addition to imposing gag orders, judges can remove "unruly" spectators and "troublesome" members of the press from the courtroom. Judges have less freedom to control disruptive defendants, however, because the Sixth Amendment guarantees defendants the right to be present at their own trials. Nevertheless, if it is impossible to proceed with the defendants in the courtroom, they can be removed. More often judges keep disruptive defendants in the courtroom but order

Kenneth Lay appears in court during his 2006 fraud trial.

On May 25, 2006, Skilling was convicted on eighteen counts; Lay was convicted on all counts. However, after conviction and prior to sentencing, Lay died at a Colorado ski resort.[20]

Calling and Examining Witnesses

The defense and the prosecution both have broad powers to subpoena (command by a court order) witnesses to testify. Ordinary witnesses usually get travel money and a small daily fee (rarely enough to compensate them for lost wages). Expert witnesses (fingerprint specialists, psychiatrists, psychologists, and so on) are well paid for their testimony.

The rules for direct examination and cross-examination differ. During *direct examination*, witnesses on the side of the case the lawyers represent are examined, whereas during *cross-examination*, witnesses on the opposing side are questioned. Questions on direct examination call for narrative answers, like the answer to "Where were you on October 8 at about 8:00 p.m.?" In direct examination, lawyers cannot ask leading questions—questions steering witnesses to the answers the lawyers want. Leading questions, which call for simple "yes" or "no" answers, are common during cross-examination.[21]

intends. Here is a sample prosecution hook from the 2006 fraud trial of Enron executives Jeffrey Skilling & Kenneth Lay:

> *The government will take you inside the doors of what was once the seventh-largest corporation in this country, Enron. In the year before Enron declared bankruptcy, two men at the helm of the company told lie after lie about the true financial condition of Enron, lies that propped up the value of their own stock holdings and lies that deprived the common investors of information that they needed to make fully informed decisions about their own Enron stock. You will see that the Defendants Lay and Skilling knew key facts about the true condition of Enron, facts that the investing public did not know. With that information, Defendants Lay and Skilling sold tens of millions of dollars of their own Enron stock. The victims in this case, the investing public, their employees, those who did not have that information, those who were not able to sell their stock before Enron entered bankruptcy were not as fortunate as these two men. These men are Defendants Ken Lay and Jeffrey Skilling. This is a simple case. It is not about accounting. It is about lies and choices. This case will show you that these Defendants worked to lie and to mislead. They violated the duty of trust placed in them. They violated it by telling lie after lie about the true financial condition of Enron.*

Zacarias Moussaoui represented himself boisterously in court after being indicted on six felony charges relating to his involvement in the terrorist attacks of September 11, 2001. During the proceedings, he initially declared that he was not involved in the attacks, but Moussaoui later admitted guilt and involvement with the extremist group al-Qaeda. In May 2006 Moussaoui was sentenced to life in prison without the possibility of parole.

Admissible Evidence

The law of evidence recognizes two types of evidence: physical evidence (weapons, stolen property, and fingerprints) and testimonial evidence (witnesses' spoken, written, or symbolic words). Lawyers cannot use just any evidence they want to present. Evidence has to help prove the elements of the crime; that is, it must be **relevant evidence**.[22] But even relevant evidence is not admissible in three instances:

1 If it is **prejudicial evidence**, meaning that its power to damage the defendant is greater than its power to prove the government's case

2 If the government obtained it illegally, as in an unreasonable search

3 If it is **hearsay evidence**—evidence not known directly by the witness, such as a police officer testifying to the facts of a robbery told to him by the bank teller who actually witnessed it

Closing Arguments

After both sides have presented all their evidence, they make their closing arguments. The goal is to summarize the case and influence the jury one last time. This is often the most dramatic phase of a trial. New evidence cannot be presented during closing arguments, and the attorneys often use emotion and appeals to values in an attempt to sway the jury in their favor. Prosecutors have to temper their use of emotion in closing arguments because overuse of emotion can be grounds to reverse a verdict on appeal.[23]

Charging the Jury

After the closing arguments, the judge "charges" the jury. The charge is given in the form of jury instructions. **Jury instructions** explain the role of the jury—to decide whether the facts prove the elements of the crime. The instructions also explain the law—define the elements of the crime the jurors have to apply the facts to—and explain what "proof beyond a reasonable doubt" means. This sounds simple enough, but, in reality, the often long, complex, and technical legalese found in instructions demands a lot—maybe too much—from jurors.[24]

Jury Deliberations

After the charge, the jurors retire to a room to decide whether the prosecution proved its case beyond a reasonable doubt. When they have decided, they go back to the courtroom to reenact the centuries-old scene of returning their verdict. Formally, judges have the last word: if the verdict is "guilty," they turn defendants into offenders by entering a judgment of guilty; if the verdict is "not guilty," they turn defendants into ordinary individuals by entering a judgment of acquittal.[25]

Jury deliberations can become a long process as juries struggle to determine the outcome of a case. The jury deliberation was a "trial in itself" for a 2009 Pennsylvania fraud case. In this case, Vincent Fumo, a former State Senator, and Ruth Arnao, a former director of a non-profit organization, were tried concurrently. Fumo, facing 10 or more years in prison, was charged in a 137-count indictment for defrauding the Senate and two non-profits, and for obstruction of justice. Arnao, facing less than 10 years in prison, was charged with 45 counts of obstruction and fraud. Their trial jury deliberated for six hours a day for five days, followed by a three-day weekend, culminating in verdicts of guilty on the following Monday. An article in the *Philadelphia Inquirer*

The 1957 film **12 Angry Men** *depicts the heated deliberations of a murder trial jury. In the film, one juror (played by Henry Fonda) works to convince the others that as long as there is reasonable doubt, they cannot return a guilty verdict.*

published on the Sunday before the verdict was announced described how hard the wait was during the deliberation for the attorneys and the defendants. The prosecution and the defense teams could not move on from the case until the verdict was announced, and the lives of the defendants were paused indefinitely, as they did not know what their futures held. Former Senator Fumo took up the hobby of cooking while waiting on the verdict. Arnao, the former non-profit director, stayed at home on the days the jury deliberated so she could get to the courthouse immediately. On the Friday that the jury did not deliberate, she took her grandson to the movies and a museum. This extended deliberation reveals just how long the process can put lives on hold, forcing the defense and prosecution to anxiously await an outcome that impacts the lives and careers of all those involved.

LO3 The Guarantee of a Speedy Trial

t he government must apply the trial process in a timely manner. The Sixth Amendment guarantees the accused the right to a speedy and public trial. The goal of the founders was to prevent people from languishing in prison or having to wait an undue amount of time to have the outcome of their cases determined. How long is too long? The federal Speedy Trial Act of 1974 established time limits for when an individual must be tried or the charges dismissed. Three provisions apply to the time duration, and they resulted in a 100-day maximum at the federal level.

- The defendant must be charged with an indictment or information within 30 days of arrest.
- The arraignment must be held within 10 days of the official charging of the defendant.
- The trial must be held within 60 days of the arraignment.[26]

At the state level, the maximum time varies by state. The guarantee of a public trial means that the trial cannot be held in secret and the public must have knowledge of the proceedings.[27]

LO4 Plea Bargaining

t he criminal trial you have just learned about is the way most cases are decided in TV crime dramas. But in real life, less than 5 percent of cases are decided by a trial, where the question is, "Is the defendant guilty?" You are about to learn about the other 95 percent or so of cases, where defendants plead guilty, and the question is, "What's the punishment?" These cases are decided by plea bargaining.

Given all of the constitutional protections relating to defendants in criminal trials, is plea bargaining constitutional? According to the U.S. Supreme Court, defendants can give up their constitutional rights to trial by jury and protection against self-incrimination if there is evidence that the defendants are guilty and if they give up their rights voluntarily and knowingly. There are constraints on the use of plea bargaining, however. At both the federal and state levels, plea bargains must be made voluntarily and with comprehension. The standards of due process dictate that defendants not plead guilty assuming that they have a deal. This would seem to make plea bargaining unacceptable, but the courts have dealt with this constraint by having the judge make sure that the defendant realizes that any sentence within the law can be given, regardless of any understanding the defendant has regarding a plea deal.

Let's begin by looking at the types of guilty pleas that emerge from plea bargaining. Later sections will examine other aspects of the plea-bargaining process.

THE TYPES OF GUILTY PLEAS

All guilty pleas are not alike. In **straight pleas** ("mercy of the court" pleas), defendants plead

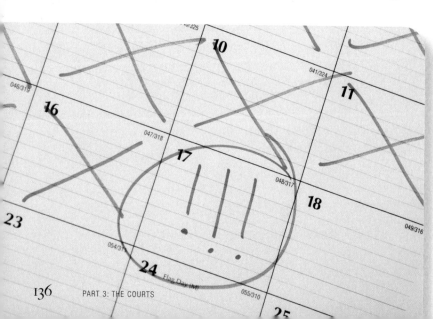

guilty, hoping for a more lenient sentence *after* pleading guilty. In **negotiated pleas**, defendants arrange some kind of deal for a reduced charge or sentence *before* pleading guilty.[28] Let's look at each type of guilty plea.

Straight Pleas

Most pleas are straight (mercy of the court) pleas. Why do defendants plead guilty without a promise of getting something in return? The strength of the case of clear guilt against them (called *dead-bang cases*) is the primary reason. Another reason for a straight plea is the "honorable" reason—hoping that cooperating without bargaining will speak well for the defendant at sentencing. Straight pleas do not always stem from such noble reasons. Defense attorneys admit that guilty pleas benefit them as much as they do their clients. Guilty pleas help lawyers avoid spending the three to four days in court required for a felony trial, plus the time needed to prepare for court. Sometimes a lawyer will advise a client to plead guilty because of the only too human reluctance to appear foolish in public. Defense attorneys also believe that insisting on a trial results in harsher penalties. Finally, going to trial is expensive. Those who can afford a lawyer can measure that cost in dollars, but even those who have court-appointed counsel face a cost in the form of time. Not even indigent defendants want to draw out their cases for months.

Negotiated Pleas

In negotiated pleas, defendants make a deal with the government; they plead guilty in exchange for less punishment. The exact deal is accomplished by bargaining over the charges, the number of charges (called "counts"), or the sentence:

1. *Charge bargaining.* Prosecutors file charges less serious than the facts justify in exchange for defendants' guilty pleas. For example, a defendant who has committed first-degree murder carrying a mandatory life term might plead guilty to second-degree murder with a term of 20 years to life. The plea to second-degree murder gives the judge discretion to sentence the defendant to less than life imprisonment.

2. *Count bargaining.* Prosecutors drop some of the charges (counts) against the defendant in exchange for a guilty plea. For example, a defendant is charged with five robberies; the prosecutor drops two of them in exchange for the defendant's guilty plea.

3. *Sentence bargaining (pleading guilty "on the nose").* Defendants plead guilty to charges actually justified by the facts in the case but with the understanding that the judge will grant (or at least the prosecutor will request) a lenient sentence, such as probation instead of jail time for writing a bad check.[29]

Plea bargaining can be either express or implicit. In express bargaining, prosecutors, defense lawyers, and sometimes trial judges meet face to face to work out a deal. Implicit bargaining involves no direct meetings. Instead, the "going rate for guilty pleas" informally accepted within the courthouse work group (local legal culture) dictates the terms of the deal. In implicit bargaining, defense attorneys can fairly assume that if their clients plead guilty to "normal" crimes, they will receive concessions in line with the going rate.

Public opinion affects local legal culture, too. Cases the public does not care about are probably going to be decided by plea; sensational cases will probably go to trial. Examples include O.J. Simpson's criminal trial for the homicides of his ex-wife, Nicole, and her friend, Ronald Goldman; Michael Jackson's trial for child molestation; and Scott Peterson's trial for the homicide

negotiated pleas defendants arrange some kind of deal for a reduced charge or sentence before pleading guilty

Straight plea → "I'm guilty"

Negotiated plea → give and take to get to "I'm guilty" plea

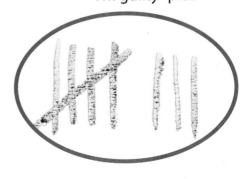

Scott Peterson's homicide trial became a media sensation, seizing the interest of the nation. On November 12, 2004, Peterson was found guilty by a 12-member jury and was later sentenced to death.

© David Paul Morris/Reuters/Landov

the defendants, the seriousness of the offense, and the dangerousness of the defendant. Two other criteria, caseload pressure and defendant pressure, also affect the negotiations. Here we will look at the three main criteria and how they are applied by prosecutors, defense counsel, and judges in negotiated pleas. We will also examine the role of heavy caseloads in negotiations. We will consider the role of the defendant in the next section.

THE STRENGTH OF THE CASE

We begin with the strength of the case because prosecutors, defense lawyers, and judges repeatedly indicate that this is the most important of all the criteria (see Figure 10.1). What makes a strong case? Even if the defendant really *did* commit the crime, lawyers know there is a huge gap between knowing that someone committed a crime and proving it—especially proving it beyond a reasonable doubt, the highest standard of proof known to our law. **Factual guilt**—what we know to be true outside court—is not good enough. Only **legal guilt**—what we can prove in court— counts.

THE SERIOUSNESS OF THE OFFENSE

How do prosecutors, defense lawyers, and judges decide how serious an offense is? The answer begins with the going rates for crimes—the local "market value" measured in prison time or the fine for particular crimes. Market values are not the same as the punishments spelled out in the state's criminal code. How is the going rate determined? There is an informal understanding among prosecutors, defense lawyers, and judges about what punishment cases deserve. Each community has its own going rates. The going rate may not be in writing, but the price of not pleading guilty is clear. Defendants can count on sentences in line with the going rate if they plead guilty.

> **factual guilt** guilty in fact but not proven (or provable) in court

> **legal guilt** guilt proven (or provable) in court

of his pregnant wife, Laci.[30] Less famous defendants who are charged with similar crimes are likely to plea-bargain; if they do go to trial, it will probably receive much less media attention.

According to James Eisenstein and Herbert Jacob, the courtroom work group also contributes to the local legal culture's influence on plea bargaining.[31] They found that defense attorneys, prosecutors, and judges have created norms for the "way things are done." Members of the work group rarely try to do things differently. They would feel uncomfortable if they insisted on going to trial when negotiating is the "way things are done."[32]

However accomplished, the exchange boils down to this: Defendants give up their right to go to trial and take a chance on getting a "not guilty" verdict that will result in no punishment at all. In return, they plead guilty and get a guarantee of *less* punishment than they would get if they went to trial and were convicted.

LO5 Plea-Bargaining Criteria

t he courtroom work group (prosecutors, defense lawyers, and judges) have different emphases when they bargain, but they all have the same criteria in mind when they negotiate.[33] Three criteria should not surprise you: the strength of the case against

JAIL

© James Steidl/iStockphoto.com

FIGURE 10.1
Reasons Prosecutors Negotiate

Bar chart with y-axis from 0 to 250. Legend: Jury, Guilty plea.

Category	Jury	Guilty plea
Violent	192	80
Property	116	41
Drug	104	43
Weapons	77	37

Source: Based on data in Herbert S. Miller, James Cramer, and William McDonald, *Plea Bargaining in the United States* (Washington, DC: National Institute of Justice, 1978).

THE DANGEROUSNESS OF THE DEFENDANT

In previous chapters, when we have referred to the "dangerousness of the defendant," we have meant only the defendant's criminal history (past criminal behavior). Now, we extend the concept of dangerousness to include "bad people" as well as "bad records." Here "bad defendants" means people that are known to the police as being particularly reprehensible. Lawyers do not look at the case strength, offense, and offender seriousness in isolation. In a weak case involving a serious offense and a "bad news" offender, the prosecution is likely to push for some kind of guilty plea, figuring that half a loaf is better than nothing.

HEAVY CASELOADS

We have mentioned several times that the work group wants to dispose of cases efficiently, quickly, and

harmoniously. But the work group subculture is not all that pushes members. Heavy caseloads drive them to dispose of cases and to do it quickly and smoothly. As administrators, prosecutors manage caseloads, which most of them believe are too heavy.

Although the courthouse work group believes heavy caseloads force them to plea-bargain, empirical research casts doubt on this belief. No simple relationship exists between caseload pressure and guilty pleas. A comparison of trial rates in districts with an extremely high volume and those with minimal caseload pressures revealed no significant differences between the percentage of cases disposed of by trial and those disposed of by guilty plea.[34]

LO6 Various Roles in Plea Negotiations

We have already indicated that all members of the courtroom work group play a role in plea bargaining. Here, we look at those roles in more detail and also examine the role of the defendant.

THE PROSECUTOR AND PLEA BARGAINING

Plea bargaining varies according to the roles its key participants (prosecutors, defense counsel, and judges) play. Prosecutors' discretion in charging and sentencing decisions conditions their role in plea bargaining. Discretion not only affects decisions in individual cases but also determines general charging policies in prosecutors' offices. In small or rural jurisdictions, individual case discretion, not general charging policies, constitutes the norm. In large urban jurisdictions, however, general charging policy includes plea bargaining.[35]

© ballyscanlon/Photodisc/Getty Images / © Stockbyte/Getty Images

DEFENSE COUNSEL AND PLEA BARGAINING

Formally, defense counsel have to look at the effect their bargaining decisions have on their clients because plea bargaining is essential to their constitutional and professional duties to vigorously and effectively defend their clients. But these formal professional duties run up against their informal connections to the work group.[36] Defense attorneys have an obligation to make sure their clients are defended appropriately from an adversarial perspective, but at the same time, defense counsel have numerous incentives to induce their clients to bargain. Case processing, time constraints, getting a good deal for the client, and working cooperatively with the rest of the courtroom work group all compete with the adversarial, zealous defense of the client.

In March 2008, Kwame Kilpatrick, former mayor of Detroit, Michigan, was forced to resign from office after being charged with 10 felony counts, including misconduct in office, obstruction of justice, and perjury. A successfully negotiated plea bargain resulted in a $1 million fine, four months in the Wayne County jail, and other penalties. Kilpatrick pled no contest to a count of assaulting and interfering with a law officer so that a second assault charge would be dropped.

JUDGES AND PLEA BARGAINING

Judges enter into plea bargaining in one of two ways: they either participate during the negotiations or supervise after lawyers have struck bargains. Sometimes they do both.[37] Judicial participation in plea bargaining varies according to the individual judge's style and from jurisdiction to jurisdiction. Some judges gently pressure lawyers to complete a bargain, others use heavy pressure to obtain a plea bargain, and others will negotiate with lawyers on the sentence. Some judges will not involve themselves in negotiation at any level. Judges who refuse to participate at all just look over what the lawyers have already decided. These judges believe they cannot impartially supervise a process when they are an active part of it.[38]

There is considerable opposition to judges participating in plea bargaining. In fact, some statutes and court rules go so far as to ban judges from plea bargaining. For example, the *Federal Rules of Criminal Procedure* (2004) say that judges "shall not participate in any such discussions."[39] In *United States v. Werker* (1976), a federal appellate court interpreted this rule to prohibit sentencing judges from taking any part "in any discussion or communication regarding the sentence to be imposed prior to the entry of a plea of guilty, conviction, or submission to him of a plea agreement."[40]

DEFENDANTS AND PLEA BARGAINING

It is a myth that defendants always want their lawyers to do full battle in court for them. Asserting the constitutional right to go to trial is more than time-consuming. For defendants not familiar with the criminal justice system, it is scary, embarrassing, and risky.

Many defendants have been through the system before. Their prior experiences affect their attitude toward plea bargaining. For some (especially minorities and "outsiders"), these experiences have led them to believe that going to trial is a poor option because the system is not in their favor. For others, trials are not worth their time because they think their cases are not "that big a deal" or are "nothing to worry about." They just want to "get it over with" as soon as possible, and the way to do that is to plead guilty.[41] Defendants who have had experience with the system are not naïve. They are familiar with the lesson of the **penalties/rewards system**: defendants who go to trial pay a penalty for their adversary stance, and defendants who plead guilty get rewarded.

Speak Up!

CJUS was built on a simple principle: to create a new teaching and learning solution that reflects the way today's faculty teach and the way you learn.

Through conversations, focus groups, surveys, and interviews, we collected data that drove the creation of the current version of CJUS that you are using today. But it doesn't stop there— in order to make CJUS an even better learning experience, we'd like you to SPEAK UP and tell us how CJUS worked for you. What did you like about it? What would you change? Are there additional ideas you have that would help us build a better product for next semester's criminal justice students?

At **4ltrpress.cengage.com/cjus** you'll find all of the resources you need to succeed in principles of criminal justice— **Printable Flash Cards, Interactive Quizzing, Downloads, Games, Video Activities,** and more!

Speak Up! Go to **4ltrpress.cengage.com/cjus**.

After a jury returns a verdict of "guilty,"

one step remains in a criminal trial: sentencing.

II

Sentencing

"I have little children and a woman. They depend on me. I'm so worried about them." This is part of the statement Khan Mohammed, a 38-year-old Afghan Taliban member, made to a federal judge at his sentencing hearing in 2008. Mohammed sobbed and begged the court for mercy as judge Colleen Kollar-Kotelly determined his sentence for convictions on drug trafficking and narco-terrorism. Mohammed was extradited from Afghanistan and tried in the United States under a 2006 law that allows stiffer penalties for offenders involved in terrorism and drug trafficking. Mohammed was charged and convicted for plotting a rocket attack on U.S. military forces and Afghan civilians at Jalalabad Airfield, and for distributing between $1 million and $3 million worth of heroin in the United States "to kill Americans as part of a jihad."

Judge Kollar-Kotelly showed no mercy, sentencing Mohammed to maximum life sentences despite his attorney's plea for 20 years and his own plea for one or two years. Kollar-Kotelly said to the defendant,

> *Terrorists stand unique among criminals. Deterrence is very important here. I heard your concerns for your family but no acceptance of responsibility for your action. Defendants often express worry for their families, but if they considered the consequences of their actions beforehand, maybe they would have acted differently.*

This judge is making her sentencing philosophy clear as she hands down her sentence. In this chapter, we will explore the punishment process and how sentences are determined.[1]

After a jury returns a verdict of "guilty," one step remains in a criminal trial: sentencing. Although sentencing is a judicial function, the judge is not all-powerful

Learning Outcomes

LO1 Recognize the major purposes of punishment

LO2 Identify the types of sentences judges can impose

LO3 Explain how sentences are determined using sentencing guidelines and presentence reports

LO4 Explain the death penalty debate

© AP Images

Colleen Kollar-Kotelly

retribution punishes criminals for past crimes because they deserve it

prevention punishes criminals to deter future crimes

restitution offenders pay back victims in money for losses they caused

restoration aims to heal victims and restore relationships

culpability assumes offenders are responsible for their actions and have to suffer the consequences if they act irresponsibly

when it comes to handing out sentences. For one thing, public demands to "get tough" on crime, reformers' dissatisfaction with judicial discretion, and scholars' research on the ineffectiveness of sentencing practices have produced reform laws limiting judges' sentencing power. Also, the structure of our criminal justice system distributes the power to sentence among legislatures, prosecutors, and judges. Finally, the judge's power is subject to constitutional limits: the Eighth Amendment bans "cruel and unusual punishments;" the Fifth and Fourteenth Amendments provide that no one can be deprived of life, liberty, or property without due process of law; and the Fourteenth Amendment guarantees that no one will be denied the equal protection of the laws.

Sentencing also affects public policymakers, particularly during times of heightened concern about crime. Since the 1970s, politicians, criminologists, reformers, and the public have subjected sentencing to careful scrutiny. The public has demanded that we "get tough" on violence, illegal drugs, and juvenile crime. And although crime rates have fallen since the late 1990s, they have not returned to the levels they were at before the great crime boom of the 1960s to 1990s. As a result of these influences, almost all legislatures have enacted some kind of sentencing reform laws. Certain justice *and* flexible mercy are still parts of the practical reality of sentencing in the twenty-first century.

In this chapter, we will look at the purposes of punishment, the types of sentences imposed, the sentencing process, and the death penalty debate.

LO1 The Major Purposes of Punishment

Criminal punishment has four main purposes: retribution, prevention, restitution, and restoration. **Retribution** (sometimes called "just deserts") looks *backward* to punish criminals for their

Though it has evolved over time in methodology and purpose, punishment has been levied against convicted offenders throughout the history of criminal justice.

completed criminal *conduct* because they deserve it. **Prevention** looks *forward* to change criminals, punishing them to prevent future crimes. **Restitution** looks *backward* to make offenders repay victims for property losses. **Restoration** looks *backward* and *forward* to heal victims (not just compensate them in money for what they lost) and restore relationships. Let's look at these four purposes of criminal punishment and their components.[2]

RETRIBUTION

Striking out to hurt what hurts us (*retribution*) is a natural impulse. From the Old Testament's philosophy of taking an eye for an eye, to the nineteenth-century Englishman's claim that it is right to hate and hurt criminals, to the modern idea of "three strikes and you're out" and "lock 'em up and throw away the key," the desire for retribution has run strong and deep in religion, criminal justice, and society.

The long and strong life of retribution can be attributed mainly to its dependence on two appealing ideas: culpability and free will. **Culpability** means that offenders are responsible for their actions and have to suffer the consequences if they act irresponsibly. Simply put, we cannot punish those we cannot blame, and we cannot blame those who are not responsible. But justice demands that we *do* punish the blameworthy. Retribution assumes that we all have free will. Applied to the idea of culpability, this means that offenders are free to choose between committing and not committing crimes. Because offenders have this choice, society can blame them for making the wrong choice. Retribution is two-edged: it benefits society by allowing for retaliation, and it benefits criminals by having them "pay their debt to society."

There are three problems with retribution, however. First, it is difficult to translate abstract justice into specific penalties. What are a rapist's just deserts? Is castration justice? How many years in prison is a robbery worth? How much suffering by the offender will repay the pain of a disfigured assault victim? Critics of retribution answer, "We can't achieve just retribution! And we shouldn't even try." Why not? The answer lies in a second problem: Retributionists cannot prove that human nature craves revenge. Third, and probably the strongest argument against retribution, is that most criminal laws are not based on moral blameworthiness because they do not require criminal intent.[3]

In March 2004, U.S. civil administrator in Iraq L. Paul Bremer spoke in front of a large bronze relief of Babylonian ruler Hammurabi (depicted right) at Al-Nahrain Law School in Baghdad. Hammurabi, who lived from 1792 to 1750 B.C.E., established one of the earliest codes of law in human civilization. His precepts, which specified explicit and often strict punishments for common offences, were carved into massive stone monuments and placed in public spaces so that all citizens could view them.

© AP Images/Nabil Mounzer

PREVENTION

Like retribution, *prevention* inflicts pain, but for a totally different reason. Prevention looks *forward* and inflicts pain to stop criminals and criminal wannabes from committing crimes in the future. There are four types of prevention: special deterrence, general deterrence, incapacitation, and rehabilitation. The idea of prevention by deterrence was born in the eighteenth-century Enlightenment and is based on the English philosopher Jeremy Bentham's concept of utility. Utility starts with two assumptions about human nature: (1) people seek pleasure and avoid pain, and (2) they have the free will to choose their own actions.[4]

In deterrence, the aim of punishment is to inflict just enough pain (or threaten to inflict pain) to make criminals (or wannabes) avoid the pain of the consequences of committing crimes. **Special deterrence** hopes to teach convicted criminals the lesson that "crime doesn't pay" by inflicting actual pain on them—pain that "costs" more than the pleasure they received from committing the crime—so that when they get out of prison, they will not commit more crimes. **General deterrence** sends the message that "crime doesn't pay" to people who are thinking about committing crimes. Whether that message gets through depends on three things—the swiftness, the certainty, and the severity of the punishment. According to deterrence theorists and researchers, swiftness and certainty are more important than severity.[5] For example, knowing that you are really going to prison next week for one year—no ifs, ands, or buts—is more effective than knowing that *maybe* you will go to prison for five years starting in the year 2030.

Incapacitation is based on the straightforward idea that criminals cannot commit crimes while they are locked up. It is *present* oriented because it is aimed at preventing locked-up criminals from committing crimes they would be committing if they were not locked up. It is not concerned with what they might do in the future when they get out. The ultimate incapacitation is, of course, death.[6]

The basic idea of **rehabilitation** is to change criminals into people who "work hard and play by the rules." Rehabilitation inflicts pain but not on purpose—the

special deterrence teaches convicted criminals that "crime doesn't pay"

general deterrence "sends a message" to people thinking about committing crime that "crime doesn't pay"

incapacitation confines criminals so they can't commit crimes while they're locked up

rehabilitation aims to change criminals into people who "work hard and play by the rules"

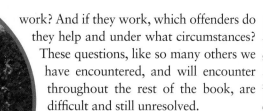

pain is only a necessary side effect of changing criminals. Various treatment programs are designed to rehabilitate the offender, such as drug treatment programs, education programs, job skills training programs, and even psychological treatment programs developed to treat the common forms of psychoses among offenders.

While there has always been considerable opposition to rehabilitation, proponents of the practice often focus on the rehabilitative prospects of youth. Minors are often perceived as more likely to benefit from rehabilitation than adults. In opposition to the construction of a planned $15 million minimum security facility for male offenders age 18 to 22, the Washington Criminal Lawyers Association publicly asserted that the money would be better spent on community-based rehabilitation programs. Having defended many underage offenders in court, the lawyers of the association said the community-based rehabilitation programs were underfunded, understaffed, and under pressure. The money to build new facilities, the association concluded, would be better spent keeping youth out of jail in the first place.[7]

In practice, none of the aims of punishment is either completely distinct from or totally in harmony with the others. So punishment in specific cases is usually based on several conflicting aims. For example, a rapist is sentenced to prison to suffer the pain of confinement for its own sake, to send him a message that rape does not pay, to incapacitate him so he will not be raping while he is in prison, to send a message to rapist wannabes that if they rape they will go to prison, and to rehabilitate him through sex-offender treatment.

Like punishments based on retribution, punishments for the purpose of prevention raise difficult questions. How much and what kind of pain is a rape worth? How much pain exceeds the pleasure of satisfying the urge to rape? Does locking up a rapist really incapacitate him or just shift the pool of his victims? Which sex-offender treatments

work? And if they work, which offenders do they help and under what circumstances? These questions, like so many others we have encountered, and will encounter throughout the rest of the book, are difficult and still unresolved.

RESTITUTION AND RESTORATION

Restitution means that offenders (almost always property offenders) pay back their victims in money for losses they caused. Restorative justice is more ambitious than simply repaying victims' losses. It starts with the proposition that the essence of crime is the harm that it causes to individuals (victims, offenders, and their friends and families) and their relationships, a harm that has to be repaired and healed.[8] (Contrast this view of crime with retribution and prevention, which view crime as a violation of the criminal law and all of society as the victim.)

The goal of restorative justice is to heal and repair the damage to the individuals and relationships directly involved. It replaces punishment of offenders with efforts to heal the injuries to crime victims, offenders, their families, and others who care about them. Retribution and prevention in the current criminal justice system "respond to harm with more harm but restorative justice responds to harm with healing. Only acts of restoration, not further harm, will effectively counterbalance the effects of crime."[9]

To accomplish restoration, victims, offenders, their families, and others who care about them have to participate in resolving the conflict. Since the victim and offender "own the conflict," restoration is impossible without their participation. They have to work together (but of course not alone) to satisfy the victim's needs and enable the offender to realize the consequences of the criminal behavior.

LO2 Types of Sentences

j udges can impose a wide range of sentences. The less serious forms include probation, fines, and restitution. Prison time is considered a serious penalty because of the deprivation of liberty involved. For more than a thousand years, officials, academics, and (in modern times) the public have debated whether sentences should fit the crime or be tailored to individual criminals. In **determinate sentencing** (sometimes called fixed sentencing), legislatures focus on the crime and attach specific punishments to it, such as a sentence of 25 years for the crime of armed robbery. In **indeterminate sentencing**, legislatures set only the outer limits of possible penalties, like 0 to 25 years for robbery. Corrections officials then tailor the actual time served using specialized programs to suit the individual offenders and release them when they are "corrected."

Both determinate (fixed) and indeterminate sentencing are essential elements of criminal justice. Fixed sentences reflect the desire for certain, predictable, and evenhanded formal rules in administering criminal justice. Indeterminate sentencing responds to the need for flexibility, the "play in the joints" of informal discretionary decision making that is essential to fair criminal justice.

THE RETURN TO DETERMINATE SENTENCING, 1971–PRESENT

Fixed sentences were the norm in the United States until about 1870 when a desire for a more flexible system with more scope for rehabilitation led many states to adopt indeterminate sentencing systems. Indeterminate sentencing remained dominant until the 1970s, when several forces combined to bring about a return to fixed sentencing. At that time, the country was in the midst of the biggest crime boom in its history. Prison riots in the late 1960s made rehabilitation seem to be only talk and revealed prisons as seething cauldrons of discontent that sometimes erupted into extreme violence. Prisoners' rights advocates challenged the broad informal discretionary powers of criminal justice officials. And a band of activist judges demanded that criminal justice officials justify their decisions in writing and empowered defendants to dispute their sentencing.

At the same time, professionals and academics were becoming disillusioned with rehabilitation. Several statistical and experimental studies strongly suggested that poor people and blacks received harsher sentences than whites and more affluent Americans. Disillusionment and the troubling statistical studies led to the creation of a distinguished panel of the National Research Council to review sentencing practices. The panel concluded that by the early 1970s, a "remarkable consensus emerged among left and right, law enforcement officials and prisoners groups, reformers and bureaucrats that the indeterminate sentencing era was at its end."[10]

What led to this remarkable consensus? A powerful alliance of civil libertarians and conservatives agreed that the aim of sentencing is swift and certain punishment. But there the agreement ended. They disagreed over two fundamentals: the length and the kind of sentences. To civil libertarians, determinate sentencing meant short, fixed sentences, with programs to prepare prisoners for playing by the rules and paying their way in life. To conservatives, punishment meant long, fixed uncomfortable sentences (prisons are not "country clubs"). The public was firmly on the side of the conservatives. Americans were frustrated and angry with judges who were "letting too many criminals off with a slap on the wrist." The conservatives and the public view of fixed sentencing won.[11] By 1996, the United States was sentencing more people to prison for longer terms than almost any other country in the world.

There are two types of fixed sentences: (1) mandatory minimum sentences, which require convicted offenders to spend at least some time in prison, and (2) sentences from sentencing guidelines, which base sentences on a combination of the severity of the crime and the criminal history of the offender. Here we will look more closely at mandatory minimum sentences. We will examine sentencing guidelines in the next section.

indeterminate sentencing legislatures set only the outer limits of possible penalties, and judges and corrections professionals decide actual sentence lengths

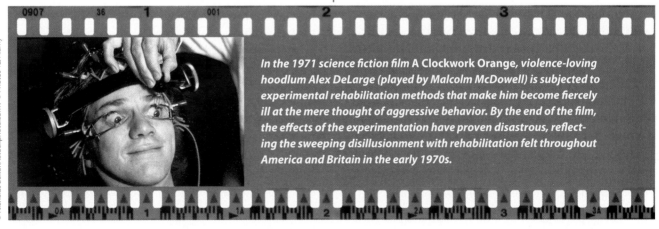

In the 1971 science fiction film A Clockwork Orange, violence-loving hoodlum Alex DeLarge (played by Malcolm McDowell) is subjected to experimental rehabilitation methods that make him become fiercely ill at the mere thought of aggressive behavior. By the end of the film, the effects of the experimentation have proven disastrous, reflecting the sweeping disillusionment with rehabilitation felt throughout America and Britain in the early 1970s.

© Nicholas Belton/iStockphoto.com / © Photos 12/Alamy

MANDATORY MINIMUM SENTENCING LAWS

Under **mandatory minimum sentence laws**, offenders have to spend at least some time (the mandatory minimum laid out in the law) in prison. At least as far as the mandatory minimum is required, the laws take away both judges' and corrections officials' discretionary power in sentencing. Judges cannot suspend the minimum, and they cannot substitute probation for it. Prison and parole authorities cannot release offenders until they have served the minimum.

Mandatory minimums have had an on-and-off history in the United States.[12] They were used frequently during the 1800s but then fell into disuse between 1900 and 1950. In 1956, the public's concern about crime and illegal drugs led Congress to enact a mandatory minimum drug law to make sure that offenders who did the drug crime would "do the time"—in this case, 5 years in prison for a first-time heroin sale. The statute imposed stiff mandatory minimum sentences for narcotics offenses, requiring judges to pick within a range of penalties. Judges could not suspend sentences or put convicted offenders on probation; they had to sentence them to at least 5 years in prison. Offenders were not eligible for parole if they were convicted under the act. For second offenders, the mandatory minimum was raised to 10 years. The penalty for the sale of narcotics to persons under 18 years of age ranged from a mandatory minimum of 10 years to a maximum of life imprisonment or death.[13]

Congress repealed the 1956 law in 1970 because it concluded that the longer sentences "had not shown the expected overall reduction in drug law violations."[14] Further, they alienated youths from the general society, hampered the rehabilitation of drug law offenders, infringed on judicial discretion, and reduced the deterrent effect of drug laws. Prosecutors had stopped charging offenders because even they believed the laws were too severe.[15] The retreat from mandatory minimum sentences did not last, however. By 1991, 46 states and the federal government had enacted mandatory minimum sentencing laws, mainly aimed at drug and weapons offenses.

According to criminal justice officials, mandatory minimum sentences further five fundamental principles of criminal punishment:

1 *Equality.* Similar offenses receive similar sentences.

2 *Certainty.* Offenders and the public know that offenders will really do the minimum prison time the statute prescribes.

3 *Just deserts.* Violent and drug offenders, habitual criminals, and criminals who use guns to commit crimes deserve mandatory long prison terms.

4 *Deterrence.* Mandatory prison sentences deter crime by sending the strong message that those who "do the crime" really will "do the time."

5 *Incapacitation.* Mandatory prison terms protect public safety by locking up drug dealers and violent armed criminals.[16]

But do mandatory minimum sentences really work? Let's look more closely at this issue. Then we will examine two types of mandatory minimum sentencing laws: "truth-in-sentencing" and "three strikes and you're out" laws.

Do Mandatory Minimum Sentence Laws Work?

Mandatory minimum sentences are supposed to satisfy three aims of criminal punishment: retribution, incapacitation, and deterrence. According to this view, retribution is satisfied because the laws promise that serious crimes will receive severe punishment. Violent criminals, criminals who use weapons, and drug offenders cannot harm the public if they are in prison, so the goal of incapacitation is achieved. Finally, the knowledge that committing mandatory minimum crimes will bring certain, severe punishment will deter criminal wannabes.

Evaluations suggest, however, that in practice mandatory minimum penalties do not live up to these promises. A rigorous Department of Justice study concluded that "the threat embodied in the words of the law proved to have teeth for relatively few offenders" because "mandatory sentencing laws directly affect only an end product of a long criminal justice process—the convicted offender." The laws also had some serious side effects. They slowed down the criminal process and worked a real hardship in some cases. One 38-year-old woman with no prior criminal record, for instance, was sentenced to life imprisonment for possessing one ounce of heroin.[17]

In 1990, Congress ordered the U.S. Sentencing Commission to evaluate federal mandatory minimum sentencing statutes.[18] After studying presentence reports, sentencing hearings, plea agreements, sentencing guideline worksheets, and a random sample of drug and firearms cases, the commission concluded:

- Only 41 percent of defendants who qualify for mandatory minimum sentences actually receive them.

- Mandatory minimum sentences increase disparity in sentencing.

- Whites are less likely than blacks and Hispanics to be indicted or convicted at the mandatory minimum.

- Whites are also more likely than blacks and Hispanics to receive reductions for "substantial assistance" in aiding in the prosecution of other offenders.[19]

Defendants who provide prosecutors with "substantial assistance" in investigating other offenders are eligible for an exception to the mandatory minimum sentences. The substantial assistance exception creates more than racial disparities. It also favors the very peo-

Pablo Escobar was one of history's most infamous and successful drug kingpins. After growing up as a petty thief on the streets of Medellín, Colombia, Escobar began to accrue wealth and influence by selling and trafficking cocaine. During the 1970s, Escobar founded the Medellín Cartel, a powerful and ruthless syndicate which oversaw cocaine transportation throughout the Americas and into Asia. Using bribery and murder, Escobar evaded authorities until 1991, when he was sentenced to up to five years in a private prison, which he escaped the following year. An international manhunt ensued, and in 1993 Escobar was shot to death in his hometown by Colombian police.

© AP Images

ple the law was intended to punish ("drug kingpins") because underlings do not have anything substantial to offer the government.

Mandatory minimum sentences do not eliminate discretion either; they just shift it from judges to prosecutors. Prosecutors can use their discretion in a number of ways, including not charging defendants at all with mandatory sentence crimes. Or they can charge offenders with less serious mandatory minimum crimes. Prosecutors can also manipulate the substantial assistance exception to suit their purposes. Although the Sentencing Commission recommended further study before drawing any final conclusions about the effectiveness of mandatory penalties, its findings suggest that mandatory minimum penalties are not the easy answer to the crime problem that politicians promise and for which the public hopes.[20]

"Truth-in-Sentencing" and "Three Strikes and You're Out" Laws

Despite the shortcomings of mandatory minimum sentences, they remain popular with the public and some professionals. Truth-in-sentencing laws are intended to make sure serious offenders spend some time locked up. Three-strikes laws are supposed to make sure that offenders who are convicted of a third felony are sent to prison for a very long time (sometimes for life). Supporters claim that both types of laws will "help restore the credibility of the criminal justice system and will deter crime." Opponents believe the harsh penalties will not have much effect on crime and that imprisoning offenders for such long terms will cost states more than they can afford to pay.[21]

© Koji Aoki/Sport/Jupiterimages

LO3 Determining Sentences

the other type of fixed (determinate) sentences used today are sentences that are determined by using sentencing guidelines. In states without sentencing guidelines, judges use their discretion to determine sentencing based on legal statutes. To curb the misuse of discretion and to reduce sentence disparity, many states have established sentencing guidelines. **Sentencing guidelines** provide for fixed (but flexible) sentences based on balancing the seriousness of the offense and the criminal history of the offender. Guidelines establish narrow ranges of sentences that judges can impose. Guidelines have four purposes:

- *Uniformity.* Improving the chances that similar offenders who have committed similar offenses will receive similar penalties.

- *Neutrality.* Reducing the chances that race, gender, ethnicity, age, and class will affect sentencing by restricting the criteria for sentencing to the seriousness of the offense and the criminal history of the offender.

- *Truth.* Ensuring that the type and length of sentences that offenders actually serve nearly equal the sentences judges impose. In other words, "You do the crime, you do the time."

- *Control.* Preventing rapidly growing prison populations from overtaking prison space and state resources.

In this section, we will see how judges use sentencing guidelines and presentence reports to determine sentences. First, though, let's look at the types of guidelines.

TYPES OF GUIDELINES

Sentencing guidelines may be presumptive or voluntary. With presumptive sentencing guidelines, either legislatures or special commissions set the types and ranges of sentences. Judges have to contain their sentences within the prescribed ranges, unless they can justify their departures from the guidelines in writing using criteria that are usually prescribed in a guidelines manual. Voluntary sentencing guidelines merely suggest possible sentences. Judges can (and often do) follow the suggested sentences, but they do not have to.

The specific types and exact ranges of sentences are either descriptive or prescriptive. In descriptive sentencing guidelines, the guidelines are based on existing sentencing practices within the state; they merely state in writing what judges have actually been doing. Prescriptive sentencing guidelines develop new sentencing norms based on what decision makers decide the type and range of penalties should be.

AN EXAMPLE OF SENTENCING GUIDELINES

As an example of how sentencing guidelines are used, let's consider the Minnesota Sentencing Guidelines, which were the first set of model guidelines to be developed and have served as a model for other states in developing their own sentencing guidelines. A commission has been set up to support the use of the guidelines in Minnesota. According to the commission's website:

> *The Sentencing Guidelines Commission embodies the goals of the criminal justice system as determined by the citizens of our state through their elected representatives. This system promotes uniform and proportional sentences for convicted felons and helps to ensure that sentencing decisions are not influenced by factors such as race, gender, or the exercise of constitutional rights by the defendant. The guidelines serve as a model for the criminal justice system as a whole to aspire to, as well as provide a standard to measure how well the system is working.*[22]

The Minnesota guidelines regulate both the kind of disposition (incarceration or probation) and the length of jail and prison terms. Figure 11.1 reproduces the 2008 Minnesota grid (also called a matrix) for determining sentences under the modified deserts model.[23]

The rows on the grid contain offenses, and the columns represent a score for criminal history. The bold line, called the disposition line, represents the boundary separating presumptive stayed sentences—that is, those cases in which judges suspend prison sentences for the number of months specified in the grid. The numbers above the bold line are the presumptive executed sentences (prison sentences). The numbers in the cells present the range of months judges can sentence offenders to. For example,

FIGURE 11.1

Minnesota Sentencing Guideline Grid

Italicized numbers within the grid denote the range within which a judge may sentence without the sentence being deemed a departure. Offenders with non-imprisonment felony sentences are subject to jail time according to law. Presumptive sentence lengths are in months.

SEVERITY LEVEL OF CONVICTION OFFENSE (Common offenses listed in italics)		CRIMINAL HISTORY SCORE						
		0	1	2	3	4	5	6 or more
Murder, 2nd Degree (intentional murder; drive-by-shootings)	XI	306 *261–367*	326 *278–391*	346 *295–415*	366 *312–439*	386 *329–463*	406 *346–480²*	426 *363–480²*
Murder, 3rd Degree Murder, 2nd Degree (unintentional murder)	X	150 *128–180*	165 *141–198*	180 *153–216*	195 *166–234*	210 *179–252*	225 *192–270*	240 *204–288*
Assault, 1st Degree Controlled Substance Crime, 1st Degree	IX	86 *74–103*	98 *84–117*	110 *94–132*	122 *104–146*	134 *114–160*	146 *125–175*	158 *135–189*
Aggravated Robbery, 1st Degree Controlled Substance Crime, 2nd Degree	VIII	48 *41–57*	58 *50–69*	68 *58–81*	78 *67–93*	88 *75–105*	98 *84–117*	108 *92–129*
Felony DWI	VII	36	42	48	54 *46–64*	60 *51–72*	66 *57–79*	72 *62–84²*
Controlled Substance Crime, 3rd Degree	VI	21	27	33	39 *34–46*	45 *39–54*	51 *44–61*	57 *49–68*
Residential Burglary Simple Robbery	V	18	23	28	33 *29–39*	38 *33–45*	43 *37–51*	48 *41–57*
Nonresidential Burglary	IV	12¹	15	18	21	24 *21–28*	27 *23–32*	30 *26–36*
Theft Crimes (Over $5,000)	III	12¹	13	15	17	19 *17–22*	21 *18–25*	23 *20–27*
Theft Crimes ($5,000 or less) Check Forgery ($251–$2,500)	II	12¹	12¹	13	15	17	19	21 *18–25*
Sale of Simulated Controlled Substance	I	12¹	12¹	12¹	13	15	17	19 *17–22*

☐ Presumptive commitment to state imprisonment. First-degree murder has a mandatory life sentence and is excluded from the guidelines by law. See Guidelines Section **II.E., Mandatory Sentences**, for policy regarding those sentences controlled by law.

☐ Presumptive stayed sentence; at the discretion of the judge, up to a year in jail and/or other non-jail sanctions can be imposed as conditions of probation. However, certain offenses in this section of the grid always carry a presumptive commitment to state prison. See, Guidelines Sections **II.C. Presumptive Sentence** and **II.E. Mandatory Sentences**.

¹ One year and one day

² M.S. § 244.09 requires the Sentencing Guidelines to provide a range for sentences which are presumptive commitment to state imprisonment of 15% lower and 20% higher than the fixed duration displayed, provided that the minimum sentence is not less than one year and one day and the maximum sentence is not more than the statutory maximum. See, Guidelines Sections II.H. Presumptive Sentence Durations that Exceed the Statutory Maximum Sentence and II.I. Sentence Ranges for Presumptive Commitment Offenses in Shaded Areas of Grids.

Effective August 1, 2008

Source: Adapted from Minnesota Sentencing Guidelines Commission, *Minnesota Sentencing Guidelines and Commentary*, revised August 1, 2008, p. 57 (http://www.msgc.state.mn.us/guidelines/guide08.pdf).

a first-time aggravated robbery conviction carries a recommended sentence of 48 months, but the judge can choose any time between 41 and 57 months without formally departing from the guidelines.

Allowing judges to choose within a range without departing from the guidelines builds flexibility into the system, allowing for differences in individual cases. Characteristics like the amount of money stolen, the extent of personal injury inflicted, and the criminal history of the offender can affect the sentence judges impose without undermining the basic goals of uniformity and equity.

THE PRESENTENCE INVESTIGATION

Judges also rely on information about offenders' backgrounds when they make their sentencing decisions. This is certainly true in indeterminate sentencing where judges have broad discretion, but it also applies to fixed sentencing because although mandatory minimum sentencing and guidelines sentencing *reduce* judicial discretion, they do not *eliminate* it. Also (and frequently overlooked), fixed sentences are aimed almost completely at reducing discretion in felony sentencing; that leaves judges with lots of leeway in misdemeanor sentencing. (Remember, misdemeanor cases vastly outnumber felony cases.) So, even in felony cases but much more so in misdemeanor cases, judges do not just automatically apply sentences from statutes and guidelines; they use their discretion.

This leeway in sentencing allows judges to take into account the individual offender. That is where the presentence report comes in to guide judges' discretion in sentencing. The presentence report (PSR), based on a **presentence investigation** (PSI), contains information about the offender's prior criminal record (criminal history), social history, and mental health history and psychiatric evaluation. The first part of the PSR enumerates the facts of the case based on both the police report and the defendant's version of what happened. As you might expect, the police and defendant's versions often conflict. Judges tend to accept the police version.

The second part of the PSR includes the offender's prior criminal record, including prior convictions, dropped charges, and arrests. Social histories include family history, employment record, and education.

DON'T LET DRUG DEALERS CHANGE THE FACE OF YOUR NEIGHBOURHOOD.
Call Crimestoppers anonymously on 0800 555 111.

METROPOLITAN POLICE *Working for a safer London*

Judges' discretion is influenced by a number of factors, such as a defendant's tendency to repeat offenses. When a person becomes addicted to drugs such as methamphetamine (as this repeat offender has), she is more likely to face multiple arrests and prosecutions. As judges observe a persistent refusal to amend criminal behavior, their sentencing may become less and less merciful.

Judges say social histories help them predict the offender's potential for rehabilitation and future behavior. Psychiatric evaluations include the defendant's history of mental illness, hospitalizations, treatment, and recommendations.[24]

The impact of the crime on the victim is typically included in the PSR to help the judge understand the true nature of the crime committed. To learn about the role they play in the development of the PSR, victims in Erie County, Ohio, can access a website that explains the PSR and the role of victim impact statements in the sentencing process.[25]

The quality of information in PSRs can be a problem. Probation officers, who are in charge of presentence investigations and writing the PSRs, have to do these jobs while they are supervising heavy caseloads

Presentence Investigations

What are they? . . . When are they needed? . . . When are they ordered?

When the defendant has appeared in court and pled guilty or no contest to an offense and the Judge feels that there may be a need for more information before the defendant is sentenced, a presentence investigation may be ordered by the Judge.

Who does it?

A presentence investigation is done by the court's adult probation officer (or department).

What happens?

The defendant is given a questionnaire to fill out and is told to make an appointment, and will be interviewed. (Sometimes this can happen immediately.)

From this questionnaire the probation department will review and will verify the information.

Victim Impact Statements

The Victim Impact Statement is an essential part of the presentence investigation, because this helps the Judge, Probation Department, and the Prosecutor to understand how this crime has affected you.

What happens next?

Upon completion of the information gathering and verification process, a sentencing hearing date will be scheduled.

What happens in court?

The information gathered by the Probation Department and the recommendations of that department will be used by the Judge to determine what type of sentence the defendants will receive and whether they will be placed on probation.

Victim's Assistance can be there for you . . .

So you should try to appear in court for the sentencing hearing if at all possible, so the Judge can speak to you in person.

Source: Erie County, Ohio (2008). *Pre-Sentence Investigations.* Retrieved February 2, 2009, from Erie County, Ohio Victim Assistance Services: http://www.erie-county-ohio.net/victim/presentence.htm.

of probationers. Always pressed for time, they often cannot get all the information they need or, equally important, make sure the information they do get is correct.

LO4 The Death Penalty

the most severe form of punishment in the United States is the death penalty. Throughout most of modern history, the American public has stood firmly behind the death penalty. An increasingly exasperated majority of the U.S. Supreme Court has also repeatedly reminded stubborn defense lawyers that the U.S. Constitution does not forbid the death penalty. Nevertheless, despite this strong public support and the clear rulings of the U.S. Supreme Court, the reluctance to actually kill criminals convicted of capital offenses is strong. Furthermore, in recent years support for the death penalty has begun to decline.

As of January 2009, 36 states have a death penalty statute and 14 states do not use the death penalty. The peak in modern-day executions was reached in 1999 with 98 executions. Since that time, executions have declined; only 37 executions were conducted in 2008—the lowest number since 1999. The number of death sentences has also dropped considerably. In 1999, 284 death sentences were imposed, down from 306 in 1998. In 2001, the decline continued with 167 death sentences, and in 2007 there were only 115 death sentences (see Figure 11.2).[26]

Attitudes toward the death penalty have shifted with the mood of the country. During the conservative 1950s, about two-thirds of the people favored it. Then, during the brief interlude of mid-1960s liberalism, support slipped to 42 percent, the lowest in 50 years. The quick return to conservatism in the wake of the 1960s crime boom brought support back to 51 percent in 1969. Support continued to grow from the 1970s to the mid-1990s as the country's tough stand on punishment hardened. In 1994, support for the death penalty reached an all-time high—80 percent.[27]

Since 1994, however, support for the death penalty has begun to falter for a number of reasons. First, DNA testing has driven home the obvious fact that human beings make mistakes, including sentencing innocent people to death. There is also a growing belief that the penalty is not administered fairly; rich people can escape it and poor people cannot. This is especially troubling because so many death penalty defendants are members of racial or ethnic minority groups. At the same time, there is growing doubt among the public that the death penalty prevents murder.

In June 2007, the Death Penalty Information Center conducted a poll that revealed the growing loss of

Seated in his office, New Mexico Governor Bill Richardson (left) signs the repeal on the death penalty bill into law while Representative Gail Chasey looks on.

confidence in the death penalty. Respondents were concerned about the mistakes made in the use of the death penalty and its inability to accomplish its intended effects. More than half of the respondents (58 percent) said they would like a moratorium on the death penalty (see Figure 11.3) while it undergoes extensive review, and 40 percent believed they would not be permitted to serve as jurors in capital cases because of their concerns about the death penalty.[28]

On March 18, 2009, New Mexico Governor Bill Richardson signed a bill abolishing the death penalty in his state. New Mexico became the 15th state to eliminate the death penalty, following New Jersey and New York, which abolished their death penalties in 2007. In New Mexico, the death penalty has been replaced by the punishment of life in prison without the possibility of parole. In defense of his decision, Governor Richardson cited the continuing problem of wrongful conviction, which makes it imperative that the absoluteness of the death penalty be removed from the sentencing process.[29]

Certainly, a major reason for the public's growing doubts

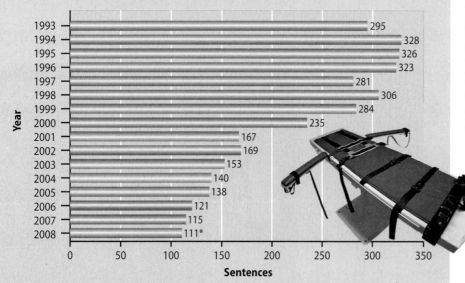

FIGURE 11.2

Number of Death Sentences in the United States 1993–2008

Year	Sentences
1993	295
1994	328
1995	326
1996	323
1997	281
1998	306
1999	284
2000	235
2001	167
2002	169
2003	153
2004	140
2005	138
2006	121
2007	115
2008	111*

*Projected based on DPIC's research.

Source: Adapted from Death Penalty Information Center, *Facts about the Death Penalty*, January 30, 2009, p. 3 (http://www.deathpenaltyinfo.org/FactSheet.pdf).

about the death penalty is the number of death row inmates who have been exonerated—that is, found innocent and released from prison. From 1973 to 1999, an average of 3.1 exonerations occurred per year. From 2000 to 2007, the average increased to 5 exonerations annually. One reason for the rise in exonerations has been the increased use of DNA and the work of the Innocence Project, which was founded by Barry Scheck and Peter Neufeld. According to the Innocence Project's website:

> *the Innocence Project is a national litigation and public policy organization dedicated to exonerating wrongfully convicted people through DNA testing and reforming the criminal justice system to prevent future injustice.*[30]

Wrongful convictions occur for various reasons including eyewitness misidentification, unreliable or limited science, false confessions, forensic science fraud or misconduct, government misconduct, use of informants or snitches, and bad lawyers. The Innocence Project works on convictions where any of these issues may be to blame to determine if the conviction can be overturned. According to the Innocence Project, "there have been 232 post-conviction DNA exonerations in United States history,"[31] of which 17 were exonerations of inmates on death row (see Figure 11.4).

THE DEATH PENALTY AND THE CONSTITUTION

Legal issues have been a major factor in the use of the death penalty. The Eighth Amendment to the U.S. Constitution prohibits "cruel and unusual punishments," but does the death penalty constitute cruel and unusual punishment? Certainly, the death penalty was well established before the Eighth Amendment was adopted and was widely practiced afterward. Nevertheless, the issue of cruel and unusual punishment has been raised at various times over the years, but culminated in 1972 in *Furman v. Georgia*.[32] In that decision, the U.S. Supreme Court set out what would be considered "cruel and unusual punishments." A punishment would be "cruel and unusual" if the punishment outweighed the severity of the crime, if the

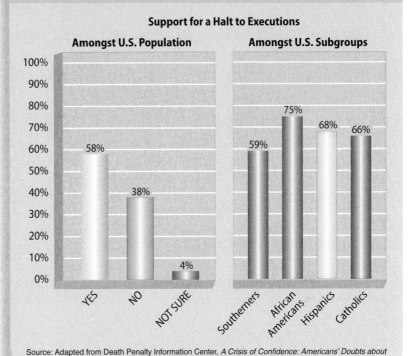

FIGURE 11.3

Support for a Moratorium on the Death Penalty

Support for a Halt to Executions

Amongst U.S. Population: YES 58%, NO 38%, NOT SURE 4%

Amongst U.S. Subgroups: Southerners 59%, African Americans 75%, Hispanics 68%, Catholics 66%

Source: Adapted from Death Penalty Information Center, *A Crisis of Confidence: Americans' Doubts about the Death Penalty*, June 2007, p. 10 (http://www.deathpenaltyinfo.org/CoC.pdf).

punishment was deemed arbitrary, if society's sense of justice was offended, or if a less severe punishment would be just as effective. By a 5-to-4 vote, the Court held that Georgia's death penalty statute was arbitrary because it gave the jury complete sentencing discretion. The decision voided death penalty statutes in 40 states, and inmates on death row at the time had their sentences commuted to life in prison.

To reinstate the death penalty, the states worked to limit jury discretion by creating guided discretion statutes that imposed sentencing guidelines for the judge and jury. These guidelines included aggravating and mitigating factors to be used in determining a sentence. The usual aggravating circumstances include killing someone while committing some other felony, prior convictions for homicide, killing strangers, killing multiple victims, especially cruel killings, and killing law enforcement officers. Typical mitigating circumstances include having no prior criminal history, mental or emotional stress, participation by the victim in the crime, and playing only a minor part in the murder. These statutes were

Willie "O" Pete Williams smiles as he answers a question during a news conference held January 2007 at the office of the Georgia Innocence Project in Atlanta. The Georgia Innocence Project was able to use DNA evidence to free Williams from prison after he spent 21 years behind bars for rape.

© AP Images

approved by the U.S. Supreme Court in 1976 in the *Gregg v. Georgia* case.[33]

This landmark decision held that the new death penalty statutes in Florida, Georgia, and Texas were constitutional under the Eighth Amendment. The death penalty then resumed in those states. The Court also introduced three procedural reforms, which, though not required by the Court, were adopted in some form

by many states. The reforms involved bifurcated capital trials with separate deliberations for guilt and sentencing, automatic appellate review of convictions and sentences, and a proportionality analysis in which a state using the death penalty would search for sentencing disparities with the goal of identifying and eliminating these disparities in the use of the death penalty. The 10-year ban on executions ended in 1977 with the execution of Gary Gilmore in Utah. Lethal injection was adopted the next year in Oklahoma. The first execution by lethal injection was in 1982 in Texas.[34] Additional legal issues that have arisen since that time include the executions of the mentally ill and juveniles.

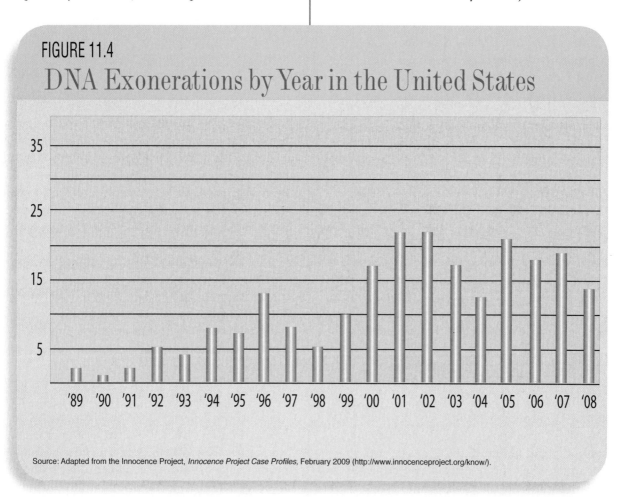

FIGURE 11.4
DNA Exonerations by Year in the United States

Source: Adapted from the Innocence Project, *Innocence Project Case Profiles*, February 2009 (http://www.innocenceproject.org/know/).

Learning Your Way

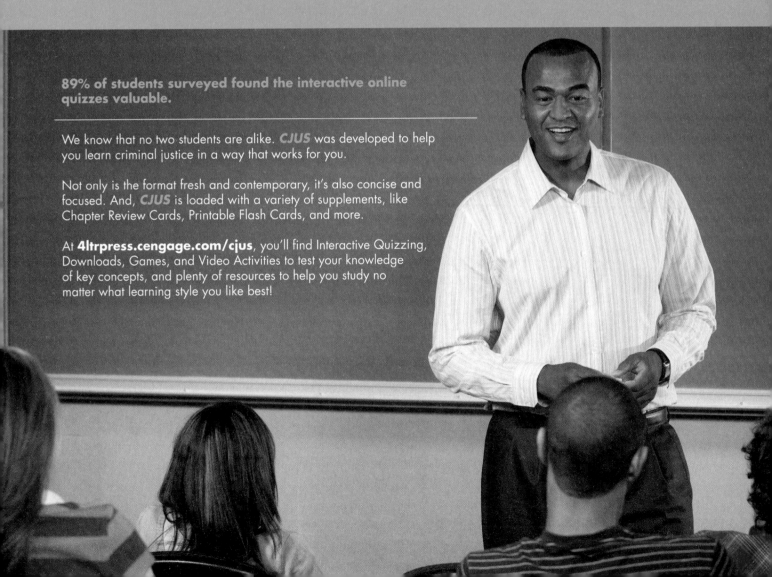

89% of students surveyed found the interactive online quizzes valuable.

We know that no two students are alike. *CJUS* was developed to help you learn criminal justice in a way that works for you.

Not only is the format fresh and contemporary, it's also concise and focused. And, *CJUS* is loaded with a variety of supplements, like Chapter Review Cards, Printable Flash Cards, and more.

At **4ltrpress.cengage.com/cjus**, you'll find Interactive Quizzing, Downloads, Games, and Video Activities to test your knowledge of key concepts, and plenty of resources to help you study no matter what learning style you like best!

All community corrections
have multiple and demanding missions.

12
Community Corrections

© Sandy Jones/iStockphoto.com / © Emrah Turudu/iStockphoto.com

Learning Outcomes

LO1 Understand the community correctional forms of probation and parole

LO2 Understand the missions of community corrections

LO3 Understand how probation and parole evolved

LO4 Explain how community corrections are implemented today

LO5 Be familiar with the legal issues of probation and parole

LO6 Know what is meant by intermediate sanctions and be familiar with the types and how they are administered

Probation, a type of community corrections, is typically the sentence given to first-time offenders and offenders who have committed crimes that do not warrant a prison sentence. Sometimes there is disagreement over whether probation is a severe enough punishment for the crime committed. In early 2009, a New Jersey man was sentenced to one year of probation for serving as an online pimp to a woman operating out of a local veterinary clinic. The man pled guilty to third-degree promoting prostitution and conspiracy to promote prostitution. In addition to the one year of probation, he was also sentenced to 50 hours of community service and a 90-day suspended jail sentence. The man's defense attorney claimed the married father of three was sorry for what he had done and that he had been going through financial difficulties that led him to engage in the crime. Do you agree he should have been sentenced to probation, or should he have received a more severe penalty? In this chapter, we will discuss how probation and parole decisions are made.[1]

Once offenders are convicted, they are sentenced and moved to the final stage of the criminal process—**corrections**. Corrections can take place in prisons and jails (incarceration), in the community (probation and parole), or in a combination of confinement and community supervision

> **corrections** the final stage of the criminal process—incarceration, probation and parole, or intermediate punishments

(intermediate punishments). Incarceration—especially confinement in prisons—gets the lion's share of public attention, tax dollars, and research efforts. But most convicted offenders are not in prison or jail; they are serving their sentences in the community. At the end of 2007, 4,293,163 adult men and women were on probation in the United States, and 824,365 were on parole; meanwhile, some 2.3 million adults were in federal or state prison or jail. Of those sentenced to probation, slightly more than half (51 percent) had committed a misdemeanor, and slightly less than half had committed a felony (47 percent); 3 percent were on probation for other infractions (see Figure 12.1). More people were sentenced to probation for drug crimes than for any other offense.[2]

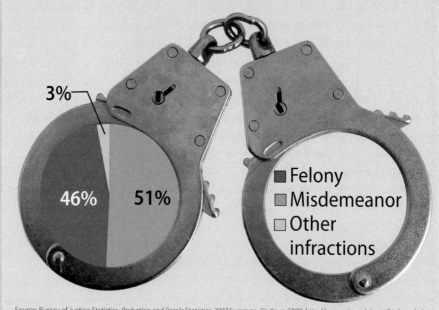

FIGURE 12.1

Offenses for Which Adults Were Sentenced to Probation

3%

46% 51%

■ Felony
■ Misdemeanor
□ Other infractions

© Maxim Lysenko/iStockphoto.com

Source: Bureau of Justice Statistics, *Probation and Parole Statistics: 2007 Summary Findings*, 2008, http://www.ojp.usdoj.gov/bjs/pandp.htm.

LO1 Probation and Parole

many people confuse probation with parole, so let's clear up the confusion before we discuss them:

1. **Probation** is a *substitute* for confinement in prison or jail; **parole** *follows* confinement in prison.

2. Probation is a *sentencing* option for *judges*, who set the conditions of release; parole is a *release* option for *administrators* (parole board), who set the conditions of release.

3. Probation is a local or state decision made in one of the more than 2,000 probation departments; parole is *always* a state decision administered by a single state agency (parole board). Local judges decide whether and under what conditions to put offenders on probation; state parole boards decide whether and under what conditions to release prisoners.[3]

Despite these differences, probation and parole have a lot in common:

1. Both probation and parole involve supervision in the community, *not* in jails and prisons.

2. Both require information to be gathered and presented to decision makers.

3. In both, decision makers have the power to release offenders into the community, to set the conditions of their release, and to revoke their release and order them to confinement.

4. Both include the core missions of holding offenders accountable for their crimes, protecting public safety, and reintegrating offenders into the community—turning them into responsible people who support themselves and obey the law.[4]

In the next several sections, you will learn more about the missions of community corrections; the history of probation and parole; and the granting, conditions, and revocation of probation and parole.

LO2 Community Corrections

a ll community corrections—probation, parole, and intermediate punishments—have multiple and demanding missions: punishing and rehabilitating offenders, protecting public safety, reducing crime, controlling costs, and relieving prison and jail overcrowding. The core missions of all community corrections are to:

1. *Punish*. Hold offenders accountable for their crimes by punishing them.

2. *Protect public safety*. Make sure offenders do not commit new crimes against law-abiding people.

3. *Rehabilitate offenders (reintegration)*. Help offenders by connecting them with resources that turn them into responsible people who support themselves and obey the law.

These missions have changed somewhat over time, however. Let's look briefly at how they have changed.

THE MISSIONS OF PROBATION

Until the end of World War II, the mission of probation was to show leniency to first-time, minor offenders. After the war, doubts that prison was "correcting" offenders led to the adoption of another mission—rehabilitation. Judges started putting repeat and even violent offenders on probation to reform them. But by the 1970s, there was a backlash against probation. The public, fed up with crime and judges who were "soft on criminals," demanded that probation accomplish a third mission—punish offenders and protect the public from "felons on the streets." But there was a problem standing in the way of accomplishing the punish-and-protect mission—paying the high price of exploding prison populations.[5]

Despite worries about its "softness," probation is still the clear punishment of choice, probably because the public is not willing to pay the high costs of confinement. According to Joan Petersilia:

> *When the prison population began to overwhelm existing facilities, probation and "split sentences" (a jail sentence followed by a term on probation) became the de facto disposition of all misdemeanors. As prison overcrowding becomes a national crisis, the courts are being forced to use probation even more frequently. Many felons without criminal records are now sentenced to probation.[6]*

Television host, author, and magazine publisher Martha Stewart (left) leaves federal court with attorney Robert Morvillo after meeting her probation officer on March 8, 2004, in New York City. In 2001, Stewart sold nearly 4,000 shares of ImClone stock after receiving an inside tip that the stock would soon decline in value. In 2003, Stewart was indicted on nine counts, including securities fraud and obstruction of justice, and served five months in a federal prison and five months of house arrest.

THE MISSIONS OF PAROLE

In the 1800s, when prisons became "warehouses for the poor," parole was viewed as a way to relieve prison crowding by making room for new prisoners. So parole was expected to accomplish this goal as well as its original missions of protecting the public and rehabilitating offenders. These missions are sometimes at odds with one another, however. Releasing more prisoners reduces prison populations but also may increase the risk to public safety. Close supervision outside prison might enhance public safety but increases the costs of rehabilitating and reintegrating offenders into the community.

LO3 The Evolution of Probation and Parole

S upervision in the community instead of confinement in prisons and jails is an ancient practice. In England, justices of the peace released minor offenders if they promised "good behavior" and if some

© Stephen Chernin/Getty Images

responsible person agreed to make sure they kept their promise. If they broke it, they were locked up. English settlers brought the idea of the **good behavior bond** to the American colonies.

THE HISTORY OF PROBATION

In the 1840s, John Augustus, a Boston shoemaker, earned the title of "first probation officer" by expanding on the good behavior bond. Augustus visited the Boston police court, where he saw "a ragged and wretched looking man" charged with being a "common drunkard." The man begged Augustus to save him from the House of Correction; "I'll never take another drink if you save me." Deeply moved, Augustus asked the judge to release the man into his custody for 30 days. During that time, Augustus fed the man and found him a job. After that, the man stopped drinking and supported himself.

Encouraged by his success, Augustus gave up shoemaking and devoted the rest of his life to "saving" Boston criminals. Magistrates released 2,000 people into his custody—mostly drunks, prostitutes, juveniles, and gamblers. Augustus treated them all the same; he took them into his home, found them jobs, and inspired them to "purify" their lives. He had great success, probably because of the powerful combination of his devotion to reform and his skill in selecting the right offenders. He threw himself totally into his "calling," and he accepted only "good risks"—first-time, minor offenders who showed promise of success.[7]

A half century later, probation became a favorite of reformers during the great Progressive reform wave of the early 1900s. By 1930, the federal government and 36 states had enacted probation legislation. By 1954, all states were using some form of probation.[8]

THE HISTORY OF PAROLE

Alexander Maconochie, a Scottish geographer and captain in the British Royal Navy, introduced the modern idea of parole in 1840, when he was appointed superintendent of the infamous English penal colonies in Norfolk Island, Australia. Believing prisoners were capable of reform, he developed a plan to prepare them for their eventual return to society. He divided his system into three grades, with each offering more life outside prison. Prisoners could earn promotions through labor, study, and good behavior.

The third grade in Maconochie's system was what we call parole—conditional liberty with a "a ticket of leave." With ticket in hand, prisoners could live outside prison as long as they obeyed the conditions of release attached to the ticket. Violating the rules of release meant returning to prison and starting all over again through the ranks. So conditional liberty, like the grades inside prison, was tied to successfully living according to the rules outside prison walls. Vast improvements in the conditions of confinement were reported, but the British government did not appreciate Maconochie's reforms and replaced him in 1844, after which it is said, prison conditions sank to the low they were in before he took over.[9]

The penologist Zebulon Brockway introduced parole to the United States when he became superintendent of the famous Elmira Reformatory in New York in the 1870s. Brockway was determined to manage prison populations and reform prisoners. To accomplish these missions, he adopted a two-prong strategy: indeterminate sentences and parole releases.[10] Within a short time, parole came to include three elements, all based on the indeterminate sentence:

1. Conditional release from confinement before sentences expire
2. Supervision until sentences expire
3. Revocation for violations of the conditions of the release

All of these remain part of parole today.

On July 23, 2007, recently paroled felons Joshua Komisarjevsky and Steven J. Hayes allegedly entered the Cheshire, Connecticut home of Dr. William Petit and Jennifer Hawke-Petit and tortured the couple and their two daughters for hours before using gasoline to set the house on fire. Komisarjevsky and Hayes were apprehended as they attempted to escape the burning house and were charged with six counts of capital murder and multiple counts of arson, kidnapping, and sexual assault. These brutal crimes led to nationwide skepticism towards the effectiveness of parole and the Connecticut parolee-tracking system in particular.

© AP Images/Claudia Wolf

LO4 Community Corrections Today

s we saw earlier, nearly 4.3 million offenders were on probation at the end of 2007,[11] and more than 800,000 were on parole (see Figure 12.2, which for comparison also shows the population of Connecticut). One in every 45 adults in the United States in 2007 was being supervised on probation or parole.[12] Who decides whether offenders will spend their time behind bars or in the community? Who decides if and when offend-ers already behind bars will return to the community before the end of their sentences? The answer is the probation and parole authorities. Who are these authorities, and what criteria do they use in making their decisions? Let's look at these questions and the answers to them.

> **discretionary release**
>
> parole boards decide the date of prisoners' release and set the conditions of their community supervision until their sentence expires

GRANTING PROBATION

Formally, probation is a criminal sentence imposed by judges. Probationers are in the custody of the state; they are legally accountable to the state and subject to conditions that limit their freedom and privacy. The judge can change the conditions of probation or revoke it altogether if probationers violate the conditions of their release. Informally, the grant of probation involves discretionary decision making to accomplish the missions discussed earlier. Probation is not a suspended sentence (release of convicted offenders without conditions or supervision). The possibility of being locked up is still "hanging over the offenders' heads," because at any time judges can revoke the suspension and send them to jail or prison.[13]

Formally, judges sentence offenders, but behind the sentencing decision is the influence of probation officers. Usually, the judge's formal sentence only approves what the probation officers have recommended in their presentence investigation report. What criteria do probation officers use in making their recommendation? Two will not surprise you—the more serious the offense and the longer the criminal history of the offender, the less the chances of getting probation.[14] Other criteria include employment, education level, financial condition, and marital or equivalent situation. All of these criteria are related to stability while on probation and are linked to successful probation completion.

GRANTING PAROLE

The United States sentences more people to prison and keeps them there longer than any other "major" country in the world. Nevertheless, most prisoners spend less than two years in prison before they are released. They are released in three ways:

1. **Discretionary release.** Parole boards decide the date of release and set the conditions of the offenders' community supervision until their sentences expire.

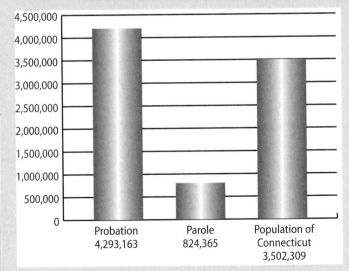

FIGURE 12.2

Number of Offenders Who Were on Probation or Parole at the End of 2007

Probation 4,293,163	Parole 824,365	Population of Connecticut 3,502,309

Source: Bureau of Justice Statistics, *Probation and Parole Statistics: 2007 Summary Findings*, 2008, http://www.ojp.usdoj.gov/bjs/pandp.htm.

Parole Board

mandatory release legislatures and judges set the date of prisoners' release and the conditions of their community supervision until their sentence expires

expiration release prisoners are released unconditionally when their sentence expires

2. **Mandatory release.** Legislatures and judges set the date of release and the conditions of the offenders' community supervision until their sentences expire.

3. **Expiration release.** Prisoners are released unconditionally when their sentences—less good time—expire.

Judges make the final probation decision; in discretionary release, parole boards decide whether to release prisoners. State governors appoint about 10 men and women to sit on the board, which has broad discretionary decision-making power. They review files; interview prisoners; and decide the date, conditions, and, when necessary, the revocation of parole. They can also issue warrants and subpoenas, order the payment of restitution to victims and fees to the state to help pay the costs of supervision, rescind release dates, restore (or continue to deny) prisoners' civil rights, and grant (or deny) final discharges from state custody.[15]

The Texas Board of Pardons and Parole is an example of a parole board with significant power over parolees. The board explains its parole review process, outlined in the box on this page, on its website.

What criteria drive the discretionary decision making of parole boards? An American Paroling Authorities' survey found the major criteria (listed here in order of importance to decision makers) to be:

1. Seriousness of the prisoner's offense
2. History of violence
3. Previous felony convictions

Parole Review Process for the State of Texas

1 A Parole Division case pull list identifies offenders 6 months prior to initial parole eligibility date and subsequent parole review cases are identified 4 months prior to next review date.

2 Notice is sent to trial officials/victims/victims' family.

3 Institutional Parole Office (IPO) interviews offender—prepares parole case summary.

4 Offender's file is sent to affected board office.
- A panel consists of 3 parole panel members.
- 1st voting member reviews/votes case.
- Case transferred to 2nd voting member— reviews/votes case.
- 2 similar votes = final vote on case.
- If the first two votes differ from each other, the 3rd voting member of the panel reviews the case and breaks the tie.
- There must be a majority of two votes for a vote to become final.

5 Offender is notified of the parole panel decision via correspondence.

6 Interviewing the offender is at the discretion of the parole panel member.

7 Granting interviews to individuals in support/ protest of an offender's release is also at the parole panel member's discretion.

8 Parole panel members must grant an interview to victims upon request.[16]

4. Possession of a firearm
5. Previous incarceration
6. Prior parole adjustment
7. Prison disciplinary record
8. Psychological reports
9. Victim input[17]

No surprises here—the ranking follows what you have learned throughout the criminal justice process: the seriousness of the offense and criminal history top the list, followed by criteria indirectly related to crime seriousness and criminal history.

Community service, such as neighborhood restoration, is a common punitive condition of probation.

Parole boards use two methods of decision making in granting parole. In the **case study method**, "the board member, case worker, or parole agency collects as much information as possible, combines it in a unique way, mulls over the results, and reaches a decision."[18] Case studies were the standard method of decision making until attempts to restrict parole boards' discretion led to the adoption of the **risk assessment method**. This method uses information about the seriousness of the crime that offenders are imprisoned for and their criminal history to derive a statistically based prediction.

The idea behind risk assessment is that the more serious the offense and the longer the criminal history, the less the chances parolees will succeed in becoming law-abiding people who can support themselves. By 1994, half of the state parole boards had adopted a risk assessment method.

Supporters say that decision making by risk assessment has several advantages. Predictions are based on legitimate objective criteria—the seriousness of the offense and criminal history. Because the criteria are objective, they are also fair; they prevent decision making from being based on gender, race, and class. Risk assessment also benefits the public because the most dangerous offenders who have committed the worst crimes remain in prison, while offenders who pose the least threat to public safety are released.[19] By identifying offenders who can safely be released, risk assessment also saves money—imprisonment costs more than parole.

THE CONDITIONS OF PROBATION AND PAROLE

Probationers and parolees are not free to do as they please. There are strings attached to their release, because they are offenders who are still under criminal sentences and in state custody. They face three types of conditions (see Figure 12.3):

- *Standard conditions.* Obey the law; do not carry a weapon; do not associate with criminals; report to your probation or parole officer; notify the office if you change your address; work or go to school; support your family; and do not leave the jurisdiction without permission.

- *Punitive conditions* (usually reserved for felony probationers). Pay your fines;

report daily to your probation office; do community service; pay victims back (restitution); do not leave the house (house arrest); and submit to drug tests.

- *Treatment conditions.* Go through a substance abuse program; get family counseling; and go through job training.

Although these conditions are reasonable, they are not necessarily realistic because there are not enough resources to supervise offenders adequately in the community. (See the Standard Conditions of Probation for Texas' Taylor County Court at Law Number 2 on page 167.)

REVOKING PROBATION AND PAROLE

What happens if probationers and parolees violate the conditions of their release? They can be sent to prison to serve the rest of their sentences. Probation and parole are revoked for one of two reasons: **recidivism**, which occurs when the offender is arrested or convicted for a

case study method a professional collects information, combines it in a unique way, mulls over the results, and reaches a decision

risk assessment method a statistical prediction based on the seriousness of the crime offenders are imprisoned for and their criminal history

recidivism falling back or relapsing into prior criminal habits after conviction and punishment, resulting in a new arrest or conviction

PAROLED

© Visions of America/Joe Sohm/Digital Vision/Getty Images

©iStockphoto.com

FIGURE 12.3

United States Probation Office Monthly Supervision Report (MSR)

This Report must be received by your officer between the 1st and 5th day of each month. Officer________________

MONTHLY SUPERVISION REPORT FOR ______________________, 20______

PART A: NAME and RESIDENCE

Name:______________________________ Street Address, Apt #:____________________
Home Phone:(____)________________ City, State, Zip:____________________
Cell/Pager #:(____)________________ Other Mailing Addresses:____________________

Persons living with you (list name and relationship):____________________________

Did you move during the month? Yes [ ] No [ ] (If yes, attach lease/purchase agreement)
List all Websites or E-Mail addresses that you maintain or control directly or indirectly:________________

PART B: EMPLOYMENT (If unemployed, list source of support under Part C)

Name of Company:____________________ Name of Supervisor:____________________
Address:____________________ City, State:____________________
Phone # of Employer:____________________ Position Held:____________________
Work Hours:____________________

Is your employer aware you are on supervision? Yes [ ] No [ ]

Did you change jobs during the month? Yes [ ] No [ ] If yes, when and why?

Did you miss work during the month? Yes [ ] No [ ] Explain: ____________________

PART C: MONTHLY FINANCIAL STATEMENT

MONTHLY INCOME

Net Income from Employment __________
(*attach proof of earnings/paystubs)

Spouse's Income: + __________

Other Income (source): + __________

+ __________

____

TOTAL MONTHLY INCOME: = __________

NECESSARY MONTHLY EXPENSES

Home Mortgage/Rent: __________
Grocery: __________
Utilities: __________
Medical/Insurance: __________
Telephone: __________
Credit Cards: __________
Car Insurance: __________
Transportation/Gas: __________
Child Support: __________
Restitution/Fine/Elec. Monitoring:__________
Other: Explain __________

TOTAL MONTHLY EXPENSES: = __________

Do you have checking/saving(s) account(s)? Yes [ ] No [ ]
If yes, give bank name, account number and balances:
Checking [ ] Savings [ ] ____________________________
Checking [ ] Savings [ ] ____________________________
Does your spouse, significant other, or dependent have a checking/savings account that you enjoy the benefits of or make contributions toward? Yes [ ] No [ ] If yes, give bank name, location and balance:

Did you file bankruptcy during the month? Yes [ ] No [ ]

Source: United States Probation Office, Middle District of North Carolina. http://www.ncmp.uscourts.gov/forms/MSR.pdf.

Standard Conditions of Probation for Texas' Taylor County Court at Law Number 2

1. Commit no offense against the laws of this or any other state, or the United States, or any governmental entity.

2. Avoid injurious or vicious habits of any nature whatsoever, including but not limited to the use of alcohol, narcotics, controlled substances, or harmful drugs, the sniffing of glue or paint, or any chemical compound which might cause intoxication.

3. Avoid persons of disreputable and harmful character. Do not associate with persons of questionable character, persons with criminal records, or past or present inmates of penal institutions.

4. Stay out of bars, lounges, dance halls, honky-tonks, beer joints, pool halls, taverns, and liquor stores.

5. Report to the Adult Supervision Officer of Taylor County, Texas as directed by the Court or Supervision Officer at the Taylor, Callahan, Coleman Counties Community Corrections and Supervision Department, 2nd Floor, Old Taylor County Courthouse, Abilene, Texas, beginning this day and continuing as directed, being not less than once each month. Obey all rules and regulations of the Taylor, Callahan, Coleman Counties Community Corrections and Supervision Department.

6. Immediately notify the Supervision Officer of any change of address, employment, marital status, or arrest not more than three (3) days from change.

7. Permit the Supervision Officer to visit him at home or elsewhere without restriction, reluctance, or delay.

8. Work faithfully at suitable employment as far as possible and support his dependents.

9. Remain within a specified place, to-wit: TAYLOR, CALLAHAN, JONES, AND SHACKELFORD counties of the State of Texas. Do not leave the confines of said counties without written consent of the Supervision Officer and/or this Court.

10. ABSTAIN FROM THE CONSUMPTION OF ALCOHOL in any form at any time.

11. Avoid possession, use, sale, or control of any narcotic drugs or controlled substances, unless taken under a physician's directive.

12. Pay his honest and just debts and not over-extend his credit to a point which may cause his undue hardship.

13. Be home each night not later than 12:00 Midnight and remain there unless his work requires him to be out later.

14. Pay all court costs in the amount of $###, as follows: In three equal payments, due on or before the first day of next month and first day of the next two following months.

15. Pay his fine in the amount of $###, to be paid as follows: In TEN (10) equal payments due and payable on or before the first day of each month.

16. Pay a supervision fee of **$35.00** per month to the Supervision Officer of this Court, on or before the first day of each month hereafter during the term of supervision.

17. If and when so directed, appear before this Court to show cause why your supervision should not be revoked.

18. Submit to testing for alcohol or controlled substances if so directed by the Supervision Officer.

19. Submit to educational testing as required by Code of Criminal Procedure Article 42.12 11(C), and if so directed immediately enroll in the Adult Education Program of the Taylor, Callahan, Coleman Counties Community Corrections and Supervision Department and attend classes on a weekly basis, during the term of supervision, until earning the GED. On proof of enrollment in another educational course this requirement may be waived in writing at the discretion of the Supervision Officer pending proof of continued satisfactory participation in such program.

20. If so directed, the Defendant will voluntarily attend and participate in Alcoholics Anonymous and/or Narcotics Anonymous meetings at least two times weekly and submit proof of attendance to his Supervision Officer.

21. If so directed by your Supervision Officer, submit to testing, provide information, and in all ways comply with the requirements of 81.083 and Chapter 81, Subchapter G, of the Health and Safety Code.

22. The Defendant was under twenty one (21) years of age at the time of the offense. The Defendant's driver's license (and/or the right of the Defendant to drive in the State of Texas) is suspended for a period of one (1) year under the terms of Art. 6687b 24. The Defendant is required to pay a tuition fee as required for Safety Education School conducted either by the Abilene Regional Council on Alcohol and Drug Abuse, Inc. or the Abilene Pro-Driving School (APDS DWI Education Program) and attend all sessions of said school.

23. The Court finds that the Date of the Offense is on or after September 1, 1993, and that no good cause has been shown why Community Service restitution should not be ordered. The Defendant is hereby ordered to complete ## hours of Community Service under the direction of the Supervision Officer.

24. Pay restitution due to any victim in this case.

25. Pay a Crime Stopper's Fee of $10.00 in two equal payments on the first day of the next two calendar months.[20]

new crime, or **technical violations**, which are violations of conditions that are not crimes, such as not notifying a probation or parole officer of a change of address. Judges and parole boards can revoke probation and parole, but they usually do not.21 During 2006, 39 percent of parolees were returned to incarceration for committing a new offense or a technical violation while 18 percent of probationers were incarcerated (see Table 12.1).22

Most parolees and probationers who commit technical violations are not incarcerated. Critics say the gap between technical violations and revocations is just one more example of criminals getting away with breaking the rules and threatening the safety of innocent people. But criminologists like Todd R. Clear and Anthony A. Braga see it differently.23 They say technical violations prove only that probationers and parolees lack discipline, not that they are a threat to public safety—just because a probationer does not tell her probation officer she moved does not mean she is going to commit a crime.

One method of dealing with probation revocations is restricting movement by attaching a GPS monitoring device to the offender. In early 2009, a sex offender who had his probation revoked was fitted with a GPS monitoring device and released back into the community. After only 49 days of GPS monitoring, the offender murdered a 13-year-old girl as she walked through a field known to be popular with transients. Electronic data from the GPS device was used to confirm the offender's confession that he was in the field at the same time the young girl was murdered. It was discovered that the GPS device attached to the offender was not being monitored in real-time, thus failing to restrict his movements. The seemingly more restrictive but actually passive monitoring of the revoked probationer did little to protect public safety.24

LO5 Legal Issues of Probation and Parole

Probationers and parolees are convicted offenders still in state custody. So—according to the U.S. Supreme Court—they have fewer rights than law-abiding people. In the words of the Court, probationers and parolees are subject to "special restrictions" on their rights (*Griffin v. Wisconsin* 1987).25 For example, probation and parole officers do not have to give them *Miranda* warnings (*Minnesota v. Murphy* 1984).26 Also, probationers and parolees have diminished protection against unreasonable searches and seizures (guaranteed by the Fourth Amendment to the U.S. Constitution).

Do not confuse *fewer* rights with *no* rights. One right they still possess is that probation and parole cannot be revoked without due process of law (*Morrissey v. Brewer* 1973).27 Due process guarantees probationers and parolees the right to a hearing where authorities decide (1) whether the probationers or parolees violated the conditions of their release and (2) if they did, whether the violation justifies revocation. Due process also guarantees suspected violators:

1. Written notice of the alleged violations *before* the revocation hearing

2. The right to see and hear the evidence against them

3. The opportunity to be heard in person and to present witnesses and documentary evidence in their favor

4. The right to confront and cross-examine the witnesses against them

5. A hearing panel made up of neutral members

6. A written statement by the hearing panel that includes the evidence relied on and the reasons for revoking probation (*Morrissey v. Brewer* 1973)28

TABLE 12.1 Adults Leaving Probation and Parole in 2006

	SUCCESSFUL	RETURNED TO INCARCERATION	ABSCONDED	OTHER UNSUCCESSFUL	DEATH	UNKNOWN
Probation	57%	18	4	12	1	8*
Parole	44%	39	11	2	1	3

*Includes 2 unaccounted for in source.

Source: Lauren E. Glaze and Thomas P. Bonczar, *Probation and Parole in the United States, 2006* (Washington, DC: Bureau of Justice Statistics, 2007).

© Photodisc/Getty Images

LO6 Intermediate Sanctions

for most of the twentieth century, convicted offenders were either locked up or put on probation. This **either/or corrections** (also called **in-or-out corrections**) policy ignored the reality that imprisonment is too harsh for a lot of criminal behavior and that, for some offenders, probation is too lenient. In other words, probation and confinement were not accomplishing their mission of doing justice—fitting the punishment to the crime and tailoring the penalty to suit the offender. **Intermediate punishments**, which are harsher than probation but milder than imprisonment, allow us to accomplish the mission of justice.[29]

Justice is not the only mission that intermediate sanctions are supposed to accomplish. Proponents have "sold" them to legislators and the public on the claims that the sanctions can reduce prison crowding, protect the public, and punish and rehabilitate offenders—all while saving tax dollars. But intermediate sanctions cannot completely accomplish all these far-reaching missions; they are not a panacea.[30]

either/or corrections (in-or-out corrections) convicted offenders are either locked up or put on probation

intermediate punishments harsher than probation but milder than imprisonment, they allow us to accomplish the mission of justice

intensive supervised probation a more intensive version of traditional probation

THE TYPES OF INTERMEDIATE PUNISHMENTS

Now, let's look at several intermediate punishments (see Table 12.2) that local, state, and federal governments adopted during the 1980s and 1990s:

- Intensive supervised probation (ISP)
- Home confinement (often called house arrest or home detention)
- Correctional boot camps (shock incarceration)
- Fines
- Community service
- Day reporting centers

Intensive Supervised Probation (ISP)

Crowded prisons, budget crunches, and the perceived threat to public safety led to the adoption of **intensive supervised probation** (ISP). Intensive supervised probation is a tougher version of traditional probation in several respects. Most programs include the following ingredients:

- Daily contact with probation officers
- Frequent alcohol and other drug testing
- Unannounced visits by probation officers

© Eliza Snow/iStockphoto.com

TABLE 12.2 Intermediate Punishments

TYPE	CHARACTERISTICS	GOALS	EMPIRICAL EVALUATION
Intensive Supervision	Frequent contacts (e.g., daily) Less privacy and freedom (e.g., unannounced officer visits, drug testing) Have to work, go to school, and/or get treatment	Protect public safety Punish Reduce prison crowding Save money Rehabilitation	More technical violations Little or no effect on arrest rates Little or no effect on the kinds of crimes arrested for Punished appropriately, fulfilling the justice mission*
Home Confinement/ Electronic Monitoring	24/7 surveillance Ankle monitor	Confine without imprisonment Maintain family ties and employment Save money Public safety	Reduce costs Participants found or kept employment Participants supported their families Younger participants failed more frequently than older participants No reduction in jail population Technical problems with equipment
Correctional Boot Camps	Strict discipline Physical training Drill and ceremony Military atmosphere Physical labor Punishment for minor violations	Deterrence Punishment	Deterrence? Mixed empirical results Succeed in punishing offenders
Fines	Money punishment	Pay debt to victim (restitution) Punishment Deterrence	Mixed empirical results
Community Service	Order to work on public property (e.g., clean parks, sweep streets, clean jails)	Punishment Help community Restitution Rehabilitation	Not enough evaluations to comment

© AP Images Photo/Jimmy May

*See Petersilia, J., Turner, S., & Deschennes, P. "Intensive Supervision Programs for Drug Offenders," in J. M. Byrne, A. J. Lurigio, & J. Petersilia, *Smart Sentencing* (Newbury Park, CA: Sage, 1992), p. 19.

- Intolerance of even minor violations of the conditions of probation

Intensive supervised probation has several ambitious visible missions:

- Reducing prison crowding
- Increasing community protection
- Rehabilitating offenders
- Proving that probation can work and that probation is punishment
- Saving money

It also has some hidden missions:

- *Institutional.* Probation has an image problem; it is often regarded as a "slap on the wrist." ISP claims to be "tough" on criminals and promises to protect the community.
- *Professional.* ISP is supposed to generate more money for probation departments so that probation officers can make a difference in probationers' lives.
- *Political.* ISP allows probation departments to get in tune with the public's "get tough on crime and criminals" attitude. This harmony with the public makes probation—and probation budgets—more salable to the public.[31]

Home Confinement: Electronic Monitoring

Home confinement—sentencing offenders to remain in their homes—became popular with advocates of intermediate punishments during the 1980s and continues to be used today. Electronic monitoring systems are used to maintain observation of the offender while on home confinement.[32] Most people sentenced to home confinement have committed misdemeanors such as DWI.

The benefits of home confinement include:

- Reducing the stigma of incarceration while still punishing offenders
  - Maintaining family ties and occupational roles that improve chances for rehabilitation
  - Saving money from reduced jail and prison maintenance and construction costs and from payments by offenders
- Protecting the public by keeping offenders "off the street"
- Satisfying the demand for punishment

Some critics of home confinement claim that it violates the right to privacy and the rights against self-incrimination, unreasonable search and seizure, and cruel and unusual punishment. But since 1929, the U.S.

In February 2009, imprisoned NFL quarterback Michael Vick was approved to be released to home confinement for the last two months of his 23-month sentence. Vick pled guilty to bankrolling a dog fighting operation out of his home. He was set to be released to a halfway house, but due to lack of bed space, home confinement with electronic monitoring was ordered.[33]

Supreme Court has ruled that there is no constitutional ban on electronic surveillance. This is especially true under the doctrine that convicted offenders enjoy only diminished constitutional rights.

Correctional Boot Camps

Correctional boot camps (a form of shock incarceration) provide an alternative to prison for young, first-time, nonviolent offenders, particularly drug offenders. They are based on the assumption that they deter and rehabilitate offenders more effectively than prisons. Boot camps are modeled on basic training in the military. Like other intermediate punishments, correctional boot camps are a response to the combined influences of prison crowding, the demand for more severe punishment, and budgetary restraints.[34]

Correctional boot camps have a number of features in common with military boot camps:

- Strict discipline
- Physical training
- Drill and ceremony
- Military bearing and courage
- Physical labor
- Summary punishment for minor misconduct

Fines

There are many positive ways in which fines serve as an appropriate criminal punishment. They are clearly aimed at both retribution and deterrence. They emphasize accountability by requiring offenders to pay their "debt to society" literally, in the form of money. All these aims are consistent with current sentencing policies.[35]

Fines also fulfill the aims of fairness and proportionality in punishment by allowing the size of the debt to society to be adjusted to the seriousness of the offenses

community service intermediate punishment that orders offenders "to work without pay at projects that benefit the public"

in our criminal law. The flexibility of monetary penalties also allows for the adjustment of the fine to the ability of the offenders to pay. Moreover, fines are already a current sentencing option in all American courts, whether large or small, urban or rural. Finally, and far from least important, fines generate revenue.[36]

Why haven't fines figured prominently in the repertoire of intermediate punishments? Some of the reasons are that they have no effect on wealthy offenders, they are unfair to poor offenders, and poor offenders cannot (or do not) pay them.[37] Lower criminal courts have always been the primary users of fines.

In June 2008, Fairfax County, Virginia, announced that its Code Enforcement Strike Team prosecuted an illegal boarding house owner, a trial that resulted in the largest amount of fines ever levied against such a criminal: more than $23,000 in fines was assessed against the boarding house owner. The man was convicted of violating zoning, building, and fire safety codes. In their first year of operation, the Fairfax County strike teams prosecuted 132 civil and criminal cases.[38]

Community Service

Sentences of **community service** order offenders "to work without pay at projects that . . . benefit the public or . . . public charities."[39] These sentences hark back to two ancient practices: restitution and hard labor.

Restitution is paying back victims for the injuries and other losses caused by offenders. Community service has several underlying purposes that have varied over time. During the 1970s, community service was acclaimed as a mechanism to serve a variety of utili-

In 2006, supermodel Naomi Campbell was charged with second-degree felony assault after hitting her housekeeper in the head with a jewel-encrusted mobile phone. Campbell pleaded guilty in January 2007 to a reduced count of reckless assault and was sentenced to five days of community service. Following a 2008 quarrel in a British airport, Campbell pleaded guilty to four charges, including two counts of assaulting a police constable, and was sentenced to 200 more hours of community service.

tarian purposes. It was touted as a form of restitution; instead of paying back individual victims, however, community service paid back the entire community. Furthermore, community service was supposed to rehabilitate offenders. Reformers hoped that by working beside law-abiding people, offenders would develop a sense of responsibility.

These justifications began to sound outdated in the atmosphere of the tougher attitudes toward crime and criminals that began in the 1970s. The philosophy of "just deserts" replaced utilitarian aims such as rehabilitation. Community service came to be seen mainly as a way to punish criminals who deserve intermediate punishment; that is, they deserve to suffer more than ordinary probationers but not as much as offenders in jails and prisons.[40]

Day Reporting Centers

A handful of states have introduced day reporting centers as an intermediate punishment.[41] **Day reporting centers** can reduce jail and prison crowding by requiring offenders to report every day instead of confining them. Day reporting centers "combine high levels of surveillance and extensive services, treatments, or activities." Their clients include:

1. Defendants denied bail before conviction
2. Prisoners released conditionally from prison
3. Offenders sentenced to day reporting instead of confinement in jails

THE EFFECTIVENESS OF INTERMEDIATE PUNISHMENTS

Intermediate punishments, especially those that seem to be really punishing offenders instead of coddling them—like correctional boot camps—are enormously popular with the public. But do they punish offenders? Do they deter crime? Do they rehabilitate offenders? Do they pro-

Weusi Olusola performs in 2003 during the Pioneers for Peace violence prevention rally at Belle Isle in Detroit, Michigan. Olusola, a former gang member, was shot and permanently paralyzed in 1986 when he was 16.

tect the public? There is a substantial amount of research (and mixed results) on the effectiveness of intermediate punishment programs, but we can boil it down into four findings researchers agree on:

> **day reporting centers**
> intermediate punishment that "combines high levels of surveillance and extensive services, treatments, or activities"

1. *Intermediate punishments add tougher conditions to probation; they do not just divert offenders from prison.* This is good if the tougher conditions are added to offenders on probation who deserve harsher penalties and do not let serious prisoners out of prison. But it is not good if it results in what we call *net widening*, meaning that harsher penalties are applied to offenders who need only ordinary supervision while intermediate punishments are denied to prisoners whose crimes and history merits them. Unfortunately, net widening is a problem in most intermediate punishment programs. So intermediate punishments have not reduced prison populations.[42]

2. *Intermediate punishments do justice by implementing a graduated punishment system.* Policy makers, judges, corrections personnel, and the public strongly support intermediate punishment for nonviolent offenders, especially first-time offenders. Offenders see intermediate punishments as tougher than being locked up, especially if they have to work and get regular drug tests.[43]

3. *Intermediate punishments can be cost-effective.* Intermediate punishments are cost-effective if they are managed well, are directed at nonviolent offenders, and are not net widening.[44]

4. *Most intermediate punishment programs fail.* According to Michael Tonry and Mary Lynch, "There is no free lunch. The failure of most intermediate sanctions to achieve promised reductions in recidivism, cost, and prison use is not surprising. Expectations for the programs were never realistic. . . . Intermediate sanctions can reduce costs and divert offenders from imprisonment, but those results are not easy to obtain."[45]

The dominant missions of prisons

are retribution, incapacitation, and general deterrence.

13
Prisons, Jails, and Prisoners

© AP Images

How would you define a "humane" prison? Can a prison be humane and still deprive inmates of certain freedoms? An examination of how the Abu Ghraib prison in Iraq has changed over time may help us understand what "humane" means in regard to prison life. In 2009, officials in Iraq made the claim that Abu Ghraib prison was "now a humane prison." This statement is a result of the democratic Iraqi government taking control of the prison after years of operation by the now executed dictator Saddam Hussein, followed by control of the prison by U.S. troops after the Iraqi invasion. Under Hussein, prisoners were tortured, abused, and executed without trial. In 2004, abuse by U.S. troops was reported. The Brigadier General in charge of the prison was demoted to colonel over the scandal, other soldiers were sanctioned, and Defense Secretary Donald Rumsfeld made the statement that "the day the scandal broke was the worst in his tenure as defense secretary."

In 2009, under the public relations campaign of the Ministry of Justice, improved conditions have been reported at the prison. Abu Ghraib is now called Baghdad Central Prison, and it has water fountains, a new garden, and a gym with weights and the jerseys of sports teams on the walls. Rooms have been remodeled and renovated to reduce overcrowding and assist security. A wing of the prison under Hussein's control housed over 3,000 inmates. Today that same section of the prison houses 160 inmates.[1]

Here are some highlights about imprisonment in the United States.

Learning Outcomes

LO1 Contrast the penitentiary theories of the 1800s and understand the models of corrections that have predominated since the 1940s

LO2 Discuss the increase in prison populations after 1975 and the factors that have caused that increase

LO3 Classify the different types of federal and state penal institutions

LO4 Understand the role of corrections officers in a prison

LO5 Indicate the difference between traditional jails and new-generation jails

LO6 Understand the major characteristics of prisoners

© iStockphoto.com

- The prison population grew by 1.8 percent during 2007, a slower rate of growth than the 2 percent experienced from 2000 to 2006.

- The rate of growth in prison admissions and releases also slowed in 2007.

- Growth in admissions in 2007 slowed in states with the largest prison populations.

- One out of every 198 U.S. residents was serving a prison sentence in 2007.

- The imprisonment of black offenders has decreased since 2000.

- Black males age 30 to 34 have a higher incarceration rate than any other racial, age, or gender group.

- The total number of inmates at the end of 2007 was nearly 2.3 million (see Table 13.1).

- Non-U.S citizens in state custody increased during 2007.[2]

Now that you've had a brief look at the highlights, let's examine prisons, jails, and prisoners in more depth.

LO1 Prisons in the United States

Prisons are ancient, but until 1700, they were not used for punishment; instead, they confined suspects and defendants to make sure they showed up in court. Prisons were not used for punishment throughout most of North American colonial history either. Capital punishment was an option but was used infrequently. Occasionally, early American judges sentenced offenders to whipping or mutilation, including cropping their ears or slitting their nostrils. Judges also used public shaming—stocks, ducking stools, pillories, dunce caps, or signs such as "I'm a fornicator" and the like. The punishments of choice were fines and restitution.[3] Not until the late eighteenth century did confinement begin to be used as a punishment.

TABLE 13.1 Inmates in Custody in State or Federal Prisons or in Local Jails, 2000–2007		
NUMBER OF INMATES		
2000	2006	2007
1,937,482	2,258,983	2,293,157

Source: Heather C. West and William J. Sabol, *Prisoners in 2007* (Washington, DC: Bureau of Justice Statistics, December 2008), Table 8, p. 6.

© Maria Toutoudaki/iStockphoto.com / © Prints & Photographs Division, Library of Congress, LC-DIG-ggbain-31930

Let's look at the origins of the penitentiary, the correctional institution, and finally, modern-day prisons.

THE PENITENTIARY, 1785–1890

During the period from 1785 to 1890, Massachusetts, Pennsylvania, and New York each contributed to the development of what was known as the *penitentiary*.

The Massachusetts System

Massachusetts was the first state to use prisons to punish convicted offenders. In 1785, the state passed a law allowing judges to sentence offenders to long-term confinement instead of the older punishments. The law named the Castle Island fortress, built to guard Boston Harbor, as the nation's first prison. According to the law, prisoners were sentenced to hard labor because being idle was thought to lead to deviant behavior. Hard labor would reform those who needed activity to occupy their time. Convicts were ruled by a competent staff, including a doctor and a chaplain, and subjected to military discipline and strict dietary and sanitary conditions. Isolation from society and hard work were supposed to redeem their souls, reform their bodies, and instill in them the habits of law-abiding citizens. Armed with these, they would be ready, willing, and able to pay their way and stay out of trouble.[4]

The Pennsylvania System

The Pennsylvania Quakers soon stole the limelight from Massachusetts as prison innovators. The Quakers believed that inflicting pain for the sake of retribution was barbaric and cruel. To reclaim "fallen" citizens, the Quakers designed the Walnut Street Jail in Philadelphia.

The jail was completed in 1790, followed by the Western Penitentiary in 1826 and the Eastern Penitentiary in 1830.

The Walnut Street Jail was the first penitentiary in the world. The basic idea of the **penitentiary** was to isolate offenders in their cells. In solitary confinement, they could think about what they did wrong and how they would make it right by living useful lives when they went back into the world. To encourage prisoners to think, they were not allowed to talk. But they were required to work—alone in their cells, making nails and cutting stones. They received adequate food, shelter, clothing, bedding, and medical care for free. This was a major reform because previously prisoners had to pay for their keep in money. Thus, in the *Pennsylvania system*, prisoners spent all day—every day—in silent, solitary confinement, either working or meditating on their misdeeds.[5]

The Auburn System

In 1817, New York built its own version of the penitentiary based entirely on solitary confinement in small cells and a strict rule of silence. But since so many prisoners committed suicide or had mental breakdowns due to being locked up in tiny cells with nowhere to go and nothing to do, authorities modified the system. Under the *Auburn system* or *congregate system*, prisoners worked in silent groups during the day and meditated and slept in solitary confinement at night. Anyone who broke the rules was whipped on the spot.[6]

Except for working together versus working alone, the Auburn and Pennsylvania penitentiary systems were alike. Prisons were separate worlds of huge, walled fortresses where breaking the rules of silence and work spelled instant, hard punishment and wardens ruled with absolute power. Both systems were considered humane—and they were, compared with capital punishment, mutilation, and whipping. Once the prisoners were reformed, the penitentiary would send them back into the free world as people who worked for a living and obeyed the law instead of preying on others to survive.

Most observers quickly noticed, however, that penitentiaries were not accomplishing their mission of reforming prisoners. They also discovered that reforming prisoners was not the penitentiaries' only—perhaps not even their primary—mission. If prisons were not penitentiaries, then what were they? They were custodial warehouses for criminals where, despite the honest reform efforts and humanitarian rhetoric, the keepers were sometimes extremely cruel.

THE "CORRECTIONAL" INSTITUTION, 1891–1970

The Progressive reformers attacked penitentiaries as cruel and barbaric, just as the creators of the penitentiary had attacked capital, corporal, and mutilation punishments as cruel and barbaric. The Progressives' mission was to reform or rehabilitate offenders into law-abiding people who worked to support themselves. Their strategy was to combine the tactics of humane treatment, counseling, vocational training, and discipline into a coherent, scientifically sound program in **correctional institutions**.

The Progressives led a successful campaign to establish the indeterminate sentence and the pillars of community corrections, probation, and parole. According to the Progressives, if they were going to accomplish their mission, they had to first rid criminal justice of rigid formal decision making by legislators, lawyers, and judges. Next, they had to arm experts in the new

penitentiary places of confinement to remove offenders from a corrupting environment and make them work, isolating them in cells

correctional institution places of confinement to reform offenders into law-abiding people who work to support themselves through a coherent, scientifically sound program

Rehabilitative prison programs, such as the training of guide dogs, are a staple of the Progressives' reformative process.

© AP Images/Charlie Riedel

social and medical sciences with discretionary decision-making power to "diagnose," "treat," and "cure" offenders, who were "sick" with the "disease" of criminal behavior. According to this **medical model of corrections**, decisions about whether to send offenders to prison in the first place, what kind of prison to send them to and when to release them conditionally and then finally from state custody should depend on their rehabilitation, not on their past crimes.[7]

By the 1940s, the correctional institution, which was based on the mission of rehabilitation, had replaced the penitentiary. In principle, correctional institutions were more humane and accommodating than penitentiaries. They provided softer discipline; more yard and recreational privileges; more liberal visitation and mail policies; more amenities, such as movies; and more programs, including education, vocational training, and therapy.[8]

During the 1960s, politicians dragged the issue of correctional institutions into politics. Both conservatives and liberals attacked them—sometimes ferociously.[9] Liberals attacked correctional institutions because they put prisoners' needs over their rights. According to liberals, prison treatment programs were unjustified invasions of prisoners' privacy and autonomy. They also attacked the broad discretionary decision making of probation, parole, and prison officials as badly infected with individual, ethnic, racial, gender, and class discrimination. Conservatives attacked correctional institutions as "soft on crime," describing them as "country clubs" where prisoners were freeloading on hardworking, honest people's money. With prisons like these, conservatives asked, how can we expect them to deter criminals and send a message to criminal wannabes that crime does not pay?

Academics joined the chorus of criticism by claiming that indeterminate sentences for the purpose of rehabilitation did not work and that it was time to do something about it. Liberals and conservatives could agree with that. So could a frightened, frustrated, and angry public, as the 1960s witnessed a wave of prison riots, a huge crime boom, and high rates of recidivism.

The agreement ended there. What to do became a heated controversy. Liberals wanted fewer people locked up, and they wanted those who were to stay behind bars for a short, fixed time. Further, liberals wanted prisoners' lives in confinement to be enriched with programs that would improve their chances of returning to productive and law-abiding lives outside prison. They called this process reintegration. Conservatives wanted long, fixed sentences under conditions that would punish offenders for their crimes (retribution), keep them from committing crimes (incapacitation or special/specific deterrence), and be so unpleasant that prisoners would never want to come back (general deterrence).

PRISONS, 1971–PRESENT

The debate over prisons was hot and loud and political, but the future was with the conservatives. By the end of the 1970s, the dominant missions of prisons had become retribution, incapacitation, and general deterrence. Rehabilitation was still around but more as an incidental aspect than a central mission.[10]

The conservative victory accompanied four major changes in U.S. prisons:

1. Massive growth in prison populations
2. Heavy reliance on prison time for drug offenses
3. Increasing proportions of black and Hispanic prisoners
4. Rising power and influence of prison gangs

LO2 Prison Populations since 1975

After 50 years (1925–1975) of stable prison populations, the United States experienced an enormous prison population boom that started in 1975 and continues at a slightly slower pace today (see Table 13.2, which shows how stable the prison population has been since 2000). It is easy to track the increase in prison populations after 1975. It is quite another matter to explain this increase. In the explanations that follow, keep in mind that the experts agree on one thing: policy makers decided to increase prison populations; it did not just happen. So the question we want to answer is, "Why did they decide to increase the prison population?" To find some answers, let's look at the public's response to the crime boom, the role of political opportunism in the change, the impact of the "war" on drugs, and the effects of a more efficient law enforcement system.

TABLE 13.2 Number of Sentenced Prisoners Admitted and Released from State or Federal Prisons, 2000–2006

YEAR	ADMISSIONS			RELEASES		
	TOTAL	FEDERAL	STATE	TOTAL	FEDERAL	STATE
2000	625,219	43,732	581,487	604,858	35,259	569,599
2001	638,978	45,140	593,838	628,626	38,370	590,256
2002	661,082	48,144	612,938	630,176	42,339	587,837
2003	686,437	52,288	634,149	656,384	44,199	612,185
2004	699,812	52,982	646,830	672,202	46,624	625,578
2005	733,009	56,057	676,952	698,459	47,981	650,478
2006	749,798	57,495	692,303	713,473	47,920	665,553
Average annual change, 2000–2006	3.1%	4.7%	2.9%	2.8%	5.2%	2.6%
Percent change, 2005–2006	2.3%	2.6%	2.3%	2.1%	−0.1%	2.3%

Source: William J. Sabol and Heather Couture, *Prison Inmates at Midyear 2007* (Washington, DC: Bureau of Justice Statistics, June 2008), Table 4, p. 4.

PUBLIC RESPONSE TO THE CRIME BOOM

The most common explanation for the imprisonment boom that began in the 1970s is the crime boom that began in the 1960s. The public's reaction to the crime boom—"get tough on crime" by locking up criminals—was a combination of society's natural moral outrage and a rational desire to control crime.[11] Legislatures' and criminal justice agencies' decisions to "get tough" by locking up criminals followed.

Still, rising crime rates are only *part* of the explanation for the prison population boom.[12] We had other crime booms in the twentieth century—Prohibition in the 1920s and 1930s and drug offenses during the 1950s—and the public demanded a "lock 'em up" response then, too. But none of those crime booms produced explosions in prison populations. Significantly, the prison population boom and public support for it lasted right through the high-crime plateau of the 1980s and the crime bust of the 1990s.

POLITICAL OPPORTUNISM

To conflict theorists, another group of social scientists and penal experts with a distinguished history, morality may have driven the community's demand for punish-ment, but the decision by legislatures and criminal justice agencies to increase prison populations was motivated by political opportunism. Politicians preyed on public outrage and fear in order to win votes. But there is more to the story of the decision making behind the prison population boom than political opportunism and community demands to control crime.

THE "WAR" ON DRUGS

Another element in the story was the decision to fight still another war on drugs.[13] Getting tough on crime can raise prison populations only if there are available offenders to lock up. Most murderers, rapists, robbers, burglars, and thieves are not available to keep the population boom growing. Why not? The worst criminals are already caught, locked up, or executed, leaving only a few roaming around uncaught, on probation, parole, or furlough. So that left drug offenders to keep the prison populations growing—and they did.[14] Also, legislatures lengthened sentences for violent offenses, and keeping violent offenders locked up longer also contributed to the prison population growth.[15]

When crack cocaine and the violence associated with it spread in the 1980s, legislatures responded by passing mandatory sentencing laws that created new drug crimes with stiff prison sentences and lengthened the sentences of drug laws already on the books. As a result of the tougher drug laws, every large city came to have such a large pool of potential prisoners that law enforcement officers could arrest as many as they had the time and resources to pursue. The same was definitely not true of violent and property crimes.

Glass pipes like this one are used to smoke crack cocaine.

© Karen Mower/iStockphoto.com

IMPROVED CRIMINAL JUSTICE SYSTEM EFFICIENCY

In 1960, state criminal justice agencies were inefficient offices run in highly personal ways by highly independent officials. By the 1980s, these same agencies had become modernized bureaucracies that could respond faster to public demand and political pressures. At the same time, the mission of criminal justice agencies was shifting from changing offenders into law-abiding citizens to controlling what was increasingly believed to be a permanent criminal class. So the efficient, modern agencies could respond quickly to the public demand to control crime by locking up criminals.[16]

All criminal justice agencies—police, prosecution, defense lawyers, courts, and corrections—formed a rapid response team to satisfy public demand and political pressure for more incarceration. Police could make more arrests and make them stick because they were more efficient and knew the law better than they did in 1960.[17] The members of the courtroom work group were more efficient too, and could process greater numbers of defendants into offenders. Furthermore, judges could no longer use their discretionary sentencing power to put the brakes on the new efficiency in locking up more people. Just the opposite was true: Mandatory sentencing laws and sentencing guidelines had put the brakes on judges by restricting their discretion to sentence.

LO3 Penal Institutions

1ocking up offenders is expensive. In 2005, the average annual cost was more than $22,000 per offender.[18] Figure 13.1 shows how the Florida Department of Corrections allocated the $19,308 it spent per inmate in 2008. Nearly 60 percent was spent

on security and just over 20 percent on medical services; the remainder was spent on feeding, clothing, and educating inmates, as well as some administrative costs. Of course, costs vary considerably by the type of prison; the higher the security classification of the prison, the higher the cost. To better understand the issues surrounding prisons, we will look at the various prison security levels, women's prisons, and private prisons.

PRISON SECURITY LEVELS

There are many types of prisons in the United States. We will concentrate on three—maximum security, medium security, and minimum security. Security is the first mission of all prisons and is the dominant criterion for building prisons and managing prisoners. Security against what? Three things: escape, harm to staff and other prisoners, and smuggling contraband into the prison.

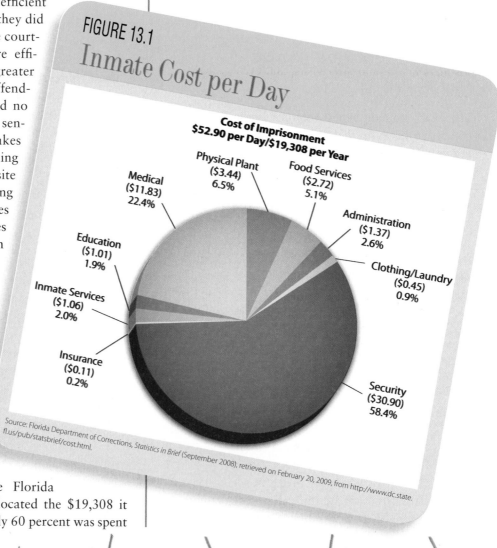

FIGURE 13.1
Inmate Cost per Day

**Cost of Imprisonment
$52.90 per Day/$19,308 per Year**

- Medical ($11.83) 22.4%
- Physical Plant ($3.44) 6.5%
- Food Services ($2.72) 5.1%
- Administration ($1.37) 2.6%
- Clothing/Laundry ($0.45) 0.9%
- Education ($1.01) 1.9%
- Inmate Services ($1.06) 2.0%
- Insurance ($0.11) 0.2%
- Security ($30.90) 58.4%

Source: Florida Department of Corrections, *Statistics in Brief* (September 2008), retrieved on February 20, 2009, from http://www.dc.state.fl.us/pub/statsbrief/cost.html.

Maximum Security Prisons

Maximum security prisons focus almost exclusively on the three goals of security—preventing prisoners from escaping, keeping them from hurting the staff or one another, and keeping out contraband. Maximum security prisons can be traditional facilities, supermaxes, or new-generation facilities. In 2005, 20 percent of all correctional facilities were maximum security prisons.[19]

Traditional Facilities Traditional maximum security prisons are like fortresses, surrounded by thick, high walls or fences topped by electrified barbed or razor wire. Armed guards in fortified towers watch the walls at all times, using searchlights and even electronic devices to prevent prisoner escapes. Inside maximum security prisons, supervision, surveillance, and control are extensive. Prisoners are moved only in groups under close guard by officers.

In older maximum security prisons, large cell blocks arranged in tiers permit a single guard to observe hundreds of cells at one time. Bars replace doors and windows. Television surveillance makes it easier to watch prisoners, not only in their cells but also in the shower, at meals, and even in the toilet. Officers may strip-search prisoners before and after visits, and even visitors are subject to pat-downs. Officers also take "head counts" throughout the day; anyone not accounted for prompts major efforts to locate the "missing" prisoner. Metal furniture built into the walls and floors improves security by preventing chairs and tables from being used as obstacles and weapons. Scraping, clashing, and echoing metal causes high noise levels. It is an understatement to say that prisons are not quiet places.

Supermaximum Facilities Sometimes we build whole prisons for "the worst of the worst." These special prisons are called **supermaximum security prisons**, or **supermaxes**. The primary purpose of a supermax prison is to isolate and control inmates to prevent disciplinary problems of extreme proportion, such as riots and violence.[20] The legendary Alcatraz, a federal prison built in 1934 on an island in San Francisco Bay, was the first supermax prison, although it was not called that. Until 1963 when it closed, Alcatraz housed the nation's most notorious criminals, "most sophisticated prison escape artists," prison riot leaders, and most violent prisoners. The prison was based on the philosophy of "lock 'em up and throw away the key." (See page 182 for An Example of an Alcatraz Inmate's Daily Schedule.)

Alcatraz introduced the *concentration model* of managing prisoners who most threaten prison security and safety. The model assumes it is easier to manage troublemakers if they are completely removed from the general prison population.[21] When Alcatraz was closed in 1963, rehabilitation was still the dominant penal policy, and the *dispersion model* of handling troublesome prisoners had come into favor. Following this model, authorities spread the Alcatraz prisoners around the country in many different prisons.[22] Several assumptions lie behind the dispersion model. Spreading problem prisoners around prevents them from joining together to cause trouble. This relieves prison staff from having to spend all their time controlling the same troublemakers. Dispersion also allows the prison administration to break up cliques and gangs, and prisoners can participate in rehabilitation programs.[23]

By 1978, a combination of rising assaults on prison staff, prisoner unrest, and "get tough on criminals" attitudes led to a return to the concentration model. In that year, the U.S. Bureau of Prisons opened a "special high security control unit" in the federal prison at Marion, Indiana. The unit housed the nation's most dangerous prisoners. Assaults on staff and prisoners increased sharply around the country and at Marion in the early 1980s. Throughout these years, there were 54 serious inmate-on-inmate assaults, 8 prisoner killings, and 28 serious assaults on staff at Marion—not counting group disturbances. Marion remained the nation's only supermax until 1994, when the U.S. Bureau of Prisons opened the Administrative Maximum Penitentiary at Florence, Colorado. Florence (ADX) became the nation's state-of-the-art supermax.

In 2007, *60 Minutes* (CBS) news correspondent Scott Pelley reported on conditions at the United States Penitentiary Administrative Maximum, commonly known as the ADX. Pelley reported that the ADX, a supermax prison, is like a twenty-first-century Alcatraz. Located in the mountains outside of Denver, Colorado, the ADX holds inmates too violent for any other prison. It housed over 40 terrorists in 2007 and currently hosts the shoe bomber, Richard Reid, the Unabomber, Ted Kaczynski, Olympic Park bomber Eric Rudolph, and Oklahoma City bomber Terry Nichols. Fellow Oklahoma City bomber Timothy McVeigh was imprisoned there until his execution in 2001. While the ADX holds

maximum security prisons the highest priority security (preventing prisoners from escaping, keeping them from hurting staff or each other, and keeping out contraband)

supermaximum security prisons (supermaxes) prisons for "the worst of the worst"

An Example of an Alcatraz Inmate's Daily Schedule

07:00 hours: Prisoners are awakened by cell house bell. Prisoners are expected to get up, shave, get dressed, make their beds, and clean their cell before leaving.

07:20 hours: Second morning bell. Prisoners' cell doors are opened. All inmates are to stand quietly outside their cell facing forward. The inmates are expected to remain standing until the second bell sounds indicating a correct count. Absolute silence is the rule during every count process. Inmates are marched into the mess hall in line numbers by order of tier. Inmates are expected to sit in cell order.

07:30 hours: Breakfast. Prisoners are allowed to take as much food as they like as long as they eat everything. The motto is well known among inmates "Take what you like, eat what all that you take." Inmates are allowed to talk quietly during meals, and when finished, they are expected to prominently place all of their silverware on their trays. In order, correctional officers count silverware for each place set and validate counts.

07:50 hours: Breakfast concludes. Inmates line up for their work details. Inmates with no work assignments are led back to their cells by order of tier. Inmates with work assignments in the industries are led to the recreation yard and lined up by work detail (primary details are laundry, tailor shop, glove, shoe, gardening, standard labor, and metal shop).

08:00 hours: Inmates are led by division to their respective assignments down the steep stair ledge and through the snitch box (metal detector) and expected to line up at their duty post for counts. Counts are completed and validated by correctional officers.

08:20 hours: Work details begin.

10:00 hours: Inmates are given an eight-minute break. Inmates are allowed to smoke during the break in designated areas.

10:08 hours: Prison industries' whistle signals end of break and allows inmates two minutes to return back to their duty assignment.

11:35 hours: Prison industries' whistle signals end of work period. Inmates are lined up and marched through the snitch box (metal detector), up the stair trail into the recreation yard for counts before lunch. After counts are validated, inmates are led into the mess hall.

12:00 hours: Lunch begins.

12:20 hours: Lunch period concludes. In order, correctional officers count silverware for each place set and validate counts. Inmates are lined up and marched back to their cells for the 12:30 count and then locked up for a short break.

13:00 hours: Inmates assigned to work details are marched back to the recreation yard awaiting counts. Inmates are led back to their duty post and counts are validated by correctional officers.

13:20 hours: Work resumes. . . .

15:00 hours: Prison industries' whistle signals end of work period. Inmates are allowed to break in designated areas to smoke.

15:08 hours: Prison industries' whistle signals end of break and allows inmates two minutes to return back to their duty assignment.

15:10 hours: Work resumes. . . .

16:10 hours: Work period ends. . . .

16:20 hours: Prisoners are led back to recreation yard, lined up, and prepared for counts. Prisoners are counted and led back to the dining hall for dinner.

16:35 hours: Prisoners not on work assignments are released from cells and marched into the dining hall for dinner meal.

16:40 hours: Supper.

17:00 hours: Dinner period concludes. In order, correctional officers count silverware for each place set and validate counts. Prisoners are lined up and led back to their cells for count. Inmates are permitted to enter cells and locked down for the night.

17:30 hours: Final lock-up count. . . .

21:30 hours: Inmate evening count and then lights out.[24]

less than 500 inmates (who spend 23 hours a day in windowless prison cells), parts of the prison are understaffed, creating certain security and safety problems. In order to keep the peace, concessions are made to Muslim prisoners, who make considerable demands on the staff, reports Pelley. When convicted al-Qaeda terrorists protested poor living conditions by refusing to eat, they were force-fed by the prison staff. Still, despite the aggressive population, most prisoners live without fear of attack: there have been only two prisoner deaths and four prisoner suicides since the prison opened in 1994.

Supermaxes cost a lot of money—about twice as much as maximum security prisons.[25] Are supermaxes worth the price? Relying on anecdotes, supporters of supermaxes say they have reduced assaults and other serious incidents against prisoners and staff throughout the prison system, not just in the supermaxes.

New-Generation Maximum Security Prisons
Some maximum security prisons do not fit the description of either the traditional maximum security prison or the supermax. In the 1970s, a new idea for both building and managing maximum security prisons arose. **New-generation maximum security prisons** are based on the idea that offenders are sent to prison *as* punishment, not *for* punishment. These prisons are built to allow architecture and management to contribute to a safe, humane confinement where the confinement itself is supposed to be the punishment.

New-generation prisons usually contain six to eight physically separated units within a secure perimeter. Each unit contains 40 to 50 prisoners, with a cell for each inmate. Each unit also has dining rooms, a laundry, counseling offices, game rooms, and an enclosed outdoor recreation yard and work area. Because these units are only two levels high, corrections officers in secure "bubbles" can conduct continual surveillance, monitoring all prisoners' interactions with one another and staff. These self-contained units can keep many prisoners secure in groups small enough to participate in group activities. The design also permits specialization. One unit focuses on drug dependency. Another unit houses prisoners attending school. A third unit concentrates on work projects. Another unit is reserved for those with disciplinary problems.[26]

Medium and Minimum Security Prisons

Most prisoners are not in maximum security prisons; they are confined in medium security prisons surrounded by barbed wire fences. **Medium security prisons** are less focused on security than maximum security prisons. In 2005, 27 percent of all correctional facilities were medium security prisons.[27] Newer medium security facilities commonly have dormitories or other shared living quarters. Prisoners work without constant supervision. But medium security prisons do have several security practices, including head counts and surveillance, that resemble the measures at maximum security prisons.[28]

Minimum security prisons tend to be newer than maximum and medium security prisons; most were built after 1950. In 2005, just over 50 percent of all prison facilities were minimum security facilities.[29] Vocational training and treatment, not security, are their main focus. Minimum security prisoners are mainly first-time, nonviolent, white-collar and younger offenders who are not considered dangerous or likely to escape.

Minimum security prisons look a lot like college campuses, with low buildings surrounded by a recreational area. These prisons emphasize trust and a normal lifestyle. Prisoners eat in small groups, often at tables for four instead of at long rows of tables that all face in one direction, a common feature of maximum and medium security prisons. Minimum security prisoners also have some privacy, including private rooms with doors prisoners can lock.

Most minimum security prisons also offer various programs, including vocational training, academic education, and counseling. A number of prisoners are released for the day on work-study programs that allow them to hold jobs and attend neighboring schools and colleges. Some prisons provide family visiting facilities for conjugal visits where prisoners can stay with their families for up to three days at a time.[30]

WOMEN'S PRISONS

Most women's prisons combine maximum, medium, and minimum security levels in the same prison.

new-generation maximum security prisons a combination of architecture and management to provide a safe, secure, humane environment based on the idea that offenders are sent to prison *as* punishment, not *for* punishment

medium security prisons less focused on security than maximum security prisons and with more programs

minimum security prisons for young, first-time, and other offenders not considered dangerous or likely to escape, where vocational training and treatment, not security, are emphasized

© iStockphoto.com

In the early 1980s, pediatric nurse Genene Jones allegedly killed between 11 and 46 infants and children in San Antonio, Texas, by injecting lethal overdoses of heparin and succinylcholine. After chemical detection tests revealed two of Jones's murders in 1985, she was sentenced to 99 years in prison. However, because of a Texas law enacted to reduce prison overcrowding, Jones will receive automatic parole in 2017.

Generally, a single cottage, dormitory, or wing is all that is needed to house maximum security women prisoners. At the other end of the security level, "honor cottages" confine minimum security prisoners. There are separate sections based on age groups, programs, and sentence lengths. Most women's prisons are less gloomy than men's because they tend to be located in rural settings, there is hardly any security equipment, and many have a cottage architecture style and private rooms.

PRIVATE PRISONS

Private prisons are built and managed by private companies under contract with the government. In 1989, Texas became the first state to open a private prison in the United States—four of them, in fact—two operated by Corrections Corporation of America and the other two by Wackenhut Corrections Corporation. In 2002, privately operated prisons housed 90,542 prisoners, or 6.5 percent of all prisoners in federal and state facilities. By 2007, 118,239 prisoners were housed in private prisons. On average, from 2000 to 2006 private prison populations grew at an annual rate of 2.1 percent; they rose by 3.3 percent from 2006 to 2007.[31]

LO4 Corrections Officers

Corrections officers used to be called "guards" because of the belief that their primary missions were protecting the public by preventing escape and controlling prisoners by keeping order. Newer thinking takes into account the reality that officers have to do a lot more than "merely opening and closing doors." Nevertheless, their primary mission is still to watch and guard prisoners. They watch them while they work, go to school, eat, exercise, relax, and sleep. They escort them to the doctor when they are sick or injured, to court when they have hearings, and to visits with their families on visiting day. They sit in towers to watch the prison walls and in cubicles to guard the areas inside prison and the gates between the outside world and prison.[32] The most important duty officers have is accounting for every prisoner at all times (called "the count"). Even one prisoner unaccounted for shuts down all operations and movement. Officers face disciplinary action for miscounting.

Guarding and watching prisoners is dangerous. Prisoners outnumber officers, so officers have to depend more on their communication skills than on their physical power to protect themselves, control prisoners, and prevent escape. On "ordinary" days, prisoners could assault and injure them. During riots, prisoners might take them hostage, beat, rape, or kill them.[33]

To better understand the world of corrections officers, let's look more closely at the supervision hierarchy, women and minority corrections officers, and officer education and training.

THE SUPERVISION HIERARCHY

Sergeants, lieutenants, and captains supervise the line officers (corrections officers). Sergeants supervise cell blocks, work units, kitchens, and hospitals. They check corrections officers' work, assign them to specific tasks, and even fill in for absentees. In traditional prisons, social distance separates line officers from lieutenants and captains. True to the operations of any paramilitary organization, corrections officers receive orders from their superior officers and are expected to carry them out efficiently and effectively.

Lieutenants act as prison police officers who keep the peace by stopping fights and other prison disturbances. They have to maintain order by "walking" prisoners to isolation or forcibly removing them from cells when necessary. When they are not settling disturbances, they go on preventive patrol, checking and "shaking down" prisoners for weapons and other contraband. Lieutenants police not only the prisoners but also the line officers. They search lower-ranking officers for contraband and weapons, just as they do the prisoners. Lieutenants check on both prisoners and officers to make sure they are doing their jobs. Lieutenants also write disciplinary reports, called "tickets," on officers, just as officers write them on prisoners. The few captains manage the loads of paperwork required by bureaucracy—personnel evaluations, budget preparations, and disciplinary committee reports.

WOMEN AND MINORITY CORRECTIONS OFFICERS

Traditionally, the process for selecting officers gave high priority to physical standards—height, weight, and general strength. So male officers always guarded male prisoners until the 1970s when affirmative action lawsuits and federal and state legislation started to change that. By 1998, 22 percent of corrections officers were women.[34] By 2000, women made up one-third of the ranks.[35] More members of minority groups are now employed in corrections as well.

OFFICER EDUCATION AND TRAINING

State and local prisons require a high school diploma or graduation equivalency degree. The Federal Bureau of Prisons requires new corrections officers to have a bachelor's degree; three years of full-time experience in a field providing counseling, assistance, or supervision to individuals; or a combination of the two. Law enforcement or military experience may be substituted for some of the education requirement. There is debate in the corrections field regarding whether a college degree for corrections officers is helpful. Some argue that requiring a college degree reduces the pool of potential corrections officers and that additional on-the-job training for corrections officers would be more useful. Others maintain that college-educated corrections officers have enhanced leadership and analytical thinking skills and are better able to deal with the stress and alienation of corrections work.[36] A corrections officer must be at least 18 to 21 years of age, be a U.S. citizen or permanent resident, and have no felony convictions.

Using guidelines established by the American Correctional Association and the American Jail Association, federal, state, and some local departments of corrections provide training for corrections officers. Regional training academies are available to local agencies in some states. The training curriculum typically includes institutional policies, regulations, and operations, as well as custody and security procedures. All state and local corrections agencies provide in-service training, including training on legal restrictions and interpersonal relations. Some agencies mandate firearms proficiency and self-defense skills training. Although requirements vary widely, most agencies require their new officers to work for several weeks or months under the supervision of an experienced officer.[37]

© Jack Kurtz/The Image Works

jail a county or municipal facility for either keeping adults while they wait for trial or for punishing them for less than a year after they're convicted

prisons state institutions where prisoners are locked up after they're convicted if their sentence is for more than a year

LO5 Traditional versus New-Generation Jails

do not confuse jails with prisons. A **jail** is a county or municipal facility for *either* keeping adults while they wait for trial *or* for punishing them for less than a year after they are convicted. In contrast, **prisons** are state institutions where prisoners are locked up after they are convicted if their sentence is for more than a year.

In addition to detention before and incarceration after conviction, jails hold all of the following people:

* Juveniles waiting to be transferred to juvenile facilities

- Adults waiting to be transferred to facilities in other counties or states, the federal government, or the military
- Adults waiting for mental facility commitment hearings
- Adults held as material witnesses
- Adults in protective custody
- Adults in contempt of court
- Probationers waiting for revocation hearings
- Parolees waiting for revocation hearings
- Felons waiting for transfer to prison after conviction
- Prison inmates waiting for trial on new charges, to testify as witnesses, or to appear as plaintiffs in lawsuits against the government[38]

To better understand the role of jails in the punishment of offenders, let's look at jail conditions and new-generation jails.

JAIL CONDITIONS

Some jails are modern, safe, clean, and efficiently and humanely administered. Many jails, however, are overcrowded and provide poor conditions for inmates. Jail overcrowding occurs when jails exceed design capacity or rated capacity (the capacity estimate that a correctional expert deems safe; it is usually smaller than design capacity). As jail inmates have challenged overcrowding and poor conditions, courts have moved to correct these conditions.[39]

In 2006, the U.S. Department of Justice (DOJ) undertook an investigation of the King County jail in downtown Seattle, Washington. The investigation was sparked by media accounts of jail inmates committing suicide and by criminal charges of sexual misconduct brought against jail guards. In 2007, the DOJ handed down a strongly worded report that highlighted "medical bungling by health care staff at the King County jail" as the most likely reason for the recent death of an inmate. According to a story in the local newspaper:

> As described in the report, the incident involved an inmate with a history of alcohol withdrawal seizures and with skin infections on his legs who was admitted to the jail and sent the same day to the emergency room at Harborview Medical Center, where he was diagnosed with multiple abscesses, anemia and either cellulitis (a potentially serious bacterial infection) or deep vein thrombosis.
>
> 'Although arguably the hospital should have admitted him, it did not do so,' the report says. Instead, the inmate was returned to the jail, where he was not examined by a doctor 'even though he should have been' and was forced to wait more than 30 hours for his first dose of the antibiotics prescribed for his skin infections, the report says.
>
> When the inmate requested care and finally was checked by a doctor, the examination detected abdominal tenderness, indications of intestinal distress and 'highly abnormal and unstable vital signs,' the report says. But the doctor did not send him back to the hospital.
>
> The following day, his third at the jail, the inmate experienced severe abdominal pain and was sweating and doubled over. Still, it was seven hours before he was re-examined by a doctor, who sent him to the hospital, where the inmate died—'apparently of a perforated gastric ulcer,' the report says.[40]

The DOJ's investigation also found that the jail was below the legal standards for medical treatment, suicide prevention, and safeguards against physical and sexual abuse of prisoners by jailers. According to the report, inmates at the jail routinely faced unnecessary uses of serious force. Staff regularly used pepper spray and the "hair-hold technique," in which guards grab an inmate's hair to exert control, against inmates who were not resisting or were handcuffed. The report concluded that the jail had violated the inmates' constitutional rights by failing to provide adequate medical care, protect inmates from physical harm and sexual

A New-Generation Jail

© AP Images/Chet Brokaw

© Shane Cummins/iStockphoto.com

Some prisoners are forced to live in grossly unhygienic environments.

abuse, and take steps to keep inmates from harming themselves.

NEW-GENERATION JAILS

New-generation jails combine new approaches to architecture, management philosophy, operation, and training. This combination has changed a few jails. When the Federal Bureau of Prisons, traditionally an innovative force in American corrections, developed the new-generation jail concept based on the confinement model of imprisonment (lock people up *as* punishment, not *for* punishment), its basic directive was, "If you can't rehabilitate, at least do no harm." Three federal Metropolitan Correctional Centers (MCCs) were built in Chicago, New York, and San Diego to provide humane, secure detention.[41]

Architecturally, new-generation jails have a podular design, which allows constant surveillance (see Figure 13.2). In contrast, traditional jails have a linear design—a corridor lined with cells that officers can see into only when they walk down the hallways (see Figure 13.3). In traditional jails, officers can control only the area they see; prisoners control the rest. In new-generation jails, officers control most of the jail most of the time.

The podular design includes the following characteristics:

- Security concentration along the outside perimeter with impregnable walls and windows

- Restricted movement inside the jail (unit officers do not have keys; an officer in a control booth can allow movement in and out of the unit by closed-circuit TV and intercom)

- Free movement and as few barriers as possible inside living units

- Living units with fewer than 50 prisoners to give officers an unobstructed view of the entire area

- Private rooms for prisoners

- Standard building materials for both cost and appearance

At first, new-generation jails were viewed as soft on criminals; critics accused them of providing inmates with a luxury motel at public expense. But the new jails report as much as 90 percent fewer violent incidents. Private rooms allow prisoners to go to their own rooms to cool off, thereby preventing violent responses to incidents. Homosexual rape has almost disappeared. Vandalism and graffiti have nearly vanished.

Architecture is not the only reason for the success of new-generation jails; direct supervision has replaced old-style management. Direct supervision places officers in constant contact with prisoners, which allows them to get to know prisoners and thereby recognize and respond to trouble before it escalates into violence. Negotiation and verbal communication replace physical force.

new-generation jails

combine architecture, management philosophy, operation, and training based on the goal of incarceration *as*, not *for*, punishment

FIGURE 13.2
New-Generation Jails: Podular Design

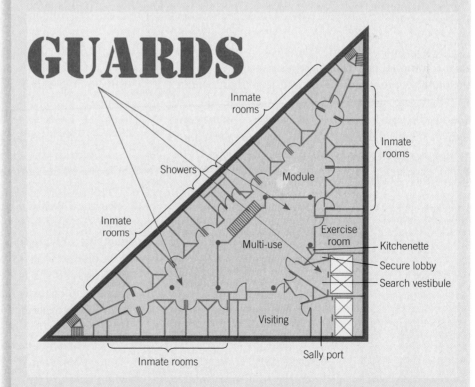

Source: Figure supplied by Federal Bureau of Prisons, Metropolitan Corrections Center, Chicago.

FIGURE 13.3

Traditional Jails: Linear Design

GUARD

Source: Figure supplied by Federal Bureau of Prisons, Metropolitan Corrections Center, Chicago.

New-generation jails are much more expensive than traditional jails. They are also harder to "sell" to the public because they are viewed as not harsh enough and therefore are susceptible to the charge that they "coddle" criminals. Also, administrators and managers remain skeptical of direct supervision, despite support among hard-line corrections officers and criminal justice researchers.[42]

LO6 Major Characteristics of Prisoners

most prisoners are male, young, black or white. In 2007, 93 percent were males and only 7 percent were females. Still, the number of female inmates in 2007 was 25 percent higher than it was in 2000. Between 2006 and 2007, the number of white male

inmates decreased by 1.5 percent, black inmates increased by 4.1 percent, and Hispanic inmates increased by 3.5 percent.[43] More than half of all state, federal, and jail inmates are under the age of 35. Between 2000 and 2007, the custody population increased by over 350,000. The increase was primarily male and more than half were Hispanic or white males.[44]

To learn more about prisoners, let's look more closely at women prisoners, repeat offenders, and special-management prisoners.

WOMEN PRISONERS

From 1925 until 1980, the number of women in prison never exceeded 10 for every 100,000 people. Since 1980, however, the rate of women prisoners has increased sharply, to 62 for every 100,000 people in 2003.[45] Nevertheless, we should keep this steep rise in perspective—in 2007, men were 13 times more likely to be imprisoned than women, and only 7 percent of prisoners in 2007 were women.[46] In the 2000 Census of State and Federal Correctional Facilities, only 150 of the almost 1,700 correctional facilities housed women.[47]

What are the reasons for the increase in women prisoners? Many are the same ones driving up the general prison population boom. But, according to Barbara Owen and Barbara Bloom, who profiled women prisoners in California, it is also because of the growing numbers of women prosecuted for and convicted of drug offenses, the increasingly harsh sentences for drug offenses, and the lack of both treatment and community sanctions for women drug offenders. In fact, Owen and Bloom argue that the "war on drugs" is really a war on women.[48]

The increase in women prisoners is not distributed evenly according to race and ethnicity. The rate for white women increased nearly 7 percent between 2000 and 2006, and the rate for Hispanic or Latina women increased nearly 5 percent; but the rate for black women dropped 2 percent.[49] Less than half of white female offenders and less than half of black female offenders are under the age of 35, while nearly 60 percent of Hispanic female offenders are under the age of 35.[50]

The primary concern of women prisoners is not security and the threat of violence in prison but rather how to care for their children. Female inmates express much less physical aggression than male inmates. Most conflicts occur over personal relationships and tend not to affect the management of female inmates.[51] Most of the offenses committed by female inmates are nonviolent drug crimes. Because so many women are being incarcerated for drug crimes—more than for any other offense—and because of stiffer drug penalties, there are increasing numbers of mothers with children in prison. Crawford refers to the problems this poses for the children of female inmates as collateral damage because imprisonment separates many of these children from their primary caregivers.[52] Since there are so few female prisons, female offenders are housed on average more than 160 miles from their children, making it hard for them to stay connected. Often, there is no one except perhaps a grandmother to care for the children. The psychological and emotional damage created by the broken bond can be intense and very damaging to the child. The depression and post-traumatic stress that result can lead to early deviance and developmental problems for the child. Some prisons have created programs to help mothers of children rehabilitate more quickly and to help them maintain bonds with their children. Most of these programs deal with domestic abuse, drug addiction, and job skills.

REPEAT OFFENDERS

Which offenses count in calculating *recidivism* (repeat offending) depends on the researcher. The three main measures are rearrest for another crime, reconviction, and recommitment to prison. The rearrest, reconviction, or recommitment does not have to be for the same crime; any other felony or "serious misdemeanor" counts.[53]

The longer former prisoners remain out of prison, the less likely they are to return. Nearly 70 percent of prisoners are rearrested for a new offense within three years of release.[54] Also, recidivism varies according to offense. Property offenders return to prison more frequently (33.5 percent) than violent offenders (22.5 percent). Burglars return most frequently, followed by robbers. Drug offenders, forgers, embezzlers, and sex offenders follow robbers; homicide is last with the

lowest recidivist rates.[55] The more times prisoners are confined, the greater the likelihood they will return to prison. About one-quarter of all prisoners with no prior record will return to prison; 37 percent of all prisoners with one or two prior prison terms will return; and 42.7 percent of those with three or more prior terms will be back in prison.[56]

Recidivism also varies according to age, gender, and race. The younger prisoners are when they leave prison, the greater the chance they will be back. Gender also affects recidivism (see Figure 13.4). Men recidivate

Two years after she pleaded no contest to charges of hit and run, drunken driving, and driving with a suspended license in 2003, actress Michelle Rodriguez pleaded guilty to driving under the influence, which violated probation for the previous offences. Rodriguez was sentenced to a 30-day alcohol rehabilitation program, 30 days of community service, and 60 days in prison, but she served less than a day in prison before being released due to overcrowding. In September 2007, Rodriguez was again found in violation of her probation for failing to complete the community service and rehabilitation program. She was sentenced to 180 days in prison but served only 18 days before again being released due to overcrowding.

at substantially higher rates than women. In New York State, for example, 36 percent of released men return to prison; 12.1 percent of women return. Women are less likely to recidivate when support services are available in the community. Most imprisoned women have "serious economic, medical, mental health, and social difficulties which are often overlooked and frequently intensified" in prison.[57] Community programs are more effective at enabling women to lead law-abiding lives than is imprisonment. In Pennsylvania, for example, the Program for Women Offenders found that its services reduced recidivism. In a random sample of more than one thousand clients, 3.2 percent recidivated. Intermediate sanctions such as home confinement and intensive supervision may also provide alternatives to imprisonment, if they include direct services.[58]

SPECIAL-MANAGEMENT PRISONERS

Special-management prisoners fall into these groups:

1. *Vulnerable prisoners.* A rapidly growing group of inmates who need protection from other prisoners to survive in prison

2. *Troublemakers.* Prisoners who need added restraints to protect other inmates, staff, or the security of the institution

3. *Prisoners with AIDS or other infectious diseases.* Prisoners who have infectious diseases that are communicable to other inmates and staff

4. *Elderly inmates.* Inmates past the age of 55 with special needs

5. *Mentally disordered inmates.* Prisoners with mental problems who cannot function in the general popula-

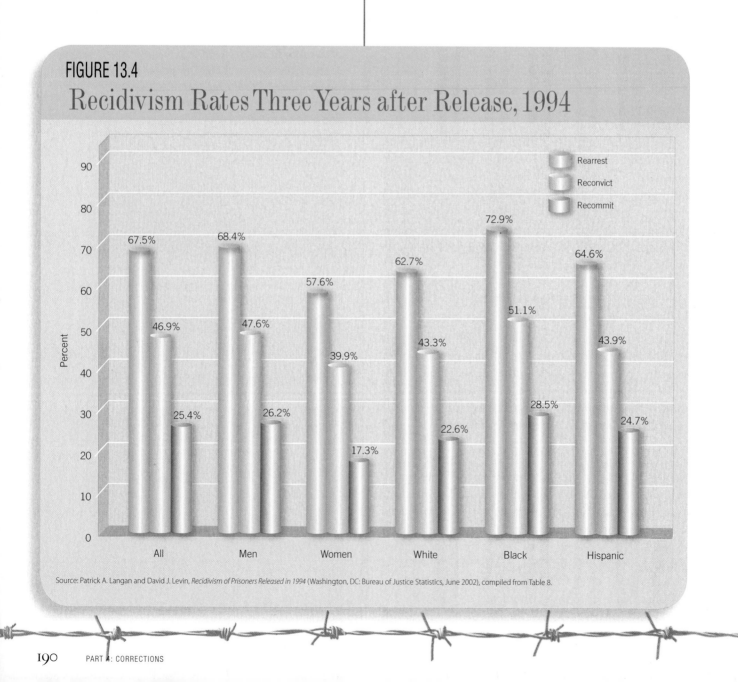

FIGURE 13.4
Recidivism Rates Three Years after Release, 1994

Source: Patrick A. Langan and David J. Levin, *Recidivism of Prisoners Released in 1994* (Washington, DC: Bureau of Justice Statistics, June 2002), compiled from Table 8.

tion without assistance or who need professional treatment and medication

Correctional administrators prefer a one-size-fits-all approach to the management of inmates, but special-needs offenders require specialized management to either protect them or to protect other inmates and staff. Medical conditions and problems of the elderly have to be managed.[59] Prisons have specialized medical programs and education programs, such as HIV Peer Programs. Violent inmates or inmates who cause disturbances may be segregated in special locations within prisons—a practice called *administrative segregation*.

INFAMOUS INMATES OF THE ADX

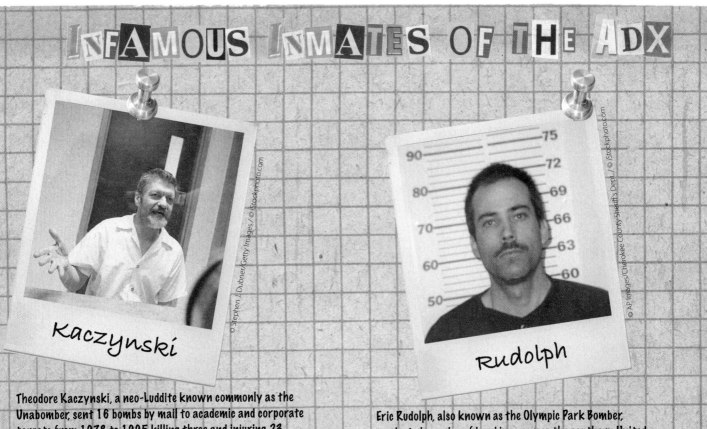

Kaczynski

Rudolph

Theodore Kaczynski, a neo-Luddite known commonly as the Unabomber, sent 16 bombs by mail to academic and corporate targets from 1978 to 1995, killing three and injuring 23 people. After a nationwide search aided by Kaczynski's brother, the Unabomber was arrested in April 1996. He pleaded guilty to all charges and was sentenced to life without the possibility of parole.

Eric Rudolph, also known as the Olympic Park Bomber, conducted a series of bombings across the southern United States. Most infamous for his 1996 bombing of the Centennial Olympic Park in Atlanta, Georgia, Rudolph killed two and injured at least 150 others in a radical campaign against liberalism, abortion, and homosexuality. After he was captured in the Appalachian wilderness, Rudolph pleaded guilty to all charges levied against him and was sentenced to five consecutive life terms in prison.

Nichols

On April 19, 1995, 168 people died and over 800 were injured in the bombing of the Alfred P. Murrah Federal Building in Oklahoma City, Oklahoma, the deadliest act of domestic terrorism in American history. After meeting in the U.S. Army, Terry Nichols (pictured) and Timothy McVeigh conspired to destroy the building in retaliation for the government's handling of the Waco Siege of 1993. McVeigh was arrested within 90 minutes of the bombing, and Nichols turned himself in two days later.

Prisons are islands of poverty
stranded in seas of plenty.

14

Prison Life

In what type of conditions should prison inmates be confined? Do they have rights to clean and safe facilities? An Idaho inmate sent to a private prison in Texas committed suicide as a result of the new living conditions he was sentenced to. While serving time for child molestation, the inmate wrote letters to his family describing the horrific nature of his confinement. He described standing water on the floor, odorous pillow cases, sheets with blood stains, and access to just one dirty towel. Seven months into his sentence, he used a razor blade to slash his throat. While some may believe that prisoners should not expect any better, prisoners do have rights, and correctional institutions must provide clean and safe conditions. This chapter explores the nature of prison life and the realities of prison confinement.[1]

LO1 Prison as a Total Institution

early prison research focused primarily on male prison society.[2] This early research identified two worlds where two completely separate societies existed—free society and prison society. Prisons were defined as **total institutions**, meaning that a prison was a whole society in itself, separate and isolated from free society.[3] Inside prison walls, prison administrators had so much power that they could force prisoners to give up their personalities and live completely controlled lives.

INDIGENOUS AND IMPORTATION THEORIES

The theory that prison society is created inside prison walls independent of the outside world is called the **indigenous theory of imprisonment**. The early indigenous theory researchers concentrated on how prisoners adapted to life in

total institutions prisons are societies, separate and isolated from free society

indigenous theory of imprisonment prison society is created inside prison walls independent of the outside world

Learning Outcomes

LO1 Explain the concept of prison as a total institution and discuss other theories of prisons

LO2 Understand the lives and cultures of male inmates

LO3 Understand the nature and causes of prison violence

LO4 Understand the nature of common prison programs for male inmates

LO5 Understand the special needs and problems of incarcerated women

LO6 Understand the issue of prisoner reentry

prison. In 1940, Donald Clemmer introduced the concept of *prisonization*, the process by which prisoners adapt to the prison world.[4] Clemmer based his prisonization theory on the detailed observations he made while working at Menard Penitentiary in Illinois. According to this theory, prisoners adapted to prison life by following the inmate code, an unwritten law based on the values of "noncooperation and hostility toward staff."

Do not confuse this unwritten informal inmate code with either formal prison rules or the informal adaptations of the formal rules that occur. In 1958, Gresham Sykes identified the unwritten rules of the inmate code, which included "Never rat on a con," "Be cool," "Do your own time," and "Don't exploit inmates."[5] Although Sykes saw the code as an ideal, not a description of how prisoners actually behaved, it became the basis of most indigenous theory research.[6] We will look at today's version of the inmate code in the next section.

Prisons have changed a lot since the indigenous theory was introduced by Clemmer and Sykes. Prisons are bigger and so is the proportion of the public that is locked up. The numbers of black and Hispanic prisoners have outpaced those of whites, increasing an already disproportionate number of minorities in prison. Prison gangs have gotten a lot bigger, too; their influence is stronger; and their connections with the outside world are firmer. More staff members have joined unions, and unions have become a lot more powerful. The chances have increased that courts will interfere with prison management and life in prison. And prisons and imprisonment have become hot political issues.

All these changes have led to a new theory to explain prison society, the **importation theory of imprisonment**. The theory assumes that the roots of prison society lie outside prison. All prisoners bring with them a long history of life in public institutions—almost all have gone to school, many have spent time in juvenile and adult facilities, and some have been confined in psychiatric hospitals and other treatment facilities. They also bring

to prison other individual attributes—their race, ethnicity, and criminal history. Once in prison, prisoners still watch television, read magazines, listen to music, talk to visitors, bring lawsuits, and maintain contacts with gangs outside prison. All these aspects of their background and life in prison break down the clear barriers, if there ever were any, between life inside and outside prison.

Prison gangs are an example of how the outside world can penetrate prison society. Outside gang affiliations are imported inside prisons and create a gang culture that the corrections staff must manage. In the Florida prison system, for example, there are six known major gangs:

- Neta
- Aryan Brotherhood
- Black Guerrilla Family
- Mexican Mafia
- La Nuestra Familia
- Texas Syndicate

The Neta and Aryan Brotherhood are the largest gangs in the Florida prison system.[7] The Texas prison system has six Hispanic gangs, three white gangs, and two black gangs.[8] We will consider the role that gangs play in prison violence in a later section.

A prison dining tray with gang insignia drawn on it.

© AP Images/Bob Anez

LO2 The Lives of Male Inmates

in 1958, Sykes identified five deprivations at the core of life in a male maximum security prison:

- Goods and services
- Liberty
- Straight sexual relationships
- Autonomy
- Security[9]

Recognizing these deprivations, called the **pains of imprisonment**, is essential to understanding the way prisoners deal with confinement. Let's look first at how inmates cope with two major prison deprivations—the lack of goods and services and the absence of straight sexual relationships—and then at how inmates deal with the stress of imprisonment.

ENFORCED POVERTY

Prisons are supposed to be islands of poverty in a sea of plenty. Prisoners are not supposed to be comfortable in confinement. Part of their punishment is to lose their freedom, their privacy, and all of the things associated with the "good life." This means that prisoners are to live lives of enforced poverty, where the state provides only the bare essentials—plain food, clothing, medical care, and shelter.

Prisoners can augment this subsistence living by obtaining some amenities legally. For example, they are allowed to receive gifts from friends and relatives. They can also get some of the comforts of life from the prison commissary. Cash is banned from prisons, so prisoners have to purchase these comforts by using scrip or credit drawn on accounts supplied with money from the outside or that they have earned in prison.

Still, the approved list of gifts and the stock of items in the commissary are rarely enough to satisfy the wants of most prisoners. Prisoners are well aware of all the comforts of life that they are not allowed to have. It is hard to satisfy their desires with available resources and within the enforced poverty of confinement.

Deprived of luxuries, prisoners do their best to get them, usually by obtaining contraband that finds its way inside prison walls. Hustling contraband goods and services—mainly food, clothing, weapons, drugs, and prostitution—breaks prison rules and frustrates the goal of punishment by enforced poverty. Nevertheless, the prison authorities realize that getting these small luxuries eases the pain of imprisonment and promotes prison stability. Therefore, the authorities tolerate contraband goods and services to some extent because they make prisoners easier to manage.

pains of imprisonment
deprivations suffered by prisoners as part of life in prison society

Prisoners put great stake in these amenities, and trouble looms when they do not get them. Trouble also brews when prisoner leaders lose the profits from controlling contraband goods and services. In some prisons, these leaders form symbiotic relationships with corrections officers. Both have an interest in maintaining stability, so they make tradeoffs: Officers allow some illegal trafficking, usually in "nonserious" contraband such as food; prisoner leaders, in return, maintain peaceful cell blocks.[10]

BAN ON SEX

All prisons prohibit sexual relationships. Why? The denial of sex is another legitimate pain of imprisonment. Despite

On October 22, 1983, two prison guards were stabbed to death by Aryan Brotherhood members at the United States penitentiary, Marion, which at the time housed the Federal Bureau of Prisons' most dangerous prisoners. In response to the stabbings, prison officials initiated a permanent lockdown, transforming Marion into a temporary supermax. Inmates were restricted to solitary confinement for 23 hours every day and could not congregate, even for religious services. It was not until 2006 that the Marion lockdown was terminated.

this formal ban, anecdotes about prison life for generations have told of routine consensual sex behind prison walls. But the spread of AIDS has spurred a demand for more knowledge about consensual sex in prison. Prison systems today try to educate prisoners about the dangers of sexually transmitted diseases, and they work to treat and manage these diseases within prisons.

COPING WITH STRESS FROM THE PAINS OF IMPRISONMENT

All new inmates ask themselves, "How shall I do my time?" Or, "What shall I do in prison?" A few cannot cope at all; they either commit suicide or sink into psychosis. There are four basic ways in which male offenders adapt to prison life:

- Doing time
- Gleaning
- Jailing
- Becoming a disorganized criminal[11]

Offenders "doing time" see prison time as the cost of doing business. It will be brief so they attempt to do their time with minimal suffering and maximum comfort. They live by the inmate code (see Table 14.1)—the informal social control created by the inmates to define proper and improper behavior.[12] Inmates doing time strive to avoid trouble and to fill their time. They just want to survive and get out.

Inmates who "glean" try to take advantage of prison programs for education and vocational training to improve their chances of success after release. Some inmates are able to learn skills, obtain jobs on the outside, and never return to crime.

Some inmates cut themselves off from the outside world and live an institutional life inside the prison. They are said to be "jailing." These are often inmates who entered the system as young juveniles and have never accepted the values of free society. They become part of the politics and economy of the prison world. Jailing is about obtaining power within the prison society.

The "disorganized criminals" are inmates who are unable to make any of the other three adaptations. They often are easily manipulated because of low intelligence, mental or physical disabilities, or problems functioning in prison society. They often develop emotional problems, attempt suicide, and break prison rules.

In his review of the literature on coping, Kenneth Adams discusses research that asked inmates how they handle problems.[13] Most male inmates choose "real-man strategies," relying heavily on personal strength and self-reliance. Some long-term prisoners choose another coping strategy—sticking to minimum expectations based on focusing on today and not hoping for too much tomorrow. Hispanics sometimes join gangs as family surrogates to ease the pain of separation from their real families.

LO3 Prison Violence

racial and ethnic conflict, gangs and violent prisoners, bans on consensual sex, and enforced poverty can lead to violence against other prisoners. Assaults and homicides in maximum security men's prisons have increased to the point that the possibility of being attacked or killed is now the major concern of offenders incarcerated in these prisons or anticipating going to one.

Prison violence is not limited to the United States. In 2008, for example, the British media reported that in one British prison seven inmates had committed suicide between 2006 and 2008 and that 50 cases of self-inflicted injury had occurred in just February and March of 2008. According to the news story, violence at the prison had become so pervasive that it was not only driving inmates to attempt suicide but was also increasing tensions between prison gangs and eroding prison programs designed to assist inmates. The increased

TABLE 14.1 Basic Tenets of the Inmate Code

Do not rat or squeal on other inmates.
Do not interfere with the interests of other inmates.
Do not steal from, exploit, or cheat other inmates.
Do not be a "sucker" or make a fool of yourself by supporting prison policies.
Do not lose your cool.
Be a man, be tough, and don't weaken.

Source: Champion, D. J. "Prison," *Microsoft Encarta Online Encyclopedia* (2008), http://encarta.msn.com/encyclopedia_761573083/Prison.html.

Prisoners sometimes fashion crude weapons from the materials at their disposal. This slashing weapon was created by inserting a shaving razor into a melted plastic pen.

© Mikael Karlsson/Alamy

violence was attributed to the drug trade, overcrowding, and the aging facilities at the prison, among other things. Efforts by the staff to improve prison conditions and reduce drug trafficking within the prison subsequently resulted in reductions in violence.[14]

Similar causes have been cited as factors contributing to the violence in American prisons. Crowding, for example, is a common characteristic of prison life that probably accounts for some of the increased violence. Economic victimization, which occurs when violence or threats of it accompany gambling, fraud, loan sharking, theft, robbery, protection rackets, con games, delivery of misrepresented contraband, or failure to deliver promised goods, may be another factor. When promised commodities are not delivered—or are not as promised—victims may retaliate. Drug trafficking is a good example. To get drugs into prisons requires sophisticated smuggling operations. Violence erupts if drugs are stolen, misrepresented, overpriced, or not delivered. Prisoners use violence to prevent these distribution irregularities from happening in the first place or to retaliate for them if they do take place.

Let's look at how escalating prison violence is manifested in prisoner-officer violence, sexual assaults, the growing strength of gangs, and prison riots.

PRISONER-OFFICER VIOLENCE

Prisoners do not just attack each other; they attack officers, too. Officers take risks attempting to break up fights, managing intoxicated prisoners, and escorting them to segregation. These situations are known to provoke assaults. But not all violence is predictable, especially random violent acts like throwing dangerous objects at officers or dropping items from catwalks above as officers patrol cell blocks below.[15] Violence against officers is perceived to be related to an absence of administrative support for corrections officers. Officers report that a lack of support by administration, unclear guidelines, and lack of participatory decision making can make managing inmates more difficult and make it harder to deter threats of assaults by offenders.[16] Not all prisoner-officer violence involves attacks by prisoners. Officers also attack prisoners. Some officers use violence against inmates to enforce rules and maintain order.[17]

SEXUAL ASSAULT

Some prisoners are victims of sexual assault. It is estimated that 60,500, or 4.5 percent, of the nation's prisoners in state and federal facilities have experienced sexual violence. In a 2007 survey, 2.1 percent of inmates said they had been sexually assaulted by another inmate,

and 2.9 percent reported that they were the victims of sexual assaults by staff members.[18] Less than 1 percent said that they had been victimized by both inmates and staff (see Table 14.2).

As Table 14.2 shows, 1.3 percent reported having had nonconsensual sex with another inmate, which was defined as giving or receiving sexual gratification and oral, anal, or vaginal sex; 0.8 percent had experienced an abusive sexual contact, defined as unwanted touching by another inmate of specific body parts in a sexual way. Inmates victimized by staff reported that they were just as likely to "willingly" have sex or sexual contact as they were to be victims of physical force, pressure, or offers of special favors or privileges. A majority of the reported incidents of sexual abuse by staff went beyond simple touching.

Some evidence indicates that the more crowded the prison, the higher the likelihood of sexual victimization. The following inmates are at higher risk for sexual victimization:

- Young, inexperienced inmates
- Physically small/weak inmates
- Inmates with mental disabilities and/or developmental problems
- Middle-class inmates who are not "tough" or "streetwise"

TABLE 14.2 Sexual Victimization of Inmates in State and Federal Custody, 2007

TYPES OF VICTIMIZATION	NATIONAL ESTIMATE OF SEXUAL VICTIMIZATION IN PRISON	
	NUMBER	PERCENT
Total	60,500	4.5%
Inmate-on-inmate	**27,400**	**2.1%**
Nonconsensual sexual acts	16,800	1.3
Abusive sexual contacts only	10,600	0.8
Staff sexual misconduct	**38,600**	**2.9%**
Unwilling activity	22,600	1.7%
Excluding touching	16,900	1.3
Touching only	5,700	0.4
Willing activity	22,700	1.7%
Excluding touching	20,600	1.5
Touching only	2,100	0.2

Source: Allen J. Beck and Paige M. Harrison, *Sexual Victimization in State and Federal Prisons Reported by Inmates, 2007* (Washington, DC: Bureau of Justice Statistics, December 2008), p. 1.

- Inmates who are not members of gangs or affiliated with gangs
- Inmates who are known homosexuals or overly effeminate
- Inmates who have been convicted of sex crimes
- "Code of silence" violators or "rats"
- Inmates who are strongly disliked by other inmates/staff
- Previous victims of sexual assault
- Inmates in prisons with high racial tensions[19]

Sexual relationships between officers and inmates have become more problematic, especially as more female staff are working with male inmates. Inappropriate relationships between staff and inmates are prohibited. Increasingly, however, female officers have been sexually manipulated by offenders, even though laws prohibited staff from engaging in sexual relationships with inmates.[20] Inmates also have been the victims of sexual demands from staff.[21] Some female corrections officers have been raped by inmates.

In 2009, an inmate in a South Carolina prison, serving time for sexually assaulting a minor, raped a female corrections officer. The officer was in a locked control area from which she could watch the inmates. The inmate forced entry into the room and used a makeshift weapon to subdue the officer. While the attack was taking place, three other inmates stormed the room and rescued the officer. These inmates testified against the attacker at trial, and he was sentenced to life in prison for the sexual assault on the officer.[22]

PRISON GANGS AND VIOLENCE

Gangs have been in prisons for a long time, but only since the 1970s have they became problematic for prison administrators. Today, prison gangs are a major part of men's prison life, despite strong prohibitions against them. Gang members rob, assault, and otherwise prey on members of other gangs and members of the general prison population. Gang members are already hostile to authority when they come to prison. By challenging authority, they gain status.

The emergence of gangs in prisons has changed the prison subculture. It is no longer inmates against staff, but rival gangs against each other. Specific allegiance to these inmate associations has complicated the dynamic of prison society. The gangs are divided along racial, ethnic, or religious lines. The power struggles between these groups intensifies the violence and desire for vengeance within prisons. Because gangs engage in criminal behavior,

On April 24, 2007, helicopters from Indianapolis, Indiana, television station WISH-TV filmed a prison riot in progress at the New Castle Correctional Facility, a medium-security men's prison. The riot occurred after a group of prisoners, recently transferred against their will from another facility, refused to wear state-issued smocks during a meal in the prison dining hall. The prisoners attacked a guard, inciting others to riot as well. Though prisoners set fire to mattresses and other furniture, full order and authority was restored within two hours, and neither prisoners nor guards suffered serious injuries.

they have been given alternate names such as "disruptive groups" or "security-threat groups," which make them easier to target with prison policies to maintain security.[23]

COLLECTIVE MALE VIOLENCE (RIOTS)

Riots are part of U.S. history; they are part of U.S. prison history, too. Two modern examples are the famous riot at Attica State Prison in New York in 1971 and the bloody riot at New Mexico Penitentiary in 1980. Although riots like those at Attica and New Mexico rightly deserve their notorious reputation, riots are a rare part of prison life. Some riots are spontaneous; others are planned in advance. A highly organized inmate force held together by racial solidarity and political consciousness planned and executed the Attica riot in 1971. To a considerable extent, that riot was a product of the 1960s—a political protest against "white oppression."

Modern riots have complicated causes. According to Jeanne B. Stinchcomb, environmental stressors such as regimentation, personal deprivations, limits on freedom, boredom, idleness, brutality, racial conflicts, and gangs can lead to riots.[24] Substandard facilities lead to stress that can lead to riots. Crowded conditions, the depersonalization of surroundings, bad food, and poor plumbing, heating, lighting, or ventilation create stress for inmates subjected to these conditions.

Inappropriate staffing caused by budget cuts, hiring freezes, or just inadequate administration of personnel can lead to a lack of basic services for inmates, improper supervision, and poor security. This creates tension among inmates and between inmates and staff that can lead to riots.

Public apathy and a "get tough" attitude against prisoners can lead to a heavy emphasis on incapacitation and less emphasis on treatment and programming. As inmates internalize this ostracization from society, they can become alienated and this can lead to riots.

LO4 Common Prison Programs

As you read about prison programs, keep in mind that in too many prisons there are disappointingly few programs or, perhaps more accurately, there are too many programs with far too little money and staff.[25] It may surprise you to learn this, especially in view of the two important missions that prison programs are supposed to help accomplish:

1. Rehabilitate prisoners
2. Manage prisons by keeping prisoners busy and out of trouble

Why do too many prisons either lack programs or have programs without adequate support? The easy answer is the public's enthusiastic, but not well-informed, response to an article published in 1974 by Robert Martinson. Entitled "What Works? Questions and Answers about Prison Reform," the article concluded: "With few and isolated exceptions, the rehabilitative efforts that have been reported so far have no appreciable effect on recidivism."[26] Martinson had conducted the most extensive review of prison programs (231 programs) in the history of evaluation research. The professionals and the public saw the facts and concluded, "'Nothing works,' so why do anything?"

This knee-jerk reaction to the "nothing works" pronouncement was followed by a heated debate that led to a more balanced assessment of the effectiveness of rehabilitation programs. As some commentators pointed out, prison programs have broader missions than just reducing recidivism. These include reducing misbehavior in prison; contributing to peaceful, humane punishment; and improving prisoners' chances of getting a job when they get out of prison. Practically, rehabilitation programs are aimed at "correcting" deficiencies that have the strongest links to criminal behavior. We will focus here on five types of programs—education, work, recreation, religious programs, and substance abuse.

EDUCATION IN PRISONS

Prison education programs can be academic or vocational. Teaching prisoners to read and write is the oldest rehabilitation program; it has been a prison mission and a part of prison life since the birth of the reformatories in the 1870s. By the 1930s, primary and secondary education had become primary rehabilitation programs. By the 1960s, college education had been added.[27]

Academic education can reduce recidivism in three ways. First, education improves the chances of getting a job, and getting a job reduces the chances of recidivism. Second, the process of learning itself makes inmates more mature, conscientious, and committed to achievement. These qualities can lead to better decision making, and better decision making reduces the chances of returning to prison. Third, the classroom is a chance for inmates to "interact with civilian employees in . . . a nonauthoritarian, goal-directed relationship."[28]

College education programs are available in many prisons either through distance learning or from local colleges and universities. Research has shown that the higher the level of education, the more successful the inmate is after release. Inmates with more education are less likely to reoffend.[29]

Vocational training can include skill training in various fields such as auto mechanics, welding, printing, construction, woodworking, horticulture, data processing, and bookkeeping. The goal of these programs is to teach marketable skills that will allow the released inmate to obtain work after release.[30]

WORK IN PRISON

Education is the oldest rehabilitation program, but work is the oldest prison activity. And just as prisoners come to prison with major educational deficiencies, they also bring major deficiencies in their work history—poor to no work records, few if any marketable skills, and a poor work ethic or none at all.[31] So work programs have multiple missions. Some of these missions are directed at inmates, such as developing positive attitudes toward work, self-discipline, and marketable skills. Two other missions are aimed at prison management:

1. Maintain order and safety by keeping prisoners busy and out of trouble.
2. Reduce the cost of imprisonment by using prison labor.

Prisons have to provide all the services most communities in the outside world have to provide—and more. They require utilities (sewer and water, electricity, telephones), restaurants, bakeries, laundries, hospitals, mail delivery, fire protection, record keeping, and janitorial services. Prisoners do most of the work that provides these services. Obviously, the resources of prisoner labor and time are in great supply in prisons. Prison jobs reveal a great deal about the prestige of the prisoners who hold them. The most prestigious jobs are those closest to decision makers. Record keeping ranks highest because it puts inmates in charge of a valuable commodity—information (who is eligible for release or reclassification to lower or higher security prisons). Desk jobs provide regular access to administrators; food and other commodities service jobs give prisoners access to better food and other amenities *and* to goods that they can sell to other prisoners. The lowest prestige job is also the most available—janitorial work. Not only does it involve menial work like mopping floors, but there is no access to information, goods, or services.[32]

Prison work also includes working in prison industries that produce for the outside world. Prison industries were a major part of prison life from 1900 to 1925. They were considered a major element in the rehabilitation of prisoners. According to the Progressive prison reformers, work was therapeutic as well as useful. But prison industries faced stiff opposition from labor and small business because they took jobs away from union labor and profits away from small businesses. The industries ran into the firmly entrenched principle of less eligibility (prisoners cannot make as much money as free workers).

In the 1980s, though, prison industries returned to prison life. By 2000, prisons were engaged in a long list of enterprises, including car repair, lumbering, ranching, meat processing, making flags, printing, data entry, telephone answering services, Braille translation, microfilming, and CD-ROM copying.[33]

The South Carolina Department of Corrections describes its Prison Industries Program on its website:

> The Prison Industries (PI) Program allows the inmates to return to society with skills that will enable them to become useful and productive citizens. In pursuit of this objective, the cost of incarceration is offset through inmate wages, and quality products and services are provided to qualified businesses and organizations at substantial savings. Three programs operate within Prison Industries: Traditional, Service, and Prison Industry Enterprise (PIE).

The Traditional Program

> Inmates working in the Traditional Program manufacture products such as desks, credenzas, bookcases, mattresses, seating, office modular systems, and janitorial products. These items are sold to state, county, and municipal offices and school districts. Inmates working in this program may receive a wage of up to $.35 per hour. PI offers comprehensive printing services to a wide range of customers. The purchase of all new equipment in the "quick copy" center provides improved quality and service at reduced cost.

The Service Program

> In the Service Program, inmates rebuild/reupholster furniture for both public and private sector customers, disassemble transmissions, recycle textiles, and launder linen items. Additionally, PI packages hosiery, plastic cutlery, and tennis balls. Service work is not original equipment manufacturing, and inmate wages can be negotiated with private sector companies since it does

not fall under Federal Minimum Wage requirements. Inmates earn from $.35 to $1.80 per hour. Donated computers are recycled and upgraded for distribution to local school districts.

The Prison Industry Enterprise (PIE) Program

In the PIE Program, strict guidelines must be followed which require that inmates voluntarily work in the program and acknowledge that taxes, victim compensation, and room and board will be deducted from their gross pay. Inmates in this program are paid the prevailing wage of the local area for the particular jobs they perform. Also, PI does not displace currently employed workers in the community. Since this work is manufacturing and goods are placed in interstate commerce, the PIE guidelines must be followed. Currently hardwood flooring, apparel, computer wire harnesses, furniture, and faucet handles are being produced. Pay ranges from $5.15 to $10.00 per hour.

Currently 2,233 inmates are working in Prison Industries. The Prison Industries Program is completely self-supporting, providing valuable training for the inmates while generating funding for the Agency.[34] ,,

The major justification for the revival of prison industries is the idea that prisoners should pay for their imprisonment. But this rarely happens; only a small percentage of prisoners work in prison industries. Further, many of the prison industry programs cost taxpayers more money than they save. People in charge of prison industries say that potential profits are eaten away by security and other concerns, such as rehabilitating inmates and protecting private businesses from unfair competition. "The goal is really to create work, reduce idleness, and help manage the prison," said Pamela Jo Davis, president of Florida's PRIDE (Prison Rehabilitative Industries and Diversified Enterprises) and chair of Correctional Industries Association, a national umbrella group for prison industries.[35]

Prison work provides all the essential services to maintain prison society, and it occupies prisoners' time and keeps them out of trouble. But what about work *programs* aimed at reducing crime when prisoners leave prison? Some of these programs have focused on vocational training (as discussed earlier); others emphasize job placement, subsidized employment, or temporary financial assistance.[36]

Most evaluations of well-designed programs (randomly selected, strongly matched experimental groups and control groups, and some nonexperimental) from the 1970s until recently have shown little difference in future criminal behavior between experimental groups that received job training or financial assistance and control groups that did not.[37] But not *all* programs have received such a negative evaluation. Arrests for domestic abuse had a greater deterrent effect on *employed* men. Also, an observational study found sex-offender treatment programs were more effective for probationers who had a steady employment history than those who did not.[38] In another study, researchers found that federal offender participants in a nonexperimental vocational apprenticeship had higher employment rates when they left prison than a comparison group. And compared to a control group, participants in prison industries and participants who completed either vocational or apprenticeship training were 24 percent and 33 percent less likely to recidivate, respectively.[39]

RECREATION

Most prisons have athletic teams; many prisoners work out in prison exercise rooms; virtually all watch movies; and some participate in drama, music, art, and journalism. Recreation is an important part of prison life—and, of course, is desired by most prisoners. Recreation programs are good for prisoners: They help to accomplish the mission of rehabilitation to the extent that they teach inmates social skills such as engaging in fair competition, working together, and building self-esteem. They are also part of the reward and punishment system that helps to enforce prison discipline. Few inmates want to lose their recreation privileges. Finally, recreation definitely fits in with the philosophy of humane punishment. Perhaps nothing humanizes prisons more than allowing prisoners to participate in social activities they really enjoy. Of course, recreation programs also pose safety risks. Fights can—and do—erupt during competitive sports, for example. And there is considerable controversy over whether recreation is consistent with punishment.[40]

RELIGIOUS PROGRAMS

Every prison has some religious programs. The First

Amendment guarantees the "free exercise" of religion, so prisons have to provide religious programs. Like most other prison programs, religious programs help prisoners fill time, are supposed to aid in rehabilitation, and contribute to a humane punishment.[41]

In 1992, Todd Clear and his colleagues conducted one of the few national studies of religion in prison.[42] Interviews with inmates indicated that religion helps prisoners by providing a psychological and physical "safe haven." Religion also enables inmates to maintain ties with family and religious volunteers. The study also found that participation in religious programs contributed both to helping prisoners adjust to prison and reducing disciplinary infractions.

DRUG TREATMENT

There is compelling evidence that drug use increases criminal activity among significant numbers of offenders.[43] Almost two-thirds of state prisoners say they use drugs regularly; nearly half of federal prisoners say the same.[44] This has created enormous pressure on corrections departments to create drug treatment programs for prisoners. Most of these programs are therapeutic communities (TCs), which isolate drug-dependent prisoners from the general prison population. This isolation is supposed to increase group pressure on prisoners to commit themselves to the program and decrease peer pressure from outside the group to use drugs. In 2006, there were more than 13,000 drug treatment facilities in the United States. The states with the highest number of drug treatment facilities in 2006 were California, New York, Florida, Illinois, Michigan, and Texas (see Table 14.3).[45]

LO5 The Special Needs of Incarcerated Women

Life in prison is very different for women than for men. Why? There are several reasons including that there are fewer women criminals than men and that women commit lesser offenses. Other reasons include the belief that women are more "reformable" (some say "tractable") than men, assumptions about women's psyche, and conceptions about the role of women.[46]

In 2006, there were more than 112,000 female prisoners in state and federal facilities. Nearly 100,000 of them were in state facilities. The incarceration rate of women in 2006 was 68 incarcerated females per

TABLE 14.3 States with the Most Drug Treatment Facilities, 2006

STATE	NUMBER OF FACILITIES	PERCENT OF U.S. TOTAL (13,771)
California	1,820	13.2%
New York	1,030	7.5%
Florida	688	5.0%
Illinois	588	4.3%
Michigan	539	3.9%
Texas	523	3.8%

Source: "Drug and Alcoholism Treatment Facilities," *Sourcebook of Criminal Justice Statistics Online* (2006), http://www.albany.edu/sourcebook/pdf/t6622006.pdf.

100,000 female residents.[47] Women aged 35 to 39 make up the largest age group among female offenders.

More than half of the increase in women prisoners in recent years is due to the imprisonment of drug offenders. Nearly 30 percent of female inmates are incarcerated for drug offenses.[48] According to Owen and Bloom in 1995, "the legal response to drug-related behavior has become increasingly punitive, resulting in a flood of less serious offenders into the state and federal prison systems."[49] In fact, the number of women serving time for violent offenses has dropped since 1991. One-third of the women serving time for either murder or manslaughter killed relatives.[50]

THE PAINS OF WOMEN'S IMPRISONMENT

Women cope with prison life differently from men. It is harder for women to adjust to prison. Women value privacy more than men do, so communal living, numerous rules, and body searches are more difficult for women trying to adjust to prison life. They also do not have the same levels of support from spouses and family that male inmates tend to have. Female inmates develop emotional intimacy with other inmates to create a quasi-family pattern to help meet their familial needs. They develop power and authority relationships using the family model of relationships. Sexual relations between women are more about mutual affection and caring relationships than the dominance and force that characterize homosexual activity in male prisons.

Female prisons are less violent than male prisons because of the familial relationship model of behavior

In 2006, the American Civil Liberties Union (ACLU) filed a class-action lawsuit against the Taycheedah Correctional Institution, a Wisconsin prison for women. The ACLU alleged that the prison's medical, mental, and dental care was grossly deficient, far below standards set at men's prisons around the country. The ACLU proposed a number of solutions such as employing licensed practical nurses to dispense prisoners' medications and overhauling the prescription ordering process to ensure that prisoners receive the correct drugs on time. In April 2009, Judge Rudolph T. Randa ruled in favor of the ACLU and ordered sweeping reforms at the prison.

that permeates female prisons, but that does not mean that female prisons are more peaceful or easier to manage. In fact, many corrections officers prefer working in the less secure male prisons because they perceive female prisoners as less cooperative and respectful than male prisoners. There are also more disciplinary infractions in female prisons because there are more rules than in male prisons. Female prisoners tend to get more upset by disciplinary actions against themselves or their fellow inmates.[51]

Female inmates are often victimized sexually by prison staff. The abuse ranges from the less serious forms of inappropriate language and verbal degradation to the more serious forms of intrusive searches and sexual assault. In Michigan, for example, more than 500 female inmates are suing the state for sexual assaults that occurred in Michigan facilities during the 1990s while prison officials ignored or dismissed claims by human rights groups that these abuses were being perpetrated by prison staff. A class-action lawsuit has already yielded damages awards totaling almost $50 million for just the first 18 women. More verdicts are expected.[52]

Because there are fewer female inmates, there is less custodial classification in female prisons than in male prisons. As a result, female offenders convicted of a

wide range of offenses with varying degrees of seriousness are housed together. There are also fewer prisons, so women find themselves in remote locations, making it harder for family to visit. Female prisons are also smaller than male prisons, but actually less oppressive and less institutional. There is typically more emphasis on rehabilitation in female prisons.[53]

prisoner reentry the process of prisoners' leaving prison and returning to society

WOMEN'S PRISON PROGRAMS AND SERVICES FOR WOMEN

Because of the smaller female inmate population, state corrections systems are unable to economically justify the same programs and services for female inmates that are provided to male inmates as well as any programs that might be uniquely suited to female inmates. Medical services may not be directed specifically or completely to meet female needs. Educational and vocational programs are limited and may not provide the range of education levels and the vocational skills found in male prison programs. The programs offered tend to be gender stereotyped—sewing, typing, and cosmetology—which do not provide the highly marketable skills women will need when they reenter society. There are fewer institutional work assignments for women, and they are paid less than male inmates for prison work. Women also have less access to work release programs than men do.[54]

LO6 Prisoner Reentry

In 2006, more than 700,000 prisoners were released from prison, while more than 350 persons per 100,000 residents were on parole. Nearly 90 percent of the parolees were male, and most were white or black. Most parolees had been incarcerated for drug crimes (39 percent), followed by violent crimes (26 percent). Of the parolees, 44 percent completed their parole, but 39 percent were returned to prison either because they committed a new offense or because parole was revoked. Just over 10 percent absconded from parole supervision.[55]

Of course, prisoners have always gone home, and corrections officials have always struggled with the problem of **prisoner reentry** (the process of leaving prison and returning to society). But since the early 1990s, reentry has changed dramatically. The huge increase in the numbers of released prisoners has stretched resources to the point that officials worry that they cannot carry out their two main missions: protecting the public and assisting in successfully reintegrating released prisoners.

Research confirms that today's reentering prisoners have more problems and therefore need more supervision and assistance than prisoners in the past (see Table 14.4). According to Amy Solomon and her colleagues at the Urban Institute, a survey of reentry programs found the following:

> *Not only are more prisoners returning home than ever before, but they are also returning less prepared for life outside the walls. Many will have difficulty managing the most basic ingredients for successful reintegration—reconnecting with jobs, housing, and their families, and accessing needed substance abuse and health care treatment. Most will be arrested in three years, and many will be returned to prison for new crimes or parole violations. The cycle of incarceration and reentry into society carries the potential for profound adverse consequences for prisoners, their families, and communities.*[56]

Since the 1980s, reentering prisoners have served more time in prison, especially for drug crimes, than previous prisoners.[57] Nevertheless, this does not deter two-thirds of all released prisoners from being rearrested and half from committing another crime within three years.[58] Paradoxically, while the number of "churners" (offenders who are returned to prison for technical violations or for committing new crimes) is rising, so is the number of prisoners released for the first time.[59]

WHERE DO RELEASED PRISONERS GO?

The vast majority of prisoners go back to where they came from. That means they reenter high-crime, large-city neighborhoods with high unemployment rates,

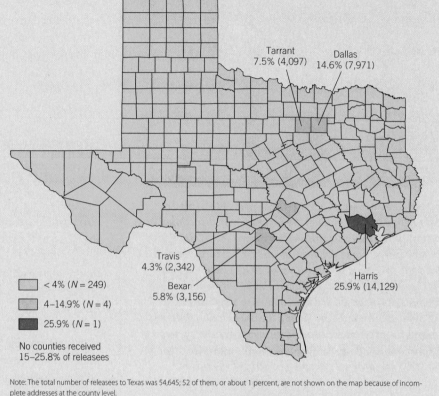

FIGURE 14.1
Portrait of Prisoner Reentry in Texas

Tarrant
7.5% (4,097)

Dallas
14.6% (7,971)

Travis
4.3% (2,342)

Bexar
5.8% (3,156)

Harris
25.9% (14,129)

☐ < 4% (N = 249)

☐ 4–14.9% (N = 4)

■ 25.9% (N = 1)

No counties received
15–25.8% of releasees

Note: The total number of releasees to Texas was 54,645; 52 of them, or about 1 percent, are not shown on the map because of incomplete addresses at the county level.

Source: Jamie Watson, Amy L. Solomon, Nancy G. LaVigne, and Jeremy Travis, *A Portrait of Prisoner Reentry in Texas* (Washington, DC: The Urban Institute, March 2004), p. 53, Figure 6.2.

few affordable housing choices, and hardly any social services. Texas provides a typical example of this concentration of released prisoners.[60] Almost 60 percent of Texas prisoners are released to five counties (see Figure 14.1). More than 25 percent go to Houston, the largest city in the state, and Harris County (where Houston is located).[61] Not only does Houston have the highest rate of supervised released prisoners per 100,000 residents (3.1), but they are concentrated in neighborhoods in five zip codes (see Figure 14.2). Furthermore, these neighborhoods are among the areas in Houston most affected by poverty, unemployment, crime, and other characteristics linked to crime and other problems, including a large number of high school dropouts, a low percentage of owner-occupied housing, and a much higher than average number of female-headed households.[62]

WHICH REENTRY PROGRAMS "WORK"?

Opinions vary widely about the best programs for prisoner reentry. Some say programs with more community

TABLE 14.4 Problems More Acute among Reentering Prisoners Today Than in the Past
• Prisoners are more disconnected from the potential support of their families and friends.
• There are more health problems linked to untreated substance abuse and physical and mental illnesses.
• Prisoners are less educated.
• Prisoners are less employable.
• Prisoners are barred from receiving public assistance, such as food stamps, health care, and housing.

Sources: Joan Petersilia, "What Works in Reentry? Reviewing and Questioning the Evidence." *Federal Probation* (September 2004), p. 4. Amy Solomon, Michelle Waul, Ashley Van Ness, and Jeremy Travis, *Outside the Walls: A National Snapshot of Community-Based Prisoner Reentry Programs.* (Washington, DC: Urban Institute, 2004), p. 12.

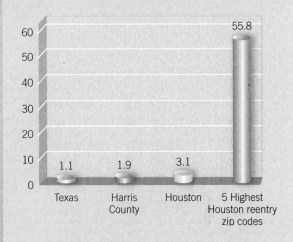

FIGURE 14.2

The Rate of Texas Prisoner Reentry per 100,000 Residents

Source: Jamie Watson, Amy L. Solomon, Nancy G. LaVigne, and Jeremy Travis, *A Portrait of Prisoner Reentry in Texas* (Washington, DC: The Urban Institute, March 2004), p. 69, Figure 7.4.

involvement are the answer; others recommend that judges control reentry. Others would put the responsibility on the reentering prisoners themselves. Some advise a mixed strategy of increasing supervision for high-risk offenders and reducing it for the rest; still others would follow a "broken windows" theory of reentry, putting safety first and enforcing even small violations.[63]

In her 2004 review of research on "what works in prisoner reentry," Joan Petersilia estimated that since 1975 states have tried more than 10,000 programs.[64] Which ones work? In 1998, MacKenzie and her colleagues identified 184 evaluations between 1978 and 1998 that were based on some kind of control or comparison group. According to those criteria, she found six programs that reduced recidivism and two that were promising. She also found that intensive supervision and electronic monitoring by *themselves* did not reduce recidivism.[65]

Of nine credible evaluations, Seiter and Kadela *did* find a few programs in 2003 that reduced recidivism: vocational training and work release, halfway houses, and drug treatment.[66] They also found that education programs increased achievement scores even if they did not reduce recidivism. And there is some evidence that prerelease programs reduce recidivism.

Model guidelines for reentry programs call for three phases of reentry to enhance the chances of success for released inmates. These phases begin while the inmate is still in prison and continue on the outside.

❝*Phase 1—Protect and Prepare: Institution-Based Programs. These programs are designed to prepare offenders to reenter society. Services provided in this phase will include education, mental health and substance abuse treatment, job training, mentoring, and full diagnostic and risk assessment.*

Phase 2—Control and Restore: Community-Based Transition Programs. These programs will work with offenders prior to and immediately following their release from correctional institutions. Services provided in this phase will include, as appropriate, education, monitoring, mentoring, life skills training, assessment, job skills development, and mental health and substance abuse treatment.

Phase 3—Sustain and Support: Community-Based Long-Term Support Programs. These programs will connect individuals who have left the supervision of the justice system with a network of social services agencies and community-based organizations to provide ongoing services and mentoring relationships.❞

Recommended program elements for reentry programs include institution-based readiness programs, institutional and community assessment centers, reentry courts, supervised or electronically monitored boarding houses, mentoring programs, and community corrections centers.[67]

Like adults, juveniles are subject to
law enforcement, courts, and corrections agencies.

15

Juvenile Justice

Learning Outcomes

LO1 Explain the history and development of juvenile justice, including the child-saving movement and the doctrine of *parens patriae*

LO2 Understand the rights of juveniles in the juvenile justice system

LO3 Understand juvenile delinquency and describe the nature of juvenile delinquency

LO4 Describe the juvenile justice system

LO5 Describe the nature and purpose of law enforcement for juveniles

LO6 Describe the purpose and operation of the juvenile court

LO7 Understand the dual system of justice and the waiver process for juveniles

LO8 Describe the nature and purpose of juvenile corrections

When you were younger, did your parents ever ground you or tell you that you couldn't play video games for several weeks because of your bad behavior? If so, did you consider hiring a hit man to get even? In 2007, a 16-year-old Maryland youth did hire a hit man to kill his parents. Most kids would think about running away or doing something defiant like getting a tattoo—but not this kid. He was grounded and told that he could not use his PlayStation or watch television for several weeks for stealing, not attending school, and getting arrested. He then stole $45 from his sister and got into a heated argument with his parents. When he threatened to have the family killed, his mother contacted the police, and an undercover officer posed as a hit man. The youth offered the undercover officer his father's truck as payment. He was charged with attempted murder and sent to the adult system to await trial as an adult. Although his mother wanted him tried as an adult, he was ultimately tried as a juvenile because the juvenile court felt he would benefit from its system. He pleaded guilty and was sentenced to serve up to four years in a juvenile facility. This was certainly an unusual case, but many cases of juvenile crime involve some unusual circumstances. How do we deal with juvenile crime? When should a juvenile be tried as an adult? When can we reform a juvenile offender? This chapter addresses these issues.[1]

LO1 The Juvenile Justice System

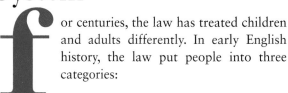or centuries, the law has treated children and adults differently. In early English history, the law put people into three categories:

1. Children under 7, who could not form criminal intent; therefore, they could not be tried for criminal behavior.

2. Children between 7 and 14, who were *presumed* to be incompetent and thus incapable of forming criminal intent unless evidence showed otherwise; then they could be tried for crimes.

3. Adults over 14, who were presumed to be *competent* and thus capable of forming criminal intent unless they were insane or retarded.

The doctrine of *parens patriae* and the legal presumptions against children's capacity to form criminal intent came to North America with the English colonists.[2]

THE CHILD-SAVING MOVEMENT AND THE PROGRESSIVES

During the 1800s, the desire for social reform led to a passionate "child-saving" movement. At the same time, a great social, economic, and intellectual transformation was taking place. People were increasingly getting their education, livelihood, and entertainment not at home with their families but in schools, factories, and places of public amusement. Not surprisingly, the child-saving movement relied on two institutions outside the home, the house of refuge and the reform school, to "save" children. Both institutions were based on the nineteenth-century idea that children's environments made them bad. Houses of refuge and reform schools would take them out of their bad homes and away from their unhealthy associations and turn bad children into law-abiding people.[3]

Child saving was also on the agenda of the Progressive Era (about 1900 to 1914) reformers. According to the Progressives, children

The ancient **doctrine of *parens patriae*** allowed the government to intervene in family life to protect children's estates from dishonest guardians. This principle expanded over time to include the power to intervene to protect children against parental neglect, incompetence, and abuse.

misbehaved because they lived in unhealthy homes with unhealthy families. "Healthy homes" were homes where the parents lived according to middle-class values. They worked hard, saved their money, went to church, did not drink or smoke, and obeyed the laws of God and the state. The Progressives maintained that families who did not have these values—particularly immigrants—should acquire them. How would they learn the right values? From the good examples set by the Progressives and with a lot of help from Progressive government experts.

The Progressives had enormous, but perhaps naïve, confidence in both the state and in experts. This confidence led them to call on the state to supply experts to "save" children by "curing" their "unhealthy" home lives. The Progressives distrusted traditional institutions dominated (they claimed) by outdated, inefficient, and ineffective formal rules. So they turned away from the criminal courts, which emphasized criminal behavior, and created a new institution. The **juvenile court** concentrated not on behavior but on children and what they needed to make them responsible.[4]

In juvenile court, judges did not sit on benches above children but beside them at a table. Proceedings

At age 13, Nathaniel Abraham was convicted of second-degree murder for using a handgun to shoot a man as he exited a convenience store in 1997. Though he was tried as an adult, Abraham was sentenced as a juvenile to serve seven years at a maximum security detention center in January 2000. After being released from juvenile custody in January 2007, Abraham was arrested at a gas station on a drug charge just 16 months later.

© AP Images/Charlie Cortez

© Image Source/Jupiterimages

were informal. Their aim was not to affix blame but to find out what caused children to "go wrong" so that it could be put right. The Progressives were great fact collectors. They gathered information about children's home life, past behavior, health, and anything else that might help them diagnose and cure youths' problems.

The Progressives were also great optimists. They had a strong faith that government could cure delinquency if it just could ensure that experts were free to make professional judgments unhampered by formal rules. Their optimistic faith in government led to the adoption of what came to be called a **medical model of crime**. The medical model is based on the idea that crime is a disease that experts can diagnose, treat, and cure. Based on these optimistic ideas, Chicago established the first juvenile court in 1899. By 1925, almost every jurisdiction in the country had one.[5]

JUVENILE JUSTICE SINCE 1960

During the 1960s, the professional interest in children shifted from needs to rights. This shift was due both to the general rights movement and a growing skepticism about the capacity of government to meet the needs of children. The increased fear of crime and disorder during that turbulent time led critics to attack juvenile justice generally and juvenile courts specifically.

During the 1970s, the fear of crime and youth rebellion continued to rise. Also rising was disillusionment with the juvenile justice system's capacity either to meet the needs of juveniles or to secure their rights. Fear and disillusionment contributed to a harsher public attitude toward youth crime and to a renewed confidence that retribution was the right response to crime and delinquency. A growing consensus among both criminal justice professionals and the public demanded that juveniles be tried as adults.

Fueling this consensus was a belief that if juveniles are old enough to commit crimes, they are old enough to take the consequences. Today, every state allows prosecutors to try juveniles as young as 14 as adults under specific circumstances. Children as young as age 10 can be tried as adults in several states, including Indiana, South Dakota, and Vermont.[6] In Pennsylvania, for example, by law anyone over the age of 10 is charged as an adult for the crime of homicide. In February 2009,

an 11-year-old boy in Pennsylvania allegedly killed his father's pregnant girlfriend. Under the law, he was charged as an adult and faces a maximum sentence of life in prison.[7]

medical model of crime a model based on the idea that crime is a disease that experts can diagnose, treat, and cure

juvenile delinquent a youth who has committed either crimes or status offenses, or both

LO2
Rights of Juveniles

Several landmark U.S. Supreme Court decisions have restricted the informal, discretionary powers of the juvenile court and other agencies dealing with juveniles. At the same time, those decisions granted to juveniles a number of rights already provided to adult criminal defendants. In 1966, for example, in *Kent v. United States* (a case involving a 16-year-old charged with housebreaking, robbery, and rape), the Court ruled that juvenile court proceedings have to provide juveniles with the basic due process right to a fair hearing.[8]

The Court extended juvenile rights further in *In re Gault* (1967).[9] The case involved proceedings against a 15-year-old Arizona boy who had made lewd remarks to an elderly woman on the telephone. The juvenile court confined the juvenile to a training school. The U.S. Supreme Court ruled that committing a juvenile to a correctional facility required:

1. Written notice that a hearing was scheduled
2. Advice about the right to counsel
3. The right to confront and cross-examine witnesses

In *In re Winship* (1970), a 12-year-old boy had been charged with purse snatching.[10] The U.S. Supreme Court ruled that due process requires proof beyond a reasonable doubt before a juvenile can be classified as a **juvenile delinquent**.

Juveniles do not have *all* the rights enjoyed by adult

juveniles those under juvenile justice jurisdiction—children 8 to 16 (or 18 in some states)

delinquency includes conduct that would be criminal if an adult engaged in it

status offenses conduct that is illegal only if juveniles engage in it

criminal defendants, so juvenile proceedings are not exactly like adult criminal court proceedings. In *McKeiver v. Pennsylvania* (1970), for example, the Court ruled that juveniles do not have the right to a jury trial. In the Court's words,

> *We do not mean to indicate that the hearing must be held to conform with all the requirements of a criminal trial but we do hold that the hearing must measure up to the essentials of due process and fair treatment.*[11]

LO3 Juvenile Delinquency

States vary considerably in their definitions of **juveniles**. Most states exclude children under 8 from juvenile justice jurisdiction. States differ about the upper age limit, though, with some using 16 and others 18 as the dividing line between juvenile and criminal justice jurisdiction. In most states, "older" juveniles, those within a year or two of the upper age limit, can be treated either as juveniles or as adults, depending on the circumstances.

The juvenile justice system processes several types of juveniles: the needy, the dependent, the neglected, and the delinquent. In this chapter, you will learn only about delinquents and their delinquency. **Delinquency** is an act committed by a juvenile for which an adult could be prosecuted in a criminal court, but when committed by a juvenile is within the jurisdiction of the juvenile court. Delinquent acts include crimes against persons, crimes against property, drug offenses, and crimes against public order, when juveniles commit such acts.[12] A **status offense** is conduct that is illegal only if juveniles engage in it. Common examples include truancy, underage drinking, curfew violations, running away, and incorrigibility.

Serious offenses by delinquents may result in their confinement in some form of detention. The state of Texas houses its convicted juveniles in facilities of the Texas Youth Commission (TYC), the state's juvenile corrections agency. The TYC provides this description of its mission and its criteria for confinement of offenders:

> *TYC provides for the care, custody, rehabilitation, and reestablishment in society of Texas' most chronically delinquent or serious juvenile offenders. Texas judges commit these youth to TYC for felony-level offenses committed when they were at least age 10 and less than age 17. TYC can maintain jurisdiction over these offenders until their 19th birthdays. (A small group of identified youth, however, who were committed to TYC prior to June 6, 2007, and were classified as sentenced offenders, can remain under TYC jurisdiction until their 21st birthdays.)*

> *TYC operates a system of 12 secure institutions and nine residential halfway house programs. The agency also contracts with private or local government providers for a wide range of services to TYC offenders.*

> *All male offenders sent to the Texas Youth Commission start at the McLennan County State Juvenile Correctional Facility, Unit I, in Mart. All female offenders are sent to the Ron*

In late 2008, an eight-year-old Arizona boy allegedly shot and killed his father, Vincent Romero, and a man renting a room in Romero's house. According to prosecutors, the boy shot each victim at least four times with a .22-caliber hunting rifle, methodically stopping to reload the weapon as he killed them. Though he was initially charged with two counts of first-degree murder, in February 2009 the young defendant accepted a plea bargain that reduced the charge to one count of negligent homicide, requiring him to undergo follow-up evaluations at ages 12 and 15, and before his 18th birthday. According to his mother at the time of the plea, the boy was still too young to understand the gravity of his actions or the plea he agreed to.

© AP Images/Dana Felthauser

Some youth are committed to TYC under the Determinate Sentencing law, which provides for sentences of up to 40 years for the most serious crimes. The sentence begins at TYC, and depending on the youth's behavior, he or she can be transferred to the adult prison system (Texas Department of Criminal Justice) to complete the sentence.[13] "

Let's look at how delinquency is measured and at juvenile arrests.

MEASURING DELINQUENCY

It is not easy to measure delinquency because many statistics are incomplete. Most criticisms of adult crime statistics also apply to measures of juvenile delinquency. In fact, juvenile statistics come from the same sources: the Uniform Crime Reports, the National Crime Survey, court records, and self-reports. Despite difficulties in measuring delinquency, we know that youths are considerably more "crime-prone than adults, that juvenile offenders tend to commit crimes in groups, and that juvenile offenders are frequently armed. Several highlights also stand out.

- In 2002, the number of homicides committed by juveniles dropped to its lowest levels since 1984.
- One of every 12 murders in 2002 was committed by a juvenile.
- The decline in juvenile homicides was driven by a significant decrease in the number of male members of minority groups killing other male minority group members.
- Most juvenile offenders do not continue their offending into adulthood. Just 25 percent of juveniles aged 16 to 17 offend again at age 18 or 19, their first two years of legal adulthood.
- In 2003, school crimes were common. One out of eight students was in a fight, and one out of three had property stolen or damaged.
- The proportion of students who carried a weapon to school dropped to 6 percent in 2003.
- More than half of high school seniors have used an illicit drug at least once.
- Youth gangs have declined in nonurban areas but remain a substantial urban problem.
- Violent juvenile crime is highest on school days during after-school hours.[14]

Jackson State Juvenile Correctional Complex in Brownwood. During the 21- to 28-day average stay, they receive:

- *A physical evaluation and survey of medical history*
- *Educational testing and assessment*
- *Psychological evaluation*
- *Social summary*
- *Introduction to the TYC treatment program and to behavioral expectations*
- *Assessment of needs for specialized treatment such as sex offender behavior, chemical dependency, mental retardation or violent crime behavior*

The evaluations help staff determine placement. Approximately 80 percent of offenders are assigned to a TYC secure correctional facility, and 20 percent go into facilities and programs run by contract providers. Halfway houses are used for some youth as a transitional assignment after they have completed their stay in a secure setting.

Time Served: Youth are assigned a minimum length of stay, which is the minimum amount of time they must spend in a residential program before parole consideration. This assigned length of stay is based on the crime they committed.

FIGURE 15.1

Proportion of Serious, Violent, and Chronic Offenses among Children Younger Than 13 versus Those 13 and Older

Child offenders had a greater proportion of serious, violent, and chronic careers than older-onset offenders. Offenders outside the Serious, Violent, and Chronic circles (yellow areas) were referred to court one to three times but never for a serious offense. Overlapping circles represent offenders who committed multiple types of offenses. The circles and overlapping areas are drawn in proportion to the numbers of offenses of each type.

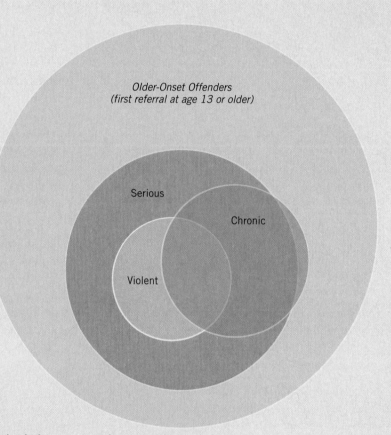

Older-Onset Offenders
(first referral at age 13 or older)

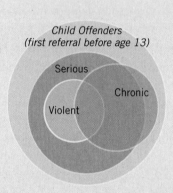

Child Offenders
(first referral before age 13)

Violent offenders: Committed murder, kidnapping, violent sexual assault, robbery, or aggravated assault

Serious offenders: Committed violent offenses plus burglary, serious larceny, motor vehicle theft, arson, weapons offenses, or drug dealing

Chronic offenders: Were referred to court four or more times

Source: Melissa Sickmund, *Juveniles in Court* (Washington, DC: Office of Juvenile Justice and Delinquency Prevention, June 2003), p. 29.

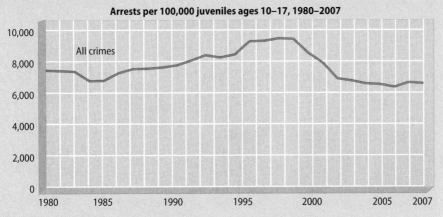

FIGURE 15.2

Juvenile Arrest Rates for All Crimes, 1980–2007

Arrests per 100,000 juveniles ages 10–17, 1980–2007

All crimes

Source: *OJJDP Statistical Briefing Book* Online (Washington, DC: Office of Juvenile Justice and Delinquency Prevention, October 24, 2008, Retrieved on March 3, 2009, from http://ojjdp.ncjrs.gov/ojstatbb/crime/JAR_Display.asp?ID=qa05200).

JUVENILE ARRESTS

Here are some of the highlights from the 2006 survey of juvenile arrests:

- Juvenile arrests increased modestly in 2005 and 2006, but because the 2004 arrest numbers were the lowest since 1987, the 2006 arrest numbers were actually relatively low.

- Property crime arrests continued to decline and were the lowest since 1980.

- The proportion of females entering the system has grown. While violent crime arrests for males declined 22 percent between 1997 and 2006, the decline was only 12 percent for females.

- Simple assault arrest rates for males dropped 4 percent while female arrest rates increased 19 percent.

- Although blacks made up only 17 percent of the juvenile population, black juveniles accounted for 51 percent of violent crime arrests and 31 percent of property crime arrests.[15]

Another part of this picture is that juveniles who begin offending at an early age are more likely to become violent offenders (see Figure 15.1 on the previous page). The good news is that the juvenile arrest rates for all crimes have declined. The 2007 juvenile arrest rate was the lowest since the 1980s (see Figure 15.2).

The picture of juvenile crime that we have painted may not be very pretty, but let's end this section on a cautiously optimistic note. Take the likelihood of becoming a violent offender, depicted in Figure 15.1. The bad news is that 16 percent of offenders who enter the juvenile justice system when they are nine years old will later become violent offenders. The good news is that 84 percent will not!

LO4 The Process of the Juvenile System

t he juvenile justice system is a state and a local affair. Like adult criminal justice, the juvenile system consists of law enforcement, courts, and corrections agencies (see Figure 15.3). Most cases are referred to the juvenile justice system by law enforcement. Law enforcement will divert some cases away from the system, and the rest will proceed into the system. The juvenile justice system is similar to the adult criminal justice system, but the phases have different names. Convictions in the juvenile justice system, for example, are called adjudications.[16] In the next section, we will take a closer look at juvenile law enforcement, courts, and corrections.

LO5 Law Enforcement and Juveniles

m ost large-city police departments have special youth divisions. Juvenile units keep records on juveniles, investigate cases involving them, and initiate referrals to the juvenile court. Juvenile officers can detain juveniles in secure facilities for brief periods. Although these special

© Steve Liss/Time Life Pictures/Getty Images

FIGURE 15.3

Juvenile Justice System Structure and Process (Case Flow Diagram)

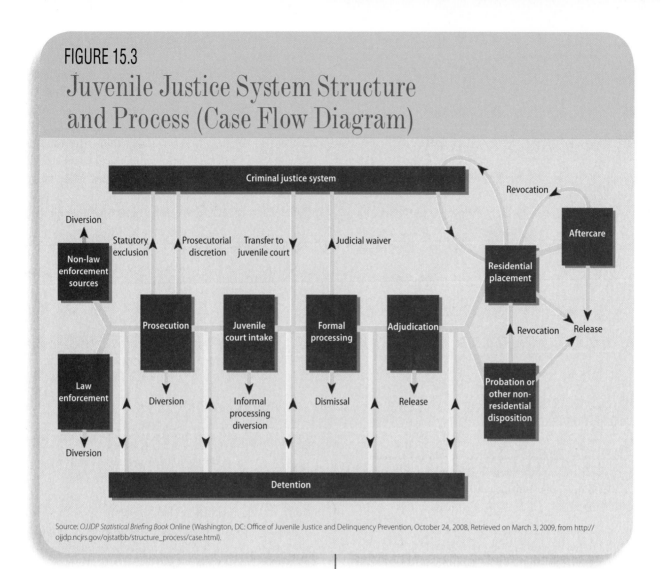

Source: *OJJDP Statistical Briefing Book* Online (Washington, DC: Office of Juvenile Justice and Delinquency Prevention, October 24, 2008, Retrieved on March 3, 2009, from http://ojjdp.ncjrs.gov/ojstatbb/structure_process/case.html).

youth divisions are responsible for juveniles, in practice, regular patrol officers encounter most juveniles and make the critical decisions whether to investigate and/or arrest them.[17]

How police handle juveniles depends on a combination of internal and external influences that differ from department to department and even among individuals within departments. Departments adopting a community-service approach emphasize helping juveniles, whereas departments stressing the crime-fighting role view rehabilitation differently. Regular patrol officers who make the most contacts with juveniles also have different philosophies when responding to juvenile activity. Their individual philosophies may be different from the philosophy their agency has toward juveniles.

Department policies and the outlooks of individual officers also affect the way juveniles are processed. The general formalization of the criminal process has had less effect on police discretion in processing juveniles than on police dealings with adults. The police have a range of options in deciding what to do with juvenile lawbreakers. Their four major choices are to:

1. Ignore them.
2. Counsel and release them.
3. Refer them to other agencies.
4. Process them further into the juvenile justice system.[18]

If officers see juveniles together in a situation where the officers "sense something is wrong," for example, they may simply pass by or stop for a brief conversation. Or they may take further actions.[19] From the least to the most invasive, the officers' actions might include:

1. Ask the juveniles for their names and addresses and what they are up to.
2. Search them.
3. Tell them to break up and move on.
4. Take them home and warn their parents to keep them off the street.
5. Take them to the station for further questioning without arresting them.
6. Take them to the station house and call in their parents. If the parents seem amenable, the officers warn the parents and kids of the consequences of further bad conduct and send them home.

In about half the cases, police decide to "counsel and release."[20] These actions may be *informal*, but informal handling can have greater consequences than you might expect. For example, police might treat this option like an informal probation system. So, if juveniles who are counseled and released commit further offenses, they will be arrested. Police also use the informal counsel-and-release option as a trade for information about other juveniles.[21] Juveniles who are not counseled and dismissed are either arrested and then released or referred to either a social service agency (diversion) or sent to juvenile court (referral).

In 2005, law enforcement agencies referred 91 percent of property offense cases, 91 percent of drug law violation cases, 87 percent of person offense cases, and 61 percent of public order offense cases to juvenile court.[22] At least one criterion for deciding whether to release, divert, arrest, or refer to juvenile court should be familiar to you by now—the seriousness of the offense. The police are almost certain to arrest and refer to juvenile court juveniles suspected of serious crimes, such as murder, rape, or major theft. They are much more likely to dismiss or divert juveniles suspected of status offenses.

Citizen complaints also are important in police decisions to arrest juveniles. Police acquire most of their information concerning juveniles in the same way they do for adults—from private persons. If complainants are present and demand action short of arrest, police comply; if they ask for leniency, police grant it; if they demand formal arrest and processing, the officers usually comply. So the presence and wishes of those who complain influence whether juveniles are counseled and released, diverted to social service agencies, or arrested.

LO6 The Operation of the Juvenile Court

In 2005, juvenile courts disposed of more than 1.7 million delinquency cases.[23] The juvenile court process starts with a referral. Law enforcement refers most of the cases to juvenile court; parents, schools, child welfare agencies, and probation officers refer the rest.[24] From the time of referral, the juvenile court process consists of three steps:

1. Intake
2. Adjudication
3. Disposition

INTAKE

Intake involves screening the cases referred to the court. Juvenile probation departments and/or prosecutors' offices are in charge of intake. Screening consists of making one of three choices:

1. Dismiss the case outright.
2. Handle the manner informally.
3. Request formal intervention by the juvenile court.[25]

The decision-making process behind the choice begins with prosecutors and/or the probation department deciding whether there is enough evidence to prove the case against the juvenile. If there is not, they dismiss the case outright.

If there is enough evidence, the next step is to decide whether formal court action (adjudication) is necessary. Intake officers dismiss about half of the cases with enough evidence; in the other half, juveniles voluntarily agree to a diversion and sign a written agreement (consent decree) to comply with specific conditions for a specific period of time.[26] Typical conditions include victim restitution, school attendance, drug counseling, and/or curfew. Probation officers monitor compliance with the conditions. If the juvenile meets the conditions, the case is dismissed; if not, the case is referred for a formal juvenile court hearing.

The Denver (Colorado) District Attorney's Office, for example, has a special diversion division for juvenile

© Creatas Images/Jupiterimages

Juvenile Diversion

When a juvenile commits a crime and lands in the criminal justice system, you have to wonder why it happened. And, you have to wonder if there is something that could be done to help that young person stay out of more trouble.

The Denver District Attorney's Juvenile Diversion Program works with eligible first-time juvenile offenders as an alternative to formal court proceedings. These young people are referred to as clients and participate in Diversion with their parent or guardian. Diversion programs focus on teaching skills and providing opportunities to practice those skills. Clients are assigned to programs based on their need and must perform community service and complete restitution. Programs include:

Cognitive-Behavioral Programming:

These are group settings in which clients learn such things as life skills, problem solving, conflict resolution, critical thinking and reasoning skills. Groups are based on gender, age, and language.

Community Service:

Clients perform community service through projects such as graffiti removal, trash pick-up, and helping at food banks, homeless shelters, and community events by request.

Specialized Client Services:

This includes Educational Enhancement and Substance Abuse Screening and Treatment. Clients in the Educational Enhancement program receive visits at school by staff members, and get regular feedback about attendance, behavior, and performance. They may also be involved in a tutoring program that provides homework help and topic-specific instruction. A full-service computer lab including Microsoft Word and the Internet is available, along with English as a second language. Substance Abuse Screening is conducted on all clients. Referrals are made to the TASC program for those clients with substance abuse issues.

Family Intervention:

Clients may take part in family therapy, which includes family sessions as well as individual counseling sessions.

Restitution Programs:

Restitution is an important piece of the Juvenile Diversion Program. Some clients participate in a program called Acquiring Restitution Through Talent (A.R.T.T.). These clients work with various art forms and crafts then sell their items to earn the money to pay back victims.

Restorative Justice Program:

In a number of cases, the victims of crime or community members affected by crime can meet face to face with the person who committed the crime. Restorative justice involves trained staff and/or community members who help ensure both the victim and offender receive answers to their questions as they work toward restoration and closure.[27]

---

delinquency petitions requests for a trial (adjudicatory hearing) to find juveniles delinquent and make them wards of the court

transfer petitions requests for a hearing to waive the juvenile court's jurisdiction and transfer the case to adult criminal court

offenders. See a description of its mission and programming for juvenile diversion in the box above.

To start formal juvenile court proceedings, intake officers have to file one of two types of petition. **Delinquency petitions** request a trial (in juvenile court, it is called an adjudicatory hearing) to find the youth a delinquent and make the youth a ward of the court. **Transfer petitions** ask for a hearing to waive the juvenile court's jurisdiction and transfer the case to adult criminal courts. Let's look at the proceedings that follow a delinquency petition.

ADJUDICATORY HEARING

During *adjudication*, judges (with a lot of help from probation officers) decide whether the allegations in the petition prove delinquency. If they do, juveniles are formally judged "delinquent." Since the U.S. Supreme Court opinions reviewed earlier in this chapter, the juvenile court's proceedings have become more formal than originally intended. Juveniles are notified of the pending delinquency charges, lawyers are more often present, evidence standards are stricter, and proceedings are more like criminal courts.

DISPOSITION

Once juveniles have been adjudicated delinquent, judges schedule **disposition hearings** to decide how best to resolve delinquency cases. In the meantime, probation officers conduct background investigations to assist judges in their disposition decisions. Juvenile court judges have wide discretion to choose from a broad range of alternative dispositions, ranging from unconditional dismissal to commitment to secure correctional facilities resembling adult prisons.

Judges may decide to order a **continuance in contemplation of dismissal**. If delinquents do not get into further trouble with the law within a specified period—often between six months and a year—judges will dismiss their cases. Continuance lets judges keep open their option for further action if juveniles do not obey the law. Judges might also continue cases until the fulfillment of specified conditions, including taking required diagnostic tests and treatment for disturbances stemming from emotional problems, substance abuse, and physical illness; observing curfew; paying restitution to victims; and performing community service. Delinquents usually are allowed one to six months to fulfill these conditions.[28]

Probation of delinquents strongly resembles adult probation. For delinquents confined in juvenile correctional facilities for status offenses and minor property crimes, confinement probably means training schools or camps. Or the confinement might consist of community-based programs, such as foster care, youth development centers, or independent living arrangements. For serious delinquency, juvenile corrections means secure facilities that resemble adult prisons.

LO7 Transfers and Blended Sentencing

he **dual system of justice** for adults and juveniles is divided mainly according to age. What about juveniles who commit serious crimes? Are their murders, rapes, and robberies merely "delinquent acts"? Or should juveniles who commit these crimes be treated like adults—either partly or completely? These questions are answered through the process for **transfer** of cases from the juvenile court, also called **waiver** of juvenile court jurisdiction or **certification** of juvenile cases for trial in adult criminal courts.

Here is how transfer works. The prosecutor or probation officer working in intake files a waiver petition when she believes an adult criminal court should handle the case.[29] After the intake officer files the petition, the juvenile court judge decides whether to waive jurisdiction of the juvenile court and transfer the case to adult criminal court. You should not be surprised to learn that the criteria for the decision boil down to the strength of the case, the seriousness of the offense, and the juvenile's delinquency and criminal record. Juvenile courts waive about 1 percent of formal waiver petitions.[30]

All states have provisions for trying juveniles as adults. There are three basic transfer mechanisms:

- Judicial waiver
- Statutory exclusion
- Concurrent jurisdiction

Those states with all three mechanisms tend to transfer older juveniles and those charged with the most serious offenses. Discretionary waiver is used more with

Community Service

© Jeff Greenberg/PhotoEdit

disposition hearings hearings to decide how best to resolve delinquency cases

continuance in contemplation of dismissal dismissal of the case if the juvenile stays out of trouble for a specific time period

dual system of justice one system of justice for adults and another for juveniles

transfer (also called **waiver** or **certification**) transfer of cases from juvenile court to adult criminal court

younger juveniles and those charged with less serious offenses. Judicial waiver provisions permit the juvenile court judge to waive the juvenile court's jurisdiction and transfer the case to the criminal court. With statutory exclusions, state statutes exclude specific serious, violent, or repeat juvenile offenders from the juvenile court. Concurrent jurisdiction permits the criminal and juvenile courts to share original jurisdiction for certain cases. The prosecutor then uses discretion to determine which court to file the case in. This type of transfer is also known as prosecutorial waiver, prosecutor discretion, or direct file.

Blended sentencing options are another way of dealing with more serious juvenile offenders and are used at both the juvenile court and criminal court levels. At the juvenile court level, the court can impose an adult sentence on juvenile offenders. Most juvenile blended sentence laws allow the court to com-

juvenile sentence

suspended criminal sentence

bine the juvenile disposition with the adult sentence, but the adult sentence is suspended. The adult sentence is imposed only if the offender fails to complete the juvenile dispositions satisfactorily. Criminal court blended sentences are used on juveniles transferred to adult court. The juvenile is given both a juvenile sentence and a suspended criminal sentence that will be

one more chance

© iStockphoto.com / © Anthony Masterson/Photodisc/Getty Images

imposed only if the juvenile fails to complete the juvenile disposition. Thus, this option gives the juvenile "one more chance."[31]

Transfers increased in the early 1990s, due in part to the shift from rehabilitation to punishment.[32] The peak year for waivers was 1994. In 2005, the number of waivers to adult court was 47 percent less than in 1994 (see Figure 15.4). However, specific jurisdictions have seen an increase in the number of juvenile waivers. In Ventura County, California, for example, the number of juveniles tried as adults nearly tripled from 10 in 2006 to 27 in 2007, an increase of 170 percent. The increase in Ventura County has been attributed to a significant gang problem (85 percent of the waivers were for gang crimes) and an increase in resources to combat the gang problem. It is important to note that since 2000 it has been easier to secure juvenile transfers in California because of Proposition 21, which gave the sole decision of waiver to the prosecutor. Prior to the passage of Proposition 21, a fitness hearing had to be held, and a judge determined the waiver.[33]

Not surprisingly, the cases most likely to be waived are those involving a serious offense (the juvenile used a weapon and injured someone) and a juvenile with a criminal history. This follows the practice approved by the U.S. Supreme Court in *Kent v. United States* (1966), discussed earlier: "An offense will be waived if it is heinous or of aggravated character, or even though less serious—if it represents a pattern of repeated offenses."[34]

LO8 Juvenile Corrections

t he history of juvenile corrections has fairly closely tracked that of adult corrections and of criminal justice in general. In the 1950s, a great interest arose in community-based alternatives to large, state-run institutions for delinquents. Local institutions, residential youth centers, group homes, and specialized probation services began to develop. From the late 1960s to the 1970s, in a second phase of this development, diversion and deinstitutionalization programs were created and were claimed to be the answer to youth crime and delinquency. These community-based corrections rested on the conviction that state reformatories failed to prevent delinquency and, in fact, made it worse by stigmatizing youths exposed to it. Such youths became part of

FIGURE 15.4

Number of Delinquency Cases Judicially Waived to Criminal Court, 1985–2005

```
6,000                                    Person
5,000         Property
4,000
3,000
2,000                        Drugs
1,000
                            Public Order
   0
      1985  1987  1989  1991  1993  1995  1997  1999  2001  2003  2005
```

Source: *OJJDP Statistical Briefing Book* Online (Washington, DC: Office of Juvenile Justice and Delinquency Prevention, September 12, 2008, Retrieved March 3, 2009, from http://ojjdp.ncjrs.gov/ojstatbb/court/qa06502.asp?qaDate=2005).

juvenile probation is community-based treatment. Juveniles can be assigned to community-based group counseling or drug counseling.

Of the 1.1 million delinquency cases that received a juvenile court sanction in 2005, 48 percent resulted in the offender being sentenced to probation. The number of probation dispositions was almost 30 percent higher in 2005 than in 1985 (see Figure 15.5). Property crimes accounted for most cases of juvenile probation. More than three-quarters of probationers were male, but the proportion of female probationers increased from 14 percent in 1985 to 24 percent in 2005.[37]

a "state youth subculture" heavily involved in patterns of both state dependence and criminality that were very difficult, if not impossible, to break.[35]

The prison population "binge" and the shift from treatment to punishment in adult corrections have their parallels in juvenile corrections, including demands for more focus on punishment, deterrence, and community safety. Not that rehabilitation was ever the sole mission of juvenile justice—informally, punishment and community protection have always been missions, even if they are not admitted to up front. Still, there are differences between adult and juvenile corrections. Rehabilitation is still a major goal; probation is widespread; and there is more variety in juvenile correctional institutions (called "residential placements"), including training schools, treatment centers, boot camps, and group homes. Let's look at juvenile community (probation) and institutional placements.

PROBATION

Probation is the primary sanction for juveniles. It is also used for diversion.[36] A juvenile on probation is supervised in the community by a juvenile probation officer. Like adult probationers, the juvenile offenders must comply with the rules and conditions of probation set forth by the court. One typical condition of

*In the 2005 case **Roper v. Simmons**, the Supreme Court ruled 5–4 that imposing capital punishment for crimes committed while under the age of 18 is unconstitutional, overturning a 1989 case that set the age limit for capital punishment at 16. Christopher Simmons was 17 years of age when he was arrested for the drowning murder of Shirley Crook. A jury found Simmons guilty and recommended the death penalty, which the trial court imposed. Simmons appealed, and after it was upheld by multiple appellate courts, the Supreme Court of Missouri overturned his sentence in favor of life without parole, a decision upheld by the U.S. Supreme Court.*

© AP Images/Missouri Department of Corrections

INSTITUTIONAL CORRECTIONS

Placement in a residential facility is the most severe sanction the juvenile court can impose. The imposition of a residential sanction has a detrimental effect on both the juvenile offender and the offender's family. The juvenile's normal routine, education, and family/social relations are severely disrupted. Furthermore, once juveniles are placed into the system, their needs must be met by the system.

Let's start with some basic information about prisoners (in juvenile justice, they are called "residents") in juvenile institutions (usually called "juvenile custody facilities"). The following highlights are from 2006 data:

- In 2006, nearly 105,000 juveniles were confined in a residential facility.
- The number of juveniles in custody fell 14 percent from 1999 to 2006.
- Of the juveniles in custody, 15 percent were females.
- The number of black juveniles in custody exceeded the rates for all other race/ethnicity groups in all but eight states.
- The custody rate for minorities to whites was 2.9 to 1.
- Sixteen-year-olds accounted for more custodial placements (25,000 placements) than any other age group
- The median time in placement was 70 days for males and 42 days for females.[38]

Juvenile correctional institutions cover a broad spectrum, from small, short-term, nonsecure facilities to long-term, highly secure facilities serving large areas. Foster homes—small, nonsecure substitutes for real families—are used at all stages in the juvenile justice process. Police might temporarily place arrested juveniles who cannot be returned to their homes in foster homes instead of detention facilities. Courts might also assign juveniles to foster homes before, or after, adjudication. Foster care is recommended as the primary placement for minor delinquency.

Shelters, nonsecure residential facilities, hold juveniles temporarily. These include juveniles who are not sent home after arrest or who are waiting for placement after being adjudicated delinquent. Shelters are reserved mainly for status and property offenders.

Group homes, also nonsecure, are residential placements that operate as a homelike setting. In these homes, groups of unrelated juveniles live together for various lengths of time. These homes typically serve 5 to 15 juveniles. Juveniles are placed in the home by court order or through public welfare agencies. The homes are run by "house parents" or rotating staff. Some group homes are also therapeutic or treatment homes that work with youths with emotional or behavioral problems. Group home residents usually attend school—in the home or in the community—or they work. They also participate in individual and group counseling and recreation. Group homes are intended to provide support and structure in nonrestrictive settings that facilitate reintegration into the community. The most commonly used treatment approach in therapeutic group homes is the Teaching Family Model, developed at the University of Kansas in the 1960s and used at Boys Town in the early 1970s. Structural behavior interventions are used by highly trained staff acting as parents.[39]

Halfway houses are large, nonsecure residential centers. They provide both a place to live and a range of personal and social services. The average halfway house serves from 12 to 20 residents, but some large programs serve as many as 40 residents. Residents' ages range from 14 to 18. Halfway

© iStockphoto.com

houses provide a range of services and emphasize normal group living, school attendance, securing employment, working with parents to resolve problems, and general participation in the community.

Camps and ranches are nonsecure facilities located in rural and remote areas. Juveniles adjudicated delinquent are generally placed in camps as an alternative to the more secure training schools. The healthful setting, small numbers of residents, and close contact between staff and juveniles are supposed to develop good work and living habits that will facilitate rehabilitation. Ranches and camps emphasize outside activity, self-discipline, and the development of vocational and interpersonal skills. Juveniles assigned to them are supposed not only to develop good work habits but also to perform "useful and necessary" work that benefits the community.[40]

Detention centers are temporary custodial facilities. But unlike shelters, detention centers are secure institutions—lockups—that hold juveniles both before and after adjudication. There are three formal purposes of locking up juveniles in detention centers:

1. To secure their presence at court proceedings
2. To hold those who cannot be sent home
3. To protect them from harming themselves or others or disrupting juvenile court processes

Juveniles who have committed more serious offenses are sent to detention centers; less serious offenders go to shelters.[41]

Before adjudication, juveniles may stay in detention centers anywhere from a day to more than two weeks, raising the troubling question of the fairness of detention prior to proven delinquency. Detention is also sometimes used as informal punishment. Judges lock up juveniles to scare them, to show them what might happen to them, or to "teach them a lesson and give them a taste of jail." Some jurisdictions have formalized detention centers as jails for children.

Training schools are found in every state except Massachusetts, which abolished them in the 1970s. They vary greatly in size, staff, services, programs, ages, and types of residents. Most, however, house from one to several hundred juveniles committed by juvenile courts. Some training schools resemble adult prisons, with congregate-style living and emphasis on security and order, whereas others are relatively open facilities that focus on treatment and rehabilitation.

Training schools are the instrument of last resort in the juvenile correctional system. They contain the most serious delinquents: those who are security risks, have substantial prior records, or have exhausted other juvenile court dispositions. Almost all training schools are state operated and controlled, unlike the other facilities discussed previously. Most legislation requires training schools to provide both safe custody and rehabilitative treatment.[42]

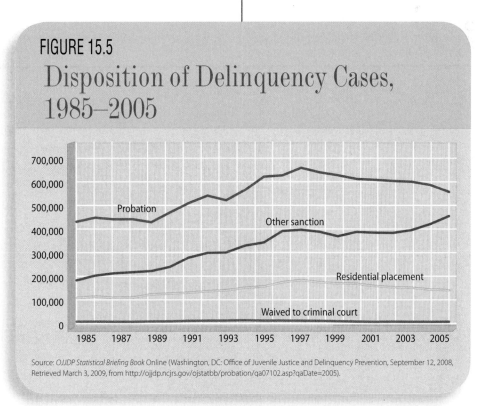

FIGURE 15.5

Disposition of Delinquency Cases, 1985–2005

Source: *OJJDP Statistical Briefing Book* Online (Washington, DC: Office of Juvenile Justice and Delinquency Prevention, September 12, 2008, Retrieved March 3, 2009, from http://ojjdp.ncjrs.gov/ojstatbb/probation/qa07102.asp?qaDate=2005).

More Bang for Your Buck

ENDNOTES

CHAPTER 1

1. Lanier, M. & Henry, S. (2004). *Essential criminology*. Boulder, CO: Westview Press.
2. Remington, F. J., Kimball, E. L., Dickey, W. J., Goldstein, H., & Newman, D. J. (1982). *Criminal justice administration*. Indianapolis, IN: Bobbs-Merrill.
3. *Police: No bail for O.J. Simpson in Las Vegas robbery arrest*. (2007, September 17). Retrieved November 14, 2008, from CNN.com: http://www.cnn.com/2007/US/law/09/16/oj.simpson/
4. *O. J. Simpson guilty of armed robbery, kidnapping*. (2008, October 4). Retrieved November 19, 2008, from CNN.com: http://www.cnn.com/2008/CRIME/10/04/oj.simpson.verdict/index.html
5. *Casey Anthony could face murder charges*. (2008, October 9). Retrieved November 14, 2008, from ABC Action News: http://www.abcactionnews.com/content/news/specialreports/caylee_anthony/story.aspx?content_id=0394D950-F565-4157-AB5A-7F1E2886082E&gsa=true
6. *Casey Anthony indicted in Orlando on first-degree murder charge, arrested in missing daughter case*. (2008, October 14). Retrieved November 14, 2008, from News-Press.com: http://www.news-press.com/apps/pbcs.dll/article?AID=/20081014/NEWS01/81014063&t
7. *Martha Stewart released from prison*. (2005, March 5). Retrieved November 14, 2008, from FOX News.com: http://www.foxnews.com/story/0,2933,149388,00.html
8. Ohlin, L. E. (1993). Surveying discretion by criminal justice decision makers. In L. E. Ohlin & F. J. Remington, *Discretion in criminal justice: The tension between individualization and uniformity* (p. 11). Albany: State University of New York Press.
9. Walker, S. (1993). *Taming the system: The control of discretion in criminal justice, 1950–1990* (pp. 18–20). New York: Oxford University Press.
10. Kelling, G. L. (1999). *Broken windows and police discretion*. Washington, DC: National Institute of Justice.
11. Walker, S. (1992). *The police in America* (2nd ed.). New York: McGraw-Hill.
12. Teplin, L. (2000, July). Keeping the peace: Police discretion and mentally ill persons. *National Institute of Justice Journal*, 8–15.
13. Lauritsen, J. L. & Sampson, R. J. (1998). Minorities, crime, and criminal justice. In M. Tonry, *Crime and punishment* (pp. 75–78). New York: Oxford University Press.
14. Sullivan, W. (2007, April 30). Racial profiling in police searches? Retrieved November 14, 2008, from *US News & World Report*: http://www.usnews.com/blogs/news-desk/2007/4/30/racial-profiling-in-police-searches.html
15. Gottfredson, M. R. & Gottfredson, D. M. (1988). *Decision making in criminal justice* (2nd ed.). Sacramento: Office of Attorney General of California; Mather, M. (1974). Some determinants of the method of case disposition: Decision making by public defenders in Los Angeles. *Law and Society Review 8*, 187–216; Spohn, C. & Cederblom, J. (1991). Race and disparities in sentencing: A test of the liberation hypothesis. *Justice Quarterly, 8*, 306.
16. Walker, S. (1994). *Sense and nonsense about crime and drugs* (pp. 29–37). Belmont, CA: Wadsworth.
17. Packer, H. L. (1964). Two models of the criminal process. *University of Pennsylvania Law Review, 113*.
18. Perron, B. A. (n.d.). *The crime controls and due process models*. Retrieved November 14, 2008, from The Criminal Defense Investigation Training Council: http://www.defenseinvestigator.com/article10.html
19. Packer, H. L. (1968). *The limits of the criminal sanction* (p. 158). Palo Alto, CA: Stanford University Press.
20. Packer (1968, p. 159).
21. Packer (1968, p. 170).
22. Cronin, T. E., Cronin, T. Z., & Milakovich, M. E. (1981). *U.S. vs. crime in the streets*. Bloomington: Indiana University Press; Halberstam, D. (1998). *The children*. New York: Random House; Skolnick, J. H. (1994). *Justice without trial* (3rd ed., p. 241). New York: Macmillan.
23. Currie, E. (1998). *Crime and punishment in America* (pp. 3–11). New York: Metropolitan Books; Flanagan, T. J. & Longmire, D. R. (1996). *Americans view crime and justice*. Thousand Oaks, CA: Sage.

CHAPTER 2

1. Essig, M. (2009, January 26). Moonshiner gets 18 month sentence. Retrieved March 2, 2009, from *Asheville Citizen-Times*: http://www.citizen-times.com/apps/pbcs.dll/article?AID=2009901250347
2. Lanier, M., & Henry, S. (2004). *Essential criminology*. Boulder, CO: Westview Press.
3. Lanier & Henry (2004).
4. Jordan, L. J. (2008, September 16). FBI says violent crime in U.S. is falling. Retrieved November 24, 2008, from *The New York Sun*: http://www

.nysun.com/national/fbi-says-violent-crime-in-us-
is-falling/85888/

5. Pratley, S. (2009, March 12). *Police warn students of spring break rapist.* Retrieved March 12, 2009, from CNN.com: http://www.cnn.com/2009/CRIME/03/12/kansas.spring.break.rapes/index.html

6. WorldNow and KVBC. (2007, July 24). *Copper theft a rapidly growing crime.* Retrieved November 24, 2008, from KVBC.com: http://www.kvbc.com/Global/story.asp?S=5109520

7. Grinberg, E. (2008). *Copper thefts leave youth sports scrambling for field time, answers.* Retrieved November 24, 2008, from CNN.com: http://www.cnn.com/2008/CRIME/10/20/copper.theft/

8. Hakim, D. & Rashbaum, W. K. (2008, March 10). Spitzer is linked to prostitution ring. Retrieved November 24, 2008, from The New York Times: http://www.nytimes.com/2008/03/10/nyregion/10cnd-spitzer.html?_r=1&pagewanted=1&incamp=article_popular

9. Lanier, M. & Henry, S. (2004). *Essential criminology.* Boulder, CO: Westview Press.

10. Federal Bureau of Investigation. (2008, September 15). *FBI releases 2007 crime statistics.* Retrieved November 24, 2008, from FBI.gov: http://www.fbi.gov/pressrel/pressrel08/ucr091508.htm

11. Jordan, L. J. (2008, September 16). FBI says violent crime in U.S. is falling. Retrieved November 24, 2008, from *The New York Sun*: http://www.nysun.com/national/fbi-says-violent-crime-in-us-isfalling/85888/

12. Schwartz, E. (2008, June 11). Crime rates shown to be falling. Retrieved November 24, 2008, from *U.S. News & World Report*: http://www.usnews.com/articles/news/national/2008/06/11/crime-rates-shown-to-be-falling.html

13. Federal Bureau of Investigation. (2008, September 15). *FBI releases 2007 crime statistics.* Retrieved November 24, 2008, from FBI.gov: http://www.fbi.gov/pressrel/pressrel08/ucr091508.htm

14. Lanier, M. & Henry, S. (2004). *Essential criminology.* Boulder, CO: Westview Press.

15. Brownstein, H. H. (1996). *The rise and fall of a violent crime wave* (pp. 19–25). Guilderland, NY: Harrow and Heston; Schneider, V. W. & Wiersema, B. (1991). Limits and use of the Uniform Crime Reports. In D. L. MacKenzie, P. J. Baunach, & R. R. Roberg, *Measuring crime: Large scale, long range efforts* (pp. 333–335). Albany: State University of New York Press.

16. Inter-University Consortium for Political and Social Research (ICPSR), University of Michigan. (2008). *National Incident-Based Reporting System resource guide.* Retrieved December 4, 2008, from National Archive of Criminal Justice Data: http://www.icpsr.umich.edu/NACJD/NIBRS/#About_NIBRS

17. Justice Research and Statistics Association. (2008). *Incident-based reporting resource center.* Retrieved December 5, 2008, from IBR: http://www.jrsainfo.org/ibrrc/background-status/nibrs_states.shtml

18. Bureau of Justice Statistics. (1997). *Implementing the National Incident-Based Reporting System: A project status report.* Washington, DC: Bureau of Justice Statistics.

19. Lanier, M. & Henry, S. (2004). *Essential criminology.* Boulder, CO: Westview Press.

20. Skogan, W. G. (1990). Poll review: National Crime Survey redesign. *Public Opinion Quarterly 54,* 256–272.

21. Rennison, C. & Rand, M. R. (2003). *Criminal victimization 2002* (p. 11). Washington, DC: Bureau of Justice Statistics.

22. Lanier, M. & Henry, S. (2004). *Essential criminology.* Boulder, CO: Westview Press.

23. Lafree, G. D. (1998). *Losing legitimacy* (p. 15). New York: Westview.

24. Hough, M. (1987). Offenders' choice of target: Findings from victim surveys. *Journal of Quantitative Criminology 3,* 356; Wright, R. T. & Decker, S. H. (1994). *Burglars on the job: Streetlife and residential break-ins* (pp. 5–6). Boston: Northeastern University Press.

25. Braithwaite, J. (1979). *Inequality, crime, and public policy* (p. 21). London/Boston: Routledge & Kegan Paul.

26. Hart, A. (2004, February 21). Report finds Atlanta police cut figures on crimes. Retrieved March 2, 2009, from *New York Times*: http://query.nytimes.com/gst/fullpage.html?sec=travel&res=880CE0D61E3DF932A15751C0A9629C8B63.

CHAPTER 3

1. Miller, J. M., Schreck, C. J., & Tewksbury, R. (2008). *Criminological theory: A brief introduction* (p. 5). Boston, MA: Pearson Education, Inc.

2. Miller, Schreck, & Tewksbury (2008, pp. 6–7).

3. Miller, Schreck, & Tewksbury (2008, p. 174).

4. Gottfredson, M. R., & Hirschi, T. (1990). *A general theory of crime* (p. 5). Stanford, CA: Stanford University Press.

5. Winslow, R. W., & Zhang, S. X. (2008). *Criminology: A global perspective* (p. 128). Upper Saddle River, NJ: Pearson Education, Inc.; Miller, J. M., Schreck, C. J., & Tewksbury, R. (2008). *Criminological theory: A brief introduction* (pp. 16–17). Boston, MA: Pearson Education, Inc.

6. True Life Crimes. (n.d.). *True life crime profile: Hilton Crawford.* Retrieved March 6, 2009, from True Life Crimes: http://www.truelifecrimes.com/hilton_crawford.html

7. Felson, M. (1986). Linking criminal choices, routine activities, informal control, and criminal outcomes. In D. B. Cornish & R. V. Clarke, *The reasoning criminal* (pp. 119–128). New York: Springer-Verlag.

8. Clarke, R. V., & Felson, M. (1993). *Routine activity and rational choice* (pp. 10–11). New Brunswick, NJ: Transaction Publishers.

9. Clarke & Felson (1993, p. 11).

10. Clarke & Felson (1993, p. 2).

11. Clarke & Felson (1993, pp. 2–3).

12. True Life Crimes. (n.d.). *Serial killer profile: Angel Maturino Resendiz*. Retrieved March 6, 2009, from True Life Crimes: http://www.truelifecrimes.com/angel_maturino_resendiz.html

13. Lafree, G. D. (1998). *Losing legitimacy* (p. 68). New York: Westview.

14. Lafree (1998).

15. U.S. Department of Justice, Bureau of Justice Statistics. (2008, August). *Criminal victimization in the United States, 2006 statistical tables*. Retrieved December 15, 2008, from U.S. Department of Justice, Office of Justice Programs: http://www.ojp.usdoj.gov/bjs/pub/pdf/cvus06.pdf

16. U.S. Department of Justice, Bureau of Justice Statistics. (2008, August); Office for Victims of Crime Resource Center, National Criminal Justice Reference Service. (2008). *2008 NCVRW resource guide*. Retrieved December 16, 2008, from National Criminal Justice Reference Service: http://ovc.ncjrs.gov/ncvrw2008/pdf/statistical_overviews.pdf

17. Winslow, R. W., & Zhang, S. X. (2008). *Criminology: A global perspective* (p. 49). Upper Saddle River, NJ: Pearson Education, Inc.

18. Bureau of Justice Statistics. (1989). *The prosecution of felony arrests*. Washington, DC: Bureau of Justice Statistics; Victims' rights amendments pass in 5 states (1992, November 8). *New York Times*, p. 156.

19. Miller, J. M., Schreck, C. J., & Tewksbury, R. (2008). *Criminological theory: A brief introduction* (pp. 34–37). Boston, MA: Pearson Education, Inc.

20. Winslow, R. W., & Zhang, S. X. (2008). *Criminology: A global perspective* (p. 99). Upper Saddle River, NJ: Pearson Education, Inc.

21. True Life Crimes. (n.d.). *Serial killer profile: Dennis Rader*. Retrieved March 6, 2009, from True Life Crimes: http://www.truelifecrimes.com/dennis_rader.html

22. Miczek, K. A., Mirsky, A. F., Carey, G., DeBold, J., & Raine, A. (1994). An overview of biological influences on violent behavior. In A. Reis, K. A. Miczek, & J. A. Roth, *Understanding and preventing violence 2* (p. 2). Washington, DC: National Academy Press.

23. Denno, D. W. (2006). Revisiting the legal link between genetics and crime. *Law and Contemporary Problems*, 209–257.

24. Bland, J. (2002). *Hormones in context: Testosterone and aggression—crimes of violence*. Retrieved December 12, 2008, from About Gender: http://www.gender.org.uk/about/06encrn/63faggrs.htm

25. Miller, J. M., Schreck, C. J., & Tewksbury, R. (2008). *Criminological theory: A brief introduction* (p. 45). Boston, MA: Pearson Education, Inc.

26. Bland, J. (2002). *Hormones in context: Testosterone and aggression—crimes of violence*. Retrieved December 12, 2008, from About Gender: http://www.gender.org.uk/about/06encrn/63faggrs.htm

27. Miller, J. M., Schreck, C. J., & Tewksbury, R. (2008). *Criminological theory: A brief introduction* (p. 46). Boston, MA: Pearson Education, Inc.

28. American Law and Legal Information. (n.d.). *Causes of crime—explaining crime, physical abnormalities, psychological disorders, social and economic factors, broken windows, income and education*. Retrieved December 16, 2008, from Crime and Punishment in America Vol 1: http://law.jrank.org/pages/12004/Causes-Crime.html

29. Miller, J. M., Schreck, C. J., & Tewksbury, R. (2008). *Criminological theory: A brief introduction* (pp. 48–49). Boston, MA: Pearson Education, Inc.; American Law and Legal Information. (n.d.). *Causes of crime–explaining crime, physical abnormalities, psychological disorders, social and economic factors, broken windows, income and education*. Retrieved December 16, 2008, from Crime and Punishment in America Vol 1: http://law.jrank.org/pages/12004/Causes-crime.html

30. True Life Crimes. (n.d.). *Serial killer profile: Jeffrey Dahmer*. Retrieved March 6, 2009, from True Life Crimes: http://www.truelifecrimes.com/jeffrey_dahmer.html

31. Psychopaths: New evidence of brain abnormalities. (n.d.). Retrieved December 12, 2008, from *Crime Times*: http://www.crimetimes.org/04c/w04cp7.htm; American Law and Legal Information (n.d.). *Causes of crime—explaining crime, physical abnormalities, psychological disorders, social and economic factors, broken windows, income and education*. Retrieved December 16, 2008, from Crime and Punishment in America Vol 1: http://law.jrank.org/pages/12004/Causes-Crime.html

32. Lawrence, F., & Fawcett, A. (2008). Crime, punishment and a junk food diet. Retrieved December 12, 2008, from *The Sydney Morning Herald*: http://www.smh.com.au/news/national/crime-punishment-and-a-junk-food-diet/2006/11/15/1163266639865.html; Winslow, R. W., & Zhang, S. X. (2008). *Criminology: A global perspective* (p. 143). Upper Saddle River, NJ: Pearson Education, Inc.

33. Miller, J. M., Schreck, C. J., & Tewksbury, R. (2008). *Criminological theory: A brief introduction*. Boston, MA: Pearson Education, Inc.

34. Hirschi, T., & Hindelang, M. (1977). Intelligence and delinquency. *American Sociological Review* 42, 572–587.

35. Herrnstein, R., & Murray, C. (1994). *The bell curve*. New York: Free Press.

36. Winslow, R. W., & Zhang, S. X. (2008). *Criminology: A global perspective* (pp. 94–96). Upper Saddle River, NJ: Pearson Education, Inc.

37. Glueck, S., & Glueck, E. (1930). *500 criminal careers*. New York: A. A. Knopf.
38. True Life Crimes. (n.d.). *Serial killer profile: Gary Ridgway*. Retrieved March 6, 2009, from True Life Crimes: http://www.truelifecrimes.com/gary_ridgway.html
39. Durkheim, E. (1951). *Suicide: A study in sociology*. New York: Free Press.
40. Merton, R. K. (1968). Social structure and anomie. In *social theory and social structure* (pp. 185–214). New York: Free Press.
41. Sutherland, E. H., & Cressey, D. R. (1978). *Criminology* (pp. 83–87). Philadelphia, PA: J. Lippincott.
42. Hirschi, T. (1969). *Causes of delinquency* (p. 34). Berkeley: University of California Press.
43. Miller, J. M., Schreck, C. J., & Tewksbury, R. (2008). *Criminological theory: A brief introduction* (p. 160). Boston, MA: Pearson Education, Inc.
44. Lafree, G. D. (1998). *Losing legitimacy* (pp. 66–67). New York: Westview.
45. Becker, H. (1973). *Outsiders*. New York: Free Press.
46. Winslow, R. W., & Zhang, S. X. (2008). *Criminology: A global perspective* (pp. 116–117). Upper Saddle River, NJ: Pearson Education, Inc.
47. Winslow & Zhang (2008, pp. 117–121).
48. Durkheim, E. (1933). *The division of labor in society*. New York: Free Press.
49. Rossi, P. H., Waite, E., Bose, C. E., & Berk, R. E. (1974). The seriousness of crimes: Normative structure and individual differences. *American Sociological Review* 39.
50. Chambliss, W. J. (1984). *Criminal law in action* (pp. 16–31). New York: Macmillan.
51. Winslow, R. W., & Zhang, S. X. (2008). *Criminology: A global perspective* (p. 121). Upper Saddle River, NJ: Pearson Education, Inc.
52. Quinney, R. (1977). *Class, state, and crime: On the theory and practice of criminal justice*. New York: David McKay Co.

CHAPTER 4

1. Sweetingham, L. (2006, July 26). *Andrea Yates found not guilty by reason of insanity in children's deaths*. Retrieved March 12, 2009, from Court TV News: http://www.courttv.com/trials/yates/072606_verdict2_ctv.html
2. Carp, R. A., Stidham, R., & Manning, K. L. (2007). *Judicial process in America*. Washington, DC: CQ Press.
3. Carp, Stidham, & Manning (2007, pp. 211–213).
4. State v. Damms, 100 N.W.2d 592 (Wis. 1960).
5. State v. Furr, 235 S.E.2d 193 (N.C. 1977).
6. Carp, R. A., Stidham, R., & Manning, K. L. (2007). *Judicial process in America* (pp. 211–212). Washington, DC: CQ Press.
7. Carp, Stidham, & Manning (2007, pp. 212–213).

8. Barkan, S. E. (2009). *Law and society: An introduction* (pp. 73–75). Upper Saddle River, NJ: Pearson Education, Inc.
9. Barkan (2009, p. 74).
10. *Toobin: Entrapment defense rarely works in case like Craig's*. (2007, August 31). Retrieved December 19, 2008, from CNN.com: http://www.cnn.com/2007/POLITICS/08/31/craig.entrapment/index.html
11. M'Naughten's Case, 8 Eng. Rep. 718 (1843).
12. Sweetingham, L. (2006, July 26). *Andrea Yates found not guilty by reason of insanity in children's deaths*. Retrieved March 12, 2009, from Court TV News: http://www.courttv.com/trials/yates/072606_verdict2_ctv.html
13. Carp, R. A., Stidham, R., & Manning, K. L. (2007). *Judicial process in America* (p. 204). Washington, DC: CQ Press.
14. TMZ. (2009, March 5). *Chris Brown charged with two felonies*. Retrieved March 12, 2009, from TMZ: http://www.tmz.com/2009/03/05/chris-brown-charged-with-two-felonies/
15. Carp, R. A., Stidham, R., & Manning, K. L. (2007). *Judicial process in America* (pp. 276–277). Washington, DC: CQ Press.
16. Carp, Stidham, & Manning (2007, p. 237).
17. Lanzetta v. New Jersey, 306 U.S. 451 (1939, 453).
18. Michael M. v. Superior Court of Sonoma County, 450 U.S. 464 (1981).
19. Carp, R. A., Stidham, R., & Manning, K. L. (2007). *Judicial process in America* (pp. 235–237). Washington, DC: CQ Press.
20. Carp, Stidham, & Manning (2007, pp. 239–252).
21. Associated Press. (2006, July 25). *Jury sequestered in Andrea Yates trial*. Retrieved March 12, 2009, from Fox News.com: http://www.foxnews.com/story/0,2933,205321,00.html

CHAPTER 5

1. Myers, L. B., & Myers, L. J. (2008). *Creation of a regional emergency planning model for continuous disaster mitigation response: A guide for regional response planning*. Retrieved March 2009, from Southeast Region Research Initiative (SERRI): http://www.serri.org/publications/Documents/Reports/WCU%20REPM%20Project%20Final%20Report%20-%20Phase%20I%20(Myers).pdf
2. Dempsey, T., & Coffey, D. (2006). *Law enforcement for the 21st century* (pp. 2–3). Charlottesville, VA: Michael Bender and Company, Inc.
3. Dempsey & Coffey (2006, pp. 3–4).
4. Dempsey & Coffey (2006, p. 11).
5. Dempsey, J. S., & Forst, L. S. (2005). *An introduction to policing* (p. 12). Belmont, CA: Thomson Wadsworth.
6. White, M. (2007). *Current issues and controversies in policing* (pp. 73–76). Boston, MA: Pearson Education.

7. White (2007, pp. 73–76).
8. White (2007, pp. 74–76).
9. White (2007, p. 74).
10. Sparrow, M. K., Moore, M. H., & Kennedy, D. M. (1995). *Beyond 911: A new era for policing* (pp. 44–50). New York: Basic Books.
11. President's Commission on Law Enforcement and the Administration of Justice. (1967). *The challenge of crime in a free society*. Washington, DC: Government Printing Office.
12. Walker, S. (1992). *The police in America*, 2d ed. (pp. 27–28). New York: McGraw-Hill.
13. Dempsey, T., & Coffey, D. (2006). *Law enforcement for the 21st century* (pp. 12–14). Charlottesville, VA: Michael Bender and Company, Inc.
14. Bureau of Justice Statistics. (n.d.). *Law enforcement statistics*. Retrieved December 27, 2008, from U.S. Department of Justice, Office of Justice Programs: http://www.ojp.usdoj.gov/bjs/lawenf .htm
15. Federal Bureau of Investigation. (n.d.). *Facts and figures*. Retrieved October 23, 2008, from Federal Bureau of Investigation: http://www.fbi.gov/ priorities/priorities.htm
16. Federal Bureau of Investigation. (n.d.).
17. http://thecaucus.blogs.nytimes.com/2009/02/26/ examine-the-budget-document/
18. U.S. Drug Enforcement Administration. (n.d.). *DEA mission statement*. Retrieved October 23, 2008, from U.S. Drug Enforcement Administration: http:// www.usdoj.gov/dea/agency/mission.htm
19. U.S. Drug Enforcement Administration. (n.d.).
20. U.S. Marshals Service. (n.d.). *U.S. Marshals Service homepage*. Retrieved December 27, 2008, from United States Marshals Service: http://www .usmarshals.gov/
21. Department of Homeland Security. (n.d.). *U.S. Customs and Border Patrol spotlight*. Retrieved December 27, 2008, from CBP.gov Securing America's Borders: http://www.cbp.gov/xp/cgov/ about/
22. WTOP. (2009, February 26). *Sausages, cigars and porn—A wacky week at Dulles*. Retrieved March 9, 2009, from WTOP.com: http://www.wtop .com/?nid=25&sid=1611830
23. Bureau of Alcohol, Tobacco, Firearms and Explosives. (n.d.). *About ATF*. Retrieved December 27, 2008, from ATF.org http://www.atf.gov/ about/mission.htm
24. Bureau of Alcohol, Tobacco, Firearms and Explosives. (2009, February 25). *Coatesville area arsons continue; ATF's work not yet finished*. Retrieved March 9, 2009, from ATF.gov: http://www.atf.gov/ press/2009press/field/022509phil_atfs-work-not -finished.htm
25. Department of Homeland Security. (n.d.). *Department six-point agenda*. Retrieved December 27, 2008, from Homeland Security: http:// www.dhs.gov/xabout/history/editorial_0646 .shtm
26. Department of Homeland Security. (n.d.). *Department six point agenda*.
27. http://thecaucus.blogs.nytimes.com/2009/02/26/ examine-the-budget-document/
28. Dempsey, J. S., & Forst, L. S. (2005). *An introduction to policing* (p. 37). Belmont, CA: Thomson Wadsworth.
29. White, M. (2007). *Current issues and controversies in policing* (pp. 132–134). Boston, MA: Pearson Education.
30. White (2007, pp. 150–151).
31. White (2007, p. 138).
32. Dempsey, T., & Coffey, D. (2006). *Law enforcement for the 21st century* (p. 30). Charlottesville, VA: Michael Bender and Company, Inc.
33. Dempsey & Coffey (2006, pp. 30–31).
34. Dempsey & Coffey (2006, p. 31).

CHAPTER 6

1. White, M. (2007). *Current issues and controversies in policing* (pp. 102–103). Boston, MA: Pearson Education.
2. White (2007, p. 85).
3. National Advisory Committee on Criminal Justice Standards and Goals. (1973). *Police* (p. 193). Washington, DC: Government Printing Office.
4. Dempsey, T., & Coffey, D. (2006). *Law enforcement for the 21st century* (pp. 209–219). Charlottesville, VA: Michael Bender and Company, Inc.
5. White, M. (2007). *Current issues and controversies in policing* (pp. 141–142). Boston, MA: Pearson Education.
6. White (2007, pp. 140–141).
7. Dempsey, T., & Coffey, D. (2006). *Law enforcement for the 21st century* (pp. 209–219). Charlottesville, VA: Michael Bender and Company, Inc.
8. Dempsey & Coffey (2006, p. 209).
9. White, M. (2007). *Current issues and controversies in policing* (pp. 85–86). Boston, MA: Pearson Education.
10. White (2007, p. 86).
11. Mastrofski, S. D. (1990). The prospects for change in police patrol: A decade of review. *American Journal of Police* 9, 31.
12. White, M. (2007). *Current issues and controversies in policing* (pp. 143–144). Boston, MA: Pearson Education.
13. White (2007, p. 331).
14. Tracy, P. E., & Morgan, V. (2000). Big Brother and his science kit: DNA databases for 21st century crime control? *Journal of Criminal Law and Criminology* 30, 649.
15. AFP.com. (2008, December 22). *Blood from mosquito traps Finnish suspect*. Retrieved December 23, 2008, from Yahoo! News: http://

news.yahoo.com/s/afp/20081222/od_afp/finlandcrimeoffbeat

16. Sherman, L. W. (1995). The police. In J. Q. Wilson, & J. Petersilia, *Crime* (p. 331). San Francisco, CA: Institute for Contemporary Studies.

17. Sherman (1995).

18. Sherman (1995, pp. 333–334).

19. Sherman, L. W., & Rogan, D. P. (1995). Effects of gun seizures on gun violence: "Hot spots" patrol in Kansas City. *Justice Quarterly* 12.

20. Sherman (1995, p. 331).

21. Sherman (1995, p. 332).

22. Pasadena (TX) Police Department. (n.d.). *Gang task force and street crimes unit*. Retrieved December 31, 2008, from City of Pasadena, Texas: http://www.ci.pasadena.tx.us/police/operations/patrol/gangs/gtf.htm

23. Sherman, L. W. (1990, March/April, 2–6). *Police crackdowns*. Washington, DC: NIJ Reports.

24. White, M. (2007). *Current issues and controversies in policing* (pp. 144–146). Boston, MA: Pearson Education.

25. Texas Commission on Law Enforcement Officers Standards and Education. (n.d.). *Training warning*. Retrieved December 29, 2008, from Texas Commission on Law Enforcement Officers Standards and Education: http://www.tcleose.state.tx.us/training_warning_05.asp

26. Federal Grants Wire. (2008). *Public safety partnership and community policing grants*. Retrieved December 29, 2008, from Federal Grants Wire: http://www.federalgrantswire.com/public-safety-partnership-and-community-policing-grants.html

27. Houston (TX) Police Department. (2008). *Crime statistics*. Retrieved December 29, 2008, from City of Houston: http://www.houstontx.gov/police/cs/stats2.htm

28. Dempsey, T., & Coffey, D. (2006). *Law enforcement for the 21st century* (pp. 13–15). Charlottesville, VA: Michael Bender and Company, Inc.

29. Zhao, J., Lovrich, N. P., & Robinson, T. H. (2001). Community policing: Is it changing the basic functions of policing? Findings from a longitudinal study of 200+ municipal police agencies. *Journal of Criminal Justice 29*(5), 365–377.

30. Jones, T. (2008, June 22). Saddle squad: As duties expand, Columbus Police horse patrol grows. Retrieved December 31, 2008, from *The Columbus Dispatch*: http://www.dispatch.com/live/content/local_news/stories/2008/06/22/Cophorse.ART_ART_06-22-08_B1_DNAI27L.html?sid=101

31. San Diego (CA) Police Department. (n.d.). *Police department neighborhood watch program*. Retrieved December 31, 2008, from The City of San Diego: http://www.sandiego.gov/police/prevention/neighwatch.shtml

CHAPTER 7

1. Dempsey, T., & Coffey, D. (2006). *Law enforcement for the 21st century* (pp. 151–152). Charlottesville, VA: Michael Bender and Company, Inc.

2. Dempsey & Coffey (2006, pp. 148–149).

3. Dempsey & Coffey (2006, p. 147).

4. Welsh v. Wisconsin, 466 U.S. 470 (1980, 748).

5. Katz v. U.S., 389 U.S. 347 (1967).

6. U.S. v. Miller, 425 U.S. 435 (1976).

7. Smith v. Maryland, 442 U.S. 745 (1979).

8. California v. Greenwood, 486 U.S. 35 (1988).

9. U.S. v. White, 401 U.S. 745 (1971).

10. Dempsey, T., & Coffey, D. (2006). *Law enforcement for the 21st century* (pp. 140–141). Charlottesville, VA: Michael Bender and Company, Inc.

11. Illinois v. Rodriguez, 497 U.S. 177 (1990).

12. Dempsey, T., & Coffey, D. (2006). *Law enforcement for the 21st century* (pp. 169–170). Charlottesville, VA: Michael Bender and Company, Inc.

13. Mapp v. Ohio, 367 U.S. 643 (1961).

14. White, M. (2007). *Current issues and controversies in policing* (p. 168). Boston, MA: Pearson Education.

15. Miranda v. Arizona, 384 U.S. 436 (1966).

16. Miranda Warning.org. (2007). *Pre-arrest questioning*. Retrieved January 2, 2009, from Miranda Warning.org: http://www.mirandawarning.org/pre-arrestquestioning.html

17. Miranda Warning.org. (2007).

18. White, M. (2007). *Current issues and controversies in policing* (pp. 171–173). Boston, MA: Pearson Education.

19. White (2007, p. 173).

20. Electronic Privacy Information Center. (2005). *The USA PATRIOT Act—Introduction*. Retrieved January 2, 2009, from EPIC.org: http://epic.org/privacy/terrorism/usapatriot/#introduction

21. Tennessee v. Garner, 471 U.S. 1 (1985).

22. White, M. (2007). *Current issues and controversies in policing* (pp. 247–248). Boston, MA: Pearson Education.

23. Bureau of Justice Statistics. (February 2001, 26). *Contacts between Police and the Public: Findings from the 1999 Survey*. Washington, DC: Bureau of Justice Statistics.

24. White, M. (2007). *Current issues and controversies in policing* (p. 249). Boston, MA: Pearson Education.

25. You Gotta Eat. (2006, November 22). *Police brutality, racial discrimination, or both?* Retrieved January 2, 2009, from yougottaeat.wordpress.com: http://yougottaeat.wordpress.com/2006/11/22/police-brutality-racial-discrimination-or-both/

26. White, M. (2007). *Current issues and controversies in policing* (p. 249). Boston, MA: Pearson Education.

27. The Associated Press. (2007, August 23). Use of tasers by police in US is again under scrutiny. Retrieved January 3, 2009, from *International*

Herald Tribune: http://www.iht.com/articles/2007/08/23/america/taser.php?page=1

28. White, M. (2007). *Current issues and controversies in policing* (pp. 250–251). Boston, MA: Pearson Education.

29. Pennsylvania State Police Department. (2008, May 15). *Police pursuits in Pennsylvania drop 9 percent.* Retrieved January 3, 2009, from Reuters.com: http://www.reuters.com/article/pressRelease/idUS261209+15-May-2008+PRN20080515

30. Tennessee v. Garner, 471 U.S. 1 (1985).

31. White, M. (2007). *Current issues and controversies in policing* (pp. 251–252). Boston, MA: Pearson Education.

32. Khanna, R., & Olsen, L. (2004, July 25). *A Chronicle special report—1 in 3 police shootings involve unarmed people.* Retrieved January 3, 2009, from Chron.com: http://www.chron.com/disp/story.mpl/special/04/shootings/2698952.html

33. White, M. (2007). *Current issues and controversies in policing* (p. 253). Boston, MA: Pearson Education.

34. Ellwanger, S. (2008). How police officers learn ethics. In M. C. Braswell, B. McCarthy, & B. McCarthy, *Justice, Crime, and Ethics* (pp. 51–79). Newark, NJ: Matthew Bender & Company, Inc.

35. Behind the Blue Wall. (2008, Feburary 26). *Connecticut state police whistleblowers seek help and protection.* Retrieved January 3, 2009, from Behind the Blue Wall: http://behindthebluewall.blogspot.com/2008/02/ct-state-police-whistleblowers-seek.html

36. Ellwanger, S. (2008). *How police officers learn ethics.* In M. C. Braswell, B. McCarthy, & B. McCarthy, Justice, Crime, and Ethics (pp. 51–79). Newark, NJ: Matthew Bender & Company, Inc.

37. Ellwanger (2008, p. 70).

38. Criminal Law Lawyer Source. (n.d.). *Police corruption.* Retrieved January 3, 2009, from Criminal Law Lawyer Source: http://www.criminal-law-lawyer-source.com/terms/police-corruption.html

39. Amnesty International USA. (n.d.). *Racial profiling laws in your state.* Retrieved January 4, 2009, from amnestyusa.org: http://www.amnestyusa.org/us-human-rights/other/racial-profiling---laws-in-your-state/page.do?id=1106665

40. Dempsey, T., & Coffey, D. (2006). *Law enforcement for the 21st century* (pp. 280–281). Charlottesville, VA: Michael Bender and Company, Inc.

41. Criminal Law Lawyer Source. (n.d.). *Police corruption.* Retrieved January 3, 2009, from Criminal Law Lawyer Source: http://www.criminal-law-lawyer-source.com/terms/police-corruption.html

CHAPTER 8

1. Rutherford, N. L. (2001). *To Kill a Mockingbird: The student survival guide.* Retrieved March 12, 2009, from Los Angeles Unified School District: http://www.lausd.k12.ca.us/Belmont_HS/tkm/

2. Nardulli, P. F., Eisenstein, J., & Flemming, R. B. (1988). *The tenor of justice: Criminal courts and the guilty plea* (pp. 373–374). Urbana: University of Illinois Press.

3. Rabe, G. A., & Champion, D. J. (2002). *Criminal courts: Structure, process, and issues* (pp. 24–25). Upper Saddle Ridge, NJ: Prentice Hall.

4. Rabe & Champion (2002, pp. 24–25).

5. Rabe & Champion (2002, pp. 25–27).

6. Carp, R. A., Stidham, R., & Manning, K. L. (2007). *Judicial process in America* (pp. 36–37). Washington, DC: CQ Press.

7. Carp, Stidham, & Manning (2007, pp. 56–61).

8. Carp, Stidham, & Manning (2007, pp. 76–77).

9. http://www.supremecourtus.gov/

10. Carp, R. A., Stidham, R., & Manning, K. L. (2007). *Judicial process in America* (pp. 63–64). Washington, DC: CQ Press.

11. LawInfo. (n.d.). *What is a plea bargain?* Retrieved January 9, 2009, from LawInfo: http://resources.lawinfo.com/en/Legal-FAQs/Plea-Negotiations-Criminal-Lawyer/Federal/what-is-a-plea-bargain-.html

12. Carp, R. A., Stidham, R., & Manning, K. L. (2007). *Judicial process in America* (pp. 63–64). Washington, DC: CQ Press.

13. Carp, Stidham, & Manning (2007, p. 63).

14. Carp, Stidham, & Manning (2007, p. 223).

15. Barkan, S. E. (2009). *Law and society: An introduction* (pp. 273–276). Upper Saddle River, NJ: Pearson Education, Inc.

16. Carp, R. A., Stidham, R., & Manning, K. L. (2007). *Judicial process in America* (pp. 104–106). Washington, DC: CQ Press.

17. American Judicature Society. (2009). *Methods of judicial selection.* Retrieved January 6, 2009, from American Judicature Society: http://www.judicialselection.us/judicial_selection/methods/removal_of_judges.cfm?state

18. Smith, C. E. (1997). *Courts, politics, and the judicial process* (pp. 153–156). Chicago: Nelson-Hall Publishers.

19. Court Watch. (2005, November 22). *Good judges/bad judges.* Retrieved January 9, 2009, from Court Watch: http://trialandappeal.blogspot.com/2005/11/good-judgesbad-judges.html

20. Ofgang, K. (2008, June 27). *CJP orders Orange superior court judge removed from bench.* Retrieved January 9, 2009, from Metropolitan News-Enterprise: http://www.metnews.com/articles/2008/cjpx062708.htm

21. Carp, R. A., Stidham, R., & Manning, K. L. (2007). *Judicial process in America* (pp. 184–186). Washington, DC: CQ Press.

22. Mellott, J. (2007, December 28). *Prosecuting priorities: Garst set for third term as commonwealth's attorney.* Retrieved January 9, 2009, from

DNRonline.com: http://www.dnronline.com/news_details.php?CHID=2&AID=14111

23. Nardulli, P. F., Eisenstein, J., & Flemming, R. B. (1988). *The tenor of justice: Criminal courts and the guilty plea* (pp. 108–111). Urbana: University of Illinois Press.

24. Los Angeles County District Attorney's Office. (2009). *Welcome*. Retrieved January 11, 2009, from Los Angeles County District Attorney's Office: http://da.co.la.ca.us/

25. Carp, R. A., Stidham, R., & Manning, K. L. (2007). *Judicial process in America* (pp. 185–186). Washington, DC: CQ Press.

26. Ethics Scoreboard. (2005, October 12). *The ethics of justice: Why criminal defense lawyers defend the guilty*. Retrieved January 11, 2009, from Ethics Scoreboard: http://www.ethicsscoreboard.com/list/defense.html

27. Blumberg, A. S. (1967). The practice of law as confidence game: Organizational co-optation of a profession. *Law and Society Review, 1*, 22.

28. Blumberg (1967, p. 20).

29. Barkan, S. E. (2009). *Law and society: An introduction* (p. 20). Upper Saddle River, NJ: Pearson Education, Inc.

30. Barkan (2009, pp. 271–272).

CHAPTER 9

1. Secret, M. (2009, January 8). *Why didn't Madoff get the slammer in the first place?* Retrieved March 18, 2009, from ProPublica: http://www.propublica.org/article/why-didnt-madoff-get-the-slammer-in-the-first-place-0108; Destefano, A. M. (2009, March 13). *Madoff stands alone, takes blame for Ponzi scheme*. Retrieved March 18, 2009, from Newsday: http://www.newsday.com/services/newspaper/printedition/friday/news/ny-bzmain136067602mar13,0,256235.story

2. Barkan, S. E. (2009). *Law and society: An introduction* (p. 270). Upper Saddle River, NJ: Pearson Education, Inc.

3. *Death penalty sought against suspect in UNC shooting*. (2007, August 31). Retrieved January 20, 2009, from CNN.com: http://www.cnn.com/2009/CRIME/01/16/unc.carson.deathpenalty/

4. Stroud, E. (2009, March 17). *Family of legendary moonshiner hoped his sentence would be reduced*. Retrieved March 20, 2009, from WBIR.com: http://www.wbir.com/news/local/story.aspx?storyid=81403&catid=2; Morrison, C. (2009, March 19). Moonshiner 'Popcorn' Sutton given a quiet mountain funeral. Retrieved March 20, 2009, from *Asheville Citizen-Times*: http://www.citizen-times.com/apps/pbcs.dll/article?AID=2009903180322

5. Barkan, S. E. (2009). *Law and society: An introduction* (p. 270). Upper Saddle River, NJ: Pearson Education, Inc.

6. Carp, R. A., Stidham, R., & Manning, K. L. (2007). *Judicial process in America* (pp. 222–230). Washington, DC: CQ Press.

7. Forst, B. (1995). Prosecution and sentencing. In J. Q. Wilson, & J. Petersilia, *Crime* (p. 367). San Francisco: Institute for Contemporary Studies Press.

8. Brakel, S. J. (2006). Individualizing justice after Atkins. *The Journal of the American Academy of Psychiatry and the Law*, 103–104.

9. Carp, R. A., Stidham, R., & Manning, K. L. (2007). *Judicial process in America* (pp. 236–237). Washington, DC: CQ Press.

10. Betts v. Brady, 316 U.S. 455 (1942).

11. Gideon v. Wainwright, 372 U.S. 335 (1963).

12. Escobedo v. Illinois, 378 U.S. 478 (1964).

13. The Oyez Project. (n.d.). *Escobedo v. Illinois, 378 U.S. 478 (1964)*. Retrieved January 16, 2009, from The Oyez Project: http://www.oyez.org/cases/1960-1969/1963/1963_615/

14. Miranda v. Arizona, 384 U.S. 436 (1966).

15. Powell v. Alabama, 287 U.S. 45 (1932).

16. Gideon v. Wainwright, 372 U.S. 335 (1963).

17. Argersinger v. Hamlin, 407 U.S. 25 (1972).

18. Scott v. Illinois, 440 U.S. 367 (1979).

19. Strickland v. Washington, 466 U.S. 668 (1984).

20. Carp, R. A., Stidham, R., & Manning, K. L. (2007). *Judicial process in America* (pp. 189–190). Washington, DC: CQ Press.

21. Miller, F. W., Dawson, R. O., Dix, G. E., & Parnas, R. I. (2000). *Criminal justice administration* (p. 616). New York: Foundation Press.

22. Carp, R. A., Stidham, R., & Manning, K. L. (2007). *Judicial process in America* (pp. 219–220). Washington, DC: CQ Press.

23. Miller, F. W., Dawson, R. O., Dix, G. E., & Parnas, R. I. (2000). *Criminal justice administration* (p. 617). New York: Foundation Press.

24. Foote, C. (1965). Vagrancy-type law and its administration. *University of Pennsylvania Law Review, 104*.

25. Miller, F. W., Dawson, R. O., Dix, G. E., & Parnas, R. I. (2000). *Criminal justice administration* (p. 618). New York: Foundation Press.

26. Rankin, C. (1964). The effect of pretrial detention. *New York University Law Review, 39*, 641.

27. Robinson, M. (2008, December 9). *Illinois governor released on own recognizance*. Retrieved March 18, 2009, from WISH TV: http://www.wishtv.com/dpp/news/national/nat_ap_chicago_ill_gov_released_200812091519

28. U.S. Code, Title 18, § 3142(f) (1999).

29. Carp, R. A., Stidham, R., & Manning, K. L. (2007). *Judicial process in America* (pp. 220–222). Washington, DC: CQ Press.

30. Neumeister, L. (2009, March 6). *Bernard Madoff plea deal seems imminent as grand jury indictment is waived*. Retrieved March 18, 2009, from Newser: http://www.newser.com/article/

d96oq5ug0/bernard-madoff-plea-deal-seems-imminent-as-grand-jury-indictment-is-waived.html

31. Carp, R. A., Stidham, R., & Manning, K. L. (2007). *Judicial process in America* (p. 222). Washington, DC: CQ Press.

32. Carp, Stidham, & Manning (2007, p. 222).

CHAPTER 10

1. *Man may get death penalty in firefighters' deaths.* (2009, March 18). Retrieved March 19, 2009, from CNN.com: http://www.cnn.com/2009/CRIME/03/18/california.fire.death.penalty/index.html

2. Carp, R. A., Stidham, R., & Manning, K. L. (2007). *Judicial process in America* (p. 223). Washington, DC: CQ Press.

3. Durose, M. R., & Langan, P. A. (2007). *Felony sentences in state courts, 2004.* Washington, DC: Bureau of Justice Statistics.

4. Smith, C. E. (1997). *Courts, politics, and the judicial process* (pp. 109–100). Chicago: Nelson-Hall Publishers.

5. Kalven, J. H., & Zeisel, H. (1966). *The American jury* (pp. 163–167). Chicago: University of Chicago Press.

6. Linder, D. (2001). *Jury nullification.* Retrieved Janaury 27, 2009, from University of Missouri—Kansas City School of Law: http://www.law.umkc.edu/faculty/projects/ftrials/zenger/nullification.html

7. Holland v. Illinois, 493 U.S. 474 (1990); Taylor v. Louisiana, 419 U.S. 522 (1975).

8. Thompson, S. (2006, December 23). *Valid excuses to get out of jury duty.* Retrieved January 27, 2009, from Associated Content: http://www.associatedcontent.com/article/105502/valid_excuses_to_get_out_of_jury_duty.html?cat=17

9. Carp, R. A., Stidham, R., & Manning, K. L. (2007). *Judicial process in America* (pp. 238–239). Washington, DC: CQ Press.

10. Williams v. Florida, 399 U.S. 78 (1970).

11. LaFave, W. R., & Israel, J. H. (1984). *Criminal procedure* (pp. 695–696). St. Paul, MN: West.

12. Ballew v. Georgia, 435 U.S. 223 (1978).

13. Apodaca v. Oregon, 406 U.S. 404 (1972).

14. Johnson v. Louisiana, 406 U.S. 356 (1972).

15. LaFave & Israel (1984, 698).

16. Florida v. Anthony (2008, November). *Order denying the state's motion concerning extrajudicial comments (gag order).* Retrieved January 27, 2009, from WESH.com: http://www.wesh.com/download/2008/1126/18152687.pdf

17. Illinois v. Allen, 397 U.S. 337 (1970).

18. Carp, R. A., Stidham, R., & Manning, K. L. (2007). *Judicial process in America* (p. 246). Washington, DC: CQ Press.

19. Carp, Stidham, & Manning (2007, pp. 239–240).

20. Moses, R. (2000). *Opening statement in criminal cases: The curtain raiser.* Retrieved March 19, 2009, from Center for Criminal Justice Advocacy: http://criminaldefense.homestead.com/Opening.html

21. Carp, R. A., Stidham, R., & Manning, K. L. (2007). *Judicial process in America* (p. 241). Washington, DC: CQ Press.

22. Carp, Stidham, & Manning (2007, p. 240).

23. Carp, Stidham, & Manning (2007, p. 242).

24. Carp, Stidham, & Manning (2007, pp. 245–246).

25. Smith, C. E. (1997). *Courts, politics, and the judicial process* (pp. 109–110). Chicago: Nelson-Hall Publishers.

26. United States Department of Justice. (1997). *Speedy Trial Act of 1974.* Retrieved January 27, 2009, from United States Attorney's Criminal Resource Manual: http://www.usdoj.gov/usao/eousa/foia_reading_room/usam/title9/crm00628.htm

27. Carp, R. A., Stidham, R., & Manning, K. L. (2007). *Judicial process in America* (p. 235). Washington, DC: CQ Press.

28. Carp, Stidham, & Manning (2007, pp. 223–224).

29. Carp, Stidham, & Manning (2007, pp. 223–226).

30. Law Library—American Law and Legal Information. (n.d.). *Media—The modern media and sensational trials.* Retrieved January 29, 2009, from JRank.org: http://law.jrank.org/pages/12146/Media-modern-media-sensational-trials.html

31. Eisenstein, J., & Jacob, H. (1977). *Felony justice.* Boston: Little, Brown.

32. Nardulli, P. F., Eisenstein, J., & Flemming, R. B. (1988). *The tenor of justice: Criminal courts and the guilty plea* (p. 286). Urbana, IL: University of Illinois Press.

33. Forst, B. (1995). Prosecution and sentencing. In J. Q. Wilson, & J. Petersilia, *Crime* (pp. 366–368). San Francisco: Institute for Contemporary Studies Press.

34. Barkan, S. E. (2009). *Law and society: An introduction* (p. 274). Upper Saddle River, NJ: Pearson Education, Inc.

35. Carp, R. A., Stidham, R., & Manning, K. L. (2007). *Judicial process in America* (p. 185). Washington, DC: CQ Press.

36. Barkan, S. E. (2009). *Law and society: An introduction* (pp. 271–274). Upper Saddle River, NJ: Pearson Education, Inc.

37. Barkan (2009, p. 274).

38. Carp, R. A., Stidham, R., & Manning, K. L. (2007). *Judicial process in America* (pp. 223–224). Washington, DC: CQ Press.

39. *Federal rules of criminal procedure.* (2004). Washington, DC: U.S. Government Printing Office.

40. United States v. Werker, 535 F.2d 198 (2d Cir. 1976), certiorari denied, 429 U.S. 926 (1976).

41. Uphoff, R. J. (1995). The criminal defense lawyer: Zealous advocate, double agent, or beleaguered dealer? In G. L. Mays & P. R. Gregware, *Courts*

and justice (pp. 82–83). Prospect Heights, IL: Waveland Press.

CHAPTER 11

1. *Taliban 'narco-terrorist' begs for mercy, gets life sentence.* (2008, December 22). Retrieved March 23, 2009, from CNN.com: http://www.cnn.com/2008/CRIME/12/22/taliban.sentencing/index.html
2. Gould, L., & Sitren, A. (2008, 206–212). Crime and punishment: Punishment philosophies and ethical dilemmas. In M. Braswell, B. McCarthy, & B. McCarthy, *Justice, crime and ethics* (pp. 205–220). Cincinnati, OH: Anderson Publishing; McDowell, L., Braswell, M., & Whitehead, J. (2008, 269–271). Restorative justice and the peacemaking ethic. In M. Braswell, B. McCarthy, & B. McCarthy, *Justice, crime and ethics* (pp. 267–296). Cincinnati, OH: Anderson Publishing.
3. Diamond, J. L. (1996). The myth of morality and fault in criminal law. *American Criminal Law Review 34*, 111–131.
4. Lanier, M., & Henry, S. (2004). *Essential criminology* (pp. 72–77). Boulder, CO: Westview Press.
5. Miller, J. M., Schreck, C. J., & Tewksbury, R. (2008). *Criminological theory: A brief introduction* (p. 20–26). Boston: Pearson Education, Inc.
6. Travis, L. F. (2008, 189). Criminal sentencing: Ethical issues and the problems of reform. In M. Braswell, B. McCarthy, & B. McCarthy, *Justice, crime and ethics* (pp. 187–202). Cincinnati, OH: Anderson Publishing.
7. *Criminal lawyers want rehabilitation not jails.* (2008, August 18). Retrieved March 24, 2009, from ABC News: http://www.abc.net.au/news/stories/2008/08/18/2338258.htm
8. McDowell, L., Braswell, M., & Whitehead, J. (2008). Restorative justice and the peacemaking ethic. In M. Braswell, B. McCarthy, & B. McCarthy, *Justice, crime and ethics* (p. 270). Cincinnati, OH: Anderson Publishing
9. McCold, P. (2004, 15). Paradigm muddle: The threat to restorative justice posed by its merger with community justice. *Contemporary Justice Review 7*(1), 13–35.
10. Blumstein, A., Cohn, J., Martin, S., & Tonry, M. (1983). *Research on sentencing: The search for reform* (pp. 48–52). Washington, DC: National Academy Press.
11. Wilson, J. Q. (1983). *Thinking about crime.* New York: Basic Books.
12. U.S. Sentencing Commission. (1991). *Mandatory minimum penalties in the federal criminal justice system* (pp. 14–16). Washington, DC: U.S. Sentencing Commission.
13. U.S. Sentencing Commission (1991, p. 6).
14. U.S. House of Representatives (1970, 11). No. 1444, 91st Cong., 2d Sess.
15. U.S. Sentencing Commission. (1991). *Mandatory minimum penalties in the federal criminal justice system* (p. 6). Washington, DC: U.S. Sentencing Commission.
16. U.S. Sentencing Commission (1991).
17. Walker, S. (1989). *Sense and nonsense about crime* (p. 89). Monterey, CA: Brooks-Cole.
18. U.S. Sentencing Commission. (1991). *Mandatory minimum penalties in the federal criminal justice system* (p. 6). Washington, DC: U.S. Sentencing Commission.
19. U.S. Sentencing Commission (1991, p. 76).
20. Campaign for an effective crime policy. (1993). *Evaluating mandatory minimum sentences.* Washington, DC: Campaign for an Effective Crime Policy. Unpublished manuscript; Schulhofer, S. J. (1993). Rethinking mandatory minimums. *Wake Forest Law Review 28*, 199.
21. Turner, S., Greenwood, P. W., Chen, E., & Fain, T. (1999). The impact of truth-in-sentencing and three-strikes legislation: Prison populations, state budgets, and crime rates. *Stanford Law and Public Policy Review 11*, 75.
22. *Minnesota sentencing guidelines.* (2009). Retrieved February 2, 2009, from Minnesota Sentencing Guidelines Commission: http://www.msgc.state.mn.us/
23. http://www.msgc.state.mn.us/guidelines/grids/grid_2008.pdf
24. Carp, R. A., Stidham, R., & Manning, K. L. (2007). *Judicial process in America* (p. 252). Washington, DC: CQ Press.
25. Erie County, Ohio. (2008). *Pre-sentence investigations.* Retrieved February 2, 2009, from Erie County, Ohio Victim Assistance Services: http://www.erie-county-ohio.net/victim/presentence.htm
26. Death Penalty Information Center. (2009). *Facts about the death penalty* (2009). Retrieved February 2, 2009, from Death Penalty Information Center: http://www.deathpenaltyinfo.org/FactSheet.pdf
27. Kohut, A. (2001, May 10). The declining support for executions. *New York Times*, p. 33.
28. Death Penalty Information Center. (2008). *Public opinion about the death penalty.* Retrieved February 2, 2009, from Death Penalty Information Center: http://www.deathpenaltyinfo.org/public-opinion-about-death-penalty
29. Death Penalty Information Center. (2009, March 23). *New Mexico to save money after abolition of death penalty.* Retrieved March 24, 2009, from Death Penalty Information Center: http://www.deathpenaltyinfo.org/new-mexico-save-money-after-abolition-death-penalty
30. *The Innocence Project.* (2009). Retrieved February 2, 2009, from Innocence Project: http://www.innocenceproject.org/
31. *The Innocence Project case profiles.* (2009). Retrieved February 4, 2009, from Innocence Project: http://www.innocenceproject.org/know/
32. Furman v. Georgia, 408 U.S. 238 (1972).
33. Gregg v. Georgia, 428 U.S. 153 (1976).

34. Death Penalty Information Center. (2008). *Introduction to the death penalty.* Retrieved February 2, 2009, from Death Penalty Information Center: http://www.deathpenaltyinfo.org/part-i-history-death-penalty

CHAPTER 12

1. Golson, J. (2009, February 27). Warren man sentenced to probation for serving as online pimp. Retrieved March 20, 2009, from *The Star-Ledger*: http://www.nj.com/news/index.ssf/2009/02/online_pimp_sentenced_to_one_y.html
2. Bureau of Justice Statistics. (2008). *Probation and parole statistics: 2007 summary findings.* Retrieved February 4, 2009, from Bureau of Justice Statistics: http://www.ojp.usdoj.gov/bjs/pandp.htm
3. Stinchcomb, J. B. (2005). *Corrections: past, present, and future* (pp. 106–107). East Peoria, IL: Versa Press for the American Correctional Association.
4. Petersilia, J. (2004). Community corrections. In J. Q. Wilson & J. Petersilia, *Crime: public policies for crime control* (pp. 483–508). Oakland, CA: Institute for Contemporary Studies.
5. Petersilia (2004, pp. 487–488).
6. Petersilia, J. (1995). A crime control rationale for reinvesting in community corrections. *Prison Journal 45*, 481.
7. *History of probation: origins and evolution.* (2005). Retrieved February 4, 2009, from SpiritusTemporis.com: http://www.spiritus-temporis.com/probation/history-of-probation:-origins-and-evolution.html
8. Stinchcomb, J. B. (2005). *Corrections: Past, present, and future* (p. 105). East Peoria, IL: Versa Press for the American Correctional Association.
9. Clay, J. (2001). *Maconochie's experiment: How one man's extraordinary vision saved transported convicts from degradation and despair.* London: John Murray Publishers Ltd.
10. Stinchcomb, J. B. (2005). *Corrections: Past, present, and future* (p. 341). East Peoria, IL: Versa Press for the American Correctional Association.
11. Bureau of Justice Statistics. (2008). *Probation and parole statistics: 2007 summary findings.* Retrieved February 4, 2009, from Bureau of Justice Statistics: http://www.ojp.usdoj.gov/bjs/pandp.htm
12. Bureau of Justice Statistics (2008).
13. Palmer, J. W. (2006). *Constitutional rights of prisoners* (pp. 208–214). Cincinnati, OH: Anderson Publishing.
14. Stinchcomb, J. B. (2005). *Corrections: Past, present, and future* (p. 108). East Peoria, IL: Versa Press for the American Correctional Association.
15. Stinchcomb (2005, pp. 344–355).
16. *Parole review process.* (2008). Retrieved February 4, 2009, from Texas Board of Pardons and Paroles: http://www.tdcj.state.tx.us/bpp/what_is_parole/review.htm
17. Stinchcomb, J. B. (2005). *Corrections: Past, present, and future* (pp. 347–348). East Peoria, IL: Versa Press for the American Correctional Association.
18. Petersilia, J. (1998). Probation and parole. In M. Tonry, *Handbook of crime and punishment* (p. 575). New York: Oxford University Press.
19. Stinchcomb, J. B. (2005). *Corrections: Past, present, and future* (pp. 355–356). East Peoria, IL: Versa Press for the American Correctional Association.
20. Taylor County, Texas. (n.d.). *Standard conditions of probation for county court at law number 2.* Retrieved March 20, 2009, from Taylor County Texas: http://www.taylorcountytexas.org/ccl2prob.html
21. Stinchcomb, J. B. (2005). *Corrections: Past, present, and future* (p. 114). East Peoria, IL: Versa Press for the American Correctional Association.
22. Glaze, L. E., & Bonczar, T. P. (December 2007). *Probation and parole in the United States, 2006.* Washington, DC: Bureau of Justice Statistics.
23. Clear, T. R., & Braga, A. A. (1995). Community corrections. In J. Q. Wilson, & J. Petersilia, *Crime* (p. 442). San Francisco: Institute for Contemporary Studies.
24. McLaughlin, E. C., & Oppmann, P. (2009, March 12). *Sex offender kills teen while under GPS monitoring, police say.* Retrieved March 20, 2009, from CNN.com: http://www.cnn.com/2009/CRIME/03/12/sex.offender.gps/index.html
25. Griffin v. Wisconsin, 483 U.S. 868 (1987, 874–875).
26. Minnesota v. Murphy, 465 U.S. 420 (1984).
27. Morrissey v. Brewer, 408 U.S. 471 (1973, 485–486).
28. Morrissey v. Brewer, 408 U.S. 471 (1973, 487–489).
29. Stinchcomb, J. B. (2005). *Corrections: Past, present, and future* (pp. 580–581). East Peoria, IL: Versa Press for the American Correctional Association.
30. Stinchcomb (2005, pp. 580–581).
31. Stinchcomb (2005, pp. 117–118).
32. Stinchcomb (2005, pp. 98–103).
33. Associated Press. (2009, February 26). *Report: Vick OK'd for home confinement.* Retrieved March 20, 2009, from ESPN: http://sports.espn.go.com/nfl/news/story?id=3936529
34. Stinchcomb, J. B. (2005). *Corrections: Past, present, and future* (pp. 461–463). East Peoria, IL: Versa Press for the American Correctional Association.
35. Ruback, R. B. (2004, p. 21). The imposition of economic sanctions in Philadelphia: Costs, fines, and restitution. *Federal Probation 68*(1), 21–38.
36. Ruback (2004, p. 21).
37. Ruback (2004, p. 21).
38. Fairfax County Office of Public Affairs. (2008, June 30). *Code Enforcement Strike Teams' prosecution results in biggest civil and criminal fines*

ever. Retrieved March 20, 2009, from County of Fairfax, Virginia: http://www.fairfaxcounty.gov/news/2008/149.htm

39. McDonald, D. C. (1992). Unpaid community service as a criminal sentence. In J. M. Byrne, A. J. Lurigio, & J. Petersilia, *Smart sentencing: The emergence of intermediate sanctions* (pp. 183–184). Newbury Park, CA: Sage.

40. McDonald (1992, p. 186).

41. Parent, D. G. (1995). Day reporting centers. In M. Tonry & K. Hamilton, *Intermediate sanctions in overcrowded times.* Boston: Northeastern University Press.

42. Petersilia, J. (2004). Community corrections. In J. Q. Wilson & J. Petersillia, *Crime: Public policies for crime control* (pp. 483–508). Oakland, CA: Institute for Contemporary Studies.

43. Petersilia (2004). Community Corrections.

44. Tonry, M., & Lynch, M. (1996). Intermediate sanctions. In M. Tonry, *Crime and research: A review of research* (Vol. 20, pp. 107, 137). Chicago: University of Chicago Press.

45. Tonry & Lynch (1996, pp. 137–138).

CHAPTER 13

1. Damon, A. (2009, February 22). *Abu Ghraib now a humane prison, Iraq officials say.* Retrieved March 24, 2009, from CNN.com: http://edition.cnn.com/2009/WORLD/meast/02/22/iraq.abughraib/index.html

2. West, H. C., & Sabol, W. J. (December 2008). *Prisoners in 2007.* Washington, DC: Bureau of Justice Statistics; Sabol, W. J., & Couture, H. (June 2008). *Prison inmates at midyear 2007.* Washington, DC: Bureau of Justice Statistics.

3. Stinchcomb, J. B. (2005). *Corrections: Past, present, and future* (pp. 63–64). East Peoria, IL: Versa Press for the American Correctional Association.

4. Hirsch, A. J. (1992). *The rise of the penitentiary* (p. 11). New Haven, CT: Yale University Press.

5. Stinchcomb, J. B. (2005). *Corrections: Past, present, and future* (p. 67). East Peoria, IL: Versa Press for the American Correctional Association.

6. Stinchcomb (2005, pp. 67–68).

7. Stinchcomb (2005, p. 17).

8. Stinchcomb (2005, p. 46).

9. Johnson, R. (1996). *Hard time: Understanding and reforming the prison.* Monterey, CA: Brooks/Cole.

10. Stinchcomb, J. B. (2005). *Corrections: Past, present, and future* (p. 79). East Peoria, IL: Versa Press for the American Correctional Association.

11. DiIulio, J. (1996). Help wanted: Economists, crime, and public policy. *Journal of Economic Perspectives.*

12. Caplow, T., & Simon, J. (1999). Understanding prison policy and population growth. In M. Tonry & J. Petersilia, *Prisons* (p. 64). Chicago: University of Chicago Press.

13. Blumstein, A. (2004, pp. 453–454). Prisons: A policy change. In J. Q. Wilson & J. Petersilia, *Crime* (pp. 451–482). Oakland, CA: Institute for Contemporary Studies.

14. Blumstein, A. (2004, pp. 453–454). Prisons: A policy change. In J. Q. Wilson & J. Petersilia, *Crime* (pp. 451–482). Oakland, CA: Institute for Contemporary Studies.

15. Zimring, F. E., & Hawkins, G. (1991). *The scale of punishment.* Chicago: University of Chicago Press.

16. Caplow, T., & Simon, J. (1999). Understanding prison policy and population growth. In M. Tonry & J. Petersilia, *Prisons* (pp. 97–110). Chicago: University of Chicago Press.

17. Blumstein, A. (2004, pp. 460–466). Prisons: A policy change. In J. Q. Wilson & J. Petersilia, *Crime* (pp. 451–482). Oakland, CA: Institute for Contemporary Studies.

18. Hearts and Minds Network. (2005). *Prison facts.* Retrieved February 10, 2009, from Hearts and Minds Network: Information for Change: http://www.heartsandminds.org/prisons/facts.htm

19. Stephan, J. J. (October 2008). *Census of state and federal correctional facilities, 2005.* Washington, DC: Bureau of Justice Statistics.

20. Pettigrew, C. A. (Fall 2002). Technology and the Eighth Amendment: The problem of supermax prisons. *North Carolina Journal of Law and Technology,* 195.

21. Riveland, C. (1999). *Supermax prisons* (p. 5). Washington, DC: National Institute of Corrections.

22. Ward, D. A. (1994). Alcatraz and Marion: Confinement in super maximum custody. In J. W. Roberts, *Escaping prison myths: Selected topics in the history of federal corrections.* Washington, DC: American University Press.

23. Riveland, C. (1999). *Supermax prisons* (p. 1). Washington, DC: National Institute of Corrections.

24. *Alcatraz Inmate Daily Routine.* (n.d.). Retrieved February 10, 2009, from Alcatraz History.com: http://www.alcatrazhistory.com/daily.htm

25. Kurki, L., & Morris, N. (2001). The purposes, practices, and problems of supermax prisons. In M. Tonry, *Crime and justice: A review of research* (p. 394). Chicago: University of Chicago Press.

26. Ward, D. A., & Schoen, K. F. (1981). *Confinement in maximum custody* (pp. 9–11). Lexington, MA: Lexington Books.

27. Stephan, J. J. (October 2008). *Census of state and federal correctional facilities, 2005.* Washington, DC: Bureau of Justice Statistics.

28. Singer, R. G. (1983). Prisons: Typologies and classifications. In *Encyclopedia of crime and justice* (p. 1204). New York: Free Press.

29. Stephan, J. J. (October 2008). *Census of state and federal correctional facilities, 2005.* Washington, DC: Bureau of Justice Statistics.

30. Singer, R. G. (1983, p. 1204). Prisons: Typologies and classifications. In *Encyclopedia of crime and justice* (pp. 1203–1204). New York: Free Press.

31. Sabol, W. J., & Couture, H. (June 2008). *Prison inmates at midyear 2007*. Washington, DC: Bureau of Justice Statistics.

32. Jacobs, J. B. (1983). *New perspectives on prisons and imprisonment* (pp. 115–132). Ithaca, NY: Cornell University Press.

33. United States Department of Labor. (2008). *Occupational outlook handbook, 2008–09 edition: Correctional officers*. Retrieved February 12, 2009, from Bureau of Labor Statistics: http://www.bls.gov/oco/ocos156.htm#nature

34. Cheeseman, K., & Worley, R. (2006, p. 87). Women on the wing: Inmate perceptions about female correctional officer job competency in a Southern prison system. *Southwest Journal of Criminal Justice*, 86–102.

35. Stephan, J. J., & Karberg, J. C. (2003). *Census of state and federal correctional facilities, 2000* (p. 14). Washington, DC: Department of Justice.

36. Bynum, R. (2009, Jan/Feb). Does a correctional officer need a college education? *American Jails*, 22–26.

37. United States Department of Labor. (2008). *Occupational outlook handbook, 2008–09 edition: Correctional officers*. Retrieved February 12, 2009, from Bureau of Labor Statistics: http://www.bls.gov/oco/ocos156.htm#nature.

38. Stephan, J. J. (2001). *Census of jails, 1999* (p. 2). Washington, DC: Bureau of Justice Statistics.

39. Stinchcomb, J. B. (2005). *Corrections: Past, present, and future* (pp. 155–156). East Peoria, IL: Versa Press for the American Correctional Association.

40. Roberts, G. (2007, November 21). Justice blasts jail conditions: Inadequate diagnosis, inordinate delay in care led to death, report says. Retrieved February 12, 2009, from *Seattle Post-Intelligencer*: http://seattlepi.nwsource.com/local/340628_jail22.html

41. Weiner, R., Frazier, W., & Farbstein, J. (1987, June). Building better jails. *Psychology Today*, 40.

42. Logan, C. H., & Gaes, G. G. (1993). Meta-analysis and the rehabilitation of punishment. *Justice Quarterly*, 256–257.

43. West, H. C., & Sabol, W. J. (December 2008). *Prisoners in 2007*. Washington, DC: Bureau of Justice Statistics.

44. Sabol, W. J., & Couture, H. (June 2008). *Prison inmates at midyear 2007*. Washington, DC: Bureau of Justice Statistics.

45. Harrison, P. M., & Beck, A. J. (2003). *Prisoners in 2002* (p. 5). Washington, DC: Bureau of Justice Statistics.

46. West, H. C., & Sabol, W. J. (December 2008). *Prisoners in 2007*. Washington, DC: Bureau of Justice Statistics.

47. Stephan, J. J. (2001). *Census of jails, 1999* (p. 1). Washington, DC: Bureau of Justice Statistics.

48. Owen, B., & Bloom, B. (1995). Profiling women prisoners: Findings from national surveys and a California sample. *Prison Journal*, 166.

49. West, H. C., & Sabol, W. J. (December 2008). *Prisoners in 2007*. Washington, DC: Bureau of Justice Statistics.

50. Sabol, W. J., & Couture, H. (June 2008). *Prison inmates at midyear 2007*. Washington, DC: Bureau of Justice Statistics.

51. Kruttschnitt, C., & Gartner, R. (2003, 1). Women's imprisonment. In M. Tonry, *Crime and justice: An annual review of research* (pp. 55–135). Chicago: University of Chicago Press.

52. Crawford, J. (2003, June, 1). *Alternative sentencing necessary for female inmates with children*. Retrieved February 16, 2009, from American Correctional Association: http://www.aca.org/publications/ctarchivespdf/june03/commentary_june.pdf

53. Langan, P. A., & Levin, D. J. (2002, June). *Recidivism of prisoners released in 1994*. Washington, DC: Bureau of Justice Statistics.

54. Stinchcomb, J. B. (2005). *Corrections: Past, present, and future* (p. 373). East Peoria, IL: Versa Press for the American Correctional Association.

55. Langan, P. A., & Levin, D. J. (2002, June). Recidivism of prisoners released in 1994. Washington, DC: Bureau of Justice Statistics.

56. Immarigeon, R., & Chesney-Lind, M. (1992). *Women's prisons: Overcrowded and overused*. San Francisco: National Council on Crime and Delinquency.

57. Immarigeon & Chesney-Lind (1992).

58. Immarigeon & Chesney-Lind (1992).

59. Stinchcomb, J. B. (2005). *Corrections: Past, present, and future*. East Peoria, IL: Versa Press for the American Correctional Association.

CHAPTER 14

1. Associated Press. (2007, July 6). *Suicide reveals squalid prison conditions*. Retrieved March 20, 2009, from MSNBC: http://www.msnbc.msn.com/id/19638219/

2. Gartner, R., & Kruttschnitt, C. (2004). A brief history of doing time. *Law and Society Review 38*(2), 22–23.

3. Goffman, E. (1961). *Asylums: Essay on the social situation of mental patients and other inmates* (p. xiii). Garden City, NY: Anchor Books.

4. Clemmer, D. (1940). *The prison community*. New York: Holt, Rinehart, & Winston.

5. Sykes, G. (1958). *Society of captives*. Princeton, NJ: Princeton University Press.

6. Gartner, R., & Kruttschnitt, C. (2004). A brief history of doing time. *Law and Society Review 38*(2), 24.

7. Florida Department of Corrections. (n.d.). *Major prison gangs*. Retrieved February 19, 2009, from Florida Department of Corrections: http://www.dc.state.fl.us/pub/gangs/prison.html

8. *Texas prison gang page.* (1998). Retrieved February 19, 2009, from Texas Prison Gang Page: http://davadnai.users.omniglobal.net/gang.html

9. Sykes, G. (1958). *Society of captives.* Princeton, NJ: Princeton University Press.

10. McCarthy, B. (2008). Keeping an eye on the keeper: Prison corruption and its control. In M. C. Braswell, B. R. McCarthy, & B. J. McCarthy, *Justice, crime and ethics* (pp. 299–321). Cincinnati, OH: Anderson Publishing.

11. Irwin, J. (1987). *The felon.* Berkeley: University of California Press.

12. Stinchcomb, J. B. (2005). *Corrections: Past, present, and future* (pp. 312–313). East Peoria, IL: Versa Press for the American Correctional Association.

13. Adams, K. (1992). Adjusting to prison life. In M. Tonry, *Crime and justice: An annual review of research* (pp. 286–287). Chicago: University of Chicago Press.

14. Casciani, D. (2008). *Prison's drugs "feeding violence."* Retrieved February 19, 2009, from BBC News: http://news.bbc.co.uk/1/hi/uk/7680962.stm

15. Stinchcomb, J. B. (2005). *Corrections: Past, present, and future* (p. 489). East Peoria, IL: Versa Press for the American Correctional Association.

16. Stinchcomb (2005, pp. 489–490).

17. Clear, T. R., & Cole, G. F. (1994). *American corrections.* Belmont, CA: Wadsworth.

18. Beck, A. J., & Harrison, P. M. (2008, December). *Sexual victimization in state and federal prisons reported by inmates, 2007.* Washington, DC: Bureau of Justice Statistics.

19. Dumond, R. W. (2000, December, pp. 408–409). Inmate sexual assault: The plague that persists. *The Prison Journal,* 407–414.

20. United States Department of Justice, Office of the Inspector General. (2005). *Deterring staff sexual abuse of federal inmates.* Washington, DC: U.S. Department of Justice.

21. Stinchcomb, J. B. (2005). *Corrections: Past, present, and future* (p. 486). East Peoria, IL: Versa Press for the American Correctional Association.

22. Kropf, S. (2009). Prison inmate gets life sentence for sex assault on female guard. Retrieved February 19, 2009, from *The Post and Courier:* http://www.charleston.net/news/2009/jan/31/prison_inmate_gets_life_sentence_sex_ass70204/

23. Stinchcomb, J. B. (2005). *Corrections: Past, present, and future* (pp. 316–317). East Peoria, IL: Versa Press for the American Correctional Association.

24. Stinchcomb (2005, pp. 322–323).

25. Lipton, D. S. (1995). CDate: Updating the effectiveness of correctional treatment 25 years later. *Journal of Offender Rehabilitation,* 4.

26. Martinson, R. (1974, Spring, 25). What works? Questions and answers about prison reform. *The Public Interest.*

27. Gaes, G. G., Flanagan, T. J., Motuik, L. L., & Stewart, L. (1998). *Adult correctional treatment* (p. 57). Washington, DC: U.S. Bureau of Prisons.

28. Gaes, Flanagan, Motuik, & Stewart (1998, pp. 56–57).

29. The Real Cost of Prisons Weblog. (2009, January 30). *Report affirms benefits of in-prison college programs, calls for renewed funding.* Retrieved February 20, 2009, from The Real Cost of Prisons Weblog: http://realcostofprisons.org/blog/archives/2009/01/report_affirms.html; Correctional Association of New York (2009). *Education from the inside, out: The multiple benefits of college programs in prison.* New York: The Correctional Association of New York.

30. Stinchcomb, J. B. (2005). *Corrections: Past, present, and future* (p. 272). East Peoria, IL: Versa Press for the American Correctional Association.

31. Gaes, G. G., Flanagan, T. J., Motuik, L. L., & Stewart, L. (1998). *Adult correctional treatment* (p. 62). Washington, DC: U.S. Bureau of Prisons.

32. Clear, T. R., & Cole, G. F. (1994). *American corrections* (p. 334). Belmont, CA: Wadsworth.

33. American Correctional Association. (2000, September, 8). *Corrections Compendium Journal.* Washington, DC: American Correctional Association.

34. South Carolina Department of Corrections. (2008). *Prison industries.* Retrieved February 19, 2009, from South Carolina Department of Corrections: http://www.doc.sc.gov/programs/pi.jsp

35. Hoskinson, C. (1998, December 1). Prison industries often in the red. *Associated Press.*

36. Uggen, C., & Staff, J. (2001, p. 3). Work as a turning point for criminal offenders. *Corrections Management Quarterly,* 1–16.

37. Uggen & Staff (2001, p. 5).

38. Kruttschnitt, C., Uggen, C., & Shelton, K. (2000). Predictors or desistance among sex offenders: The interaction of formal and informal social controls. *Justice Quarterly,* 61–87.

39. Uggen, C., & Staff, J. (2001, p. 5). Work as a turning point for criminal offenders. *Corrections Management Quarterly,* 1–16.

40. Stinchcomb, J. B. (2005). *Corrections: Past, present, and future* (pp. 274–275). East Peoria, IL: Versa Press for the American Correctional Association.

41. Stinchcomb (2005, pp. 262–265).

42. Clear, T. R., Stout, B., Kelly, L., Dammer, H., & Hardyman, P. (1992). *Prisons, prisoners, and religion.* New Brunswick, NJ: Rutgers University Press.

43. Gaes, G. G., Flanagan, T. J., Motuik, L. L., & Stewart, L. (1998). *Adult correctional treatment.* Washington, DC: U.S. Bureau of Prisons.

44. Pelissier, B., Wallace, S., O'Neill, J. A., Gaes, G., Camp, S., Rhodes, W. (2001). Federal prison residential drug treatment reduces substance use and arrests after release. *American Journal of Drug, Alcohol Abuse,* 315–337.

45. *Drug and alcoholism treatment facilities.* (2006). Retrieved February 20, 2009, from Sourcebook of Criminal Justice Statistics Online: http://www .albany.edu/sourcebook/pdf/t6622006.pdf
46. Stinchcomb, J. B. (2005). *Corrections: Past, present, and future* (pp. 386–387). East Peoria, IL: Versa Press for the American Correctional Association.
47. *Number and rate (per 100,000 U.S. resident female population) of female prisoners.* (2006). Retrieved February 20, 2009, from Sourcebook of Criminal Justice Statistics Online: http://www .albany.edu/sourcebook/pdf/t6412006.pdf
48. West, H. C., & Sabol, W. J. (December 2008). *Prisoners in 2007.* Washington, DC: Bureau of Justice Statistics.
49. Owen, B., & Bloom, B. (1995). Profiling women prisoners: Findings from national surveys and a California sample. *Prison Journal, 167.*
50. Owen & Bloom (1995, p. 168).
51. Stinchcomb, J. B. (2005). *Corrections: Past, present, and future* (pp. 392–395). East Peoria, IL: Versa Press for the American Correctional Association.
52. Seidel, J. (2009, January 4). *Sexual assaults on female inmates went unheeded.* Retrieved February 20, 2009, from Free Press: http://www.freep .com/apps/pbcs.dll/article?AID=2009901040419
53. Stinchcomb, J. B. (2005). *Corrections: Past, present, and future* (p. 395). East Peoria, IL: Versa Press for the American Correctional Association.
54. Stinchcomb (2005, p. 395).
55. Glaze, L. E., & Bonczar, T. P. (2008). *Probation and parole in the United States, 2006.* Washington, DC: Bureau of Justice Statistics.
56. Solomon, A., Waul, M., Ness, A. V., & Travis, J. (2004). *Outside the walls: A national snapshot of community-based prisoner reentry programs* (p. 12). Washington, DC: Urban Institute.
57. Lynch, J. P., & Sabol, W. J. (2001). *Prisoner reentry in perspective* (p. 8). Washington, DC: Urban Institute.
58. Solomon, A., Waul, M., Ness, A. V., & Travis, J. (2004). *Outside the walls: A national snapshot of community-based prisoner reentry programs* (p. 128). Washington, DC: Urban Institute.
59. Lynch, J. P., & Sabol, W. J. (2001). *Prisoner reentry in perspective* (p. 8). Washington, DC: Urban Institute.
60. Watson, J., Solomon, A. L., LaVigne, N. G., & Travis, J. (2004). *A portrait of prisoner reentry in Texas.* Washington, DC: The Urban Institute.
61. Watson, Solomon, LaVigne, & Travis (2004, p. 65).
62. Watson, Solomon, LaVigne, & Travis (2004, pp. 69–72).
63. Lynch, J. P., & Sabol, W. J. (2001). *Prisoner reentry in perspective* (p. 4). Washington, DC: Urban Institute.
64. Petersilia, J. (2004, September, 7). What works in reentry? Reviewing and questioning the evidence. *Federal Probation.*
65. MacKenzie, D. L. (1998). *What works in corrections? An examination of the effectiveness of the type of rehabilitation programs offered by Washington State Department of Corrections.* Unpublished report.
66. Seiter, R. P., & Kadela, K. L. (2003). Prisoner reentry: What works, what does not, and what is promising? *Crime and delinquency,* 360–388.
67. United States Department of Justice, Office of Justice Programs. (2004, May). *Prisoner reentry.* Retrieved February 20, 2009, from Almanac of Policy Issues: http://www.policyalmanac.org/ crime/archive/prisoner_reentry.shtml

CHAPTER 15

1. Baldwin, T. (2007, November 2). *Mother's sting catches son, Cory Ryder, 'hiring hitman to kill her.'* Retrieved March 16, 2009, from Times Online: http://www.timesonline.co.uk/tol/news/ world/us_and_americas/article2789073.ece; Morse, D. (2007, November 1). Teen's rift with his mother leads to sting and murder-for-hire trial. Retrieved March 16, 2009, from *The Washington Post*: http://www.washingtonpost .com/wp-dyn/content/article/2007/10/31/ AR2007103103148.html; O'Brien, T. (2007, November 6). *Boy hires hitman to kill parents after losing his PlayStation privileges.* Retrieved March 16, 2009, from Switched: http://www .switched.com/2007/11/06/boy-hires-hitman-to -kill-parents-after-losing-his-playstation-pr/
2. American Law Encyclopedia. (2009). *Parens patriae.* Retrieved February 25, 2009, from American Law Encyclopedia: http://law.jrank.org/ pages/9014/Parens-Patriae.html
3. Platt, A. (1969). *The child savers: The invention of delinquency.* Chicago: University of Chicago Press.
4. Einstein Law. (2008). *History of America's juvenile justice system.* Retrieved February 25, 2009, from LawyerShop.com: http://www.lawyershop.com/ practice-areas/criminal-law/juvenile-law/history/
5. National Report Series, Juvenile Justice Bulletin. (1999, December). *The juvenile justice system was founded on the concept of rehabilitation through individualized justice.* Retrieved February 25, 2009, from Juvenile Justice: A Century of Change: http://www.ncjrs.gov/html/ojjdp/9912_2/juv1.html
6. American Law Encyclopedia. (2009). *Juvenile law—Trying juveniles as adults.* Retrieved February 25, 2009, from American Law Encyclopedia: http://law.jrank.org/pages/7957/Juvenile-Law -Trying-Juveniles-Adults.html
7. CNN.com. (2009, February 22). *Boy, 11, accused of killing father's pregnant girlfriend.* Retrieved March 3, 2009, from CNN.com: http://www.cnn .com/2009/CRIME/02/21/boy.homicide/index .html?iref=hpmostpop

8. Kent v. United States, 383 U.S. 541 (1966).

9. In re Gault, 387 U.S. 1 (1967).

10. In re Winship, 397 U.S. 358 (1970).

11. McKeiver v. Pennsylvania, 403 U.S. 528 (1970, 533–534).

12. Office of Juvenile Justice and Delinquency Prevention. (2009). *Glossary*. Retrieved February 26, 2009, from OJJDP Statistical Briefing Book: http://ojjdp.ncjrs.gov/ojstatbb/glossary.html

13. Texas Youth Commission. (2008). *Overview of the juvenile corrections system in Texas*. Retrieved February 25, 2009, from Texas Youth Commission: http://www.tyc.state.tx.us/about/overview.html

14. Snyder, H. N., & Sickmund, M. (2006). *Juvenile offenders and victims: 2006 national report*. Washington, DC: Office of Juvenile Justice and Delinquency Prevention.

15. Snyder, H. N. (2008, November). *Juvenile arrests 2006*. Washington, DC: Office of Juvenile Justice and Delinquency Prevention.

16. Office of Juvenile Justice and Delinquency Prevention. (2009). *Juvenile justice system structure & process, case flow diagram*. Retrieved February 26, 2009, from OJJDP Statistical Briefing Book: http://ojjdp.ncjrs.gov/ojstatbb/structure_process/case.html

17. Allen, T. T. (2005). Taking a juvenile into custody: Situational factors that influence police officers' decisions. *Journal of Sociology and Social Welfare*.

18. Office of Juvenile Justice and Delinquency Prevention. (2009). *Juvenile justice system structure & process, case flow diagram*.

19. Sickmund, M. (2003). *Juveniles in court* (p. 2). Washington, DC: Office of Juvenile Justice and Delinquency Prevention.

20. Greenwood, P. W. (2004). Juvenile crime and juvenile justice. In J. Q. Wilson, & J. Petersilia, *Crime: Public policies for crime control* (p. 86). Oakland, CA: Institute for Contemporary Studies.

21. Anderson, L., Garza, S., & Davis, T. (2003). *Juvenile justice in California, 2003*. Sacramento, CA: Criminal Justice Statistics Center.

22. Office of Juvenile Justice and Delinquency Prevention. (2008, September). *Juvenile court cases, 2005*. Retrieved February 26, 2009, from OJJDP Statistical Briefing Book: http://ojjdp.ncjrs.gov/ojstatbb/court/qa06203.asp?qaDate=2005

23. Office of Juvenile Justice and Delinquency Prevention. (2008, September). *Juvenile court cases, 2005*. Retrieved February 26, 2009, from OJJDP Statistical Briefing Book: http://ojjdp.ncjrs.gov/ojstatbb/court/qa06201.asp?qaDate=2005

24. Sickmund, M. (2003). *Juveniles in court* (p. 2). Washington, DC: Office of Juvenile Justice and Delinquency Prevention.

25. Sickmund, M. (2003, p. 2).

26. Sickmund, M. (2003, p. 2).

27. Denver District Attorney's Office. (n.d.). *Juvenile diversion*. Retrieved March 16, 2009, from Denver DA: http://www.denverda.org/Prosecution_Units/juvenile_diversion/juvenile_diversion.htm

28. Office of Juvenile Justice and Delinquency Prevention. (2009). *Juvenile justice system structure & process, case flow diagram*.

29. Sickmund, M. (2003). *Juveniles in court* (p. 3). Washington, DC: Office of Juvenile Justice and Delinquency Prevention.

30. Sickmund, M. (2003, p. 3).

31. Office of Juvenile Justice and Delinquency Prevention. (2006, March). *Juvenile justice system structure & process, statutes*. Retrieved February 26, 2009, from OJJDP Statistical Briefing Book: http://ojjdp.ncjrs.gov/ojstatbb/structure_process/qa04115.asp?qaDate=2004

32. Sickmund, M. (2003). *Juveniles in court* (p. 8). Washington, DC: Office of Juvenile Justice and Delinquency Prevention.

33. Hernandez, R. (2008, February 17). Juveniles tried as adults up 170%. Retrieved March 16, 2009, from *Ventura County Star*: http://www.venturacountystar.com/news/2008/feb/17/juveniles-tried-as-adults-up-170-da-cites-gang/

34. Kent v. United States (1966, 566).

35. Bartol, C., & Bartol, A. (2009). *Juvenile delinquency and antisocial behavior: A developmental perspective* (pp. 326–328). Upper Saddle River, NJ: Prentice Hall.

36. Office of Juvenile Justice and Delinquency Prevention. (2008). *Juveniles on probation, overview*. Retrieved February 26, 2009, from OJJDP Statistical Briefing Book: http://ojjdp.ncjrs.gov/ojstatbb/probation/overview.html

37. Office of Juvenile Justice and Delinquency Prevention. (2008, September). *Probation as a court disposition*. Retrieved February 26, 2009, from OJJDP Statistical Briefing Book: http://ojjdp.ncjrs.gov/ojstatbb/probation/qa07102.asp?qaDate=2005

38. Office of Juvenile Justice and Delinquency Prevention. (2008). *Frequently asked questions about juveniles in corrections*. Retrieved February 26, 2009, from OJJDP Statistical Briefing Book: http://ojjdp.ncjrs.gov/ojstatbb/corrections/faqs.asp

39. Office of Juvenile Justice and Delinquency Prevention. (n.d.). *Group home*. Retrieved February 26, 2009, from OJJDP Model Programs Guide: http://www.dsgonline.com/mpg2.5/group_home.htm

40. Office of Juvenile Justice and Delinquency Prevention. (n.d.). *Wilderness camp*. Retrieved February 26, 2009, from OJJDP Model Programs Guide: http://www.dsgonline.com/mpg2.5/wilderness_camp.htm

41. Office of Juvenile Justice and Delinquency Prevention. (n.d.). *Correctional facility*. Retrieved February 26, 2009, from OJJDP Model Programs Guide: http://www.dsgonline.com/mpg2.5/correctional_facility.htm

42. Office of Juvenile Justice and Delinquency Prevention. (n.d.). *Correctional facility*.

NAME INDEX

Test coming up? Now what?

With CJUS you have a multitude of study aids at your fingertips. After reading the chapters, check out these ideas for further help.

Review cards include all learning outcomes, definitions, and summaries for each chapter.

Printable Flash Cards give you three additional ways to check your comprehension of key criminal justice concepts.

Other great ways to help you study include **Interactive Quizzing, Downloads, Games,** and **Video Activities.**

You can find it all at **4ltrpress.cengage.com/cjus.**

SUBJECT INDEX

Note: *f* = figure, *t* = table

A

9/11, 15, 47, 59, 69, 91, 92, 134
911 emergency telephone number, 76
Abu Ghraib prison, 175
Accused, rights of, 56
Acquaintances, 34
  victims, 33
Actus reus, 46
Adjudication, 116
  juvenile court, 215
Adjudicatory hearing, juvenile, 216–217
Administrative Office of the U.S Courts, 64*t*
Admissible evidence, 135
Adversary process, 13
ADX, *see* United States Penitentiary Administrative Maximum
Age defense, 51
Alcatraz, 181, 182*f*
Alfred P. Murrah Federal Building bombing, 191
Alibi, 50
American Civil Liberties Union (ACLU), 92
American Law Institute, 53
Anomie theory, of criminal behavior, 40
Appeals, 104, 121
Appellate courts, 102, 104
Appointed counsel, 120
Arraignment, 121, 127
Arrest, 21, 79, 87–89, 91, 117*f*, 121
  juvenile, 211, 213*f*
  reasonable, 87–89
  warrants, 89
Arson, 21, 22*t*, 24*t*, 26, 129
Assault, 21, 22*t*, 24*t*, 26, 34, 130*t*, 151*t*, 196
Assigned counsel, 123
Atavistic theory of criminal behavior, 35
Attica State Prison riot, 198
Attorneys, 122, 123, *see also* Lawyers

B

Auburn system penitentiary, 177
Automobile vehicle monitoring (AVM), 76

Bail, 124–125
Bail bondsman, 116*t*
Bail Reform Act, 115
Bailiff, 57*f*, 70
Bargaining, *see* Plea bargaining
Beyond a reasonable doubt, 133, 135
Big Sleep, The, 66*f*
Bill of information, 127
Bill of Rights, 88*t*
Bind over, 126
Biological theories of criminal behavior, 35–38
Blended sentencing, juvenile, 218
Bond, 124, 125, 162
Brain abnormalities, 37
BTK (Bind, Torture, and Kill) Killer, 35
Bureau of Alcohol, Tobacco, Firearms and Explosives (ATF), 64*t*, 67, 68
Bureau of Justice Statistics (BJS), 26, 129
Burglary, 21, 22*t*, 24*t*, 26, 55, 130*t*, 151*t*
Burlington (Vermont) Police Department, 94
By the book, 7

C

Camps and ranches, juvenile, 221
Capital felonies, 54
Capitalist, 43
Case, strength of, 118
Case study method of granting parole, 165
Caseloads, 139
Causes, of crime, 29–33

Celebrated cases, 11
Center for Criminal Justice Advocacy, 133
Certification, juvenile, 217
Change of venue, 133
Charge, 116, 117
  decision to, 118
Chester County (Pennsylvania) District Attorney's Office, 68
Chicago Police Department, 90
Children, *see* Juvenile
Child-saving movement, 208–209
CIA Security Protection officers, 64
Civil cases, 55
Civil law, versus criminal law, 55
Civil lawsuit, 55
Classical (utilitarian) theories of crime, 30
Clockwork Orange, A, 146
Closing arguments, 135
Coatesville Police Department, 68
CODIS (Combined DNA Index System), 79
College education programs in prison, 199
Columbus (Ohio) Police Department, 84
Community policing strategies, 76, 83–85
Community service, 170, 171, 217
Community-oriented patrol, 85
Community-oriented policing (COP), 63–64, 83, 84*t*
Competent, 122, 123
Conflict theory of society, 42–43
Conflict view, 18
Consensus theory of society, 42
Consensus view, 18
Conspiracy, 47

Constable, 60
Constable/Night watch system, 60
Constitution, *see* U.S. Constitution
Continuance in contemplation of dismissal, 217
Contraband, 195
Contract attorneys, 123
COP, *see* Community-oriented policing
Correctional boot camps, 171
Correctional Industries Association, 201
Correctional institution, 177
Corrections, 4*t*, 5, 169, 173
  juvenile, 218–221
Corrections Corporation of America, 184
Corrections officers, 9, 184–185
  education and training, 185
Correlation, 29, 30*f*
Corruption, 96–98
  remedies for, 98
Counsel, 119–121
  effective, 121
Counts, 137
County law enforcement agencies, 70
Courts, 4*t*, 5, 101–112
  appellate, 102, 104
  criminal, 110
  felony, 102
  juvenile, 208–209, 215–217
  lower, 102
  mission, 106–107
  personnel, 116*t*
  trial, 104
Court reporter, 57*f*
Court system, structure of, 102
Courtroom work group, 105–107, 112
Crackdowns, 80
Crime, 17–27

WHAT'S INSIDE The first chapter introduces criminal justice and the criminal justice system. The three major crime control agencies are explained, as are their implementations within the three levels of government. The criminal justice decision-making process is also explicated. Through formal and informal decis[...]who and how to process. Fi[...]rocess models are explain[...] control that have shifted i[...]

> This short list gives an overview of chapter coverage.

Learning Outcomes

LO1 Define *criminal justice* and the *criminal justice system*

LO2 Explain the authority and relationships of the major crime control agencies

LO3 Explain the steps in the criminal justice decision-making process

LO4 Discuss the differences in formal and informal decision making used in criminal justice

LO5 Explain the wedding cake model of justice

LO6 Compare the crime control and due process models of criminal justice

LO7 Define and explain the due process and crime control periods from [...] perspective

> The list of learning outcomes and the chapter outline provide an at-a-glance view of the topics your students will encounter in the chapter.

Chapter Outline

Art Index

> An art index on each Prep Card lets you know what concepts have visual support in the chapter.

PowerPoint Highlights

Slide 2: A list of all the chapter's Learning Outcomes, with page numbers
Slides 3-4: LO1: How Criminal Justice and the Criminal Justice System Are Defined
Slides 10–12: LO4: The Differences [...] Informal Criminal Ju[...]
Slides 16–18: LO6: A Comparison [...] Due Process Models

> A quick view of the PowerPoint slides helps you organize your lecture.

Video Highlights

Title: Crime in America
Running time: 3 minutes
Description: Crime is on the rise in America, and police agencies are struggling to keep up.

Title: U.S.–Mexico Drug War
Running time: 8 minutes
Description: Drug-related violence er[...] border, resulting in numerous murder[...]

Title: Illegal Aliens
Running time: 6 minutes
Description: Illegal migration from both Canada and Mexico challenge National Guard and Border Patrol officials.

> Enhance your class with short video clips found online.

Lecture Launchers

In March 2009, the original Articles of Confederation went on public display in Washington, D.C. for the first time ever in celebration of the National Archives' 75th anniversary [...]
http://www.npr.org/templates/story[...]

In April 2009, Baltasar Garzon, a pro[...] an investigation into the alleged us[...] the U.S.-operated Guantánamo Bay [...]
http://www.npr.org/templates/story/[...]

> Interesting examples from the news provide engaging ways to start your lecture.

Key Terms

> Key terms from the chapter are here with page references.

In May 2009, the U.S. government began building a virtual wall along 23 miles of the U.S.–Mexico border. The unmanned wall, a $100 million project, uses radar, day and night vision cameras, and sensors to detect smugglers.

http://uk.reuters.com/article/marketsNewsUS/idUKN1234605920090512

Classroom Activities

1. Illustrate the following table for a discussion of legitimate versus discriminatory decision-making criteria. Ask students to choose where to place the various terms: Race, Ethnicity, Class, Sex, Sexual orientation, Serio   of offender, Relationship of offender to victim, and St

> Classroom activities help you integrate active learning into your course.

Legitimate and Discriminatory Decision-Making

LEGITIMATE CRITERIA	DISCRIMINATORY CRITERIA
Seriousness of offense	Race
Dangerousness of offender	Ethnicity
Relationship of offender to victim	Class
Strength of case	Sex
	Sexual orientation

2. Illustrate the wedding cake model of criminal justice by drawing a four-tiered "cake," the bottom "layer" being the largest and the top being the smallest. Remember,

   - On the small top tier are a tiny number of "celebrated cases."
   - In the second tier are a somewhat larger number of "real crimes."
   - Most "ordinary felonies" are in the third tier.
   - The broad fourth tier represents the vast number of minor crimes.

3. Illustrate the criminal justice funnel model by drawing a funnel shape, the widest at the top and smallest at the bottom. Remember,

   - More people are arrested than are charged with crimes.
   - More people are charged with crimes than are convicted.
   - More people are convicted than are sentenced.
   - More people are sentenced to probation than to prison.

Quick Quiz

1. According to the textbook, decision making among the criminal justice professionals is _____. (Page 5)
   - (a.) interdependent
   - b. equally distributed
   - c. concentrated in the
   - d. law enforcement fo

> A short quiz on every card lets you quickly check your students' level of understanding and can be used to initiate discussion or as an oral assessment.

2. According to the textbook, the _____ is the crimina official with the power to make the decision to nego plea. (Page 6)
   - a. judge
   - (b.) prosecutor
   - c. corrections director
   - d. law enforcement chief

3. According to the textbook, the _____ is the criminal justice official with the power to make the decision to accept a negotiated plea. (Page 6)
   - (a.) judge
   - b. prosecutor
   - c. corrections director
   - d. law enforcement chief

4. According to the textbook, there are two very different kinds of decision making in criminal justice: _____. (Page 7)
   - a. formal decision making and by-the-book decision making
   - (b.) formal decision making and informal decision making
   - c. rational decision making and irrational decision making
   - d. informed decision making and uninformed decision making

5. The U.S. Constitution and Bill of Rights, state codes, decisions _____ rules of criminal procedure are all _____. (Page 7)
   - c. informal decision making
   - (d.) formal rules

6. _____ cess in which criminal justice officials _____ ases according to their informal discretionary definition of "seriousness". (Page 10)
   - (a.) "wedding cake" model
   - b. "funnel" model
   - c. crime control model
   - d. due process model

7. According to the textbook, one of the most important missions of informal criminal justice is _____. (Page 7)
   - (a.) to satisfy the need for flexibility in the vast number of situations that don't fit neatly into the rules in the book of formal criminal justice
   - b. to provide certainty and predictability throughout the criminal justice system
   - c. to create clear and concise policies
   - d. to provide consistency in the application of policies

WHAT'S INSIDE The first chapter introduces criminal justice and the criminal justice system. The three major crime control agencies are explained, as are their implementations within the three levels of government. The criminal justice decision-making process is also explicated. Through formal and informal decision making, professionals decide who and how to process. Finally, the crime control and due process models are explained as opposing theories of social control that have shifted in focus throughout history.

CHAPTER 1 PREP CARD

Criminal Justice in the United States

Learning Outcomes

LO1 Define *criminal justice* and the *criminal justice system*

LO2 Explain the authority and relationships of the major crime control agencies

LO3 Explain the steps in the criminal justice decision-making process

LO4 Discuss the differences in formal and informal decision making used in criminal justice

LO5 Explain the wedding cake model of justice

LO6 Compare the crime control and due process models of criminal justice

LO7 Define and explain the due process and crime control periods from a history of criminal justice perspective

Chapter Outline

Art Index

PowerPoint Highlights

Slide 2: A list of all the chapter's Learning Outcomes, with page numbers

Slides 3–4: LO1: How Criminal Justice and the Criminal Justice System Are Defined

Slides 10–12: LO4: The Differences between Formal and Informal Criminal Justice Processes

Slides 16–18: LO6: A Comparison of the Crime Control and Due Process Models of Criminal Justice

Video Highlights

Title: Crime in America
Running time: 3 minutes
Description: Crime is on the rise in America, and police agencies are struggling to keep up.

Title: U.S.–Mexico Drug War
Running time: 8 minutes
Description: Drug-related violence erupts at the U.S.-Mexico border, resulting in numerous murders on both sides.

Title: Illegal Aliens
Running time: 6 minutes
Description: Illegal migration from both Canada and Mexico challenge National Guard and Border Patrol officials.

Lecture Launchers

In March 2009, the original Articles of Confederation went on public display in Washington, D.C. for the first time ever in celebration of the National Archives' 75th anniversary.
http://www.npr.org/templates/story/story.php?storyId=101925832

In April 2009, Baltasar Garzon, a prominent Spanish magistrate, opened an investigation into the alleged use of officially authorized torture at the U.S.-operated Guantánamo Bay detention camp.
http://www.npr.org/templates/story/story.php?storyId=102474382

Key Terms

In May 2009, the U.S. government began building a virtual wall along 23 miles of the U.S.–Mexico border. The unmanned wall, a $100 million project, uses radar, day and night vision cameras, and sensors to detect smugglers.

http://uk.reuters.com/article/marketsNewsUS/idUKN1234605920090512

Classroom Activities

1. Illustrate the following table for a discussion of legitimate versus discriminatory decision-making criteria. Ask students to choose where to place the various terms: Race, Ethnicity, Class, Sex, Sexual orientation, Seriousness of offense, Dangerousness of offender, Relationship of offender to victim, and Strength of case.

Legitimate and Discriminatory Decision-Making Criteria	
LEGITIMATE CRITERIA	**DISCRIMINATORY CRITERIA**
Seriousness of offense	Race
Dangerousness of offender	Ethnicity
Relationship of offender to victim	Class
Strength of case	Sex
	Sexual orientation

2. Illustrate the wedding cake model of criminal justice by drawing a four-tiered "cake," the bottom "layer" being the largest and the top being the smallest. Remember,

   - On the small top tier are a tiny number of "celebrated cases."
   - In the second tier are a somewhat larger number of "real crimes."
   - Most "ordinary felonies" are in the third tier.
   - The broad fourth tier represents the vast number of minor crimes.

3. Illustrate the criminal justice funnel model by drawing a funnel shape, the widest at the top and smallest at the bottom. Remember,

   - More people are arrested than are charged with crimes.
   - More people are charged with crimes than are convicted.
   - More people are convicted than are sentenced.
   - More people are sentenced to probation than to prison.

Quick Quiz

1. According to the textbook, decision making among the criminal justice professionals is _____. (Page 5)
   - (a.) interdependent
   - b. equally distributed
   - c. concentrated in the judiciary
   - d. law enforcement focused

2. According to the textbook, the _____ is the criminal justice official with the power to make the decision to negotiate a guilty plea. (Page 6)
   - a. judge
   - (b.) prosecutor
   - c. corrections director
   - d. law enforcement chief

3. According to the textbook, the _____ is the criminal justice official with the power to make the decision to accept a negotiated plea. (Page 6)
   - (a.) judge
   - b. prosecutor
   - c. corrections director
   - d. law enforcement chief

4. According to the textbook, there are two very different kinds of decision making in criminal justice: _____. (Page 7)
   - a. formal decision making and by-the-book decision making
   - (b.) formal decision making and informal decision making
   - c. rational decision making and irrational decision making
   - d. informed decision making and uninformed decision making

5. The U.S. Constitution and Bill of Rights, state codes, decisions of federal courts, and state rules of criminal procedure are all examples of _____. (Page 7)
   - a. formal decision making
   - b. rational discussions
   - c. informal decision making
   - (d.) formal rules

6. The _____ depicts a process in which criminal justice officials decide how to deal with cases according to their informal discretionary definition of "seriousness". (Page 10)
   - (a.) "wedding cake" model
   - b. "funnel" model
   - c. crime control model
   - d. due process model

7. According to the textbook, one of the most important missions of informal criminal justice is _____. (Page 7)
   - (a.) to satisfy the need for flexibility in the vast number of situations that don't fit neatly into the rules in the book of formal criminal justice
   - b. to provide certainty and predictability throughout the criminal justice system
   - c. to create clear and concise policies
   - d. to provide consistency in the application of policies

WHAT'S INSIDE This chapter begins by determining what constitutes a crime through the definition of social harm. The behaviors associated with the word crime are presented in three types: violent crime, property crime, and crimes against public order and morals. These types are defined by their victims. The chapter then explains how the dark figure of crime statistic makes it difficult to accurately measure crime. The final section in this chapter looks at the effectiveness of official police reports (including Uniform Crime Reports, Part I and Part II offenses, and the National Incident-Based Reporting System), victim surveys, and self-reports.

Learning Outcomes

LO1 Discuss how crime is defined

LO2 Define and explain the major crime types

LO3 Analyze how crime is measured

LO4 Explain the strengths and weaknesses of the measures of crime

Chapter Outline

Art Index

PowerPoint Highlights

Video Highlights

Title: Trafficking in Women
Running time: 20 minutes
Description: Women are kidnapped, trafficked and sold as slaves for prostitution throughout Europe.

Title: Subway Poison Plot
Running time: 3 minutes
Description: In 2003, al-Qaeda operatives were nearly able to release cyanide gas in the New York City subway system.

Title: Identity Theft
Running time: 3 minutes
Description: Identity thieves buy and sell personal information such as credit card and Social Security numbers online.

Lecture Launchers

When gasoline prices spiked in 2008, an Indiana drug dealer began adding a transportation surcharge to each illegal transaction. On two occasions, Anthony Salinas sold cocaine to an undercover police officer for $240. $215 covered the drug, and an extra $25 was added to the final price for gas money.
http://www.thesmokinggun.com/archive/years/2008/0918081gastax1.html

In April 2009 a woman was able to aid in the apprehension of a team of burglars after she witnessed them robbing her home on a live video surveillance feed.
http://www.thesmokinggun.com/archive/years/2009/0409092boynton1.html

In June 2004, District Judge Terry Ruckriegle ruled that the woman who accused basketball star Kobe Bryant of sexual assault could not be referred to as a "victim" during courtroom proceedings, as this term prematurely implied Bryant's guilt.
http://www.thesmokinggun.com/archive/0601041kobe1.html

Key Terms

Classroom Activities

1. According to the 2002 edition of *Crime in the United States*, the following table represents the reported arrests for minor crimes. Ask students to rely on their own knowledge and understanding and estimate the percentage of actual crimes the arrest figures in the table below represent. In other words, what percentage of acts of disorderly conduct resulted in a police report being developed, making up the figures illustrated below.

CRIME	NUMBER OF REPORTED ARRESTS
Driving under the influence	1,461,746
Disorderly conduct	669,938
Vandalism	276,697
Runaways	125,688
Prostitution and commercialized vice	79,733

2. Find out how many students in the class are not criminal justice majors, and ask them why they are taking the class. This exercise can lead to a discussion of the fact that criminal justice is an area of interest to almost everyone, not just those majoring in the field.

3. Prior to discussing the consensus and conflict views of crime, ask students to write down how they think crime is defined. Have students discuss their answers, and then after discussing the two views, have them determine if their answers are more closely aligned with the consensus view or the conflict view.

Quick Quiz

1. _____ crimes are only a tiny slice of the total amount of crime. (Page 19)
   a. Property
   b. Violent ✓
   c. Petty
   d. Misdemeanor

2. In 1930, the FBI collected its first set of data based on official police records, the _____ . (Page 21)
   a. Uniform Crime Reports ✓
   b. National Incident-Based Reporting System
   c. National Crime Victimization Survey
   d. none of the above

3. The _____ does not distinguish between attempted and completed crimes. (Page 23)
   a. Uniform Crime Reports ✓
   b. National Incident-Based Reporting System
   c. National Crime Victimization Survey
   d. none of the above

4. In March of 2009, Josef Fritzl was sentenced to life in prison after pleading guilty to six charges including which of the following? (Page 19)
   a. providing material support
   b. lying to federal investigators
   c. false imprisonment ✓
   d. corporate fraud

WHAT'S INSIDE   This chapter examines the natural scientific theories and the different ways they interpret crime. Classical theories are based on free will and reason. Positivist theories are based on determinism—the belief that criminal behavior is controlled by factors beyond the control of individuals. These factors might be within an individual or outside. Social conflict theories rest on the idea that crime is whatever the law says it is, and so the focus of these theories is on lawmakers and law enforcers instead of lawbreakers. The chapter also examines crime victims and their characteristics. The Routine Activities Theory includes the role of the victim in crime and is perhaps the dominant theory of victimization. One of the most critical dynamics of victimization is whether the victim knows the offender.

Learning Outcomes

LO1   Distinguish among the various views of crime causation

LO2   Explain the classical view of crime causation

LO3   Understand who becomes a victim of crime and the characteristics of crime victims

LO4   Describe the positivist view of crime causation, including social structure and social process theories

LO5   Understand social conflict theories

Chapter Outline

Art Index

PowerPoint Highlights

Video Highlights

Title: Judge Lectures African Americans
Running time: 4 minutes
Description: An Atlanta, Georgia judge excused whites from his courtroom so he could address the black defendants.

Title: Airline Terror Plot
Running time: 13 minutes
Description: In 2006, British and American authorities thwarted a terrorist plot to blow up 10 airplanes mid-flight.

Title: John Mark Karr Confession
Running time: 8 minutes
Description: John Mark Karr's confession to the murder of child model JonBenet Ramsey is proven phony by DNA evidence.

Lecture Launchers

In March 2009 a Wisconsin woman was arrested for felonious identity theft after allegedly posing as an ex-boyfriend and posting a personal ad on Craigslist. The ad, which included an explicit image and the boyfriend's business phone number, invited other men to call and "talk dirty" to the victim.
http://www.thesmokinggun.com/archive/years/2009/0305094eau1.html

In May 2009, a United States soldier was charged with five counts of murder after allegedly seizing a weapon and killing five fellow soldiers while attending a stress clinic in Iraq. Sergeant John Russell had served in the armed forces for 21 years before he was referred to counseling.
http://www.nytimes.com/2009/05/14/world/middleeast/14shooter.html?ref=global-home

In May 2009, Los Angeles Dodgers outfielder Manny Ramirez received a 50-game suspension for violating Major League Baseball's Performance Enhancing Drug policy. Ramirez, who led the Boston Red Sox to win the 2007 World Series, waived his right to challenge the suspension.
http://www.npr.org/templates/story/story.php?storyId=103908279&ft=1&f=1055

Chapter 3 Explanations of Criminal Behavior

Key Terms

Classroom Activities

1. In the 1960s and 1970s, radical criminologists developed a coherent radical criminal justice theory based on a set of propositions. Ask students to list these propositions, giving the contributors the opportunity to write their proposition on the board.

   1. The state's primary purpose is to protect the dominant class in society.
   2. This purpose requires controlling the lower classes.
   3. The ruling class exploits the working class by wringing profit from overworked laborers.
   4. Criminal law controls workers so capitalists can get richer and secure protection for their accumulated riches.
   5. Brute force isn't always necessary to protect these interests and control the workers.
   6. Capitalists sometimes have to commit crimes to maintain the existing power arrangements.
   7. Workers commit crimes mainly out of necessity.

2. In 1983, researchers asked a selected sample of Americans to rank the seriousness of various crimes. Provide students with a scrambled listing of the crimes considered as the top ten serious crimes and ask them to rank them in the order they deem appropriate. Ask them to discuss similarities between the 1983 list and the one they develop. Discuss the reasons for any differences. The following is the list in proper order: (Page 97)

3. Present students with the following scenario:

   On his way home from school, a fourteen-year-old boy from a poor family stops at a convenience store. When he thinks the clerk is not looking, he puts a bottle of orange juice under his coat and heads for the door. The clerk catches him and calls the police.
   How might one explain the boy's criminal action according to each of the following theories about causes of crime?

   a. Biological Explanations
   b. Psychological Explanations
   c. Social Structure Theory
   d. Social Process Theory

Quick Quiz

1. When observable phenomena tend to vary with each other systematically, we refer to this as _____ . (Page 29)
   a. relativeness
   c. correlation
   b. concession
   d. reliability

2. _____ are based on the twin pillars of free will and reason. (Page 30)
   a. Classical (utilitarian) theories
   b. Positivist theories
   c. Irrational theories
   d. Criminal law theories

3. Jeremy Bentham developed the _____ theory of crime causation. (Page 30)
   a. positivist theory
   c. utilitarian theory
   b. maxim theory
   d. criminal law theory

4. _____ assume the criminal justice system creates criminals. (Page 41)
   a. Social labeling theories
   c. Social learning theories
   b. Social control theories
   d. Social construct theories

5. _____ look for explanations of crime in social processes of families, peer groups, schools, churches, neighborhoods, and other social institutions. (Page 40)
   a. Social structure theories
   c. Social learning theories
   b. Social process theories
   d. all of the above

6. Anomie, strain, and opportunity theories are all a part of _____ . (Page 40)
   a. social structure theories
   c. social learning theories
   b. social process theories
   d. all of the above

7. When criminologists became wary of explanations of criminal behavior based on the individual's biology, psychology, and free will, they looked to _____ . (Page 39)
   a. social structure theories
   c. social learning theories
   b. social process theories
   d. all of the above

8. _____ focus(es) on the mental and emotional elements in criminal behavior. (Page 38)
   a. Rational choice theory
   c. Psychological theories
   b. Positivist theory
   d. Genetic theory

WHAT'S INSIDE This chapter explains the decisional framework of constitutions, statutes, and interpretive court decisions that makes up criminal justice. Criminal law is explored through its limiting bodies: The United States Constitution, the principle of economy, elements of crime requirements, and defenses to crime. Criminal intent and strict liability offenses are defined; defenses to crime are laid out; and the three classification schemes for crimes are defined. Civil law, in the private sector, is different from criminal law in the public sector because the government and the defendant are parties to the case. Finally, the chapter explains how due process protects the accused throughout all aspects of trial and how criminal procedure grants and limits public officials' power.

Learning Outcomes

LO1 Discuss the sources of criminal law

LO2 Understand how substantive criminal law defines a crime and the legal responsibility of the accused

LO3 Differentiate between excuses and justification defenses for crime

LO4 Explain the classifications and grading of crime

LO5 List the similarities and differences between criminal law and civil law

LO6 Explain the importance of due process in the criminal justice system and understand how criminal procedure protects the rights of the accused

Chapter Outline

(Continued)

Art Index

PowerPoint Highlights

Video Highlights

Title: U.S. Patriot Act
Running time: 2 minutes
Description: The United States Patriot Act was extended by the Senate in an effort to combat terrorism.

Title: Death Penalty and Legal Issues
Running time: 7 minutes
Description: The U.S. Supreme Court considers a proposal that the death penalty is unconstitutional.

Lecture Launchers

In May 2009, Texas became the 37th American state to adopt a law granting journalists limited protection for confidential sources. The law grants journalists the freedom not to turn over notes or testify in civil cases, even if a source admitted to committing a crime, unless all other reasonable efforts have been exhausted.
http://www.chron.com/disp/story.mpl/metropolitan/6423010.html

In early 2009, Jonathan Lawrence Thomas, an inmate at a Nebraska penitentiary, applied to change his legal given name to Sinner. A judge denied the prisoner's name change, citing three pending child-support cases and that because of his criminal record, authorities might need to track him by his given name.
http://www.npr.org/templates/story/story.php?storyId=103700853&ft=1&f=1051

In May 2009, Craigslist announced it would remove its erotic services category amidst legal pressure nationwide. The office of Andrew M. Cuomo, New York's attorney general, contacted the site earlier that month, as did South Carolina's attorney general, Henry McMaster, who threatened the management of Craigslist with criminal prosecution.
http://www.nytimes.com/2009/05/14/technology/companies/14craigslist.html?ref=technology

Key Terms

Classroom Activities

1. On the board, create two columns. Head one "mala in se" and the other "mala prohibita." Lead the students through the process of identifying current laws within your jurisdiction that fall into the two categories, allowing the students to determine the appropriate column for each law.

2. Ask several of the students who are seeking a career in law enforcement to act as panelists and the remaining students to serve as an audience. Begin a question-answer exchange where you interview the panelists about their motivations for wanting to become police officers.

3. Have the students debate the meaning of the terms "probable cause," "reasonable suspicion," and "unreasonable search and seizure." Students should come to a variety of conclusions regarding these terms which can be used to illustrate the discretion available to police officers in the area of search and seizure.

4 In regard to public perceptions about the severity of various offenses, Americans do not share a consensus about all of the behaviors that are defined under law as "crimes." Students can test their own perceptions about the definition of crimes and explore the moral and political issues underlying crime definitions by discussing whether the following actions should be crimes:

　　a. Exchanging money for sex between two consenting adults
　　b. Playing poker for money with friends
　　c. Taking a candy bar from a store without paying for it
　　d. An industrial company pouring pollution into a river
　　e. Attempting suicide
　　f. Public drunkenness
　　g. An employee taking a ballpoint pen home from the office for personal use
　　h. Calling someone an ethnically/racially derogatory name

The exercise works most effectively by listing the eight behaviors on the board and then asking the class to immediately vote on each one. The discussion can proceed after a rough vote tally has been recorded on the board for each behavior.

Quick Quiz

1. The _____ bans retroactive criminal laws. (Page 55)
　　a. principle of economy　　c. void-for-vagueness doctrine
　　b. ex post facto clause　　d. equal protection of the laws

2. A law so vague that an individual "of common intelligence" has to "guess" what it means violates the _____. (Page 56)
　　a. principle of economy　　**c. void-for-vagueness doctrine**
　　b. ex post facto clause　　d. equal protection of the laws

3. The term "_____", as defined by the law, also includes the failure to report when the law requires you to do so. (Page 48)
　　a. criminal procedure　　c. due process
　　b. criminal law　　**d. criminal act**

4. No matter what the Constitution allows, through long tradition the _____ has established limits of its own. (Page 47)
　　a. criminal procedure　　c. due process
　　b. criminal law　　d. criminal act

5. Factual cause is not enough to prove causation; there must also be _____. (Page 49)
　　a. factual cause　　c. defenses of excuse
　　b. legal cause　　d. criminal law

6. The _____ is/are based on the idea that the law should make allowances for the imperfections and frailties of human nature. (Page 50)
　　a. factual cause　　**c. defenses of excuse**
　　b. legal cause　　d. criminal law

7. American _____ did not recognize strict liability until the Industrial Revolution. (Page 49)
　　a. factual cause　　c. defenses of excuse
　　b. legal cause　　**d. criminal law**

8. The insanity excuse is an example of _____. (Page 50)
　　a. factual cause　　**c. a defense of excuse**
　　b. legal cause　　d. criminal law

WHAT'S INSIDE This chapter lays out the development of policing, beginning with the constable/night watch system and the municipal police department era. It moves through the reforming era and the 1960s to arrive at the present model of community policing. The levels and structure of policing show it is formally structured after the military model command structure, but informally follows the more solitary university decision making structure. Finally, the chapter lists police responsibilities of enforcing criminal law, maintaining public order, and providing other public services.

Learning Outcomes

LO1 Recount the early development of policing and how policing evolved in the United States

LO2 Identify the various levels of law enforcement and the main types of law enforcement agencies

LO3 Understand the police organizational structure

LO4 List the missions and basic responsibilities of the police

Chapter Outline

Art Index

PowerPoint Highlights

Video Highlights

Title: Tracking Phone Calls
Running time: 6 minutes
Description: Debate arises over the government's ability to track phone calls in the wake of the September 11 terrorist attacks.

Title: War on Drugs: Somalia
Running time: 9 minutes
Description: Khat, a new drug trafficked into New York City from Africa, challenges police and the DEA.

Title: War on Drugs: Policing Drugs
Running time: 9 minutes
Description: Police endeavor to curb drug use while many question the effectiveness of their tactics.

Lecture Launchers

In February 2009, a North Dakota woman was arrested and charged with a felony count of child neglect after police arrived at the woman's house on a domestic disturbance call and found her breast-feeding her six-week-old infant while visibly intoxicated.
http://www.thesmokinggun.com/archive/years/2009/0428091badmom1.html

In May 2009, members of a Neighborhood Watch program in Greenup, Kentucky helped police apprehend local resident Mary Thomas, who had been trafficking narcotics throughout the town.
http://www.dailyindependent.com/local/local_story_130230557.htmll

A May 2009 audit of the Massachusetts criminal database found that law enforcement officials had conducted thousands of inappropriate criminal record searches on celebrities such as Matt Damon and Tom Brady.
http://www.npr.org/templates/story/story.php?storyId=103888991&ft=1&f=1051

Key Terms

constable/night watch system 60

municipal police department system 60

proactive policing 61

reactive policing 61

reform model of policing 62

community-oriented policing (COP) 63

military model of policing 70

maintaining order 72

Classroom Activities

1. Draw a timeline on the board and ask students to illustrate the development of policing, including the integration of women and minorities into police work and setting apart the three eras of modern policing without looking at their book.

2. Write three headings on the board: Criminal Law Enforcement, Order Maintenance and Public Service. Ask students to identify characteristics about each of these missions, give them examples of police tasks and ask them which mission(s) the task would fall into. Examples are: Barking dog disturbance, vehicle accident, speeding stop, DWI enforcement action.

3. Present the following scenario and questions to students:

   Imagine that you are a member of Congress. One of your staff assistants brings you a proposal to nationalize law enforcement throughout the United States. The proposal calls for abolishing state police agencies, county sheriffs, and local police departments. Instead, Congress would create a new U.S. Department of Law Enforcement. A Secretary of Law Enforcement would oversee a national police agency which would have units established in each state, county, city, and town. Your assistant argues that the new organization would save resources by coordinating the work of every law enforcement officer in the nation and creating a standard set of law enforcement policies and priorities. In addition, the plan would standardize training, salary, and benefits for police officers everywhere and thus raise the level of professionalism of police, especially in small towns and rural areas.

   Before you decide whether or not to present this proposal to Congress, respond to the following questions.

   a. Are there any undesirable consequences that could develop from putting this plan into action?

   b. As a politician, you are concerned about how others will react to the plan. How do you think each group would react and why?
   - Voters
   - State and local politicians
   - Police officers

   c. Will you support the proposal? Why or why not?

Quick Quiz

1. During which era of policing was the President's Commission on Law Enforcement and the Administration of Justice formed? (Page 62)
   a. The Municipal Police Department Era
   b. The Reform Model Era
   c. The Turbulent Era
   d. The Community Policing Era

2. During which era of policing did police departments become the arms of the dominant political machines? (Page 61)
   a. The Constable/Night Watch System Era
   b. The Municipal Police Department Era
   c. The Reform Model Era
   d. The Turbulent Era
   e. The Community Policing Era

3. During which era of policing did the police shift from foot to motorized patrols? (Page 62)
   a. The Municipal Police Department Era
   b. The Reform Model Era
   c. The Turbulent Era
   d. The Community Policing Era

4. The report of the President's Commission on Law Enforcement and Administration of Justice documented widespread _____. (Pages 62–63)
   a. police corruption
   b. discrimination
   c. failure to respond to the needs and demands of communities
   d. all of the above

5. During which era of policing were the first uniformed police introduced? (Page 61)
   a. The Constable/Night Watch System Era
   b. The Municipal Police Department Era
   c. The Reform Model Era
   d. The Turbulent Era

WHAT'S INSIDE Chapter 6 begins by looking at and evaluating preventative patrol and criminal investigation. There is some empirical evidence supporting some special crime-attack strategies. This chapter also looks at support functions that allow police to operate, such as communications/dispatch, personnel, and public information. The final sections examine community-oriented policing and its related programs, and how the partnership between police and citizens benefits the community and gives residents power.

Learning Outcomes

LO1 Understand the main functions of police patrol, investigation, and special operations units

LO2 Discuss the concept of patrol and its effectiveness

LO3 Discuss key issues associated with the criminal investigative function

LO4 Explain the various police support functions

LO5 Understand the concept of community policing

LO6 Describe various community policing strategies

Chapter Outline

Art Index

PowerPoint Highlights

Slides 3–4: **The strategies of crime control: crime-attack and community policing**

Slides 10–11: **The drawbacks of vehicle patrol**

Slide 12: **The benefits of single-officer patrol**

Slides 16–17: **An overview of DNA evidence and its conditions for use**

Slide 19: **The support functions of police**

Slides 20–24: **An overview, examples and strategies of community policing**

Video Highlights

Title: Catching Criminals by Their Walk
Running time: 4 minutes
Description: New technology allows police to identify individual criminals by their unique gaits.

Title: Bait Cars
Running time: 5 minutes
Description: Police use specially-equipped vehicles to stop car thieves in the act, and to prevent further thefts.

Title: Bicycle Community Police Officer—SFPD
Running time: 4 minutes
Description: A San Francisco Community Police Officer is interviewed about her duties and insights.

Lecture Launchers

In December 2008, police found instructions titled "How To Commit Armed Robbery In Six Easy Steps" while searching the car of a woman apprehended for attempted armed robbery. The instructions, clearly written in a tongue-in-cheek manner, were printed from the Internet 11 hours before the woman attempted to rob a Dollar Tree store.
http://www.thesmokinggun.com/archive/years/2008/1212082guide1.html

In October 2008 a Tennessee man was indicted for illegally accessing former Republican vice presidential candidate Sarah Palin's email account and posting screenshots on the Internet. Police were able to trace the images to 20-year old David Kernell, who was charged with the felonious crime.
http://www.thesmokinggun.com/archive/years/2008/1008081palin1.html

In July 2008, a New Jersey man was arrested by federal agents after allegedly ordering nine films containing child pornography from a catalog he received in the mail. The catalog, authored by federal officials, was sent as part of a sting orchestrated by the U.S. Postal Inspection Services.
http://www.thesmokinggun.com/archive/years/2008/0909082letter1.html

Key Terms

Classroom Activities

1. Divide your class into small groups of 4 – 5 students. Ask them to think about their own communities and determine if community policing would fit into their neighborhood. Ask them to list some advantages community policing could bring to their neighborhood, and some disadvantages. Lead the class in a discussion of their findings.

2. Assign students to small groups and ask them to address the issue of "one size fits all justice." Is there any uniform application system that would stand the test of fairness? Pull the groups back together and let a representative from each give their group's consensus, compare the similarities that developed between groups.

3. What does the future hold for our criminal justice system's efforts to capture criminals? Many thought that DNA was the ultimate answer, but most crimes don't involve DNA evidence. Remember that once upon a time, society thought that the fingerprint was the magic key. What is next? How do we maintain the balance between effective detection techniques, which require some intrusion into our private lives, and the protection of our civil liberties? Prompt students to discuss their thoughts.

4. Present students with the following scenario:

   You are the members of the city of Smalltown's police community council, a group of citizens who work with the police to improve the quality of life and police-citizen relationships in Smalltown. Two days ago a Smalltown police officer was captured on a video camera brutally beating a Smalltown resident, who remained motionless on the ground. The tape was turned over to a local cable station which has played it numerous times each day, causing many residents to complain openly of police brutality and harassment. Smalltown police officers have reported that numerous teens are screaming insults at them as they pass in their police cars. One officer reported that a teenager openly challenged him to a fight. The police chief has called the community council into session and asks for advice in correcting the rapidly deteriorating relationship between the police and the community. What would be your recommendations to the chief?

Quick Quiz

1. The strategy of _____ has two objectives: controlling crime and reassuring law-abiding people they are safe. (Page 76)
   a. crackdowns
   b. preventive patrol
   c. SWAT mobilization
   d. surveillance

2. One way in which departments hoped to speed up response time was the _____. (Page 76)
   a. strategic placement plan
   b. multi-precinct strategy
   c. increase in patrol cars on duty
   d. 911 system

3. The hybrid bicycle patrol has practically all the benefits of _____. (Page 77)
   a. aggressive exercise programs
   b. investigation
   c. foot patrol
   d. mobilization

4. Police _____ has serious drawbacks and contributes to poor police-community relations, especially in poor neighborhoods. (Page 77)
   a. vehicle patrol
   b. mentality
   c. SWAT operations
   d. uniform style

5. Police returned to the old practice of _____ in the 1970s and 1980s because it brought them closer to the community. (Page 77)
   a. mooching
   b. foot patrol
   c. vice operation
   d. nightstick tricks

6. In preliminary investigations, _____ collect information at crime scenes and write incident reports. (Page 78)
   a. patrol officers
   b. detectives
   c. dispatchers
   d. civilian volunteers

WHAT'S INSIDE The chapter begins by examining what makes arrests and searches reasonable under the law. Probable cause is needed for both arrests and searches, and most also require warrants. The exclusionary rule bans the use of evidence gained in violation of rights, though there are exceptions to the rule. The USA Patriot Act of 2001 lessened restrictions on arrest and search and seizure substantially, particularly through the controversial use of roving wiretaps. *Miranda v. Arizona* resulted in the decision that custody is inherently coercive and the development of *Miranda* warnings. Police use of force is covered in the fourth amendment and by the objective standard of reasonable force. The final section covers police corruption, which pertains to a wide variety of behavior.

Learning Outcomes

LO1 Understand what an arrest is and when an arrest is reasonable

LO2 Explain when searches can be made without a warrant

LO3 Understand the exclusionary rule and the situations in which it applies

LO4 Explain the *Miranda v. Arizona* decision and how the *Miranda* warnings are used

LO5 Describe how the USA Patriot Act of 2001 changed the guidelines for electronic surveillance of suspected terrorists

LO6 Understand the objective standard of reasonable force

LO7 Explain what constitutes excessive force and describe deadly and nondeadly force

LO8 Explain police corruption

Chapter Outline

Art Index

PowerPoint Highlights

Slides 3–8: **Reasonable arrests and searches, and the use of warrants**

Slides 11–12: **An overview of *Miranda v. Arizona* and the *Miranda* warnings**

Slides 15–17: **The use of reasonable and excessive force**

Slide 20: **The use of deadly force**

Slides 21–26: **The causes and categories of police corruption, and its remedies**

Video Highlights

Title: Crime in Philadelphia
Running time: 10 minutes
Description: Police deal with the unique challenges of patrolling one of America's most violent cities.

Title: Crime in New Orleans
Running time: 8 minutes
Description: Post-Katrina New Orleans remains a hotbed of looting and violence amidst social and political strife.

Title: Crime in Los Angeles
Running time: 8 minutes
Description: America's second-largest city is invigorated by a new police chief after years of gang violence.

Lecture Launchers

In September 2008, Kenneth Smith was arrested and charged with disorderly conduct in Riviera Beach, Florida for wearing his pants below his waist, exposing blue and white boxer shorts. Earlier in 2008, Riviera Beach voters approved an ordinance criminalizing the urban fashion statement. http://www.thesmokinggun.com/archive/years/2008/0903081pants1.html

In recent years, Texas police have come under fire for over-patrolling the U.S.–Mexico border in order to apprehend and seize drug trafficking money, a portion of which they get to keep. Critics claim that Texas officers are more interested in seizing money than drugs, which are destroyed upon seizure. http://www.npr.org/templates/story/story.php?storyId=91490480

In 1990, Donald Rochon filed a discrimination suit against the FBI after being threatened and humiliated by coworkers because he was black. In May 2009, Rochon filed another suit claiming that his pension was being withheld out of spite, a claim that went under review by Attorney General Eric Holder. http://www.npr.org/templates/story/story.php?storyId=104074962

Key Terms

arrest 87
probable cause to arrest 88
public safety exception 91
reasonable suspicion 92
**objective standard of
   reasonable force 93**
less-than-lethal force 94
racial profiling 98

Classroom Activities

1. This activity can lead to an interesting discussion about the validity of eyewitness testimony and the exclusionary rule. Immediately as class starts, write "Henry Clay Boothe" on the board, without referencing it in any way, leave it for approximately one minute and then erase your writing. Continue with your discussion in the class for about twenty minutes. Ask students to, without discussion, write on a piece of paper the name that you had previously written on the board. Determine how many were able to accurately recall the exact name you had written. Explain that this could have been like a crucial piece of information in a criminal investigation—in fact, a man named Henry Clay Boothe robbed a convenience store one night. He was wearing his construction hard-hat with his name clearly printed on the side—not a single witness remembered that fact, but the store video cameras captured it and police found him at his construction site, still wearing his hard-hat.

2. Warrantless searches are important for police officers in regard to gathering evidence that might otherwise be lost or endanger the safety of others in society. Pose the following to students:

   a. What purposes are served by allowing law enforcement officers to conduct searches without a warrant?

   b. Are the following warrantless searches justifiable given the purposes that you listed? Why or why not?
      • A man is stopped and frisked on the streets because he fits the profile of a rapist in the neighborhood.
      • Hispanic-Americans are ordered out of their car and searched 5 miles from the Mexican border.
      • A cavity search is performed on a woman seen running from the scene of a gun homicide.
      • The trunk of a teen's car is searched after she receives a speeding ticket.
      • Luggage is searched at random by an airline after unknowing passengers board the airplane.

Quick Quiz

1. The Fourth Amendment protects the individual's privacy in a variety of settings, none more clearly defined than an individual's _____ . (Page 89)
   a. home
   b. sex life
   c. workplace
   d. vehicle

2. Absent exigent circumstances, searches of houses are reasonable only if police officers _____ . (Page 89)
   a. have reasonable suspicion
   b. give fair warning
   c. get a warrant
   d. know they will find something

3. According to the U.S. Supreme Court, the justification for the exclusionary rule is that it _____ . (Page 90)
   a. reduces trial case loads
   b. deters unconstitutional police behavior
   c. increases conviction rates
   d. is set forth in the First Amendment

4. In one of the most famous cases in U.S. Supreme Court history, _____ , the Court decided police have to give suspects in custody four warnings before they interrogate them. (Page 91)
   a. *Miranda v. Arizona*
   b. *Hoyle v. Clements*
   c. *Indianapolis v. Edmond*
   d. *Harwood v. United States*

5. The objective basis for backing up stops and frisks is called _____ . (Page 92)
   a. police intuition
   b. suspicion
   c. probable cause
   d. reasonable suspicion

WHAT'S INSIDE Chapter 8 begins by introducing the three-tier structure of our federal judiciary system and the duties of each tier. The difference between the appellate and trial courts is explained, as is the way that a trial gets to the U.S Supreme Court. The chapter explains the two types of petitions the Supreme Court receives and the decision making process. Courtroom work groups and their efficacy in disposing of cases are covered, followed by the judge selection process. The final two sections look at prosecutors' missions, their organizational structure, and the defense counsel mission. Both prosecutors and defense counsel have the informal mission of getting along with the courtroom work group.

Learning Outcomes

LO1 Describe the structure of the various U.S. court systems

LO2 Explain the difference between trial courts and appellate courts

LO3 Describe how a case gets to the U.S. Supreme Court

LO4 Understand the courtroom work group and its organizational mission

LO5 Discuss the selection and qualifications of judges

LO6 Identify the role played by prosecutors in the courtroom work group and understand how prosecution offices are organized and managed

LO7 Identify the role played by defense counsel in the courtroom work group

Chapter Outline

Art Index

PowerPoint Highlights

Video Highlights

Title: Ethics Charges in the Duke Rape Case
Running time: 3 minutes
Description: A district attorney faces ethics charges by the North Carolina Bar Association for hiding evidence and lying.

Title: Judges at Risk
Running time: 3 minutes
Description: Family court judges from across the country face threats of violence from disgruntled defendants.

Title: Superior Court Judge Anne Bouliane
Running time: 5 minutes
Description: A Superior Court judge is interviewed about her experiences, insights, and challenges.

Lecture Launchers

In August 2008, Cincinnati Bengals wide receiver Chad Johnson was approved to change his legal surname to OchoCinco in recognition of his uniform number, 85.
http://www.thesmokinggun.com/archive/years/2008/0905081ocho1.html

Actress Charlize Theron was sued in 2007 by luxury watch manufacturer Raymond Weil for the breach of a lucrative endorsement contract. Theron was paid between $3–5 million to promote Weil's watches exclusively for 18 months, an agreement she violated by wearing competitors' jewelry.
http://www.thesmokinggun.com/archive/years/2007/0206072charlize1.html

In May 2009, prominent New York City lawyer Marc Dreier pleaded guilty to securities fraud, wire fraud and money laundering, which netted him more than $670 million between 2004 and 2008. Until his arrest in December 2008, Dreier ran a seemingly successful hedge fund firm housing 250 attorneys.
http://www.npr.org/templates/story/story.php?storyId=104038599

Key Terms

Classroom Activities

1. Discuss the development of the court system in the United States, then ask students to identify the federal and state jurisdictions the local area of the university falls under.

2. Create three columns on the board, one labeled "Defense Attorney," another "Prosecutor," and a third "Judge." Ask students to use their knowledge of the chapter to define the various tasks of each of these in the court process.

3. Assign students to small groups and ask them to develop a model to illustrate the criminal justice process from the beginning of law enforcement interest in a case to the point where a suspect is developed and charged, through the courtroom process up to conviction. Let each group present their model to the rest of the class.

4. Divide the class into small groups. Each group is a legislative committee assigned the task of proposing legislation concerning the best method for selecting state trial judges. In considering selection methods, students should consider the following issues:

   a. Should the voting public have a direct voice in the selection and removal of judges?
   b. Do elected judges have sufficient independence to make proper decisions?
   c. Can voters vote for judges intelligently without having a party label on the ballot to tell them about the candidates' partisan affiliations?
   d. What kinds of issues should judges be permitted to discuss in judicial elections?
   e. Can a merit selection process remove political considerations from the selection of judges?
   f. Should trial judges be required to have any special qualifications?
   g. What kinds of people would be selected for judgeships if choices were determined by governors or legislatures?

   When the students later discuss the exercise in class, there may be a strong attraction to the concept of purely merit-based selection, which can still be marred by political influence and personal bias. Many students don't immediately recognize that it is difficult for anyone to choose among a range of experienced lawyers in order to say with any precision that one lawyer is "most qualified." Raise these issues and have the class discuss them.

Quick Quiz

1. _____ courts decide minor cases, like traffic offenses, drunk and disorderly conduct, shoplifting, and prostitution. (Page 102)
   a. Lower
   b. Felony
   c. Appellate
   d. Administrative

2. Most states and the federal judiciary have two levels of _____ court: Intermediate and last resort. (Page 104)
   a. lower
   b. felony
   c. appellate
   d. administrative

3. The Supreme Court issues the writ of _____ if four justices vote to issue it. (Page 105)
   a. habeas corpus
   b. shur nurita
   c. certiorari
   d. maximas demetrius

4. The petition for a writ of _____ asks the Supreme Court to order some official to come to a trial court and justify a prisoner's imprisonment. (Page 105)
   a. habeas corpus
   b. shur nurita
   c. certiorari
   d. maximas demetrius

5. The _____ mission is to keep the organization running smoothly, efficiently, and, above all, harmoniously. (Page 106)
   a. courtroom work group's
   b. star chamber's
   c. Supreme Court's
   d. bailiff's

WHAT'S INSIDE   This chapter begins by explaining the criteria prosecutors use to make the charging decision, what occurs at the first court appearance after charging, and the right to effective counsel. The chapter then distinguishes between bail and pretrial detention, as well as the circumstances and specifications relating to each system. The final sections of the chapter describe how the government's case is tested through preliminary hearings or grand jury review and the process of arraignment.

CHAPTER 9 PREP CARD
Proceedings before Trial

Learning Outcomes

LO1   Understand the pretrial process in criminal cases, including the role of prosecutorial discretion

LO2   Recognize when the right to counsel applies and in what types of cases

LO3   Understand the bail process and the legal right to bail

LO4   Understand the context of pretrial detention

LO5   Explain how the government's case against a defendant is tested

LO6   Understand the authority to try a defendant

Chapter Outline

Art Index

PowerPoint Highlights

Slides 3–12:   **The decision to charge a suspect with a crime, and the influences on that decision**

Slides 14–21:   **The right to counsel, and an overview of "effective" counsel**

Slides 22–23:   **The standard of indigence and the provision of counsel**

Slide 24:   **The legal right to bail**

Slides 26–30:   **Testing the government's case via the preliminary hearing and the grand jury**

Video Highlights

Title: CSI Real Life
Running time: 3 minutes
Description: Forensics experts demonstrate some of the high-tech equipment that assists them in solving crimes.

Title: Entertainment Hearing
Running time: 3 minutes
Description: Politicians condemn the entertainment industry for marketing violent and hypersexual material to children.

Lecture Launchers

In May 2009, Wal-Mart agreed to pay nearly $2 million in a deal that releases the retail giant of any criminal charges for the trampling death of a temporary worker in November 2008.
http://www.npr.org/templates/story/story.php?storyId=103856154&ft=1&f=1001

In April 2009, U.S. Magistrate Judge Andrew J. Peck determined that Abdiwali Abdiqadir Muse, the sole surviving suspect from a pirate attack on American cargo ship Maersk Alabama, was age 18 and should be tried as an adult, though his defence claimed he was only age 15.
http://www.npr.org/templates/story/story.php?storyId=103336392&ft=1&f=1001 l

In December 2008, 12,000 unopened rape kits were discovered in an audit of the Los Angeles Police Department and Sheriff's Office. Police stated that they did not have the money or technology to wade through the massive backlog.
http://www.npr.org/templates/story/story.php?storyId=98001964&ft=1&f=1012

Key Terms

Classroom Activities

1. Assign students to small groups, giving them the following list of factors that research indicates prosecutor's use in deciding whether or not to charge defendants in sexual assault cases:

   • The offense is serious.

   • The suspect has a criminal record.

   • It's clear the victim has suffered "real harm."

   • There's strong evidence against the suspect.

   • The victim's willing to cooperate.

   • The odds in favor of conviction are high.

   Have the members of each group rank the order of precedence and submit their answers to you. Using the board, plot the responses and compare the outcomes. Explain to the class that any differences may reflect the reasons we see prosecutors in different jurisdictions handle similar cases in different ways.

2. Have students imagine that they are judges responsible for setting bail. For each of the following cases, have them indicate whether they would release the defendant, set bail at some specific amount (state the amount), or deny bail and order preventive detention. Have students provide brief comments that explain each decision.

   a. Jane Williams is a new assistant professor of literature at the local university. She is twenty-six years old. She has no relatives in the area and her family lives 500 miles away in the city where she went to college for the eight years it took to earn her undergraduate and graduate degrees. She is charged with fraud in obtaining $50,000 in student loans during the previous three years by lying about her income and assets on student loan application forms. Seven years earlier she pleaded guilty in her home town to a misdemeanor charge of underage drinking.

   b. Karl Schmidt is charged with attempted rape. He is accused of attacking a woman in his car while giving her a ride home from the bar where he met her. He is a twenty-two year old, rookie police officer (now suspended from the force) who has lived in the city for his entire life and has no prior record.

   c. Susan Claussen is charged with theft for ordering and eating dinner at an expensive restaurant, and then leaving without paying the bill. She has been charged with and entered guilty pleas to the offense on five previous occasions over the past three years. She has been placed on probation several times and served one thirty-day jail sentence. She is unemployed and a life-long resident of the city. She lives with her parents.

Quick Quiz

1. The prosecutor's decision to charge starts the formal process of _____ . (Page 116)
   a. adjudication
   b. bonding
   c. sentencing
   d. trial

2. If the evidence adds up to what prosecutor believes is _____, the suspect will be charged. (Page 118)
   a. reasonable belief
   b. proof beyond a reasonable doubt
   c. circumstantial
   d. collected legally

3. The Supreme Court has determined that states have to provide a lawyer for defendants charged with any offense punishable by _____. (Page 121)
   a. death
   b. the state
   c. incarceration
   d. fine or imprisonment

4. Research indicates that only 5 percent of all _____ defendants see a lawyer before their first appearance. (Page 123)
   a. indigent
   b. guilty
   c. charged
   d. innocent

5. The _____ Amendment to the U.S. Constitution bans excessive bail. (Page 124)
   a. Fifth
   b. Sixth
   c. Eighth
   d. Fourteenth

6. The _____ offers the first opportunity for judicial screening of the case. (Page 126)
   a. trial
   b. appeal
   c. preliminary hearing
   d. prosecutor's review

WHAT'S INSIDE The chapter begins with a detailed look at how juries function both in deciding a case and as an indicator of community values. The steps of the trial process are summarized and the Sixth Amendment's guarantee of a speedy trial is defined. This chapter looks more in depth at plea bargaining, detailing types of guilty pleas and reasons defendants plead guilty, as well as why plea bargaining occurs at all. The chapter ends with explanations of the prosecutor, defense attorney, judge and defendant in plea negotiations. The role of the defendant is explored more deeply than in Chapter 9.

Learning Outcomes

LO1 Explain the use of juries in the trial process

LO2 Summarize the trial process

LO3 Define the concept of a speedy trial

LO4 Explain what is meant by the term *plea bargain* and identify the types of guilty pleas

LO5 Recognize how and why plea bargaining occurs

LO6 Explain the roles of the prosecutor, defense attorney, judge, and defendant in plea negotiations

Chapter Outline

(Continued)

Art Index

PowerPoint Highlights

Video Highlights

Title: Courtney Love
Running time: 3 minutes
Description: A warrant was issued for rock star Courtney Love for failing to appear in court on an assault charge.

Title: Klan Member's Verdict
Running time: 4 minutes
Description: A former member of the KKK was found guilty of the murder of three civil rights leaders in the 1960s.

Title: U.S. Serial Killer: BTK
Running time: 2 minutes
Description: Former church leader Dennis Rader confessed and pleaded guilty to being infamous serial killer BTK.

Lecture Launchers

In April 2009, a Montana resident was threatened with jail time after he wrote a lewd request for excuse from jury duty. Among other reasons put forth in the notarized affidavit, Erik Slye called court officials morons and jury duty a complete waste of time.
http://www.thesmokinggun.com/archive/years/2009/0430091jury1.html

An in-depth report released April 2009 by the Constitution Project's National Right to Counsel Committee concluded that the American public defender system grossly and consistently fails to provide adequate representation for indigent defendants.
http://www.npr.org/templates/story/story.php?storyId=103108229&ft=1&f=1012

Between 2005 and 2007, Neil Rodreick II, age 31, posed as a 12-year-old boy at a number of Arizona middle schools. Rodreick was arrested after school officials became suspicious of his forged birth certificate, presuming him to be an abducted child.
http://www.npr.org/templates/story/story.php?storyId=102858745&ft=1&f=1001

Key Terms

Classroom Activities

1. Develop a descriptive list of several felonious crimes including murder, robbery, theft, and assault (local news stories are a good source). Divide the class into small groups, giving each group a list. Ask each group to independently determine a fair sentence for each crime situation if the defendant wishes to plea bargain. When the groups are finished, compare and explain that this is how courthouse work groups determine plea bargains and why we see discrepancies between jurisdictions.

2. Prompt students to discuss the differences between direct and cross examination. Which is more adversarial? From a witness's standpoint, which would be more difficult to endure? Why? Ask students to give examples of examinations they've seen in movies and television, and instruct them to analyze the realism of these portrayals.

3. Present the following scenario to students:

   After arresting a suspect for burglary, police officers learned that the suspect's nickname was "Butch." A confidential informant had previously told them that someone named "Butch" was guilty of an unsolved murder in another city. The police in the other city were informed about this coincidence and they sent officers to question the suspect about the murder. Meanwhile, the suspect's sister secured the services of a lawyer to represent her brother on the burglary charge. Neither she nor the lawyer knew about the suspicions concerning the unsolved murder case. The lawyer telephoned the police station and said she would come to the station to be present if the police wished to question her client. The lawyer was told that the police would not question him until the following morning and she could come to the station at that time. Meanwhile, the police from the other city arrived and initiated the first of a series of evening questioning sessions with the suspect. The suspect was not informed that his sister had obtained the services of a lawyer to represent him. The suspect was not told that the lawyer had called the police and asked to be present during any questioning. During questioning, the suspect was informed of his *Miranda* rights, waived his right to be represented by counsel during questioning, and subsequently confessed to the murder.

   a. If you were the defense attorney, what arguments would you make to have the confession excluded from evidence?

   b. If you were the judge, would you permit the confession to be used in evidence? Provide reasons for your decision.

Quick Quiz

1. Juries are the _____ element of the court system; they represent the community and its values. (Page 131)
   a. adversary
   b. republican
   c. controlling
   d. democratic

2. The Supreme Court held in _____ that six-member juries do not violate the Sixth Amendment. (Page 132)
   a. *Eldridge v. Clark*
   b. *Miranda v. Arizona*
   c. *Williams v. Florida*
   d. *Gideon v. Wainwright*

3. To win _____, all defendants have to do is cast a reasonable doubt on the government's case. (Page 133)
   a. retrial
   b. appeal
   c. acquittal
   d. denial

4. In their _____, prosecutors and defense lawyers give an overview of their side of the case. (Page 133)
   a. trial briefs
   b. opening statements
   c. pre-trial motions
   d. jury charge

5. After the closing arguments, the judge gives the jury the _____ in the form of jury instructions. (Page 135)
   a. instructions
   b. verdict
   c. evidence
   d. charge

6. In _____, defendants arrange some kind of deal for a reduced charge or sentence before pleading guilty. (Page 137)
   a. mercy pleadings
   b. direct testimony
   c. negotiated pleas
   d. covert meetings

WHAT'S INSIDE Chapter 11 grounds its explanation of sentencing by looking at the four major purposes of punishment: retribution, prevention, restitution, and restorative justice. The types of sentences (determinate and fixed) are examined in terms of satisfying criminal punishment, including the implementation of mandatory minimum sentences. Sentencing guidelines and their purposes are outlined, as well as presentence reports. Finally, this chapter examines the death penalty in terms of its recent history and current levels of support.

Learning Outcomes

LO1 Recognize the major purposes of punishment

LO2 Identify the types of sentences judges can impose

LO3 Explain how sentences are determined using sentencing guidelines and presentence reports

LO4 Explain the death penalty debate

Chapter Outline

Art Index

PowerPoint Highlights

Video Highlights

Title: DNA and the Death Penalty
Running time: 8 minutes
Description: DNA evidence is used to verify the guilt of a man executed for the murder of his sister-in-law.

Title: War on Drugs: Imprisonment of Drug Offenders
Running time: 5 minutes
Description: Protesters advocate personal freedom and question why jails are filled with non-violent drug offenders.

Title: Death Row
Running time: 3 minutes
Description: Crips founder Tookie Williams faces the death penalty as many fight for mercy.

Lecture Launchers

Because of old laws on the books in Ireland, people can be incarcerated for outstanding debts. Although seldom used in recent history, the high rates of mortgage foreclosure are prompting some lenders to initiate proceedings to send defaulting homeowners to debtors' jail.
http://findarticles.com/p/articles/mi_qn4161/is_20081019/ai_n30925557/?tag=content:col1

In April 2009, convicted felon Ronald Rajcok asked for his 36-year sentence to be reviewed in hopes of obtaining an early release. The Sentence Review Board, however, decided to *increase* Rajcok's sentence to 42 years for his role in the kidnapping, rape, beating, and drowning of a 13-year-old girl.
http://www.zwire.com/site/news.cfm?newsid=20303940&BRD=1655&PAG=461&dept_id=13091&rfi=6

Bernard Madoff, the 70-year-old former NASDAQ chairman who created a billion-dollar Ponzi scheme, turned himself in to authorities in March 2009 because he realized he would eventually get caught. Madoff pleaded guilty to 11 felony counts of defrauding investors out of billions

Key Terms

of dollars. The maximum sentence for his crimes was 150 years, but if he serves concurrently, Madoff could serve a mere 20 years for his massive fraud.

http://online.wsj.com/article/SB123685693449906551.html

Classroom Activities

1. Is there disparity in sentencing in the United States? Or, are there rational reasons that African Americans and Hispanics are disproportionately represented in prisons? Why are women underrepresented in the prison population? Does race and gender actually play a significant role in the application of sentencing? Prompt students to discuss.

2. Develop a list of misdemeanor violations including such violations as jay-walking, driving without a license, public intoxication, speeding, etc. Divide the students into small groups and task them with developing alternative approaches to punish and/or rehabilitate violators of these laws. Compare the findings and discuss the Constitutional and public opinion views of each.

3. Have students define, discuss, compare and contrast sentencing disparity and sentencing discrimination.

   Some main points:
   Discriminatory sentencing is sentencing which is based on illegal considerations such as race, ethnicity, gender, etc. Numerous studies have probed the extent to which economic status, age, gender, and race improperly influence the sentence. The results of such studies are mixed. Disparity refers to inconsistencies in sentencing. There is disparity between states because of state law, and judicial backgrounds and attitudes contribute to disparity.

4. Have students debate the constitutionality of the death penalty for the following defendants who each have committed heinous murders. This should illustrate to the students the difficult question of drawing a line between life and death.

   Case #1: mildly retarded person
   Case #2: moderately retarded person
   Case #3: severely retarded person
   Case #4: seventeen-year-old male
   Case #5: seventeen-year-old female
   Case #6: fifteen-year-old male
   Case #7: fifteen-year-old female
   Case #8: accomplice to a murder who did not actually commit the murder

Quick Quiz

1. The _____ Amendment to the U.S. Constitution bans cruel and unusual punishments. (Page 144)
   a. First
   b. Fourth
   c. Eighth
   d. Tenth

2. _____ means offenders are responsible for their actions and have to suffer the consequences if they act irresponsibly. (Page 144)
   a. Applicability
   b. Culpability
   c. Destitution
   d. Amenability

3. The goal of _____ is to heal and repair the damage to individuals and relationships directly involved. (Page 146)
   a. restorative justice
   b. deterrence
   c. fixed sentences
   d. indeterminate sentences

4. To _____ , determinate sentencing means long, fixed uncomfortable sentences. (Page 147)
   a. conservatives
   b. liberals
   c. judges
   d. politicians

5. In _____ guidelines, either legislatures or special commissions set the types and ranges of sentences. (Page 150)
   a. Supreme Court sentencing
   b. restorative justice
   c. prescriptive sentencing
   d. presumptive sentencing

WHAT'S INSIDE This chapter examines correctional supervision in the community, beginning with the differences between probation and parole and their missions. Community corrections missions include holding offenders accountable, protecting public safety, and reintegrating offenders into the community. The chapter then outlines the history of probation and parole and moves into their current implementation. Details of release, conditions of parole and probation, and consequences for violations are explained. The chapter then explains the rights of probationers and parolees. The final section discusses types and effectiveness of intermediate sanctions used on those for whom probation is too lenient and incarceration is too harsh.

Learning Outcomes

LO1 Understand the community correctional forms of probation and parole

LO2 Understand the missions of community corrections

LO3 Understand how probation and parole evolved

LO4 Explain how community corrections are implemented today

LO5 Be familiar with the legal issues of probation and parole

LO6 Know what is meant by intermediate sanctions and be familiar with the types and how they are administered

Chapter Outline

Art Index

PowerPoint Highlights

Video Highlights

Title: Parole Agent 3 and Supervisor—California Youth Authority
Running time: 5 minutes
Description: A California juvenile parole officer is interviewed about his mission and experiences.

Title: 12 Regional Parole Administrator—Parole and Community Services
Running time: 5 minutes
Description: Parole administrator Robert Meeks is interviewed about his life and work.

Lecture Launchers

While doing community service for a previous offence, a Michigan teen vandalized a court office and stole a gavel, which prompted a judge to sentence the teen to 56 days in correctional boot camp. The consequences of not completing the boot camp were steep—180 days in jail.
http://www.redorbit.com/news/oddities/476883/teen_gets_boot_camp_for_angering_judge/

In 2009, Ryan LeVin ran over and killed two tourists in Florida with his car. Within ten days of the *Florida* incident, however, LeVin was incarcerated in an *Illinois* prison for violating probation related to a 2006 conviction for running over a Chicago policeman.
http://www.chicagobreakingnews.com/2009/05/ryan-levin-florida-illinois-probation-violation-sentence.html
http://www.tmcnet.com/usubmit/-owner-car-fatal-crash-gets-2-years-probation-/2009/05/12/4176628.htm

Key Terms

corrections 159

probation 160

parole 160

good behavior bond 162

discretionary release 163

mandatory release 164

expiration release 164

case study method 165

risk assessment method 165

recidivism 165

technical violations 168

either/or corrections (in-or-out corrections) 169

intermediate punishments 169

intensive supervised probation 169

community service 172

day reporting centers 173

Cynthia Horvath, a 45-year-old teacher and mother, was convicted of having unlawful sex with one of her students and sentenced to one year of community control and seven years of sex offender probation. While under community control, Horvath received a warning for chatting on Facebook with a "teenager" who turned out to be an undercover officer.
http://www.orlandosentinel.com/news/local/breakingnews/orl-teacher-sex-court-violation-051309,0,793449.story

Classroom Activities

1. Develop a scenario for parole decision making. Have the students decide if they would allow parole for a murderer who has served one-third of his sentence, with an excellent institutional record. Do the same with a drug offender with a poor institutional record. Ask, "Why did you grant or deny parole? What are some factors that make the parole decision so difficult?"

2. Ask students to list the following intermediate sanctions in order that they believe are most effective (1 for most effective and 8 for least effective). For each list item, have students describe its strengths and weaknesses with respect to the goals that should be accomplished:

   a. Fines

   b. Restitution

   c. Boot camps

   d. Intensive probation supervision

   e. Forfeiture

   f. Day reporting centers

   g. Community service

   h. Home confinement

3. Have students debate the following question:

   Has the correctional system within the United States become a prison commercial complex? Have a small group of students research this question from the perspective of corporations using government officials in order to profit from the "tough on crime" policies and have a separate group of students research the issue from the perspective of the prison system getting larger simply because the space is needed and must be developed due to the increased rate of incarceration.

4. Have students collect newspaper clippings on intermediate sanctions and community corrections in the news. Have students comment on the image of community corrections portrayed by the newspapers and compare that with what is presented in the chapter.

Quick Quiz

1. _____ follows confinement in prison. (Page 160)
   a. Retribution   c. Probation
   b. Parole   d. Reinstatement

2. Formally, _____ is a criminal sentence imposed by judges. (Page 160)
   a. retribution   c. probation
   b. parole   d. reinstatement

3. _____ sentences more people to prison and keeps them there longer than any major country in the world. (Page 163)
   a. The United States   c. China
   b. Japan   d. The United Kingdom

4. Probation and parole _____ relates to the offender being arrested or convicted of a new crime. (Page 165)
   a. technical violation   c. retrial
   b. recidivism   d. reentry

5. In the case *Morrissey v. Brewer*, the Supreme Court ruled that probationers and parolees cannot have their parole or probation revoked without _____. (Page 168)
   a. retrial   c. Supreme Court review
   b. due process of law   d. conviction of new crime

WHAT'S INSIDE   The chapter begins by looking at the rise of the penitentiary system, the evolution into correctional facilities, and the retribution, incapacitation, and prevention system of today. After 1975 the prison population increased, largely due to the decision get tough on crime. Types of federal and state penal institutions are discussed, along with the various roles of corrections officers. Next, jails and their environments are distinguished from prisons. Finally, the chapter looks at the characteristics of prisoners, explaining the rising number of women and minority prisoners.

CHAPTER 13 PREP CARD

Prisons, Jails, and Prisoners

Learning Outcomes

LO1 Contrast the penitentiary theories of the 1800s and understand the models of corrections that have predominated since the 1940s

LO2 Discuss the increase in prison populations after 1975 and the factors that have caused that increase

LO3 Classify the different types of federal and state penal institutions

LO4 Understand the role of corrections officers in a prison

LO5 Indicate the difference between traditional jails and new-generation jails

LO6 Understand the major characteristics of prisoners

Chapter Outline

(Continued)

Art Index

PowerPoint Highlights

Slides 5–10: The history of the prison system in the United States
Slides 16–23: Varieties of prisons and the origin of the supermax
Slide 27: The difference between jails and prisons, and the functions of jails
Slides 28–29: Jail conditions, and the introduction of new-generation jails
Slide 30: The major characteristics of male and female prisoners

Video Highlights

Title: Women in Maximum Security Prison: Mental Illness
Running time: 9 minutes
Description: Prison counselors help women cope with mental illness and the psychological pain of confinement.

Title: Women in Maximum Security Prison: Murderers
Running time: 4 minutes
Description: Women face life in jail or the death penalty for killing their husbands and children.

Title: Women in Maximum Security Prison: Sex and Love
Running time: 10 minutes
Description: When facing years in prison, women turn to each other for love, intimacy, and support.

Lecture Launchers

Two inmates escaped from a county jail by digging a hole through a cinderblock wall. Four months later, one convict was recaptured in an apartment only 6 blocks from the jail, and the other in Mexico City. http://www.cnn.com/2008/CRIME/01/08/nj.jailbreak/index.html

Senator James Webb (D, Virginia) introduced the National Criminal Justice Act of 2009 to create a bipartisan committee focused on a comprehensive examination and reformation of the U.S. prison system. http://politics.theatlantic.com/2009/03/a_push_for_prison_reform.php http://www.washingtonpost.com/wp-dyn/content/article/2008/12/28/AR2008122801728.html

In 1974, Susan LeFevre was convicted of selling heroin and sentenced to ten years in prison. One year into her sentence, she jumped the barbed wire fence of her minimum-security prison and spent the next 32 years

Key Terms

penitentiary 177

correctional institution 177

medical model of corrections 178

maximum security prisons 181

supermaximum security prisons (supermaxes) 181

new-generation maximum security prisons 183

medium security prisons 183

minimum security prisons 183

jail 185

prisons 185

new-generation jails 187

as a fugitive. She was arrested in 2008 in a wealthy suburb of San Diego where she lived with her husband and three children.

http://www.10news.com/news/16165874/detail.html

http://www.groundreport.com/US/Susan-LeFevre-aka-Marie-Walsh-Returns-to-Prison-32

Classroom Activities

1. Divide the class into small groups. The students are consultants for a state department of corrections. The state needs to build a new prison because of overcrowding at its aging correctional institutions.

   The consultants' task is to design a new prison, including the physical layout of the building(s), plans for living space for the prisoners, and plans for programs and facilities. In designing the prison, the students need to consider a number of objectives:

   a. Making the facility safe and secure without employing an excessive number of staff personnel or otherwise producing excessive costs.

   b. Creating living conditions that meet constitutional standards for avoiding overcrowding and that create an environment that can be stable and controlled.

   c. Planning programs and facilities to achieve correctional goals. Because the state officials show great deference to the expert consultants, the consultants should also discuss and specify which goals (e.g., rehabilitation, incapacitation, retribution, etc.) their programs and facilities are intended to achieve.

   After each group is finished, the entire class can compare the plans produced by each group. The exercise is intended to make students think seriously about the challenges that face corrections officials who must attempt to strike the appropriate balance between a variety of objectives: safety, security, staff morale, constitutional standards, rehabilitation, punishment, etc.

2. Have the students discuss potential options for dealing with inmates who have contracted the HIV virus. Should special allowances be granted to prisoners who contracted HIV as victims of rape? What method of housing these inmates would the students support? Why? If the students argue that the inmate with AIDS should be released, how does their solution comport with the various goals of punishment (i.e., rehabilitation, deterrence, retribution, and incapacitation).

3. Have students respond to the following:

   If you were a prison warden, what three things would you do to address each of the following issues? How effective do you think your strategies would be?

   a. Racial tensions flare up between groups of inmates and violence breaks out throughout the prison.

   b. Prison gangs assume total control of the internal prison economy by bribing guards.

   c. Mothers of small children are serving long sentences in an isolated institution.

Quick Quiz

1. The _____ reformers attacked penitentiaries as cruel and barbaric, just as the creators of the penitentiary had attacked capital, corporal, and mutilation punishments as cruel and barbaric. (Page 177)
   - a. Progressive
   - b. Liberal
   - c. Quaker
   - d. Catholic

2. In the debate of criminal justice reform in the 1960s and 70s, the conservative victory accompanied heavy reliance on prison time for _____ . (Page 178)
   - a. murder
   - b. bank robbery
   - c. drug offenses
   - d. terrorism

3. Women represent a _____ part of the prison population. (Page 188)
   - a. dominant
   - b. equal
   - c. small
   - d. large

4. Maximum security prisons can be traditional facilities, supermaxes, or _____ facilities. (Page 181)
   - a. new-generation
   - b. limited capacity
   - c. campus
   - d. new age

5. Alcatraz introduced the _____ model of managing prisoners who most threatened prison security and safety. (Page 181)
   - a. concentration
   - b. control
   - c. rehabilitation
   - d. punitive

6. Most minimum security prisons look a lot like _____ , with low buildings surrounded by a recreational area. (Page 183)
   - a. college campuses
   - b. fortresses
   - c. private homes
   - d. military barracks

WHAT'S INSIDE Chapter 14 begins by defining total institution and the other theories of prisons, particularly importation theory. The chapter then looks at prisoners' lives and how they cope with the stress of deprivation. That stress can lead to violence, as can gangs and violent prisoners. Programs directed at male inmates are only sometimes effective and can be controversial, as with recreational programs. Life in women's prisons is very different: prisoners form more intimate relationships and programs rarely meet their needs. The chapter ends by explaining the need for greater supervision and reentry programs.

Learning Outcomes

LO1 Explain the concept of prison as a total institution and discuss other theories of prisons

LO2 Understand the lives and cultures of male inmates

LO3 Understand the nature and causes of prison violence

LO4 Understand the nature of common prison programs for male inmates

LO5 Understand the special needs and problems of incarcerated women

LO6 Understand the issue of prisoner reentry

Chapter Outline

Art Index

PowerPoint Highlights

Slides 4–5: The indigenous and importation theories of imprisonment
Slides 6–10: The lives of incarcerated men
Slides 11–16: Prison violence, sexual victimization, gangs, and riots
Slides 17–25: An overview and the types of common prison programs
Slides 27–28: The lives of incarcerated women

Video Highlights

Title: Nightline: Corrections
Running time: 9 minutes
Description: A day in the stressful lives of two Orange County Jail correctional officers.

Title: Prison Anger Management Program
Running time: 5 minutes
Description: A novel prison program teaches inmates at San Quentin State Prison to control their anger.

Title: Gang Prevention
Running time: 6 minutes
Description: A convicted murderer establishes a 12-step program to rehabilitate gang members.

Lecture Launchers

In 2008, Jennifer Wilkov, a New York financial planner, spent several months in Rikers Island jail for conducting a real-estate scam. After being released, Wilkov wrote an article for *Marie Claire* about life inside Rikers. http://www.marieclaire.com/world-reports/news/latest/jennifer-wilkov-rikers-island-prison?click=main_sr

For 60 days in 2008, Reggie Townsend was placed in a solitary confinement cell so small that its shower regularly doused his mattress. Guards allegedly ignored repeated requests to replace the moldy, foul-smelling mattress, so Townsend filed a civil suit and was awarded $295,000 in punitive damages. http://www.thesmokinggun.com/archive/years/2008/0919082mattress1.html

Inmates at the Utah State Prison can earn associate degrees from Salt Lake Community College (SLCC) while incarcerated. Inmate students are

Key Terms

total institutions 193

**indigenous theory of
    imprisonment 193**

**importation theory of
    imprisonment 194**

pains of imprisonment 195

prisoner reentry 203

held to the same requirements as other SLCC students and pay a heavily discounted tuition—only
$88 per semester.

http://findarticles.com/p/articles/mi_qn4188/is_20080523/ai_n25464738/?tag=content;col1

Classroom Activities

1. Ask students to call out some programs that exist in men's prisons to assist them in
   preparing to return to life in the free world. After you have a substantial list, go through
   and discuss the merits and burdens of each item. Finally, prompt students to discuss
   which program they feel is the most useful in transition.

2. Present students with the following scenario:

   A woman becomes romantically involved with a drug-dealer, and she and her infant
   son move into his apartment. The woman eventually becomes addicted to drugs, but
   continues to take care of her child. A year later, the apartment is raided, and both the
   drug-dealer and the mother are arrested, each facing years in prison.

   Ask students: what should happen to the son? Should the woman receive a reduced
   sentence so she can continue to care for him? Should the child be placed in foster
   care regardless of the mother's legal outcome? Instruct students to consider some of
   the pains of women's imprisonment. How do issues such as motherhood, sexual and
   physical abuse and drug addiction affect women in prison, and once they're released?

3. Present students with the following scenarios:

   Corrections officers at the main gate receive a report that a fight involving twelve
   prisoners has broken out in Cellblock C and that the corrections officers in Cellblock C are
   unable to break up the fight. Seven corrections officers run down the corridor from the
   main gate toward Cellblock C. As they round a corner, they practically run into inmate
   Joe Cottrell who is mopping and waxing the corridor floor. One officer grabs Cottrell by
   the shoulders and throws him aside while saying, "Get out of the way!" Cottrell falls into a
   wall, dislocates his shoulder, and later files a lawsuit against the officer by claiming that the
   rough treatment and resulting injury violated his Eighth Amendment right against cruel
   and unusual punishment. Were his Eighth Amendment rights violated? Explain.

   A prison chapel is used every Sunday for Christian services. A small group of prisoners
   reserve the chapel for each Tuesday evening where they meet to study Buddhism. For
   two years, they use the chapel every Tuesday to meditate and discuss books about
   their religion, and they do not cause any trouble. Then, one year, Christmas falls on a
   Wednesday, and the Asian religion group is told that they cannot have their meeting
   because the chapel is needed for a Christmas Eve service. They file a lawsuit claiming
   that their First Amendment right to free exercise of religion is being violated because
   they cannot use the chapel on Christmas Eve. Are their rights being violated? Explain.

Quick Quiz

1. In times past, the standard explanation for how prisoners
   adapted to life in prison was the _____ . (Page 194)
   a. transference theory   c. warden's code
   b. compliant sex theory   (d.) inmate code

2. The _____ theory of imprisonment assumes that the roots of
   prison society lie outside prison. (Page 194)
   (a.) importation   c. indigenous
   b. utilitarian   d. permeation

3. Prisoners live lives of _____ , where the state provides only the
   bare essentials. (Page 195)
   a. thievery   (c.) enforced poverty
   b. bribery   d. penance

4. Prisoners can legally buy some of the comforts of life from the
   _____ . (Page 195)
   (a.) prison commissary   c. correctional officers
   b. Internet stores   d. authorized prison peddlers

5. _____ is a common characteristic of prison life that probably
   accounts for some of the increased violence. (Page 197)
   a. Officer beatings   c. Lack of food
   (b.) Crowding   d. Poor healthcare

WHAT'S INSIDE The final chapter examines the role of juveniles in the justice system. After presenting the historical background of juvenile justice, the chapter explores the rights of modern juvenile offenders, the definition and measure of delinquency, and the processes of the juvenile system. The interaction between police and juveniles is explicated, as is the process of juvenile arrest. The chapter contains an extensive review of the operation of juvenile courts from intake, through adjudication, to disposition. Finally, the chapter discusses various community and institutional corrections for juveniles.

Learning Outcomes

LO1 Explain the history and development of juvenile justice, including the child-saving movement and the doctrine of *parens patriae*

LO2 Understand the rights of juveniles in the juvenile justice system

LO3 Understand juvenile delinquency and describe the nature of juvenile delinquency

LO4 Describe the juvenile justice system

LO5 Describe the nature and purpose of law enforcement for juveniles

LO6 Describe the purpose and operation of the juvenile court

LO7 Understand the dual system of justice and the waiver process for juveniles

LO8 Describe the nature and purpose of juvenile corrections

Chapter Outline

Art Index

PowerPoint Highlights

Slides 3–7: The establishment and evolution of the juvenile justice system

Slides 10–12: An overview of delinquency and its measurements

Slides 16–19: Law enforcement and juveniles

Slides 20–24: The operation of the juvenile court from intake to disposition

Slides 25–28: Transfers and blended sentencing

Slides 29–32: Probation and institutional corrections

Video Highlights

Title: Teen Charged with Killing Her Parents, Parts 1-6
Running time: 40 minutes
Description: In 2003 a 16-year-old Idaho girl shot and killed her parents after they voiced opposition to her boyfriend, a 19-year-old alleged drug dealer. Though she maintained her innocence throughout her trial, the girl was found guilty of first degree murder.

Title: Girls Behaving Badly: Violent Girls
Running time: 9 minutes
Description: The G.A.P. program helps young girls raised in harsh environments turn away from violence.

Lecture Launchers

In February 2009 a 14-year-old Wisconsin girl was arrested and issued a criminal citation for refusing to stop sending text messages during a high school math class.
http://www.thesmokinggun.com/archive/years/2009/0217092samsung1.html

In November 2008 a 10-year-old girl was suspended from school after drafting a list of 21 classmates and four teachers to target in a school shooting spree. After the list was confiscated by a teacher, the girl told police that she did not actually intend to carry out the act.
http://www.thesmokinggun.com/archive/years/2008/1120081list1.html

In early 2009 a 17-year old was charged with unlawful eavesdropping or surveillance after allegedly using his cell phone to take pictures of a teacher's exposed legs and underwear.
http://www.thesmokinggun.com/archive/years/2009/0212091teacher1.html

Key Terms

doctrine of *parens patriae* 208

juvenile court 208

medical model of crime 209

juvenile delinquent 209

juveniles 210

delinquency 210

status offenses 210

delinquency petitions 216

transfer petitions 216

disposition hearings 217

continuance in contemplation
    of dismissal 217

dual system of justice 217

transfer (waiver,
    certification) 217

Classroom Activities

1. Ask the class to discuss the question "Should juveniles receive the death penalty for murder"? As the students explore the question, their attention should be directed to the philosophical underpinnings of juvenile justice which dictate that juvenile offenders should be treated differently than adults with respect to culpability and punishment.

   In particular, competing goals of retribution, incapacitation, deterrence, and rehabilitation come into sharp focus when considering which objectives are arguably advanced by executing or not executing juvenile murderers. Should there be a cut-off age for juvenile's eligibility for the death penalty? If a nine year old intentionally takes his parents' gun and shoots another child because of a dispute over baseball cards, should that child be subject to the death penalty? Is there any specific age that is too young to be subject to the death penalty? Does it depend on the heinousness of the crime or upon the characteristics of an individual child? Finally, if children can be subject to the death penalty, then is there any reason to treat children differently than adults by having a separate juvenile justice system?

2. Have the students develop a juvenile probation plan for a juvenile who has committed one of the following crimes...

   a. Possession with intent to deliver crack cocaine

   b. Burglary of an automobile

   c. Aggravated assault on a 70-year old lady

   d. Vandalism

   e. Shoplifting

   f. Pick pocketing

   g. Or any other offense.

   Assume that the juvenile in question has no past criminal record.

3. Find out what the statutes are in your state concerning waiver to adult court. Discuss these with the class. How do they feel about the issue of trying juveniles as adults? At what age do they think juveniles should be tried as adults?

Quick Quiz

1. The _____ movement relied on two institutions, the house of refuge and the reform school. (Page 208)
   a. progressive
   b. child-saving
   c. responsibility
   d. conservative

2. In _____, the U.S. Supreme Court ruled that juveniles do not have the right to a jury trial. (Page 210)
   a. *In re Winship*
   b. *Treat v. Meyers*
   c. *Kent v. United States*
   d. *McKeiver v. Pennsylvania*

3. Most juvenile court delinquency cases result in _____. (Page 221)
   a. parole
   b. minor prison terms
   c. probation
   d. detention

4. _____ petitions ask for a hearing to waive the juvenile court's jurisdiction and transfer the case to adult criminal courts. (Page 216)
   a. Transfer
   b. Juvenile
   c. Certiorari
   d. Habeas corpus

5. From the time of referral, the juvenile court process consists of three steps: _____, adjudication, and disposition. (Page 215)
   a. capture
   b. intake
   c. observation
   d. evaluation

6. Truancy is a _____ offense. (Page 210)
   a. status
   b. non-regulated
   c. heavily policed
   d. rare